P9-CQN-553

DATE DUE			
NOV 15			
NOV 24			
APR 18			

65332
Zabel

St. Procopius College Library
Maple Ave. & College Rd.
Lisle, Illinois

CRAFT AND CHARACTER

Also by Morton Dauwen Zabel

The Romantic Idealism of Art

The Critical and Popular Background of
Art in England: 1800–1848

Literary Opinion in America

The Situation in American Criticism: 1939

Two Years of Poetry: 1937–1939

A Book of English Literature
(*with others*)

A Literatura dos Estados Unidos

Historia de la Literatura Norteamericana

Edited by Morton Dauwen Zabel

The Portable Conrad

The Portable Henry James

Os Norte-Americanos

CRAFT AND CHARACTER

Texts, Method, and Vocation

IN
MODERN FICTION

by
Morton Dauwen Zabel

WITHDRAWN

NEW YORK : THE VIKING PRESS

1957

PR
823
.23

Copyright © 1932, 1935, 1936, 1938, 1940, 1941, 1942, 1943, 1946, 1947, 1949, 1950, 1951, 1956, 1957 by Morton Dauwen Zabel.

Published in 1957
by The Viking Press, Inc.
625 Madison Avenue, New York 22

Published in Canada by
The Macmillan Company of Canada Limited

The Note on Sources, pages 329–31, lists original publication of essays incorporated in part or in revised form in essays in this volume. The copyright lines above cover these except for portions of the Samuel Butler chapter, copyright 1950 by Random House, Inc., and of "Conrad: The East and the Sea," copyright 1951 by Harper & Brothers.

Library of Congress catalog card number: 56-11065

Printed in U.S.A. by the Vail-Ballou Press

65332

TO

BARBARA A. DAUWEN ZABEL

MDCCCLXVII

MCMXLI

Meide den Irrtum, dass es Entbehrungen gebe
für den geschehnen Entschluss, diesen: zu sein.
Seidener Faden, kamst du hinein ins Gewebe.

R. M. R.

Contents

Foreword

The subjects of the essays collected in this book have engaged the author, usually on more than one occasion, over the past three decades, and represent a selection of topics from a much larger body of critical writing published during that time. The present volume of studies in modern fiction will be followed in 1958 by one devoted to studies in modern poetry, from Baudelaire, Rimbaud, Hopkins, and Yeats to the representative poets of contemporary America. Taken together, the two collections will offer a view, from one point of critical vantage, of some forty of the representative talents who have written and dominated the fiction and verse of the past hundred years. The essays now appear in a form usually different from that of the first appearance of the material on which they are based. All of them have been revised; most of them have been wholly rewritten; a number are entirely new; and the date of their present writing is in most cases 1955–56.

It is customary to say in books of this kind that while the form and style of the discussions have been changed, their intention or substance has not. This is not the case here. A large number of the writers considered are or have until recently been our contemporaries. Their careers have taken shape, their ideas or purposes have altered, their art has changed, matured, in some cases shifted its ground, within the lifetime of living readers, including this one. Even in the cases of Nineteenth Century writers—Dickens, Hardy,

James, Conrad—critical interest has been spurred by so much in
the way of scholarly discovery, or by changes in taste, approach,
and sympathy, that new aspects and qualities in their work have
been disclosed or made apparent. They have not stayed fixed under
scrutiny; some of them have become in current acceptance wholly
different writers from what they were taken to be thirty or forty
years ago. So, of course, has any critic who has read and attempted
to interpret them during that span of time—including, again, this
one.

One definition of the critic—it must be one of the most popular
ever arrived at; it is certainly one of which a collector of his own
work becomes acutely conscious—is that he is a man who conducts
his education in public. Leaving aside the possibility that there are
worse things being conducted in public these days than an education; leaving aside also the likelihood that if the serious pursuit of
literature is anything it is an education, one may say that the nature
of the critic's work makes this inevitable. If he is qualified by any
degree of serious enthusiasm for his task, he is not content to remain
a silent reader. He commits himself to print; he neglects to wait until
full maturity, infallibility, or final judgments are arrived at. Another useful remark on the critic's operations has it that "in a sense,
one can never read the book that the author originally wrote, and
one can never read the same book twice." [1] There are students and
critics of literature to whom both these statements may be distaste-
ful. And it is agreed that it is not books and authors that change so
much as times and readers. But for present purposes, both these
axioms are accepted. While the opinions and interpretations offered
in these pages are of present date, the point at which they have
now arrived, and the statement now given them, have been reached
through three decades of reading, reaction, and empirical trial and
error. It is not to be assumed (it will not be so assumed by the
reader, and the writer himself has no wish to assume it) that they
will now stay fixed and final. They make a claim to being based on

[1] Edmund Wilson, "Foreword," *The Triple Thinkers* (revised edition, 1948),
p. ix.

careful consideration and as much scruple as I am capable of mustering, but I hope these are still capable of improvement, and that my study of these authors and problems is not a closed or settled account.

A sentence in one of these essays, I now conveniently find, says that "a notable fact about most serious writers is how early their prepossessing subject seizes them"—how soon, in their work, a characteristic bent or preoccupation engages their minds. This can evidently be true in modest cases as well as in distinguished ones. Hence the title of this book.

Craft and Character has the appearance of an equation. It is not so intended in any literal, moralizing, or scientific sense. "Character" as we commonly know, recognize, and judge it may be so radically at odds with the craft or art that issues from it that it is generally a safe rule to make no co-ordination whatever between a writer's work and his nature or conduct as a man. But in another sense, a radical and important one, there is a profound and inescapable connection between what the artist essentially is (quite apart from any personal information, legend, or reputation that may attach to him) and the work he produces. It is the sense in which his work, thought, and craft show him to be a nature capable of producing valuable and original art, of persisting in it, and of declaring himself as a character through it—the only character in which, as an artist, he is knowable or definable. In this meaning there is a valid and urgent equation of craft and character, and it is hoped that some modern instances of it are presented here.

Forty years ago one of the most distinguished modern critics gave it as a warning, an axiom that has become classic in the criticism of our time, that "the more perfect the artist, the more completely separate in him will be the man who suffers and the mind which creates." This remark has had a valuable corrective influence in our century, even among critics of biographical or psychological emphasis whose chief concern it has been to disprove it. It has acted to check a long-standing tradition of personal bias, historical approach, and moralistic distortion in the study of literature. When, however, the same critic went on to say that "the more perfect the artist," the "more completely will the mind digest and transmute the passions which are its material"; when he said further, some years later, of Yeats that he could "think of no poet, not even among the very greatest, who has shown a longer period of development," and that "development to this extent is not merely genius, it is character, and it sets a standard which his juniors should seek to emulate, without hoping to equal," [2] he allowed that the "mind," intelligence, and personal force of a writer have a great deal to do with the work he produces, his "sufferings" and what he makes of them with his creation; and that character in this sense is not only a major concern of criticism but possibly the crucial test of art itself. It is the test of *vocation*, and the presence of that word on the title page of this book is intended to refer to an emphasis which I trust will be apparent in these studies and in those of the companion volume which will follow it.

In any event, it became evident in collecting and organizing these essays that the relevance of the writer's moral personality and intelligence to his work, the relation of his character to his craft, emerged as an interest of the present critic in his first reviews and articles during the 1920s, and has persisted as a method of approach, an angle of interpretation, during the ensuing years. Admittedly this way of discussing literature should be a means and not an end. The true object of criticism is the work of art itself, its definition, analysis, and evaluation, arrived at with the fullest combination of sympathy, insight, and justice the critic can muster for himself. Such evaluation may, of course, be achieved quite impersonally, on a basis of abstract, ideal, or normative principles. Perhaps the purest criticism is so written. But "pure" or absolute criticism has been the rule in no century, least of all in ours. The agility or astuteness with which some present-day doctrinaire critics have changed their premises and methods (not to mention their judgments on indi-

---

[2] T. S. Eliot, "A Commentary" in *The Criterion,* Vol. XV, pp. 610–13 (July 1935); earlier in "Tradition and the Individual Talent" (1917) in *The Sacred Wood* (1920), p. 48.

vidual cases) from phase to phase of their careers has indicated
that absolute standards or procedures can be as unstable as the
realistic or relativistic ways of less dogmatic interpreters—can seem
to be more so by reason of the very authority they boast.

The "conditioning" of literature during the past century and a
half has, moreover, been extremely mixed. Romanticism gave the individual personality an importance which no amount of impersonality in aesthetics or critical theory has been able to cancel. That importance has, in fact, increased rather than lessened among artists
and writers. Social, political, moral, and public pressures have combined to emphasize it. Ever since Coleridge gave it as a "mandate"
that "the postulate of philosophy and at the same time the test of
philosophic capacity, is no other than the heaven-descended KNOW
THYSELF" ("and this at once practically and speculatively"), and
likened the man who lacks this capacity to one for whom philosophy—he also evidently meant art—"is a mere play of words and mo-
tions, like a theory of music to the deaf, or like the geometry of light
to the blind," the forces of moral and social regimentation, as of
political and ethical coercion, have enhanced the value of personal
insight and private judgment to a degree no fully conscious artist
has been able to ignore. And when writers like Baudelaire, Hopkins,
Rimbaud, James, Yeats, and Conrad join—in texts quoted in this
book and its companion—in their agreement on the artist's necessity of finding his strictest standard of values in himself, there can
be little question that the test of character, of personal consciousness, responsibility, and identity, remains one of the most useful,
perhaps one of the most conclusive, tests of creative capacity and
moral achievement we have at our disposal.

It is a test that is attempted, for what it is worth and for such
worth as the present writer can give it, in most of the following essays. The test will probably always find its most intense expression
in poetry. But it is the craft of fiction—and especially of modern
fiction, with its experimental and empirical conditions, its freedom
from convention, and its availability to personal use and vision—
that is likely to exercise and prove the test in a freer, more dramatic

and intimate way. While the fourteen novelists discussed here do not represent the full range and originality of modern fiction, they may be taken as showing their art in certain of its important crises and challenges during the past century, and as offering the test of vocation in fiction some of its typical occasions and opportunities. I hope other tests and considerations will also appear. I have noticed in collecting and revising these studies that while they make much of character, they make comparatively little use of biography; that while they call on whatever evidence offers itself in the moral and imaginative development of the writers they consider, they refer that growth or capacity less to external events and influences than to the evidences of insight, originality, and craftsmanship their work shows. I hope this balance is evident in what follows; I wish it were more evident than it probably is. Students or critics of literature are well advised to keep certain ancestral counsels or mottoes before them. One of my own long-standing favorites among these is one that appears here in the essay on Henry James. It bears repeating:

> To lend himself, to project himself and steep himself, to feel and feel till he understands, and to understand so well that he can say, to have perception at the pitch of passion and expression as embracing as the air, to be infinitely curious and incorrigibly patient, and yet plastic and inflammable and determinable, stooping to conquer and serving to direct—these are fine chances for an active mind, chances to add the idea of independent beauty to the conception of success. Just in proportion as he is sentient and restless, just in proportion as he reacts and reciprocates and penetrates, is the critic a valuable instrument. . . .

This unquestionably continues to set a standard which James's juniors and followers "should seek to emulate, without hoping to equal," even where, as here, the hope is the reverse of confident and the seeking fully conscious of its inadequacies.

A large part of the material in this book has appeared in earlier versions elsewhere, and I am grateful to the following magazines for publishing it: *The New Republic, The Nation, The Southern Re-*

view, The Sewanee Review, Poetry: A Magazine of Verse, The American Scholar, the *Times Literary Supplement* (London), *Sur* (Buenos Aires), *A Manhã* and *Correio da Manhã* (Rio de Janeiro), *Orígenes* (Havana), *Les Nouvelles Littéraires* (Paris), *Der Monat* (Berlin); also to publishers of books in which earlier forms of certain essays appeared as introductions: Harper and Brothers, Houghton Mifflin Company, the Modern Library (Random House), New Directions, and The Viking Press; as anthology contributions: Henry Holt and Company, the Ronald Press Company, and the University of Minnesota Press; or as chapters in my own books: Editora Agir (Rio de Janeiro) and Editorial Losada (Buenos Aires). I owe a special debt of gratitude to several editors for hospitality and encouragement over many years: to the late Harriet Monroe, during the decade in which I was associated with her as contributor and associate editor of *Poetry: A Magazine of Verse;* to Margaret Marshall for her generosity during her literary editorship of *The Nation;* to Edmund Wilson and Malcolm Cowley during their years of literary editorship of *The New Republic;* and to Cleanth Brooks and Robert Penn Warren as editors of *The Southern Review.* The unbracketed dates at the ends of the essays refer to the first or earlier appearance of material now incorporated in them; dates within brackets to the revision or present form of the essays. A more detailed acknowledgment of sources appears in the note at the end of the volume.

November 1, 1956

PART I

The Terms

of the Appeal:

Nineteenth to Twentieth Century

The house of fiction has in short not one window, but a million—a number of possible windows not to be reckoned, rather; every one of which has been pierced, or is still pierceable, in its vast front, by the need of the individual vision and by the pressure of the individual will. . . . But they have this mark of their own that at each of them stands a figure with a pair of eyes, or at least with a field-glass, which forms, again and again, for observation, a unique instrument, insuring to the person making use of it an impression distinct from every other.

—HENRY JAMES,
Preface to *The Portrait of a Lady*

. . . our literary deeds enjoy this marked advantage over many of our acts, that, though they go forth into the world and stray even in the desert, they don't to the same extent lose themselves. . . . Our relation to them is essentially traceable, and in that fact abides, we feel, the incomparable luxury of the artist.

—HENRY JAMES,
Preface to *The Golden Bowl*

. . . the artist descends within himself, and in that lonely region of stress and strife, if he be deserving and fortunate, he finds the terms of his appeal. . . . The changing wisdom of successive generations discards ideas, questions facts, demolishes theories. But the artist appeals to that part of our being which is not dependent on wisdom: to that in us which is a gift and not an acquisition—and, therefore, more permanently enduring.

—JOSEPH CONRAD,
Preface to *The Nigger of the "Narcissus"*

The novel: a crossroads, a meeting-place of problems.

—ANDRÉ GIDE

Dickens

I. THE REPUTATION REVISED

Poets, Homer the first among them, have always rivaled heroes, saints, and martyrs in the mythology of cultures. It remained for Romanticism, with its cult of symbolic individualism, heroic force, and the representative man, to render every man of letters susceptible to the inflation or distortion of personal and ethnic legend. When Keats called Shakespeare's a "life of allegory" on which his works are "the comments," he doubtless took his cue from examples nearer at hand—Rousseau, Goethe, Byron: cases that initiated a modern tradition that was to accelerate in impetus with each succeeding decade.

France, in the Nineteenth Century, became particularly rich in instances of what Raymond Mortimer has called the "idiosyncrasies that edify a legend," characters who "made themselves vivid by public energy or personal eccentricity"—"Lamartine in the February Revolution, Victor Hugo hurling chastisements from his island exile, Musset tossed by turbulent amours, Nerval hanging himself top-hatted from a lamp-post, Baudelaire enslaved simultaneously by his mother, by drugs, and by an angry drab, Verlaine reeling between the confessional and the lupanar, Rimbaud ruthlessly discarding his genius to trade in Ethiopian slaves"; even Mallarmé, "indefatigably distilling essences and intricating spells, living in poetry as the saints have sought to live in God," while leading the outward life of "a schoolmaster, just not too inefficient to keep his job, his poverty genteel rather than picturesque . . . alternating between his class-room and the poky flat where his wife and daughter darned in the lamplight." But neither America nor England has lagged in examples: America with a succession that extends from Franklin and Poe to Stephen Crane and Fitzgerald, England with a varied progeny that followed Byron in figuring the fortunes of the "culture hero" or scapegoat—it includes men as diverse as Dickens, Swinburne, Wilde, and, in a more recent generation, both the Lawrences.

Where once the accretion of fable was slow, requiring centuries for its visible accumulation, the past century and a half has seen the process accelerate to the point where the legend may claim the author well before his death. Byron, Rimbaud, and D. H. Lawrence became mythologized within their lifetimes; Kafka, Joyce, and Hart Crane from the moments of their demise. Such legend has its undoubted function in the publicity of literature, the propaganda of culture, the apotheosis of *Zeitgeist*. Equally it imposes its handicap on the historian or biographer, never more so than when it is discovered that the legend proves to be at odds with fact. A truth, hitherto suppressed or ignored, suddenly punctures the benign or simplifying screen of fiction. A benignant Wordsworth yields to the research of Legouis and Harper, a diabolic Baudelaire to Porché, Enid Starkie, and René Laforgue, Shelley to Robert Metcalf Smith, Ruskin to R. H. Wilenski and Admiral William James. Standard biographies must suddenly be revised or questioned. More seriously, since nothing influences criticism so much as a legendary reputation, the standardized interpretation of the artist's achievement must also be checked or corrected. A random fact, sprung unawares, is often enough to instigate a fresh reading or appraisal of a writer's work. The case of Dickens is instructive.

In 1928 J. W. T. Ley brought out his modern edition, "edited and annotated," of John Forster's *Life*. As an appendix this printed, like earlier editions, the text of Dickens' will. The first name in it was that of Ellen Ternan, to whom Dickens made his first bequest of a thousand pounds. Her name, again as in all earlier editions, appeared nowhere else in the book. The Stracheyans—Ralph Straus, Hugh Kingsmill, C. E. Bechhofer-Roberts with a paltry piece of "fictionized biography" called *This Side Idolatry*—had been busy with Dickens from the twenties onward, all of them deflationary and anti-Victorian in bias, all of them intent on dispelling Carlyle's, and Chesterton's, version of "the good, the gentle, high-gifted, ever-friendly, noble Dickens, every inch of him an honest man," but all of them missing the clue that might have turned the trick of reducing the fabulous Dickens to human and credible proportions. It remained for that "nosiest of literary snoopers," the Reverend Thomas Wright of Olney, who had already set the mortal remains of Cowper, Blake, Fitz-Gerald, and Walter Pater revolving in their graves, to ferret out the identity of Ellen Ternan when he published his *Life of Charles Dickens* in 1935. Presently, in 1938, the Nonesuch Edition furnished the first comprehensive edition of Dickens' letters. In 1939 a Miss Gladys Storey published an ill-written, undocumented, frankly amateurish, but highly suggestive book called *Dickens and Daughter*, purportedly based on evidence supplied her by Dickens' last surviving daughter, Kate Dickens Perugini, and laying open the distresses of Dickens' family life, his separation from his wife, his liaison with Ellen Ternan, and a distracted, exacerbated character beyond anything the earlier memoirists had recorded.

The sentimentalized Dickens of popular fancy, laureate of the English hearth, saint of Victorian domesticity, the aging dreamer depicted in a celebrated picture surrounded by the fairies, gnomes, and ogres of his benevolent imagination, was roughly dislodged. The hint to both biographers and critics was unmistakable. Edmund Wilson was the first to make use of it in his essay "Dickens: The Two Scrooges" in 1940, but others soon followed—George Orwell also in 1940, Humphry House in a fine study of *The Dickens World* in 1941, the French critic Alain in a sensitive reading called *En lisant Dickens* in 1945, F. R. Leavis extolling the poetic realism of *Hard Times* in his study of *The Great Tradition* (1948). All of them repudiated the folkloristic approach of Chesterton. All of them reclaimed and extended the serious view of Dickens that had inspired his three greatest Victorian critics—Taine, Gissing, and Bernard Shaw. All of them were concerned to correct the *niaiserie* of what had become—less, to be sure, during Dickens' lifetime than in the six or seven decades following his death in 1870—the popular fable.

Meanwhile another line of inquiry had been set in motion. Dickens in his role of social historian, critic of tradition and institutions, moralist and reformer, had always called for serious attention. Gissing had laid particular stress on this aspect of his work and had attempted to come to grips with it in a chapter on "The Radical" in his book of 1898. Shaw naturally emphasized it, and a good many scholars had undertaken to treat of Dickens' authority in such fields as education, law, philanthropy, religion, and government. It was, perhaps inevitably, a Marxist who tried to prove a consistent line of social and political criticism in the novels—T. A. Jackson in his book of 1938, *Charles Dickens: The Progress of a Radical*—and though what resulted was to a large extent a strait-jacketing of the novels in the interests of proving an argument on behalf of "radicalism," their weight as historical and social documents was suggested with greater effect than by any other writer except Shaw. (Another English Marxist, Jack Lindsay, was to push this kind of interpretation to even greater lengths in his book of 1950—as also a reckless use of Freudian clues and formulas.)

Meanwhile also the biography of Dickens began to call for drastic revision. Ley's edition of Forster in 1928 had been little more than a service of official piety on behalf of the orthodox Dickens Society and its magazine, *The Dickensian*, both of which were meanwhile viewing the new discoveries, undocumented or otherwise, with a dismay amounting to horror and a scandalized repugnance that spared the discoverers nothing in the way of contempt and vituperation. Dame Una Pope-Hennessy produced a new biography in 1945, writing with an honesty almost plodding, supplying few documents but adhering painfully to the letter of her evidence, building a picture of Victorian life quite Victorian in its oppressive density, the result of her long saturation in Dickens' works and lore, but betraying her critical ineptitude by supplying a pedes-

trian summary of each novel in its turn. Hesketh Pearson followed
this in 1949 with *Dickens: His Character, Comedy, and Career.* This,
the work of a professional popular biographer, followed Dame Una
in not abusing its privilege of becoming a facile exposé in the style of
Strachey's imitators or the debunking vogue of the twenties. Mr.
Pearson showed the racier hand that had already served him in his
books on Sydney Smith, Hazlitt, Shaw, and Wilde, an expert scissors-
and-paste skill in culling and mounting a great fund of anecdotes,
a narrative ease born of the higher journalism, a cavalier disregard
(as in his Shaw and Wilde books) for the aesthetic and political
bearings of his subject, and some awkward efforts to arrive at his own
estimate of the novels, as when he said of *Great Expectations* that
"it has been over-praised in relation to Dickens's other novels, perhaps because it is shorter than most, possibly because it is less complicated than most," or of *Bleak House* that "sometimes one is tempted
to define the work of Dickens as a blazing volcano of genius almost
entirely surrounded by a morass of imbecility."

It remained for two scrupulous American scholars to bring this
succession of biographical revaluations to a climax in 1952—Miss
Ada Nisbet with her brief account of *Dickens and Ellen Ternan,*
which laid out the full evidence on Dickens' marriage and its failure,
his association with the young actress, his infatuation with whom
became a major event in the last twelve years of his life, and the
bearings of this liaison on his public and domestic life; and finally
Edgar Johnson, in his monumental and exhaustive book, *Charles
Dickens: His Tragedy and Triumph,* comprehensive both in its biographical record and in its critical treatment, which at once became
a major authority not only on Dickens but on the age he lived in, and
one of the biographical landmarks of the century.

It was inevitable that the sentimental hero worship attending
Dickens' immense success in his own lifetime and during the fifty
years that followed it should have stimulated a reaction of contempt
or resistance. This came to include even those artists who, like James,
Proust, Shaw, and Gide, had felt the powerful appeal of the untidy
colossus who dominated the imaginative literature of his age from

England and America to Russia. But Dickens was always too much the creator of a world, the all-embracing exponent of a moment in the moral and social consciousness of the Nineteenth Century, to submit to the declining fortune of a Thackeray or a George Eliot. Moreover, critical detraction, in the heat of its specific aims, came to show as much disregard of the specific force, scope, and detail of Dickens' powers as did the devotional indulgence which brought into existence a vast agglomeration of myth-making adulation calculated to suffocate any but the ruggedest triumphs of the human imagination. It is by the ruggedness of his substance, as much as by his verbal and imaginative resources, that Dickens has survived. Both of these, given new relevance and focus by the biographical discoveries, came to lay their inescapable claim on his readers and critics.

Edmund Wilson spoke of the "pseudo-poetic booziness [of the kind sponsored by Chesterton] which verbalizes with large conceptions and ignores the most obtrusive actualities" in Dickens' novels. An opposite kind of laxity appears when the sophisticated critic or novelist becomes so impatient of popular tradition that he destroys the hero with the hero-worship and deflates the novels to the status of inanity because of the abuses they have inspired in manufacturers of popular fictional entertainment. But Dickens has never been without his persistent, if for a long time underground, claim on serious critical attention. Taine saw the creative as well as the historical power of the books. Gissing's various essays, despite their excesses of sympathy and crudity in dealing with the specific gist of the novels, raised most of the major critical arguments. Shaw, Santayana, Percy Lubbock, and T. S. Eliot variously proposed Dickens' aesthetic stature. Even Henry James, who in 1865 reviewed *Our Mutual Friend* as the work of an exhausted mechanism and helpless victim of popular compromise and took its author as the great point of attack for a new generation of aesthetic reformers in the art of fiction, could acknowledge in old age the ineradicable mark laid by Dickens on his own imaginative development, and showed, in ultimate refinements of his craft like *The Wings of the Dove* and *The Golden Bowl,* the

fruition of methods of indirection and suspense, of the slow surrounding of event and action by the processes of conscience, moral inquisition, and retributive justice, which placed the author of *Bleak House*
and *Little Dorrit* unmistakably in their artistic ancestry.

The first task of rehabilitation is to determine the scope and authenticity of a writer's content. Where Edmund Wilson's essay aimed
chiefly to recover the personal origins and psychic relevance of the
novels, Humphry House's *The Dickens World* undertook to verify
Dickens' authority as a historian and social observer. It is, he said,
their "minute attention to the business of life [that] gives Dickens'
novels their immense solidity," and he made it his business to determine the fidelity and richness of that attention, the almost official
responsibility Dickens felt in recording the social revolution he witnessed and the processes and abuses of change that were bringing
it about. He not only reconstructed the conditions out of which developed Dickens' hatred of evangelical cant, moral humbug, and
Biblical authoritarianism (Chadband, Pecksniff, Mrs. Clennam,
Stiggins, Mrs. Nubbles, the Reverend Melchisedech Howler), his
detestation of organized philanthropy (Mrs. Jellyby, Mrs. Pardiggle's Puseyism, Luke Honeythunder), his contempt of Malthusian
cynicism, Benthamite economics, and sectarian charity (*Oliver Twist,
Hard Times, Little Dorrit, Our Mutual Friend*), his loathing and at
the same time his ambivalent sharing of the casuistry of Victorian
morality and economic hypocrisy (Dombey, old Casby, Fledgeby,
the Veneerings, the Merdle connection), his disgust with legal apathy, government machinery, and caste nepotism (Chancery, the
Circumlocution Office, the Dedlock dynasty), his dislike of the
magistracy (Nupkins, Fang), and his dramatization of the huge
industrial and monopolistic forces that were transforming the English world from its legendary tradition of taverns, country-houses,
agrarian stability, and generous manhood to the railroad-racked,
factory-blackened, speculative and piratical nightmare of the later
novels. He also showed in full detail—as Edgar Johnson was to show
with even greater documentation, especially in his edition of Dickens'
letters to Angela Burdett Coutts in 1952—Dickens' lifelong concern

with reform movements in his public speeches, petitions, circulars, articles in *Household Words* and *All the Year Round*—a continuous flow of pamphlets, protests, and agitations that punctuated his fiction-writing.

He revealed what is most important still in the artistic ingenuity of the novels—the devices of anachronism Dickens used in order to expose the scandals or public outrages of the immediate present in a setting of the slightly remote past and thus to heighten his critical advantage without sacrificing his popular status as a propagandist. (The Merdle swindle, based on the debacles of promoters like Hudson and Sadlier in the forties and fifties, is distanced in *Little Dorrit* to the 1820s; the Chartist agitation of the thirties and forties is translated into the Gordon Riots of the 1780s in *Barnaby Rudge;* Chancery, in *Bleak House,* is pilloried the more effectively in a setting of the 1820s; class inequalities and injustices in 1859 are highlighted by the drama of the French Revolution in *A Tale of Two Cities.*) Dickens continually heightened the absurdity or enormity of modern evils by couching them in the barbarism or predatory violence of historic distance. House ends by showing Dickens in a far more convincing historical and critical light than that permitted by Jackson's or Lindsay's Marxist thesis. He shows him creatively independent in his methods even beyond the formulas and exactions of the Victorian forms in which he worked; eclectic in ordering and invigorating his materials; experimental in his dissection of moral and social situations; stubbornly resistant to social or political special-pleading at the same time that he kept his intimate authority over the public he aimed to reach. "He seemed topical to thousands," says Humphry House; "he was not too topical for them to see the point, nor too advanced to have the public conscience on his side . . . he so exploited his knowledge that the public recognized its master in knowing."

What thus emerges both from such socio-historical studies as House's and Edgar Johnson's—to a lesser but still serious degree from Jackson's—and from the recent biographical interpretations, is a full-bodied Dickens, compact to the errors, vigor, confusions, and obsessive dilemmas of his age, that has given new force and a new meaning to his powerful, his radical and essential, talent. His books, like all books, remain what they were when he wrote them. It is our reading of them that has been extended in vital interest, and that interest has been stimulated by a complex character and imaginative thinker only lately disclosed in his full dimensions.

Shaw was one of the first readers of Dickens privileged by such interest. He, like Dostoevsky, Henry James, Proust, and Joyce, shows the real impact of Dickens on the modern imagination, rather than the DeMorgans, Wellses, and Priestleys usually taken to be his descendants. It was, by Shaw's own account, *Little Dorrit* read in youth, not Marx or Nietzsche, that made him a social revolutionary, and he twice acknowledged this debt in some detail, in prefaces to *Hard Times* and *Great Expectations*. Dickens, Shaw said, "in spite of his exuberance, was a deeply reserved man—his imagination was ceaseless, and his outward life a feat of acting from beginning to end." And after noting that "Marx and Dickens were contemporaries living in the same city and pursuing the same profession" he added that "Marx knew that he was a revolutionist whilst Dickens had not the faintest suspicion of that part of his calling." Furthermore, an H. G. Wells "hated being a draper's assistant as much as Dickens hated being a warehouse boy, but he was not in the least ashamed of it" and would have known only too well that Dickens' "agonized sensitiveness about the blacking bottles and his resentment of his mother's opposition to his escape from them was . . . too snobbish to deserve all the sympathy he claimed for it." Put this remark together with Dickens' truculent behavior in the affair with Miss Ternan, his efforts to square the situation with conventional Victorian respectability by publishing his defense of it in his respectable domestic magazine, *Household Words,* his demand (obeyed) that his wife likewise square Miss Ternan's position by making a call on her, and his living, in the final years of his life, between his official shrine at Gad's Hill and the house he maintained for Miss Ternan in London, and we get what is probably the essential clue to Dickens' character and point of vantage in his age. It is a clue that corrects both the virtuously humane Dickens of Chesterton and the convinced revolutionary of Jackson.

The actual Dickens was neither of these. Taine sensed the fact, Gissing got hold of it though with some uncertainty, Wilson has traced its line through the novels until it arrives at what is without much question its crucial and final development in the character of John Jasper, divided between the laws of society and the compulsive outlawry of selfhood, in *Edwin Drood*. A critic in the English quarterly *Scrutiny* in 1942, R. C. Churchill, referred to it when he said that "it is a mistake to look in Dickens's writings for 'solutions'"; that "the sentimentality and vulgarity of the age he accepted with open arms; he was an important part, himself, of that sentimentality and vulgarity"; and that "the very confusion which would attend any attempt to view Dickens's labors as a whole has an attraction, and a certain value." The impurest of novelists, Dickens was also an impure thinker, as impure on both scores as Balzac, Hugo, and those of the Russians who took a part of their impetus from him. He perhaps never wrote a syllable in complete detachment or cool control of himself. His critical intelligence, his resistance to institutions, his struggling grasp of his century's events and causes, were persistently threatened by his immersion in the heat and confusion of his world. But for all the devices and compromises he traded in, the melodrama and comedy he inherited, the social and moral dilemmas he accepted, the scientific pretensions he shared with Balzac, he did not essentially simplify humanity, society, or morals.

Incapable as an aesthete, he was also incapable as a theorist. But this makes emphatic his survival as an artist, of the kind who generates and fecundates the art which he leaves purer craftsmen and moralists to distil or perfect. His mere range as a writer makes an inexhaustibly fascinating study, if only because, like Beethoven in music, he can be seen to anticipate, from style to style, a whole range of writers who followed him—Meredith, James, Conrad, Proust, Joyce. Mr. Leavis, in his rigorous challenge to the standardized view of the English novel in *The Great Tradition*, admits him to the company of the greatest—Austen, Eliot, James, Conrad, Lawrence—on the strength of *Hard Times* alone, defining in that

novel powers which certainly have a wider if qualified and neces-
sarily more complicated relevance: a "comprehensive vision"; a
"full critical vision, a stamina, a flexibility combined with consistency, and a depth that he seems to have had little credit for"; a
"triumph of ironic art"; a power to see "the common manifestations
of human kindness, and the essential virtues, asserting themselves in
the midst of ugliness, squalor, and banality" before which "his
warmly sympathetic response has no disgust to overcome"; above
all, "the truly dramatic and profoundly poetic whole" he made of
his insights and responses.

The task of criticism lies exactly in the discernment of this vision
and poetry, and of the means—so vexedly personal, so deeply involved in human and social confusion, so radically faithful to experience, so copiously varied and instinctively creative—by which
Dickens realized them. Where biographical research aids the restitu-
tion of this larger and greater Dickens it makes a radical contribution to criticism and to something more—to an understanding of the
vital sources out of which the genuine art of the modern novel has
emerged and on which it must count in the future. Those sources
have, during the past fifty years or more, yielded to another and
corrective order of discipline of which the novel stood in need after
the popular standards of the Nineteenth Century and the techniques
they encouraged—romantic or sentimental, realistic or naturalistic—
had almost succeeded in demoralizing it as a means of serious art
and thought. The principles of form, style, selection, analysis, and
symbolism came as a moral imperative to the novelist. They rescued
his medium from confusion and aesthetic collapse, stiffened it
against the inroads of a destructive vulgarization, restored it to its
necessary alliance not only with the discoveries of modern thought
and intellectual discipline but with the poetic, symbolic, and
mythopoeic bases of all great narrative art. Their danger lay in what
they have done to estrange the novelist from the substance and force
of experience, of life and action in their full amplitude and energy.

The gains in style and form, selectivity and formal rigor, moral emphasis and psychological subtlety, have shown their accompanying liabilities—the tenuity of content, alienation of human appeal, esoteric disproportion and self-sufficiency, which rigorists as far apart as James, Conrad, and D. H. Lawrence have feared as shaping a new crisis of exhaustion or impasse in the novel's history. Dickens, more than any other English novelist, joins the greatest of the French and Russian masters in the power he shows of joining social and historical substance with symbolic and mythic vision, of bringing the dramatic instinct to terms with allegoric insight and moral metaphor. He depended on no aesthetic instruction in this; he had probably the vaguest of conceptions about it; his acumen as a craftsman, his sizable body of comments on the novel and its future, do little to account for its workings in his books. What he brought to his craft was a distracted temper and rebellious impulse that kept him from submitting helplessly to the sentimental and didactic usages with which he compromised, as much as they set him apart from the disciplines of detachment and aesthetic calculation that were beginning to assert themselves in his lifetime.

The temper and impulse are to be traced in his books, of course; but they are equally evident in his actions and personality. They are now apparent in these as they never were when piety, official sentimentalism, and the scandal-fearing custodians of his fame combined to deny their existence. It is not with scandal or sensationalism that serious biography is concerned; it is with what biography can do to reveal an artist in his essential humanity, his experience in suffering and moral disturbance, and with what these have contributed to the truth, complexity, and authority of his work. The Dickens we know today can be seen much more clearly in his capacity for these than the simplified and sanctified figure his legend-makers so long projected on what they conceived to be his behalf. What we have come to learn of the man has made possible what we have rediscovered in his books. His stature as a major modern writer has gained a new lease on life. And as a consequence his books have re-established their claim on readers, critics, and novelists who might otherwise have forgotten what that claim, in its full dimensions and serious authority, requires of them in the way of respect, sympathy, and honor.

1943-49 [1956]

II. THE UNDIVIDED IMAGINATION

Bleak House

I

When Dickens began the writing of *Bleak House* late in 1851 he was advancing steadily across the high zenith of his career. He was now in his fortieth year. The swift success that had come to him at twenty-five, with the publication of the *Pickwick Papers* in 1837, was already fourteen years behind him. From that astonishing triumph he had passed without interruption to success after success in his books and in his conquest of a great public of readers, who soon came to include not only the English-speaking world of Great Britain and America but the countries of Europe as far east as Russia.

By 1851 he was a man of family and public prominence, master of a large home near Regent's Park in London and presently of a larger one on Tavistock Square, a London clubman and orator whose voice was heard on questions of the hour, a conscientious worker in causes of charity and reform, a traveler whose success had taken him not only to France and Italy but across the Atlantic on his first visit to America in 1842, and an editor who now had at his disposal a popular magazine, *Household Words,* in which to bring his prestige to work on the domestic taste, moral concerns, and problems at issue in Victorian England.

Besides the great bulk of his journalism and occasional writing, he was already the author of eight long novels and a series of Christmas tales which had seized the imagination of his contemporaries and quickly become part of the folklore and familiar mythology of their lives. He was prosperous, authoritative, read by thousands, surrounded by a growing troop of admirers and protégés, and recognized as a peer and equal by the literary masters of the time —an eminent Victorian and man of mark in his age. He had conquered the great world to whose fame he had aspired from the years of his young manhood when, his family fallen in its fortunes and its precariously achieved standing in respectable society slipping from its grasp, he had resolved to make a success of himself by the skill of his mind and pen.

His success was squarely founded on the taste and temper of the time. Few writers in the history of literature have been more sharply aware of the conditions of popular success, the tests of social approval, the demands and challenge of the reading public which, in its huge modern dimensions, was still a comparatively new thing in the world. Dickens' apprenticeship had been served in popular journalism. His first book, the *Sketches by Boz* in 1836, was a product of London newspapers and magazines. All his books and stories, through the almost forty years of his professional career, were addressed to the general reader, either as magazine serials, holiday books, or publications in monthly parts. His writing hand was never off the pulse of public response and approval. The temper of the age was in his ink, the voice and accent of the Nineteenth Century at the tip of his pen. That age and century was his great subject— had become so from the early moment when he had scanned his prospects, judged his task, taken stock of his future, and applied himself to the achievement of his great ambition. As systematically as Balzac, as industriously as Scott, as deliberately as Byron or Hugo or Tolstoy, he had resolved to master his century. He took for his subject the formidable drama of change, conflict, and progress which the century offered him as material for his imagination to work on.

He met that drama on its own terms. His driving energy, his zest and bravado of temperament, his moral sentiment and conflicting loyalties, his social aggressiveness and his critical acumen, his tact in compromise and the challenge of his moral resistance—all these were equally matched with equivalent elements in the spirit and ethos of Victorian England. Though he was possessed by a more powerful sense of his vocation and pride as an artist than he is commonly credited with, he never wrote solely, or even primarily, as an artist. The concentrated reserves of Jane Austen, the passionate aesthetic dedication of Flaubert, the scrupulous artistry of Turgenev, the rigor in formal and stylistic discipline of Henry James—none of these was his privilege. He began by being a public entertainer and he never abdicated from that role. If he enlarged upon it, it was to add the further popular functions of the public conscience, the exponent of public causes, the exhorter of moral welfare, the invoker of right and justice, the critic of institutions. He was in and of his age, and his age is in everything he wrote.

There are two principal ways in which a writer can become a spokesman of his age—the way of compromise and the way of challenge. He meets his time on its own terms or he compels it to meet him on his. He submits to its claims and prejudices or he bends it to his will. He flatters or indicts, complies or resists: he becomes its complaisant image or he becomes its critic and its prophet. It would be as difficult—and perhaps as much beside the point—to decide how much greater a writer Dickens would have become had he addressed himself wholly to the second of these functions as it would be to compute the exact degree of his superiority to the common practice in the first of them. It was as little Dickens' destiny to become a systematic thinker and reformer—a Carlyle, a Mill, an Arnold, Ruskin, or Shaw—as it was to remain cheerfully submerged in the ruck of popular or sentimental values that assured the success of the popular entertainers of Victorian England—Pierce Egan, Harrison Ainsworth, Bulwer-Lytton, Charles Reade, Charlotte Yonge, and a host of others, the elements of whose work he shared in some degree or other at every stage of his career. It is as unjust to accuse him of being a sentimental compromiser as it is to expect of him the rigorous intellectual superiority of Ibsen or Dostoevsky or the absolute sufficiency in moral contempt of Rimbaud. The melodrama, sentimentality, piety, pathos, and bathos that spell the defect of mid-Victorian art are all in him, parts of his moral and imaginative constitution. He never imperiled his success by excluding them from his equipment, even supposing that he had the power to do so. Nor did he subject his success to the risk of their opposites —the extremes of moral logic, ruthless inquisition, and conscious insult that impel the unsparing antinomian.

There is, admittedly, a more relevant measure of Dickens' mind and stature. He requires comparison with the supreme masters of the modern novel—with Stendhal, Balzac, Tolstoy, Dostoevsky, Henry James, and Proust: the men who have combined moral vision with aesthetic judgment in the most nearly perfect proportions the art of fiction has seen, and who achieved by the fusion their power of philosophic or metaphysical judgment of their materials. By that test Dickens reveals his lower station. He is neither the consistent and self-mastered artist these other novelists were, nor did he achieve what must count as an original discovery or revelation concerning human nature and experience. But that test, however imperative to the final commitments of criticism, is a supreme one. It might, flexibly applied, admit to the rank of pre-eminence several English novelists who are, in the strictest estimate, talents of narrower range and creative powers than Dickens himself—Fielding, Jane Austen, George Eliot, Thomas Hardy. In Dickens the elements were "so mixed" that he refuses to be categorized or arbitrarily ranked. He still comes to us as many things—storyteller, moralist, and entertainer; historian, journalist, reformer, and prophet. But perhaps most of all he appears as a fact, a phenomenon, a prodigious comprehensive sensibility, a witness of history in the great crisis at which it arrived in mid-Nineteenth Century Europe. When every defect or excess in his work has been tabulated, when every impurity in his art has been registered, when every concession he made to his age has been allowed, he still declares his claim to the noble title applied to one of his French contemporaries by another.[1] He is a moment in the conscience of man.

----

[1] To Zola by Anatole France in his tribute at Zola's funeral, Paris, 1902.

How Dickens came into that recognition, not only among his contemporaries but among more skeptical readers—Shaw, Proust, Gide, George Orwell—makes a significant chapter in modern criticism. How he links, in the evolution of the modern novel, with the most original geniuses which that form of writing has yet produced—with Balzac, Dostoevsky, and Henry James in the Nineteenth Century, with Proust, Joyce, Mann, Kafka, and Faulkner in the Twentieth—forms a problem in the genealogy or genetics of creation that calls for close scrutiny. One clue is particularly convenient.

It has now been for almost a century a persistent claim among Dickens' critics—Taine the first among them, Shaw, Gissing, Chesterton, Alain, and Edmund Wilson more recently—that Dickens achieved what only the greatest writers can achieve—the sense and dimensions of a moral universe of his own; that he is not only "the greatest dramatic writer that the English [have] had since Shakespeare" but that he rivals only Shakespeare among English authors in having "created the largest and most varied world." [2] To create such a world, to give it the weight and body of a valid organism of moral and human values, means more than is commonly supposed. It means not only the realization of a complete and rounded scene, a physical milieu of which the imagination can take full, instinctive, and free-ranging possession; and it means more than the populating of the scene with a gallery of human types of every rank or degree of society, every possible size and shape of human existence. Dickens' scene, rich though it is, is not nearly so generous as Balzac's or as historically comprehensive as Tolstoy's, nor is his research of human nature as profound or fathoming as Shakespeare's. Neither his language nor his moral powers permitted that supreme penetration. But to "create a world" also means—and this is perhaps as high a test as any—that a writer's "world" must communicate its human wholeness, its moral unity and relevance, to us, and convince us that they are real, authentic, inclusive.

---

[2] Edmund Wilson, "Dickens: The Two Scrooges," in *The Wound and the Bow* (1941), p. 3.

Such unity may exist in small compass: in the microcosmic form of Jane Austen, Turgenev, or Flaubert; in the effect of moral self-containment and symbolic precision which has been one of the principal aims of the modern novel as an art form. The unity may be attempted also in terms the reverse of these: in the panoramic dimensions of Balzac, Tolstoy, and Zola, whose projects of historical or social scope established the ambition of a large class of modern novelists who have addressed themselves to tracing the processes of social, family, or proletarian experience—writers of the *romans fleuves,* documentary histories, or massive inventories of the past hundred years. Such writers give us "worlds" of various kinds, but a genuine world requires for its achievement more than massive scope and detail. It requires both extension of scene and continuity of value; both scope of drama and unity of idea; both multiplicity of means and singleness of vision. Comprehensiveness of sympathy must join with coherence of judgment. The complex must come to terms with the simple. The creator of such a world is at once inclusive and radical—compendious in the material he undertakes to master; radical in the root-values to which he refers the truth or significance of the life he portrays.

Dickens lived and wrote in a time and conditions of distraction. His own nature—restless, responsive, impressionable, ambitious—spared him none of the claims of the restless age around him. It was an age continuous in change, disturbance, dislocation: an age, in fact, of continuous revolution. Whatever stability had once existed in the social and moral order, or was conceived to have existed there in the retrospective pathos of Nineteenth Century historians, had been shattered by the succession of revolutions that had transformed the modern world—American, French, Agrarian, Industrial. The demon of progress possessed Victorian Europe. "Things fall apart, the center cannot hold": however true this condition may have become in the Twentieth Century, it was fully as present in the Nineteenth. The spectre of anarchy—the fear that haunted the prophecies of Michelet, Carlyle, Arnold, and Nietzsche—obsessed the contemporary mind. Dickens is as much the novelist of this drama of change and revolution as he is the critic of the hereditary institutions that had come to represent the tyranny of the past over human life. His great images are alternately those of stagnation and ferment, of captivity and violence, of the Dead Hand and the Incendiary Torch. The fog smothers—the railway shrieks and gashes the landscape; prisons confine and bury men—mobs break and shatter them; dark dungeon-houses and rotting slums stifle their inhabitants —but houses and slums may crash and fall into dust; men passively or willingly submit to forces that oppress them—but they also defy their enslavement.

It became Dickens' task to confront in his drama these twin evils, these equal threats to the virtue and stability of mankind. He attempted to mediate between tyranny and anarchy, the dead past and the violent future. His principle of mediation required him to be at one and the same time a conservative and a radical: radical in the justice he demanded for humanity but conservative in the moral authority he saw as a necessary cognate of such justice. He combined in himself the moral sentimentalist and the moral revolutionary. The paradox is not Dickens' alone. It is part of the Victorian England in which revolution and reaction, authority and license, were forces almost equally, and certainly fatefully, matched. On their rival claims the theorist or philosopher was required to pass a decisive verdict. The purist in art might relegate the claims of both to the domain of skepticism or nihilism. Dickens was neither theorist nor philosopher, aesthete nor skeptic. He was a dramatist of history and of the moral life. A judgment of humanity was required of him, but not an abstract program of beliefs or prophecy. He was primarily responsible to the world of actualities and living people, and to the recreation of that world in his books. By the time he wrote *Bleak House* he had made himself an imaginative master of his age and was prepared to write the most ambitious judgment on it which he had yet attempted. *Bleak House* shows him working on a larger scale and in more complex terms than he had hitherto arrived at. The novel not only stands at the apex of his career. It perhaps forms the central buttress, the decisive moment, in his achievement. It has the effect of bringing to a climax everything in his work that preceded it, and of preparing the way for all he was to write afterward.

II

David Copperfield, Dickens' immediately preceding novel, had been finished in October 1850; its monthly numbers had appeared over a span of fourteen months and the book was published at the end of that year. Dickens was meanwhile deeply involved in launching his new magazine, *Household Words*, on its successful career and in the other teeming concerns of his family, friends, and public life. In the autumn of 1851 he moved his household from Devonshire Terrace, Regent's Park, to the larger home in Bloomsbury, Tavistock House, where they were to live for eight years. The idea of a new novel had been working in his mind for several months, bringing with it the familiar nervousness and impatience that possessed him at the outset of every new venture throughout his life: "violent restlessness and vague ideas of going I don't know where, I don't know why."

Titles and subtitles flitted through his mind: *Tom-all-Alone's: The Ruined House—Bleak House Academy—The East Wind—Tom-all-Alone's: The Solitary House where the Grass Grew—Tom-all-Alone's: The Solitary House that was always Shut up and never Lighted—Tom-all-Alone's: The Solitary House where the Wind howled—Tom-all-Alone's: The Ruined House that Got into Chancery and never got out—Bleak House and the East Wind: How they both got into Chancery and never got out—Bleak House.* Several images seem to have possessed him—a blighting wind, a ruinous slum, a house fated and doomed, and enclosing or connecting these, the trap of the Court of Chancery. Once settled in his new home and study, the new furnishings installed, the decorating finished, the family once more disposed in its new quarters, he began writing. By December seventh the first number was almost completed. It was published in March 1852, and the succeeding parts came out through the next eighteen months. Immediately more successful even than *Copperfield,* the novel sold some thirty-five thousand copies on each of its eighteen monthly appearances. By the end of August 1853, the book was finished. "I have never had so many readers," Dickens jubilated as he rounded off one of the most prodigious feats of his career.

Bleak House is the second in the sequence of seven novels of realistic social analysis and revolutionary implications that form the high span of Dickens' work. *Dombey and Son,* coming three years after *Martin Chuzzlewit* of 1843–45, had initiated that most serious phase of his genius in 1846–48. *Bleak House* came next in the sequence; then *Hard Times* in 1854; then *Little Dorrit* in 1855–57; *A Tale of Two Cities* followed in 1859; *Great Expectations* in 1860–61; and *Our Mutual Friend,* his last completed book, in 1864–65. *David Copperfield* in 1849–50 had been an interruption.

Copperfield hearkens back to an older England and a simpler world. In some respects it connects with the satirical humor and reminiscential vein of *Chuzzlewit,* in others with the sentimental mood of *The Old Curiosity Shop,* in still others with the buoyant spirit of the vanishing England that had found its great memorial in *Pickwick.* But its spell of charm, memory, and enchantment had more intimate roots. The book had begun as something close to autobiography; and though it abandoned the autobiographical framework once Dickens had transmuted his memories of childhood and the bitter experience in the blacking factory to which his impoverished parents had condemned him in the darkest moment of his youth, it remained personal in basis, an *Erziehungsroman* of David's encounter with life, hardship, love, misfortune, and final happiness in work, a second marriage, and parenthood. Its characters were conjured out of Dickens' deepest affections, closest likes and dislikes, most intimate sense of fate and life-wisdom. The glow and magic of its early chapters, though giving way to darker workings of evil and mischance, never wholly desert its pages. For all the personal feeling he had poured into his other books, Dickens had never before so fully translated himself, as man and spirit, into one

of his own creations; had never before made so direct an effort to
distance, objectify, and evaluate the processes that had brought him
out of his childhood's delights and suffering into the tests of maturity and the knowledge of what experience makes of a man. The
benedictory consolations that come to David in the love and death
of Dora, in the kindly ministry of his guardian Aunt Betsey, in the
griefs of Emily, Ham, and old Peggotty, in the buoyant will of
Micawber that brings the sinister Heep to justice, finally in the
blessings of his second wife Agnes, incarnation of the Victorian
"angel in the house"—these shape the faith in simple justice and
reconciliation that Dickens, at this point in his harassed and headlong progress, seized on as his ideal of experience. That ideal was
to elude him implacably in his own life, but for a moment he defined it for himself, and it must have had the effect of steadying his
nerve and reorganizing his energies for the more strenuous critical
program to which he had already addressed himself.

That program had been defined in *Dombey and Son*. Here
Dickens had in effect recreated himself as a novelist—both Gissing
and Chesterton noted the fact in their studies half a century ago.
Dombey still has the large dimensions, capacious plot, and ramifying
subplots, of his early books; it still provides most of the expected
contrasts and byplay of humor, satire, sentiment, melodrama, and
eventual catharsis. But the old ingredients of pathos, comedy, and
picaresque invention are now subdued to a larger design and more
strictly dramatic conception. Dickens had taken a swift stride in his
artistry. He had succeeded in integrating his profuse elements by
means of a focal theme, a comprehensive organism of action, and
symbolic devices wherewith to express and concentrate these and
thus to render them socially and historically significant.

His subject had a classic stamp. It was Pride—Mr. Dombey's
pride specifically, but also the pride of power and the wealth that
breeds power: the arrogance of the ruthless acquisitive ambition
which had become a new godhead of middle-class England and
Europe. His drama showed the grief, ruin, and deformation of
human instinct and passion which such Pride wreaks on the people

it dominates, and the fall to which in its blindness it is finally doomed.

The organism that embraces this theme in its devious ramifications is the great business house of Dombey and Son, symptom and epitome of selfish money power and warping tyranny. And the special symbol that spells wreckage, devastation, and the unleashed violence of the inhuman force that thus came to possess mankind is that new monster of the mid-Nineteenth Century world, brutal embodiment of mechanized energy, the railroad—the same railroad so often pictured in the *Punch* of those days or in the maledictions of Ruskin as a glaring, headlit engine of destruction, gouging open the green English landscape or the outposts of London, riding down the lives of men, and bringing the smoke and soot of industrialism in its wake: the dragon of a world grown heartless and of a future that promised to become more heartless still.[3] By shaping his book in terms of these devices, Dickens gave it a weight more solid, if less freely or spontaneously creative, than what he had achieved in *Martin Chuzzlewit*. A new equipment was now in his hands; and once he had completed *Copperfield*, where this technique does not appear, it served him in the sequence of large-scale visions of English society and modern history which were to follow as the continuous preoccupation of his last twenty years.

But another impulse was at work in Dickens' imagination. It had, in fact, been at work there from his beginnings; he was now to bring it to more serious use in the work that lay before him. It was the epic ambition. To name it may be to suggest the superficial misuse to which the term has often been reduced in modern times, whether in fiction, drama, poetry, or cinema; yet its presence in Dickens' art is unmistakable. It is not an impulse to which Dickens had any exclusive claim in the Nineteenth Century; it forms an animating ambition in the novel throughout that century and even

---

[3] Humphry House discusses the disruptive role of the railway and its symbolic use in *Dombey* in his book *The Dickens World* (1941), pp. 137–47, as well as the many other passages in which the railway figures in Dickens. His chapter on "The Changing Scene" offers a valuable background to Dickens' historical drama throughout the novels.

in our own. It was shared by Balzac, Scott, Victor Hugo, and
Manzoni; by Tolstoy, Zola, Thackeray on the lesser scale of social
drama, Hardy in the more "metaphysical" terms of cosmic allusion;
in fact, by most modern novelists who have aspired to large dimensions and comprehensive judgment. To seize and embody life in its
totality; to depict society as an organism of experience; and to make
that organism represent a moral universe—in these ambitions the
epic vision finds its compelling purpose. It seeks to create nothing
less than the image of a world—a drama of the common moral unity
of mankind.

That purpose, evident in fiction from its primitive and picaresque
European origins, came to Dickens directly from his Eighteenth
Century ancestors. His first work shows it in a tentative form. The
Sketches by Boz form an exploration of English and London life,
fragments of comedy, tragedy, and the grotesque that compose into
a conspectus of the scene the young Dickens was reconnoitering in
his early newspaper days. *Pickwick* is a comic epic straight out of
the lineage of *Don Quixote* and picaresque saga, a tour of the
English world with its episodes of farce, satire, joviality, Gothic
melodrama, and social evil strung on the thread of the adventures
of the Pickwick Club. In *Oliver Twist* the method changes. A complex, sinisterly ramifying plot comes forward in Oliver's castaway
life. He is the lost child or outcast heir in the dark forest of the
world, but that world takes on not the miscellaneous appearance of
an inventory but the more coherent spectre of a body of fate in
which all the lines are interknit, all the chances or accidents weighted
with intention, and this fate is enclosed in the dark embrace of a
haunted, crime-ridden London whose evil stalks its victims with
the deadly ruthlessness of a conscious destiny: the City of Dreadful
Night in one of its earliest Victorian renderings. Though *Nicholas
Nickleby* reverts to a cruder biographical and melodramatic scheme
it does not exclude a wide reach of social types and involvements.
The Old Curiosity Shop again engages the device of the wandering
hero—here Little Nell and her derelict grandfather: the child again,
with corrupt age in hand, threading the paths of an outcast fate.

Barnaby Rudge combines its hero's adventures with a drama of social revolution in the Gordon Riots of the 1780s, but by all but explicit reference it becomes a drama of social unrest and incipient revolution in the strike-rife, dissension-torn England of Chartism and the 1830s.

In *Martin Chuzzlewit* the primitive basis is still apparent. Martin and Mark Tapley carry out a crude Quixotic scheme in their English and American ventures, and melodrama extends its long reach of conspiracy, violence, and crime into the ramifications of the plot. But here the dispersed and heterogeneous elements are made to fit into a larger, inclusive frame. The novel, as the laborious, pastiche-like genealogy of its first chapter tells us while it ponderously delays our attention before the story proper springs into its marvelous life with Chapter II, is a family novel, a saga of the Chuzzlewit clan riddled by greed, money-lust, and interlocking hatreds. That family, before the story ends, becomes a microcosm of human life too, with the special intensity of corrupted blood and incestuous greeds: the paltry, avaricious tribe of the Chuzzlewits in time takes on the clutching, tentacular dimensions of an octopus. The epic motivation in the books of Dickens' first ten years advances from the serial and random method of *Boz* and *Pickwick*, the method essentially of the miscellany or inventory, to the method of the dramatic and moral organism.

Martin Chuzzlewit directly anticipates the family theme, now become integrated and structural, of *Dombey and Son*. And *Dombey and Son* prepares the way for the more complex, more intricate, more profoundly based and deeply riddled fate of the Jarndyce family and fortune in *Bleak House*.

III

The first chapter of *Bleak House* is consciously an overture. It sets the theme, strikes the chords, establishes the ground and motif, of the drama that follows. London—but more than London, England herself: "the Essex marshes," "the Kentish heights," river, ports,

and countryside—steam, drip, choke, and stifle in the all-enveloping
fog that becomes the dominating symbol of the tale and one of
Dickens' greatest strokes of atmospheric evocation. The fog is immediately established as the cognate of the High Court of Chancery
itself and of the "foggy glory" of its Lord High Chancellor where
he sits in state in Lincoln's Inn Hall, dispensing the suffocating
tedium and procrastinations of obsolete law. It also equates with
the eternally unresolved litigation of the Jarndyce estate case,
dragging its course through the courts decade after decade, blighting the hopes and desperate expectations of countless litigants.
When, moreover, we hear in the first paragraph that "it would not
be wonderful," in this world of mud, slime, smoke, and sooty
drizzle, "to meet a Megalosaurus, forty feet long or so, waddling
like an elephantine lizard up Holborn Hill," we know that Chancery
and Jarndyce embody frustrations that cast humanity back into
the darkest abyss of ancient blindness and primitive futility—into
a dead past whose hand will blight or deform every life, high or
low, that it touches.

"How many people out of the suit, Jarndyce and Jarndyce has
stretched forth its unwholesome hand to spoil and corrupt, would
be a very wide question": it is the great question the novel sets out
to investigate. Scarcely a noun or adjective in this opening chapter
leaves the nature of that doom unsuggested. We are in a world of
the "dim," the "sallow," the "murky," the "hopeless," the "pestilent";
of the "haggard and unwilling," the "dense" and the "muddy," the "se-
pulchral" and the "dusty," the "ill-fated" and the "grimly writhed";
a world, in a word, of a kind of "death." "This"—to make the matter
unmistakable—"is the Court of Chancery; which has its decaying
houses and its blighted lands in every shire; which has its worn-out
lunatic in every madhouse, and its dead in every church-yard; which
has its ruined suitor, with his slipshod heels and threadbare dress,
borrowing and begging through the round of every man's acquaintance; which gives to monied might, the means abundantly of weary-
ing out the right; which so exhausts finances, patience, courage,
hope; so overthrows the brain and breaks the heart; that there is

not an honorable man among its practitioners who would not give
—who does not often give—the warning, 'Suffer any wrong that can
be done you, rather than come here!' "

Dickens always handled his London geography with sure skill
and specificity. Each of his London novels has its particular setting
or group of related settings. *Bleak House* centers in legal London,
"the very heart of the fog": in Temple Bar, Chancery Lane, Lincoln's Inn, and their satellite streets and quarters—Lincoln's Inn
Fields where Mr. Tulkinghorn's gloomy house stands; Thavies Inn
where the Jellybys live; Cook's Court off Cursitor Street where the
Snagsbys have their law-stationer's shop and house, where old
Krook reigns in his rag-and-bone shop like another Lord Chancellor
over his accumulated trash, where Miss Flite lives in her eyrie of
captive birds and Nemo dies in his pauper's bed, and where the
rapacious Smallweeds nest like goblins nearby; and, not far off,
the slum of Tom-all-Alone's stinks and rots, a disease-ridden outpost
of the pervading stagnation.

All this forms the heart of the corruption, the central ganglion
of the deadly contagion which the novel will trace. That contagion
will extend its pestilence into the English world far and wide—to
Chesney Wold in Lincolnshire and the great house in London where
the Dedlocks hold their state; to Mr. Jarndyce's home near St.
Albans where Ada, Richard, and Esther find a haven from the doom
that threatens them; to the byways of Leicester Square where Mr.
George has his shooting gallery; to the Kentish suburb where the
Bagnets make their home; and even more tenuously to the house
of Mr. Boythorne in the north, to Gridley's origins in Shropshire, to
the kiln-workers' hovels in Hertfordshire, and even beyond England
to the Africa of Borrioboola-Gha where Mrs. Jellyby dreams of
civilizing the savages while her own home and family sink into chaos
and bankruptcy, or the America of the Tockahoopo Indians whom
Mrs. Pardiggle is determined to redeem with her smug philanthropic
gospel.

For we soon discover that Chancery and Jarndyce present only
one face of the blight. Moral presumption and tyranny are not

prerogatives of the past alone. They are equally active in the present. Social arrogance and parasitism can operate not only in impersonal institutions and stultified traditions. They appear with equal deadliness in modern creeds and living individuals. Fanaticism in the modern world is only a logical extension of the torpid oppressions of the dead. The sublime complacency of Sir Leicester Dedlock, with his retinue of fawning relations and political yea-sayers, instruments of a moribund parliamentary system and pride-blinded aristocracy, may join in fatuity with Chancery itself, but they have formidable rivals in another order of arrogance which Dickens viewed with equal detestation—the rapacity of moral self-importance and self-deluded idealism which preys on its victims as ruthlessly as the dead past does. Parasitism, arrogance, and moral presumption ramify the world of *Bleak House*. Chancery, Sir Leicester, and the tribes they seal—Lord Chancellor, Tulkinghorns, Vholeses, lawyers and time-servers, Coodles, Doodles, Foodles, and the rest —have their cognates in the whole gallery of tyrants and bloodsuckers that populates the novel—not only Mrs. Jellyby with her idiotic dreams for Africa and Mrs. Pardiggle with her Puseyite religious dictates but also Harold Skimpole, sponging his way through life on the pretenses of an artistic temperament, Old Turveydrop, draining the life-blood from his children on the claims of his Regency "Deportment," the Chadbands with their fatuous moral pomposity, the Smallweeds with their vulturous usury, Miss Barbary with her guilt-ridden religiosity. They are all a part of a conspiracy of pretension and tyranny which infiltrates the body of life and society. But the center of that conspiracy and of the drama that *Bleak House* unfolds will remain Chancery and Lincoln's Inn. What they represent remains from first to last the focus of the novel, and it will be to that center that all the destinies of the drama will eventually return—as Lady Dedlock herself will be drawn, when disgrace overtakes her, to the slum graveyard where her dead lover lies and at whose gate she dies.

"Ganglion: a sort of swelling or excrescence; a mass of nerve tissue containing nerve cells; a tumor caused by inflammation." The dictionary's definition is convenient, for Dickens conceived his novel in terms of morbid growth and infection, and of their pervasion throughout the body of society. As various critics have observed, he was acting in the office of an anatomist or pathologist.[4] He brought all the powers of his mature invention to tracing an infection to its farthest workings, and to devising a plot which should embody his diagnosis with scientific thoroughness—a plot which became, in the process, one of his major feats of dramatic complexity and ingenious knot-tying. Though he had little contact with Victorian science, he left some of Balzac's fascination by scientific method and theory. When he brought about the death of old Krook by spontaneous combustion, and tried to defend the phenomenon as a scientific possibility,[5] he was perhaps doing something more than exercising his dramatic ingenuity or proposing a symbol for the cataclysmic force required to blow Chancery and all its corruptions to perdition. He may also have been making a furtive appeal to the laws of science in the desperation he felt before the insoluble corruptions which had come to curse and sicken the life of humanity like an incurable disease.

That appeal, and the outlandish symbol of Krook's combustion which he planted squarely in the middle of his story, did not however exempt him from the prodigious complexities to which his social and moral analysis had committed him. He taxed his dramatic skill to the utmost in the plot he devised for *Bleak House*. In sheer invention it surpasses even the lavish actions of *Dombey, Little Dorrit*, and *Our Mutual Friend*. Such invention had been part of his equipment from the time of *Oliver Twist*. Dickens' plots belong to a fictional convention which it became one of the special objects of the art of the modern novel to reject. That art, with its standards

----

[4] Edgar Johnson, for one, calls his chapter on *Bleak House* in his *Charles Dickens* (1952), Vol. II, pp. 762–82, "The Anatomy of Society."

[5] The controversy aroused by Krook's combustion, George Henry Lewes's attack on Dickens' scientific claims in the London *Leader* (December 11, 1852, January 15, 1853, February 5 and 12, 1853) and Dickens' letters of defense, have been summarized by Gordon Haight in his article "Dickens and Lewes on Spontaneous Combustion" in *Nineteenth-Century Fiction*, Vol. X (June 1955), pp. 53–63.

of aesthetic consistency, psychological truth, and moral integration, had already before Dickens' death in 1870 taken his work as an object of attack and resistance. *Bleak House* represents the convention in which he worked at its most lavish development. The book is a feat of complex calculation, a supreme tour de force of dramatic artifice and contrivance. Unlikely chance, accident, coincidence, and melodrama operate throughout the proliferations of the plot. The test of such a novel must be the degree to which its contrivance is sustained and justified by symbolic force and logic—the power by which its moral argument vindicates the fable which it employs for its use and demonstration. The claims of *Bleak House* to a rank among the great modern novels hang on that test.

"In all Mr. Dickens's works the fantastic has been his great resource," said Henry James in his youthful criticism of *Our Mutual Friend* in 1865, "and while his fancy was lively and vigorous it accomplished great things." "But," he further announced, "the fantastic, when the fancy is dead, is a very poor business," and so was led to assert that "*Bleak House* was forced, *Little Dorrit* was laboured; [*Our Mutual Friend*] is dug out as with a spade and pick-axe." [6] James wrote this in the first severity of his reaction to the Dickens convention; he was one of the first to announce the modern resistance to it. Later he moderated his judgment. He admitted how Dickens had "laid his hand on us in a way to undermine as in no other case the power of detached appraisement"; how he had "entered so early into the blood and bone of our intelligence that it always remained better than the taste of overhauling him"; "how tremendously it had been laid upon young persons of our generation to feel Dickens, down to the soles of our shoes"; and how "no other debt in our time had been piled so high." [7]

----

[6] Henry James, "The Limitations of Dickens," in *The Nation*, December 21, 1865; reprinted in *Views and Reviews* by Henry James, edited by LeRoy Phillips (1908), pp. 153–61, and in *The Portable Henry James*, edited by Morton Dauwen Zabel (1951), pp. 433–40.

[7] See James's *A Small Boy and Others* (1913), pp. 117–18, and *Notes of a Son and Brother* (1914), pp. 253–56. The passages are quoted by Leon Edel in his *Henry James: The Untried Years* (1953), pp. 98–99, 277–78.

The modern critical reader of a novel like *Bleak House* still faces the necessity of harmonizing these two reactions as James himself felt them. The book is, on the one hand, a prodigious case, a pre-eminent Victorian instance, of what James called "the manufacture of fiction." On the other it offers, particularly to our more eclectic and experimental view, an equally prodigious example of social vision operating on a heroic scale and with a force of criticism that counterbalances the sentimentality and artifice that are integral to its conception and treatment.

Artifice of a theatrical kind is certainly integral to the tale. We feel its workings from the moment, in Chapter II, when Lady Dedlock, "bored to death" in her London house as she had already been bored to death in Lincolnshire, rests her languid glance on the Jarndyce documents Mr. Tulkinghorn has brought to show her, vaguely recognizes the script in which they have been written, suddenly rouses herself and "asks impulsively," "Who copied that?" Coincidence has shown its hand at the outset of the novel, and it will not work itself out until, fifty-eight chapters and many hundreds of pages later, Lady Dedlock dies by her lover's grave in the slum graveyard. Before that long thread is traced to its end, countless others will cross and entangle it—Esther's life as a lost daughter and child of mischance; Trooper George's life as another lost child, involved equally in the doom of his old hero Captain Hawdon, in the machinations of Mr. Tulkinghorn, and in the usuries of the Smallweeds; the street-waif Jo's martyrdom as an outcast of the London streets, victim alike of Lady Dedlock's secret guilt, of Tulkinghorn's vengeance, and of the pollution of the slum; old Krook's sinister fanaticism and spectacular death; Ada's and Richard's ruin in the snare of the "great expectations" Chancery and Jarndyce had promised them; the resistance of Mr. Rouncewell, the iron-master, exponent of the new self-made industrial power, to the hereditary social and political assumptions of the Dedlocks; the detective work of Inspector Bucket and those two other ferreters of hidden secrets, Tulkinghorn and Guppy; and then, crossing and accompanying these intermeshing lines of action, the peripheral fates of the many other characters who become involved in the action—Caddy Jellyby and her husband and their wizened child, victims of old Turveydrop's pretenses; Miss Flite and Gridley, victims of Chancery; Lawrence Boythorn and his maniacal litigations; Harold Skimpole and his parasitic cadgings; the Smallweeds with their plots and schemes; the Snagsbys with their inadvertent part in the mystery; the perverse philanthropies and sorry defeats of Mrs. Jellyby and Mrs. Pardiggle; the hard fates of the brick-makers and their wives. Merely to itemize the ramifications of the plot is to be astonished at Dickens' feat in threading the maze of complications he has devised and in keeping his reader in suspense until the center of the labyrinth has been reached. Or, to change the figure and adopt Edgar Johnson's: *Bleak House* shows a movement that "becomes a centripetal one like a whirlpool, at first slow and almost imperceptible, but fatefully drawing in successive groups of characters, circling faster and faster, and ultimately sucking them into the dark funnel whence none will escape uninjured and where many will be crushed and destroyed."

To control so vast an action, so complex a design, demands ingenuity and invention in maximum degrees, though to make a valid and impressive novel of them requires something more. No reader of *Bleak House* can close the book without an impression of inventive prodigality and dramatic manipulation perhaps unsurpassed in fiction. What is necessary to note is that these appear in a form quite different from the comprehensive amplitude and scale of Tolstoy in *War and Peace,* of Zola in the Rougon-Macquart epic, of Proust in *A la Recherche du Temps perdu,* or of Faulkner in his Yoknapatawpha saga. Those fictions, in differing degrees, work on wholly different principles of dramatic creation. Their impulse is the impulse of a purer historical logic, a natural and organic energy in their materials, a more realistic necessity in social and psychological analysis. Even Balzac yielded more instinctively to the social and moral situations in which he dealt; he is less the manipulator of events than Dickens is and less explicitly the manipulator of his moral arguments. In books like *Bleak House, Little Dorrit,* and *Our*

Mutual Friend Dickens did—the verdict seems unavoidable—"manufacture fiction." To ask what redeems these books from the artifice and contrivance of the genre to which they belong; why they have survived when countless of their Victorian rivals bred of the same method and conditions have fallen into neglect or oblivion; or what makes *Bleak House* the powerful book it remains after a hundred years, as much an artistic as a moral landmark in English fiction, is to suggest the essential test and question of Dickens' genius.

To answer it involves us in the practical problems of his craft as well as in its larger moral vision. From the first he had shown himself a born conjuror of spells. The appeal of story purely as such, basic and primitive in all fiction, was the magic that sped *Pickwick* and *Oliver Twist* to their triumphs, and it never wholly deserted Dickens, even when his purpose became more complex and his powers more strained. Yet this appeal, in spite of its supreme advantages, involves the novelist in a risk. Once his critical intelligence matures, once his sense of realism sharpens, his craft as a conjuror may become as much a liability as an asset. Dickens, whatever his skill in humor, melodrama, and artifice, was saved by an acute instinct of realism from the fate that eventually overtook most of the facile inventors of his time, but he had never been bred in the stricter authority of fact which, after 1850, asserted itself as a discipline in fiction and drama. What a recent critic, Philip Rahv, has said of Tolstoy, could never be said of Dickens: that in his work "the cleavage between art and life is of a minimal nature"; that "in a sense there are no plots in Tolstoy but simply the unquestioned and unalterable process of life itself; such is the astonishing immediacy with which he possesses his characters that he can dispense with manipulative techniques, as he dispenses with the belletristic devices of exaggeration, distortion, and dissimulation."

When Percy Lubbock dealt with Dickens in *The Craft of Fiction,* he was obliged to admit his "incurable love of labyrinthine mystification," a tendency which, "when it really ran away with him, certainly defeated all precautions." But by taking a clue from an observation made by Stevenson, Lubbock was also able to define

Dickens' skill in mastering that tendency when his genius worked at its strongest. Then his way "of dealing with his romantic intrigues was to lead gradually into them, through well-populated scenes of character and humour; so that his world is actual, its air familiar, by the time that his plot begins to thicken. He gives himself an ample margin in which to make the impression of the kind of truth he needs, before beginning to concentrate upon the fabulous action of the climax." In *Bleak House* notably, "a broad stream of diversified life moves slowly in a certain direction, so deliberately at first that its scope, its spread, is much more evident than its movement," until "presently we are in the thick of the story, hurrying to the catastrophe, without having noticed at all, it may be, that our novel of manners has turned into a romantic drama, with a mysterious crime to crown it." [8]

Lubbock took as the "chief characteristic" of Dickens' method "this careful introduction of violent drama into a scene already prepared to vouch for it," and he believed that Dickens managed it more artfully than Balzac did "because his imagination is not, like Balzac's, divided against itself." What he says emphasizes what is perhaps the major fact about Dickens' imagination: that whatever its distractions, strains, and exacerbations, and whatever its struggle toward increasingly greater moral and historical capacities, it remained basically instinctive and primitive. It succeeded, where so many other novelists have failed, in reconciling fancy with realism, fact with parable, history with fable. It may be, as George Orwell has said, that we must read Dickens at two ages of our lives: in youth, when we can take his plots and fables uncritically, and in maturity, when we can relegate his devices and dramatic apparatus to the status of a convention and devote our attention to his human and moral values.

But a novel remains finally a unity, a total organism, at whatever age we read it. Its final truth or validity must rest as much on its means as on its content, on its form as much as on its moral or

----

[8] Percy Lubbock, *The Craft of Fiction* (1921), pp. 212–17.

social vision. If in Dickens these never arrived at the wholeness or coincidence they achieve in Tolstoy or Proust, they nevertheless come to us joined and equal in appeal. *Bleak House* is massively and extravagantly plotted, and the plotting is inseparable from the social analysis which is the major concern and *raison d'être* of the book—indeed, it was conceived as a means toward such analysis. The fog, Chancery, and Jarndyce establish the continuum of theme and atmosphere that supports the fable, and they sustain it in all its ramifications. It was Dickens' greatest sign of imaginative energy that he should, in his most ambitious novels, have come into powers of symbolic control and authority which were scarcely evident in his work before 1846, or, if evident there, were chiefly based on the cruder moralistic sentiments and dramatic conventions of a now decadent romantic tradition. The fog of *Bleak House*, the prisons of *Little Dorrit*, the resurrection theme of *A Tale of Two Cities*, the river and dust-heap of *Our Mutual Friend*, dominate and sustain these novels from end to end, reinforce their plots even when the plots verge on the incredible, and so give moral strength to the drama even when the drama resorts to devices of melodrama, contrivance, coincidence, and, even in his mature work, to the old vein of willful fantasy that he was never to exorcise from his work or character. But the symbolic without a basis in truth, moral passion without a basis in character, parable without the reinforcement of conflict and solid plot structure, deprive a novelist of the substance of his art—the fact, action, and actuality which remain the stuff and basis of his craft.

By 1851 Dickens was at a stage of his career when he felt acutely the dangers of overworking his material, of repeating and exhausting his resources. His public must be kept avid at all costs. His monthly numbers must continue to sell and to increase in sales. His prodigious powers of invention were under the constant strain of renewing and alerting themselves. The old plots and spells must extend and refresh their appeal. The mounting expenses of his home, children, public undertakings and hospitality, and an increasing number of dependent relatives, his wife's as well as his own ("I never had anything left to me but relations," he once wrote with some bitterness), meant chronic anxiety that his sway over his readers must not only not diminish but increase. *Bleak House*, more than any previous novel, shows Dickens experimenting with his form and material.

It is, to begin with, a double novel, composed of two alternating narratives, the novelist's own and Esther Summerson's. Dickens' chapters (as we may call them) are written in the third person and in the present tense. Esther's are told in the first person and in the past tense. Here, at the outset, is an arbitrary scheme. What are its purpose and results? How does the incongruity of method justify itself? That it put Dickens to unprecedented effort and to a certain strain on credulity is apparent. Esther's story, Dickens' next attempt after *Copperfield* at an autobiographical novel—Pip's in *Great Expectations* was still nine years in the future—must not only tell what Esther sees and hears from the point of view of a simple, virtuous, and naïve intelligence; it must also cover a great deal of ground to which she has access by fairly factitious means, and it is bound to include many passages, observations, and insights of a sophisticated kind which can be credited less to her than to the novelist who looks over her shoulder. She must not only sustain a tone of reticence and modesty but register all the affection and tribute to which her friends treat her as the Dame Durden, Dame Trot, or Little Old Woman who discreetly ministers her love and benevolence to them. Her mock-modesty, in fact, can become one of the tiresome features of her tale, as her expeditious canvassing of events and subplots can become at times too efficient to believe.

Dickens' chapters, meanwhile, are written in deliberate contrast to hers. They sustain from the first the tone of high-stilted irony which had already appeared in large parts of *Chuzzlewit* and *Dombey*. The present tense supports this effect. Retrospective sentiment, the moderating distance of things remembered, the softening haze of historic pathos, are supplanted by the voice of acerbity, harsh immediacy, and a scathing contempt. This voice can rise to the heat of passion, exhortation, even to a sermonizing denunciation when it comes to dealing with Krook's combustion, Jo's death, or Lady Dedlock's flight; it can evoke a spectral atmosphere for Chesney Wold or a doom-struck suspense for Mr. Tulkinghorn's chambers; but it will remain from first to last a voice of ironic severity and implicit moral judgment—the sustaining critical basis of the book.

Yet it is by the alternation of his two narratives that Dickens achieves something new in his art in this book: a depth of focus, a third dimension in his perspective, a moral resonance, and an implicit ambiguity of sympathy and insight. The actual substance of the novel, moral as well as dramatic, becomes enriched in a way he had not yet defined so realistically; indeed, the complication of his form supports the complication and depth of his drama and intelligence. It gave his emotions, sympathies, and critical powers a new lease on life, a tougher energy and resilience of insight. Increasingly he had, especially after *The Old Curiosity Shop* in 1840, written in terms of a double attitude toward his material: he had come to stand both inside his story and outside of it. Sentiment and criticism, pathos and irony, had slowly achieved a high-strung balance in tales like *Barnaby Rudge, Chuzzlewit,* and *Dombey and Son*—a token, no doubt, of his own increasing ambiguity of mind and feeling, the sentimentalist at grips with the radical in his nature, the conformist at odds with the critic and social rebel. *Bleak House* certified and demonstrated the conflict in its very method, and so exercised in Dickens a complexity of moral sympathy and dramatic ambiguity which were to serve him powerfully in the books he was to write in the future—in *Little Dorrit, A Tale of Two Cities, Great Expectations,* and *Our Mutual Friend,* in all of which the significant figure of the man divided against himself —Arthur Clennam, Sydney Carton, Pip, Bradley Headstone—was to appear, until finally, in John Jasper of *Edwin Drood,* that divided self and *âme damnée* becomes the clue and center of Dickens' essential drama in a way that brings that novel into the company of a whole line of Nineteenth Century parables—Poe's *William Wilson,* Balzac's *Illusions Perdues,* Dostoevsky's *Crime and Punish-*

ment, Wilde's *Dorian Gray,* and Stevenson's *Dr. Jekyll and Mr. Hyde.*[9]

Something more, however, was needed than a double novel to sustain Dickens' plot in the proliferations of its central mystery and the solution of it. As alert as Balzac to the social and scientific phenomena which the age was offering its novelists, Dickens was almost as quick as Balzac to seize upon one of the chief of these, the police detective. *Le Père Goriot* in 1834 had transformed into the sinister police agent Vautrin the career of that phenomenal character of Napoleonic France, Eugène François Vidocq, the adventurer, forger, criminal and *galérien* who, by a feat of transformation that symbolizes the duplicity and opportunism of a new bourgeois age, became chief of the Paris *Sûreté,* dread nemesis of criminals, and publisher in 1829 of his semi-apochryphal *Mémoires* which bared the whole corrupt under-life of the uneasy century. In 1829 Sir Robert Peel, then Home Secretary, had by act of Parliament established the metropolitan Police Force in London. Law officers of an earlier time had been used by Dickens in *Pickwick, Barnaby Rudge, The Old Curiosity Shop,* and *Martin Chuzzlewit.* Now he was ready to make effective use of Peel's detective constable, who becomes the Inspector Bucket of *Bleak House.* The "sensation novel" whose great mid-Victorian vogue was already afoot was to make special use of the apparatus of modern law and police detection. Wilkie Collins, Dickens' favorite protégé and disciple, was to carry it to its highest triumphs in *The Woman in White, No Name, Armadale,* and *The Moonstone* in the sixties. Bulwer-Lytton, Charles Reade, Mrs. Henry Wood, and a host of their imitators were to capitalize on its attractions. Dickens pioneered for all of them. *Bleak House* antedates by eight years *The Woman in White* (1860) and by sixteen *The Moonstone,* which T. S. Eliot has rated "the first and greatest of English detective novels." [10] *Bleak House* is, in fact, a

---

[9] Edmund Wilson, in *The Wound and the Bow* (1941), makes the figure of the divided man the central argument in his study of Dickens.

[10] T. S. Eliot, "Wilkie Collins and Dickens," in *Selected Essays, 1917–1932* (1932), pp. 373–82; here p. 377. The whole essay traces Dickens' advances in

novel of multiple detectives. Bucket is reinforced by both Tulkinghorn and Guppy. They are all in search of secrets; they all, for
purposes unofficial as well as official, thread the maze of the mystery.
And they all cut ruthlessly across the class distinctions, protective
barriers, and social ranks that foster mystery or breed crime, alienate
souls and corrupt human instincts. No device could have served
Dickens better than the impersonal critical agency of Inspector
Bucket in carrying out what Eliot has noted in John Forster's *Life*
as a lifelong preoccupation:

> On the coincidences, resemblances, and surprises of life [said
> Forster] Dickens liked especially to dwell, and few things moved his
> fancy so pleasantly. The world, he would say, was so much smaller
> than we thought it; we were all so connected by fate without know-
> ing it; people supposed to be far apart were so constantly elbowing
> each other; and tomorrow bore so close a resemblance to nothing
> half so much as to yesterday.

It is with these links of fate, crossed lines of destiny, secret moral
alliances, this community in error, guilt, and responsibility, that
Bleak House, indeed that all of Dickens' novels, are finally concerned. When he came to write *Little Dorrit*, he first intended to
name it *Nobody's Fault*. The phrase was intended in its fullest
irony. The guilt and error in society are "nobody's" because the
whole ethic of evasion, casuistry, and moral shirking in modern
society refuses to accept it. But what Dickens meant was that the
fault is everybody's. All society is implicated in the responsibility.
If crime, subterfuge, and suffering infect and stultify life, their
consequences can be escaped by no one. "Dead, your Majesty,"
cries Dickens in the most passionate outburst in *Bleak House*, when
little Jo dies, martyr of society and pathetic sacrifice both to the
remorseless heart of Chancery and Jarndyce and to the fetid evil
of Tom-all-Alone's: "Dead, my lords and gentlemen. Dead, Right
Reverends and Wrong Reverends of every order. Dead, men and
women, born with Heavenly compassion in your hearts. And dying
thus around us every day."

----

plot construction and motivation and the connection of these with Collins'
methods.

IV

It required something more than the conventions of moral justice and his long-tested practice in the arts of sentiment and nemesis— something more even than his massive skill in plot invention and dramatic manipulation—to bring Dickens to the feat of sustained suspense and penetrating social inquisition he achieved in *Bleak House*. The novel does more than collapse society to its essential unity and singleness in moral destiny, its community in error and common participation in evil. The book is a "dark novel" in more than its atmosphere of murk, fog, rain, and suffocation; it is dark in its instinct of tragedy and, whatever its final rewards for the virtuous, in its view of the social and human future. In it, for the first time, Dickens allowed himself to do what he had shrunk from doing in Walter Gay's case in *Dombey and Son:* he shows his romantic hero, Richard Carstone, degenerate into weakness, apathy, and the demoralization that ensues from those "great expectations" which had become the *ignis fatuus* of a century deluded by false prosperity and deceiving appearance; Richard indeed shifts the whole ground of the Dickens hero, and so prepares the fates of Arthur Clennam, Sydney Carton, Pip, and Bradley Headstone that lie ahead. The title of the novel itself is a portent. "Bleak House" is more than the name of Mr. Jarndyce's home. Like the cherry orchard of Chekhov's title it names a phase of modern history; and like Shaw's *Heartbreak House,* which obviously echoes Dickens' title—possibly in tribute to the profound debt Shaw felt he owed the author of *Bleak House* (whose political criticism alone, he said, "has never been surpassed for accuracy and for penetration of superficial pretense") and of *Little Dorrit* ("a more seditious book than *Das Kapital.* All over Europe men and women are in prison for pamphlets and speeches which are to *Little Dorrit* as red pepper to dynamite")—*Bleak House* stands for the England and the Europe which, to Dickens' appalled dismay, had taken shape and form around him. When Shaw coupled *Heartbreak House* with the plays of Chekhov and Ibsen as a treatise on the "cultured, leisured Europe" of the Nineteenth Century, he may have had the equally close case of Dickens as much in his mind:

> The same nice people, the same utter futility. The nice people could read; some of them could write; and they were the sole repositories of culture who had social opportunities of contact with our politicians, administrators, and newspaper proprietors, or any chance of sharing or influencing their activities. But they shrank from that contact. . . . They did not wish to realize Utopia for the common people: they wished to realize their favorite fictions and poems in their own lives; and, when they could, they lived without scruple on incomes which they did nothing to earn. . . . They took the only part of our society in which there was leisure for high culture, and made it an economic, political, and, as far as practicable, a moral vacuum.[11]

These angry sentences echo Dickens' own. *Bleak House* is an angry novel, eloquent of the resentment, cold fury, and passionate impatience its author came to feel as he saw the generous hopes, romantic ardor, and high promise of the world of his young manhood driven headlong against the implacable materialism and hypocrisy of a new age. The anger had its source in personal conflict as much as in public conflict. Dickens was now advancing into those riddled, passionate years of his middle life when his secret desires and ambitions were to come to grief, distress, and bitter disappointment. His marriage was foundering; in 1858 it was wrecked and his wife banished from his home. His children were becoming a new source of anxiety and worry. The "old unhappy feeling" David Copperfield had felt had become chronic in Dickens himself: "a vague unhappy loss or want of something," something "incapable of realization," some "dream of youthful fancy," some desire for "renewal in another world," that could "never never more be reanimated here." None of the "dreadful insatiability" with which he threw himself into his work, his public life, his theatricals, charities, and projects, seemed able to dispel the dread of a spiritual death. To become somehow

---

11 Bernard Shaw, Preface to *Heartbreak House*, &c. (1919), pp. x–xi and *passim*. The quotations from Shaw above are from his Introduction to the Limited Editions Club edition of *Great Expectations* (1937).

"recalled to life" fixed itself on him like an obsession: was written as such into his future tales of prisons, death-traps, entombments of the living, losses of identity, imprisoning morbid states. But the England Dickens saw around him in 1851, when *Bleak House* began shaping itself in his mind, gave him practical reasons for the venting of his exasperation and undoubtedly precipitated the mood of anger in which the book was written.

Though 1851 marked a turning of the tide of depression, self-criticism, and humiliation through which England had passed during the years of Chartism, labor strife, and the "hungry Forties," Dickens viewed the return to nationalistic solidarity and public complacency with uneasiness and distaste.[12] The Great Exhibition, creation of the Prince Consort and fulsome token of England's industrial genius and imperialistic prowess, he saw chiefly as an encouragement to self-satisfaction and public self-flattery. The revival of religious enthusiasm in the wake of the Oxford reformers went hand in hand with this general taste for self-deception: the Puseyism he was to ridicule in Mrs. Pardiggle had only succeeded in "putting back the hands upon the Clock of Time, and cancelling a few hundred years of history," and helped bring about the "intolerable enormity," as he called it, of a re-established Roman hierarchy in 1850. Parliament and Government were rife with ineptitude. The session of Parliament had hardly opened in February 1851 when Lord John Russell was defeated and the country left without a government for two weeks, one leader after another trying to form a new cabinet and finally forming one too weak to last—"Boodle and his retinue, and Buffy and *his* retinue" seeming to be the incompetents "for whom the stage is reserved."

Meanwhile the condition of the English and London poor was as wretched as ever. Dickens had become almost professionally aware of it in the help he gave the heiress Angela Burdett Coutts in negotiating her projects for slum clearance and workmen's houses. The cause of sanitary reform had called public attention to the

---

[12] "*Bleak House* in the Context of 1851" is discussed and documented by John Butt in *Nineteenth-Century Fiction*, Vol. X (June 1955), pp. 1–21.

horrors of London's inadequate sewage system and the diseases it bred throughout the city. When Dr. Simon wrote his report on the Sanitary Condition of the City for the Commissioners of Sewers late in 1850, the *Times,* discussing it on December 31, 1850, and on January 2, 1851, called attention to the "definite, palpable, removable evils" that caused the "unhealthiness of towns"—the "dense overcrowding of a population," the "defective drainage," the "intricate ramifications of courts and alleys, excluding light and air," the "organic decomposition," "contaminated water," and "stinking atmosphere," all of them "distinct causes of disease and death." Twice Dickens had been chosen as speaker at the dinners of the Metropolitan Sanitary Association, in February 1850, and in May 1851; and when, shortly thereafter, he published a new edition of *Oliver Twist,* he took occasion to say that the reform of slums and sanitation "must precede all other Social Reforms," must "prepare the way for Education, even for Religion," and that "without it, those classes of the people which increase the fastest, must become so desperate, and be made so miserable, as to bear within themselves the certain seeds of ruin to the whole community." He had supported Mrs. Caroline Chisholm's Family Colonization Loan Society when it was set up in May 1850, but he remembered Mrs. Chisholm's slovenly housekeeping and dirty children as a nightmare symptom of what Carlyle had also despised: Utopia abroad and chaos at home. All these conditions and the vexation they caused him were to find place in *Bleak House;* but what found chief place there was the age-old and colossal ineptitude of Chancery.

In the first year of *Household Words* he had written two papers for its pages on "The Martyrs of Chancery." Its malpractices had been notorious for decades. The Day estate case, begun in 1834, had involved dozens of lawyers, and by 1851 had already incurred costs of seventy thousand pounds. The Jennings case, begun in 1798, and involving the disputed fortune (some one and a half million pounds) of an Acton eccentric who had died intestate, had already wasted the costs and hopes of its litigants for five decades (by 1915, when the case was still unsettled, its costs had amounted to two hundred fifty thousand pounds), and became the immediate model of Jarndyce and Jarndyce.[13] When Queen Victoria opened Parliament in February 1851, she presumed that the reform of various departments of law and equity would "doubtless receive serious attention," a suggestion which led the *Times,* which had long agitated against "the inertia of an antiquated jurisprudence," to say that "the state of the Court of Chancery is . . . an evil of extreme magnitude," and that "a suit in that court is endless, bottomless, and insatiable": "There is no word so terrible to an Englishman as this. An honest, industrious man . . . will turn pale and sick at heart at the bare mention of Chancery." "Success and defeat are alike fatal to litigants," the *Times* had said on December 24, 1850; "The lingering and expectant suitors waste their lives as well as their substance in vain hopes, and death robs them of their wished-for triumph, if ruin have not already rendered it impossible."

Here Dickens found his clue, his device for attacking the entire apparatus of inertia, casuistry, opportunism, shirking hypocrisy, and do-nothingism which he had always felt to be the curse of English tradition. The law had already been scathed in Dodson, Fogg, and Buzfuz in *Pickwick;* the poor laws in *Oliver Twist;* the predatory aristocracy in *Nicholas Nickleby;* greed, misers, and money-lust in *Chuzzlewit;* money power in *Dombey.* The turn of utilitarian economy and self-seeking trade unionism was to come in *Hard Times;* of the "Circumlocution Office" of Government in *Little Dorrit;* of corrupt wealth in *Our Mutual Friend;* of smug philanthropy, his ancient detestation, again in *Edwin Drood.* Chancery gave him an organism of irresponsibility more comprehensive than any of these. It permitted him to organize a novel in which the ramifications of legalized incompetence and the dead past reach to every stratum of English life. It became his task in *Bleak House* to treat the whole body of society as the organism of the blight and

----

[13] Edgar Johnson, op. cit., II, p. 771, quoting from *The Dickensian* (London), Vol. XI, p. 2.

desiccation to which these evils led, and to make of the novel an epic warning on the fate of England if the evil were to persist.

Thus the novel became, and remains, a fable of modern society at a point of crisis. That sense of crisis was powerful in Dickens' work throughout the two decades (1846–1865) of his major novels. They all rest on a basis of the critical and the didactic; form a sequence of exempla of social and moral wrong; are impelled by a reformer's zeal and a crusader's purpose. All of them turn on a conviction that had become for Dickens an informing passion: namely, that there is in mankind an instinct for life, self-realization, hope, liberty, and love, and that this instinct is forever preyed upon by forces of selfishness, timidity, fear, irresponsibility, and possessive greed. His books are part of a standard Victorian commodity: they are "tracts for the times." But though Dickens was always bound and tethered to his age, he had in himself a force of larger vision and humanity that over-leaped his age and enabled him to produce fables that define deep-seated and permanent elements in the condition and ordeal of mankind.

That condition is defined in his books as primarily social, yet had it remained social and nothing more, they would have long since receded to the status of merely historical documents. What has saved them from that diminution was what finally saved Dickens as an artist. He saw superficial evil as rooted in what he himself knew so intimately in his personal life and character: in the moral ambiguity and confusion of the human personality and in the psychic conflict that impels it to its crimes, if also to its ultimate heroism. He may not give us the purest drama, the truest plots, and the greatest characters the modern novel has produced. For these we must look elsewhere. An essential criticism of Dickens was suggested in what is perhaps the most acute passage of George Orwell's essay: "Why," he asks, "is it that Tolstoy's grasp seems to be so much larger than Dickens'—why is it that he seems able to tell you so much more *about yourself?*" "It is not," he believes, that Tolstoy "is more gifted, or even, in the last analysis, more intelligent," but because "he is writing about people who are growing," who "are struggling to make their souls," whereas "Dickens' are already finished and perfect." They "have no mental life. They say perfectly the thing that they have to say, but they cannot be conceived as talking about anything else. They never learn, never speculate." "In my own mind," he continues, "Dickens' people are present far more often and far more vividly than Tolstoy's, but always in a single unchangeable attitude, like pictures or pieces of furniture. You cannot hold an imaginary conversation with a Dickens character as you can with, say, Pierre Bezoukhov." [14] Or, one might add, with Flaubert's Frédéric Moreau and Marie Arnoux, with Dostoevsky's Kirilov and Prince Myshkin, with Turgenev's Bazarov and Lavretsky, with Isabel Archer, Ransom, Strether, Kate Croy, and a large number of other characters in Henry James, with the Swann, Odette, Mme. Verdurin, Saint-Loup, and Mme. de Guermantes of Proust.

But if the power of creating characters that become an intimate and self-perpetuating part of our experience was not the essential of Dickens' genius, he owned another power necessary to the novelist of moral and historical capacity. He fixed the elements of virtue and evil in human nature in essential and definitive forms; infused in his plots and fables a vision of justice that disengages itself from their artifice and applies itself to historic situations and recurring crises in society which his moral passion and instinct of conflict could prophesy as vital and constitutional. If, as Humphry House has said, "he made out of Victorian England a complete world, with a life and vigour and idiom of its own, quite unlike any other world there has ever been," the energy of his human and social insight made of that world an imaginative organism which becomes more than Victorian. It generalizes itself as an image of experience and history, and so becomes what epic and fable are by definition —modes of radical truth, and of its workings in men and society. Much as he contributed to the resources and animus of the modern novel by his invention and fantasy, it was the primitive instinct in

---

[14] George Orwell, "Charles Dickens," first published in his *Inside the Whale* (1940); later in *Dickens, Dali, and Others* (1946), pp. 1–75; here pp. 68–69.

Dickens' nature that finally made him a symbolist and prophet of human ordeal. Few novelists have worked under severer conditions of public pressure, moral vexation, and agitated conscience. But distracted as he was by the social unrest and moral duplicity of his age, confused by the impulses at conflict in his own temperament, divided in his sentimental and critical values, there worked in him a force that persisted to the end as single and integral—an imagination that remained undivided and so enabled him to combine judgment with compassion, his critical insight with his moral sympathy, in a vision that holds its authority because it is at once real and just. Of this order of genius Dickens stands a classic type, as *Bleak House,* in which his powers worked at their most ambitious, remains a fable classic not only in its own century and society, but beyond them in ours.

1956

III. THE REVOLUTIONARY FATE

A *Tale of Two Cities*

I

A Tale of Two Cities is evidently no longer what it once was. For more than half a century after its first appearance in *All the Year Round* it was one of the two or three favorites among Dickens' books and by general consent the most dramatically compelling of them all, a familiar classic on the French Revolution and a virtual textbook of popular history. Today it is likely to be called one of the "less serious" novels. Most critics since Shaw have followed his lead in brushing it aside as a product of the "sentimental romancer" in Dickens; the appeal of its sentiment has yielded to the critical realism in the social dramas and of its melodrama to the symbolic

force of the later moral subjects. But the book came at a crucial
point in Dickens' career, in 1859 when he was forty-seven. It is
the single novel in which he attempted to deal with the larger fate
of Europe. For its first readers it must have had the effect of bringing to an explicit climax the great subject that taxed him throughout
the last twenty years of his life—the crisis in English and European
society in the Nineteenth Century. Anyone who wants to know what
that crisis meant to Dickens, not only as a political but as a moral
and personal fact, is obliged to recall the impact of the book on its
time. The reasons for its Victorian fame are not unrelated to the
force of Dickens' historical vision as it concerns us today.

The novel is, for those who choose to read it as such, a historical
romance, and it must have come as a relief from the harsher realism
of its three predecessors, *Bleak House, Hard Times,* and *Little
Dorrit.* Its drama is soon set at a pitch of direct and unequivocal
eloquence, little complicated by the dramatic irony and nettling
ambiguity that had become a tendency in Dickens in the fifties.
The urgency of its appeal is immediate, even hortatory, from the
opening page. ("I have so far verified what is done and suffered
in these pages," Dickens claimed in his preface, "as that I have certainly done and suffered it all myself.") It treats a subject that
haunted the mind of England and Europe throughout the Nineteenth
Century, fully if fearfully recognized as a supreme portent in
Western history. It converted its theme into a socio-political fable
that carried a warning to the uneasy time in which it appeared.
The Revolution, already of legendary interest, especially after Carlyle's book in 1837, renewed its sinister fascination for Englishmen
in 1859 when England's old suspicion of France and the French
threat to European stability was revived by her fear of the Second
Empire and Napoleon III's Italian campaign. And since the book
is both shorter and more compact than the riddled panoramas of
modern life Dickens had lately been producing, its political topi-
cality combined with its romantic appeal in a fashion calculated to
suit the general taste of the moment.

These properties have always acted in some quarters to lessen its appeal to Dickens specialists. Chesterton found the *Tale* short in Dickens' strongest imaginative and humorous life: he felt that the Revolution was too French an event to find "a precise counterpart in so jolly and autochthonous an Englishman," and that Carlyle's "disturbed and half-skeptical transcendentalism" joined uncomfortably with "the original school and spirit to which Dickens belonged, the lucid and laughing decisiveness of the old convinced and contented Radicalism." [1] But this is to take a view of Dickens hardly tenable today, however sound it may have seemed when Chesterton wrote fifty years ago. Even Gissing felt that the novelist, by laying "a restraint upon himself," inhibited "the best" of his genius, and "whilst admitting that he has produced something like a true tragedy," thought that "many another man could have handled the theme as well, if not better." [2] It is certainly to be allowed that the *Tale* does not show Dickens' art at its highest mark of zest, spontaneity, and vividness. It lacks the free invention and exuberance that fired him from the *Pickwick Papers* to *David Copperfield*, as it also marks a lapse from the complex analysis of society he achieved in *Dombey and Son, Bleak House,* and *Little Dorrit.* The fable permits both melodrama and romantic sentiment which in his two other shorter novels, *Hard Times* and *Great Expectations,* are subdued to a stricter realism, a sharper psychological truth, a more concentrated poetry of conception and artistry. These qualifications granted, *A Tale of Two Cities* remains one of Dickens' significant books. It is his most serious essay in history, and now that a new generation of readers and a new phase of Dickens criticism have arrived; now that we see in his work as a whole not only a coherence of meaning but also a developing craftmanship and line of purpose which earlier enthusiasts were likely to miss; now that we see also, in the light of recent disclosures of his life and character, the constant relevance of his work to the forces that shaped his mind, it is important to see the part this novel plays in the creation that enabled Dickens to lay so strong an impress on his age

---

[1] G. K. Chesterton, *Charles Dickens: A Critical Study* (1906), pp. 233–34.
[2] George Gissing, *Charles Dickens: A Critical Study* (1898), p. 74.

and to remain, even in ours, one of the radical forces in modern literature. *A Tale of Two Cities* was the book that opened the final phase of his career. It shows him at an important juncture in his personal and imaginative life. To its long popularity there now succeeds a critical appeal that must be met and recognized.

When Carlyle, twenty years before Dickens, addressed himself to the theme of the French Revolution, he did so with an express purpose in mind. His most important friend at that time was John Stuart Mill (this was before the mystic vitalist in Carlyle and the Utilitarian rationalist in Mill discovered that their collaboration as fellow-reformers was doomed to conflict and incompatibility), and it was Mill who spurred Carlyle to use the great French crisis as an object-lesson for Englishmen. Here, Carlyle said in effect, is what happens to a nation when its ancient tyrannies are blind to suffering and injustice, when its masses are ground down by selfish rank and privilege, when its moral character becomes corrupted and violence must do the work that might better have been done by humane reforms and reasonable changes in law and government. His book was written as a warning. If England persisted in her course of political inertia, moral complacency, and stubborn intransigence, another such cataclysm might overtake her also, wrecking her institutions, causing a havoc more devastating than any surrender of selfish privilege would entail, and perhaps incapacitating permanently the special genius for gradualistic progress, for "noiseless revolution," on which she prided herself and which optimists like Macaulay held to be her great advantage over the other nations of Europe.

The times, in 1837 when Carlyle's *French Revolution* appeared, were ominous. The Reform Bill of 1832 had been found inadequate by the new working classes in giving them the parliamentary rights they demanded. The Chartist Movement on behalf of popular representation was rising as a threat to government and the vested interests of the mercantile and industrial capitalists. Disorder, strikes, and riots seethed over the country. The great Victorian exploit of commerce and imperialism was darkened at its outset by the threat of disruption and violence. Europe quaked with an equal disquiet, advancing toward the revolutionary crisis of 1848. Carlyle had hopes for democracy but he already felt the fear of it that was soon to produce his profound distrust of democratic processes and drive him into a reaction in favor of the heroic principle in history, the militarist control of society, so bringing him to write his histories of Cromwell and Frederick the Great—the "monstrous inverted ethic," as Strachey has called it, of his final intransigence. What he expressed in 1837 was an instinctive fear felt by Englishmen in general—a fear of France and her reckless politics, a fear of popular radicalism, a fear above all of just such a crisis as the French Revolution represented in the haunted mind of Europe.

Dickens, who knew most of his great literary contemporaries but had close friendship with few of them—his intimates were mostly his literary and intellectual inferiors—found great support in Carlyle's friendship and regarded him as a mentor. In 1854 he dedicated *Hard Times* to him, and he came to feel a deep sympathy with Carlyle's view of modern history, in which humanitarian passion joined with a distrust of theoretical radicalism and proletarian democracy. The theme of social crisis and injustice runs through all his novels. He was too faithful a historian of his age to miss it. But another thread may be traced: a dread of what the masses become when they are possessed by mob emotion or when they become the victims of a social theory or radical impulse. "It has been one of my hopes to add something to the popular and picturesque means of understanding that terrible time," he said in his foreword to *A Tale of Two Cities*, "though no one can hope to add anything to the philosophy of Mr. Carlyle's wonderful book."

Twice previously he had dramatized the theme of social revolution—first in *Barnaby Rudge* (1841), where, by means of the historical disguise or anachronism he found especially useful when writing about serious matters without alienating his huge audience of readers, he treated the Chartist unrest of the 1830s and 1840s in terms of the anti-Catholic Gordon riots of 1780; and again in *Hard Times* (1854), when he wrote a scathing indictment of Manchester industrialism, the "facts" philosophy and the tyranny of "rugged individualism" which Utilitarian doctrine has fostered in a predatory capitalism. The rioters in *Barnaby Rudge* are granted a certain justness in their cause, but they are also seen as a sinister omen. The factory slaves of *Hard Times* are shown as victims of an intolerable oppression, but their efforts to secure their rights through trade-unionism are seen as misled and unscrupulous. The divided mind of Dickens is curiously dramatized in these books, as recent students like Humphry House, Edmund Wilson, and T. A. Jackson have shown. In *Barnaby Rudge* we find a clue in the character of Dennis, the hangman of Newgate prison.[3] He is a professional executioner, hated by the people, who nevertheless joins their uprising and helps them invade his own citadel to liberate the prisoners. But once they get inside, he turns against them in order to keep the condemned men, his special charges, locked in their cells, later turning up as a stool-pigeon to betray his fellow-rioters to the police. He figures both as a violator and as a protector of prisons: "in his role of insurgent, he attacks authority; in his role of hangman, makes it odious." And in *Hard Times* we get Stephen Blackpool, the old textile-worker, one of the victims of the tyranny of the brutal manufacturer Bounderby; he argues the cause of the workers yet refuses for reasons of personal honor to join their union, and finally, on wandering off to look for a new job after he has been ousted from Bounderby's system, he falls into a disused coal-pit and dies of it, thus becoming "a martyr simultaneously to the employers and to the trade-union movement."

When common people are oppressed no one can plead their cause or defend their rights more passionately than Dickens. But when they rise to action or insurrection, he sees them possessed of a sinister and irrational violence. The mob, as Mr. Wilson rightly

---

[3] The point was made by T. A. Jackson in his *Charles Dickens: The Progress of a Radical* (1938): "From John Dennis to Madame Defarge," pp. 26–32; it was further developed by Wilson in "Dickens: The Two Scrooges," *The Wound and the Bow* (1941), and more recently by Hesketh Pearson, Edgar Johnson, and other interpreters. The two quotations here are from Wilson.

says, is something that Dickens "both sympathizes with and fears." Book after book shows his ambivalent attitude toward such matters as conventional morality, philanthropy, political radicalism, social justice. The paternal, kindly, philanthropic Cheeryble Brothers of *Nicholas Nickleby* are offset by the idiotic or atrocious busybody reformers of *Bleak House* and *Edwin Drood.* Benevolent men of wealth like Mr. Garland of *Oliver Twist,* the reformed Scrooge of *A Christmas Carol,* John Jarndyce and the pride-humbled Sir Leicester Dedlock of *Bleak House,* are set against brutal power-lords like Ralph Nickleby, Mr. Dombey, Bounderby, Jonas Chuzzlewit and the hypocrite Pecksniff in *Martin Chuzzlewit,* swindling financial Titans like Merdle in *Little Dorrit,* fish-hearted figureheads of society or government like the Barnacles of *Little Dorrit* and the Veneerings of *Our Mutual Friend.*

Dickens, it must always be emphasized, was not a theorist or "philosopher"—he was not a Carlyle, Macaulay, or Mill. He was a man of imagination, a dramatic novelist. His first loyalty was not to a reasoned consistency of ideas and attitudes. It was to the truth as he knew and felt it, the contradictory conditions of reality as he saw and experienced them. He shows a liability when we test him for the coherence of his opinions. But he also shows an advantage over those of his contemporaries who felt obliged to drive their arguments to a single, logical conclusion. Like the work of most great novelists—men as different as Balzac, Tolstoy, Dostoevsky, James, Conrad, Gide—his books show, not a set of syllogisms, an orderly program of moral findings, but a debate, continuous, perhaps inconclusive, but vital and restless in its exploration of truth. When a recent English critic, R. G. Churchill, said that "it is a mistake to look in Dickens's writings for 'solutions,'" and that "the very confusion which would attend any attempt to view Dickens's labors as a whole has an attraction, and a certain value," [4] he emphasized not only the necessity of seeing that Dickens' mind was

---

[4] R. C. Churchill, "Dickens, Drama, and Tradition" in *Scrutiny* (Cambridge, England), 1942; reprinted in *The Importance of Scrutiny,* edited by Eric Bentley (1948), pp. 182–202.

incurably divided rather than grimly "made up," but the value of finding how essentially complex, how morally representative, his involvement in his age obliged him to be. The point is notably applicable to *A Tale of Two Cities*.

The subject of the book is the greatest historical event Dickens ever tackled, acting as a focus for the entire revolutionary impulse that runs through modern history and hanging like a talisman over the Nineteenth Century. Of all modern events it is likely to demand the most emphatic decision of judgment from the historian or political moralist. This was a judgment that neither Dickens nor any other typical Englishman of his time was likely to commit himself to. He spares nothing in his denunciation of the degenerate aristocracy represented by the St. Evrémonde family. The common people of France are shown as the victims of long tyranny and oppression. The Revolution comes as a storm to cleanse the corruption of the world: "I see a beautiful city and a brilliant people rising from this abyss, and, in their struggles to be truly free, in their triumphs and defeats, through long long years to come, I see the evil of this time and of the previous time of which this is the natural birth, gradually making expiation for itself and wearing out." Yet it is the son and heir of the St. Evrémondes who is the romantic hero of the book, who redeems the evil legacy of his fathers, and for whose sake Sydney Carton dies in order to save Darney for his own lost love, Lucie Manette. And it is the oppressed poor who unleash the deadly wrath of insurrection, produce the ruthless Vengeance, sponsor the hideous Terror, and find their exponents in the bloodthirsty Defarges who would destroy the innocent with the guilty until Mme. Defarge is outwitted and killed by an honest if eccentric Englishwoman (Lucie's nurse Miss Pross), who risks her life and loses her hearing to permit the lovers to escape to an England which still offers its saner haven from a world gone mad.

The title of the book is one of the best Dickens ever hit upon. It not only indicates the two stages of the drama. It keeps before us the contrast of the two nations—France with her unjust castes and incipience of evil, England (despite the fact that, as the opening chapter tells us, she shows "scarcely an amount of order and protection to justify much national boasting") with her steadier temper, her protective liberties, her instinctive justice, even if she also is pregnant of villainies—Jerry Cruncher, Roger Cly, and their like —which serve warning that no people is ever safe from its evil genius. As the action moves between England and France we get a sense of what the opening pages emphasize: that no nation can rest in the complacency of its pride and virtues; that the whole destiny of humanity is interwoven; that injustice is an ever-present challenge to peace, and that the Woodman Fate and the Farmer Death may be preparing their forest tree and common cart to serve as guillotine and tumbril for criminals and victims alike in any part of the world.

II

By the time Dickens wrote *A Tale* he was in the fullest command of his dramatic powers. The loose picaresque narratives of his earlier years, with their freedom and melodrama, their grotesque and humorous vitality, were behind him. He had shown himself capable, in *Dombey, Bleak House, Little Dorrit,* of putting his plots to the service of a complex social analysis and his characters to the test of a deepening psychological insight. He had not however abandoned —he was fortunately never to abandon wholly—his natural skill in fabulous invention, in poetic and dramatic imagery. These arts lay at the center of his imaginative life. But he was now able to raise them to a more serious dramatic value—the level, indeed, of a dramatic symbolism in which he touches some of the most powerful novelists of modern times, Dostoevsky, Joyce, Kafka.[5]

So, as the ribbing and vaulting of his plot took on an architec-

---

[5] Dickens' progress in symbolic skill, emphasized by Wilson, is shown in its relevance to his plot structures by Robert Morse in his essay on *Our Mutual Friend* in *Partisan Review,* Vol. XVI (March 1948), pp. 277–89. And T. A. Jackson makes a good analysis of the dramatic structure of *A Tale of Two Cities* in his book (pp. 170–88), in order to show the interlocking connections of the Dr. Manette, Sydney Carton, and Revolutionary stories.

tural strength within which his fancy could play under the super-
vising control of dramatic logic, his characters, however still at
times exaggerated or simplified as "humors," could take on a richer
force through joining eccentricity with a symbolic validity as human
types. His heroine—here Lucie Manette—was still likely to be virtuously negative, even vapid, and his hero—here Darnay—an upright
automaton; his villains—Cly, St. Evrémondes, Defarges, the Vengeance, the five Jacqueses—are still likely to walk straight out of the
melodramatic theatre. Dickens was never wholly cured of idealizing
good and evil, either in life or in art. But there was another side of
himself, and of human nature, that he had no wish or power to
idealize. For all its imperfections he loved it; or if he feared it, he
was fascinated by it; or if he found it hated by the world, he instinctively defended and admired it. It was part of his own secret
self.

When Bernard Shaw, speaking with the insight of a professed
disciple, said that Dickens, "in spite of his exuberance, was a
deeply reserved man—his imagination was ceaseless, and his outward life a feat of acting from beginning to end," he referred to the
continuous life in fantasy which a man of Dickens' immense creative energy was able to sustain over a space of forty years—the
intense imaginative experience which constituted for him a reality
greater than the outward events of his career possibly could. He
stands with the greatest novelists in this—with Balzac who, while
writing *Eugénie Grandet,* happened to discuss with a friend the
serious illness of that friend's sister, expressed his sympathy, then
broke off abruptly with "Revenons à la réalité! Qui va épouser
Eugénie Grandet?" To Dickens likewise the experience of his outward self—his family, marriage, children, friends, public success
—could never measure up to the claims of his secret destiny. The
disparity urges itself increasingly in his letters and conduct; it becomes an essential clue to his character in a succession of key
figures in his later novels. The impatience of his temper was always
pulling restlessly at the tether of his practical responsibilities. The
humiliations of his youth, his secret resentment against the hard-

ships he had suffered then, the dependence of his relatives, the dullness of his wife, the problems of his children—all these demanded
compensation in a fulfillment only his art could give him. And when
his romantic conception of himself and his destiny found itself repeatedly disappointed in the girls he courted in early manhood, in
the friends on whom he laid heavier demands than they could
satisfy, in the family he raised, even in the resounding adulation of
his readers and audiences, he sought compensation more and more
in the creatures and fantasies of his mind. This histrionic need led
him to cultivate increasingly his old enthusiasm for acting and the
theatre. Private theatricals, benefit performances, collaborations
with Wilkie Collins and other writers of plays, home charades and
festivals, developed into the strenuous venture of his public read-
ings—recitals into which he threw himself with such compulsive
frenzy that they undermined his health and eventually did as much
as anything to kill him, by bringing on the stroke that ended his
life prematurely at the age of fifty-eight.

This need of his nature had other consequences. It brought him,
shortly before he began *A Tale of Two Cities*, to declare to his wife
that their marriage could not continue. He had discovered what he
soon believed to be the fulfillment of his romantic ideal in a young
actress named Ellen Ternan, successor to such earlier objects of his
adoration as Maria Beadnell, Christina Weller, and his young sister-
in-law Mary Hogarth, who lived in his home in the first years of his
marriage, died there at the age of sixteen, obsessed him morbidly
("I can't think there ever was love like I bear her!"), and whose
ring he wore on his finger "day or night" the remainder of his life.
He formed a union with Miss Ternan, breaking up his home, assign-
ing his oldest son to his wife, and keeping his eight other children
under his own custody. He defended his action before the world
in the pages of *Household Words*, and for the remaining eleven
years of his life he lived between the house he set up for Ellen
Ternan in London and the country home he now bought and established as a kind of official shrine at Gadshill, near Rochester.

He seems to have believed that he had found some fulfillment of his dream and a promise of happiness at last. In this he appears, by the fragmentary evidence available to us and the deepening note of pessimism that sounds in many of his later pages, to have been mistaken. (Of a character in *Our Mutual Friend*, five years later, who has struggled to save himself from drowning, we are told that "like us all, when we swoon—like us all, every day of our lives when we wake—he is instinctively unwilling to be restored to consciousness, and would be left dormant if he could.") Ellen Ternan—if we may take in evidence, with whatever caution, such later heroines as Estella in *Great Expectations* and Bella Wilfer in *Our Mutual Friend*, petulant, cruelty-inflicting girls who differ sharply from his former idealized heroines—brought him no lasting peace. His search for self-fulfillment broke finally against this last, elusive passion.[6]

He thus began the writing of *A Tale of Two Cities* at the most intense point of his emotional life. Its historical theme joined with a personal crisis that was bound, given Dickens' nature as an artist, to express itself in his fable. What resulted is a plot that has, superficially viewed, a traditional fairy-tale quality. It is a plot of old wrongs (Dr. Manette's eighteen-year imprisonment in the Bastille by the wicked St. Evrémondes) visited upon two romantic lovers (Lucie Manette and Charles Darnay, virtuous son of the evil St. Evrémonde) who, caught and divided in a great political cataclysm that wreaks the vengeance of the wronged upon their aristocratic oppressors, are almost made victims of that upheaval's rough justice (Dr. Manette's prison letter denouncing the St. Evrémondes and all their heirs), but are saved for a happy life and mankind's fairest hopes by the sacrifice and death of another man (Sydney Carton), Darnay's physical counterpart, who has allowed great

---

[6] Dickens' relations with Ellen Ternan, first described in a Dickens biography by Thomas Wright in his *Life* in 1935 and presently elaborated on by Gladys Storey in her *Dickens and Daughter* (1939), became the subject of prolonged controversy among Dickensians until they were documented by Ada Nisbet in her *Dickens and Ellen Ternan* (1952) and by Edgar Johnson in his *Charles Dickens: His Tragedy and Triumph* (1952). These books are discussed in the first essay, "The Reputation Revised," in the present volume.

gifts to sink into disappointment, self-disgust, and drunken habits, who loves Lucie hopelessly, and who finds salvation in giving his life that the girl may be happy and a new world may be inherited by her children. That is the fable, roughly summarized. It is a fable because it reduces life to a scheme of ideal ends and values.

It is exactly the kind of fable which, originating in the folklore and parables Dickens inherited from the past, had often furnished him with the mythic or allegorical essentials of his earlier novels, and whose basic simplicity gave him all the room he needed for substancing the myth with his humor and fantasy, the realities of his social and human insight. Here French history gave him his social substance: ancient evil defied by its victims; a sinister prison stormed by the people (prisons that shut up and debase the souls of men figure everywhere in Dickens—*Pickwick Papers, Oliver Twist, Little Dorrit, Edwin Drood*—all of them shadows of that Marshalsea that hung over his childhood); this fury in turn changing the populace into a wild mob, a world gone mad in its effort to avenge the villainies at its root.

Something closer to his personal life gave him the other part of his story—a father wrongfully imprisoned and forever haunted by fear of the dungeon; a lovely girl, his daughter, likewise threatened by that fate; two men who love that girl, look alike, and thus become in effect the divided parts of a single man, the one dying in order that the other may live and be happy. When these two parables joined in Dickens' imagination he had his story and his theme. That theme informs all parts of the novel, from the title of its first book, "Recalled to Life" (originally intended as the title of the whole novel), through the drama of the Revolution, Dr. Manette's liberation from the Bastille, Darnay's repudiation of his family's curse, even Jerry Cruncher's sinister trade as a body-snatcher ("resurrection man") which counts so intricately in tying the knot of the action, down to the Scriptural phrases that come to Sydney Carton's mind as he mounts the guillotine: "I am the Resurrection and the Life, saith the Lord. . . ." It is the idea that gives the book its informing symbol: Resurrection.

Though the *Tale* adds few characters to the gallery of Dickens' greatest creations, it creates one who is memorable—Carton himself. Jarvis Lorry of Tellson's Bank has his charm: he belongs among the gruff protecting angels that include Sam Weller in *Pickwick*, Betsey Trotwood in *David Copperfield*, John Jarndyce in *Bleak House*, Mr. Boffin in *Our Mutual Friend*. Jerry Cruncher and his "flopping" wife have their grotesque appeal: they belong among the lowly folk in Dickens who show the debasing influence of poverty and the criminal cunning it breeds. Miss Pross embodies the English courage Dickens could find in the absurdities of his race. Dr. Manette's hauntings by the prison-house repeat the amnesic terrors that Dickens had already shown in *Little Dorrit*, where old Dorrit, in his new-found wealth, is haunted by the Marshalsea prison that held him captive for years and will never let him escape its thralldom. The two lovers, Lucie and Charles, are romantically touching but beyond that conventional figures. Mme. Defarge and her fellow-knitters at the foot of the guillotine have become a classic part of the Revolutionary legend. It is Carton who gives the novel its serious life, its real center of interest.

He is Dickens' real achievement in portraiture in this book. He too has his kin in the other novels—men of high gifts or good character into whose souls some canker of disillusionment or disappointed egotism has eaten and who find themselves fatally, or almost fatally, overtaken by their own evil geniuses: Steerforth in *David Copperfield*, Richard Carstone in *Bleak House*, Arthur Clennam in *Little Dorrit*, Pip in *Great Expectations*, Bradley Headstone in *Our Mutual Friend*, John Jasper in *Edwin Drood*. They can certainly be taken as, in some sense, versions of his own alter ego—that passionate, demonic, secret self that bred his genius but also warred on his happiness and haunted his life. Sometimes, by good fortune or a helping hand, they are rescued from their "dark angels" and restored to life, like Clennam and Pip. Usually they drive themselves to self-destruction and tragedy. Sydney Carton, so charming but so feckless, human but cynical, gifted but self-condemned, knows that he too must finally be destroyed, but the sound humanity at the root of his nature directs that his end will be expiatory, that new life will be born of it; that he will do "a far, far better thing" in dying than he has ever done before. Here Dickens made a hero of his other self and created one of the most convincing and psychologically valid heroes in any of his books.

An English critic, Jack Lindsay, giving this novel one of the few close examinations it has received, sees *A Tale of Two Cities* as a direct reflection of "the lacerated and divided state of Dickens's emotions" at this moment of his life.[7] His interpretation must of its nature remain conjectural but it joins with the evidence of Dickens' other late novels in offering a suggestion which no serious reader can dismiss out of hand. The two heroes of the *Tale*, "practically twins in appearance and who love the same girl," reflect the latent conflict in Dickens himself. Carton "by his devoted death reaches the same level of heroic generosity as his rival: indeed goes higher. His gesture of renunciation completes the ravages of the Revolution with its ruthless

---

[7] Jack Lindsay, "*A Tale of Two Cities*" in *Life and Letters* (London), Vol. LXII (September 1949), pp. 191–204, this later incorporated in his book *Charles Dickens* of 1950. Lindsay's Marxist and Freudian emphasis is wildly exaggerated and his book shows many careless errors and reckless conjectures, but he offers some valuable suggestions on sources and analogies. The first is Bulwer-Lytton's novel *Zanoni* of 1842 ("in seeking the spiritual impacts behind any turn of development in Dickens it is always safe to look at Bulwer-Lytton's work . . . his *Paul Clifford* led on to *Oliver Twist*, his *Night and Morning* led on to *Martin Chuzzlewit*"). *Zanoni* has the French Revolution as its scene; it joins "the personally creative struggle with a social convulsion of change"; it combines "a symbolic account of the creative process" with the Revolutionary theme to reach "a quite different conception, in which revolution and stability, death and life, are equally accepted as aspects of process." Its characters—Zanoni who sacrifices himself, Melnour, Glyndon, the girl Viola for whom Glyndon and Zanoni compete in love—show remarkable parallels with Dickens' characters. Another analogy appears in *The Dead Heart*, a play by Watt Phillips whom Dickens knew, based on an episode in Carlyle's *French Revolution* and written about 1856 though not produced until 1859. Its hero Robert Landry, who "begins as a hopeful young artist," is "horribly changed by the hell of twenty years' imprisonment, returns to life, becomes a resolved revolutionary leader, cannot resolve his love-problem, and finds release from his inner contradictions by a redeeming death of sacrificial substitution." Lindsay believes that Bulwer-Lytton's novel and Phillips' play fused with Dickens' own material in the making of *A Tale of Two Cities. The Dead Heart* ends with "the substitution of one man for another at the guillotine in an act of self-sacrifice."

justice, and transforms them into acts of purification and redemption, without which the life of renewed love would not be possible." And it is more than the French Revolution that is put before us. It is, as everywhere in Dickens, the whole condition of conventional morality, of bourgeois venality and hypocrisy, which he saw possessing the Nineteenth Century soul "immured in a maddening cell of lies and cruelties, and seeking to break through into the truth, into a full and happy relationship" with humanity. "It was the demented sense of environing pressures," Lindsay ventures, "of an unjust and inescapable mechanism, which caught Dickens up in the midst of his wild mummery and gave him a sense of release when he determined to write the novel." Such relevances in a novel are never provable, but no one who reads *A Tale of Two Cities* in the context of Dickens' later work can fail to see in it these references to his later life and ordeal.

Potentially at least the *Tale* is the most powerful example of that now largely neglected or discredited genre, the historical novel, which Victorian England can show. Its theme has a greater historical import and modernity than anything in Scott. Its drama has a stronger modern relevance than Thackeray's *Henry Esmond* or George Eliot's *Romola*. Its social fable legitimately calls for comparison with *Les Misérables* and even with *War and Peace*. It does not of course sustain a full comparison with these mightier dramas. Dickens' personal fantasy pressed too hard as he wrote it. He sentimentalized the drama of the lovers, from whose part in the story his acute psychological penetration almost wholly drops out, just as he permitted too urgent an argument to take over the political theme: this, though treated with considerable complexity and thus rescued from melodramatic crudity, tends to become artificial where it should be realistic, and idealistic where it calls for the substance of convincing social and political conflict. But for all that, the plot makes a profoundly moving story. Where it falters in realism, Dickens' radical symbolic sense comes to its aid. The Revolution and its cognate theme of Resurrection sustain the novel as the fog symbol sustains *Bleak House*, as the prison motif integrates *Little Dorrit*, as the dust heap and the sinister

Thames, twin sources of evil wealth, dominate *Our Mutual Friend*, as the baleful rites of Kali and the Thuggee cult of death come out of the East into England's Cloisterham to create the drama of evil in *Edwin Drood*. With Lindsay's last word on the book at least, any intelligent opinion of the *Tale* must agree: that it may not be "a great work, though like anything written by Dickens it has great elements," but when it is seriously approached, it turns out to be "a work of high interest, yielding some essential clues to the workings of Dickens's mind and of creative symbolism in general."

What were the source and tendency of those workings? Every critic who has ever written on Dickens has felt obliged to formulate a theory about them. To earlier clues based on his social and moral sympathies there have now been added clues derived from what we have come to know of his emotional experience and of the bent this gave to his plots and symbols. The idea that Dickens was a sublime and irresponsible compiler of popular fantasies has been as thoroughly dismissed as the notion that he worked in terms of consistent socialist and political theses. Neither of these approaches to his genius is workable. A different consistency, a more radical and vital impulse, worked in his nature, and it was this that rescued him from the claims of his popularity, the distracting influence of his public success, and the facility of moral compromise.

He was obviously a man divided against himself and a representative Victorian in being so. The conflicts we trace in his social and moral arguments show it no less than the self-divided or self-indicting heroes he created in almost every one of his later novels. But when Shaw spoke of Dickens as a man who, "in spite of his exuberance," was "deeply reserved," and whose "outward life" was "a feat of acting from beginning to end," he did something more than point to his psychological contradictions or moral duplicity—did so, we may assume, intentionally, for he clearly aimed to define in Dickens the central integrity of purpose and imagination he ascribed by definition to any man of true genius. Behind the conflicts of Dickens' behavior, behind the ambiguity of his moral judgments, there existed an instinct for personal integration, for the wholeness and self-realization which are the animus of any vital character and an imperative claim in the character which seeks to fulfill itself creatively through imagination and art. The nature that such a man keeps in "deep reserve" is the one he hopes to realize in himself. His outward "acting" is likely to be his one means of protecting it from superficial or mistaken recognition. He knows that only his art will contain and express it justly. And while Dickens' public histrionics, imperious claims, and efforts at self-justification were too open to give him a place among the secret-keepers or self-concealers of genius; while he certainly spoke for himself in more than his art (his voluminous letters, public speeches and petitions, incessant editorializings, notably his published defiance of Victorian convention when he defended himself at the time of his separation from his wife, make as open a book of his private life as we find in any major writer of modern times), there still worked in his make-up a deeply secretive impulse. It was secretive, no doubt, because it remained to the last rooted in unconscious instinct. Graham Greene, in his essay on *Oliver Twist*, has recalled how Chesterton once emphasized a major fact about Dickens' novels: how they convey the sense of a mystery far more important than the ostensible mystery of their plots—a sense that "even the author was unaware of what was really going on." "The secrecy is sensational; the secret is tame." The outrageous, absurd, frightening, unforgettable characters are always "keeping something back from the author as well as from the reader. When the book closes we do not know their real secret. They soothe the optimistic Dickens with something less terrible than the truth."

The surface optimism of Dickens was, we may be sure, a subterfuge of his public life, his overt confidence. The very fact that it expressed itself so resolutely in his dénouements and valedictions—even in the flawed last sentence of *Great Expectations,* recommended by Bulwer-Lytton, where for once Dickens originally intended to suppress it—makes certain how much it was a function of his conscious morality, his self-constituted office as an arbiter of conventional justice. The truth it disguises is something deeper, more elusive, more "terrible." If his novels persist in power and fascination; if they have survived their Victorian artifices and contrivance; if in spite of their superficial sentiments they keep company—as they unquestionably do—with the work of greater artists and intelligences in fiction than Dickens definably was, it is because such truth is rooted in them and gives them their informing passion. What was it?

It was a truth not optimistic but tragic. Its deepest instinct was critical, doubtful, exacerbated, rather than confident. It always speaks more convincingly of perversity and evil than of goodness. It works more subtly in acts of recognition, surrender, despair, and expiation than in the easy triumphs and rewards of virtue. As the plots of Dickens deepen in their obsession with guilt and evil (so much so as to lead Greene to define a Manichean bent in Dickens' morality); as his characters struggle with a fate that is more powerful than their conscious powers of mastering or understanding it, so his fantasies take on a complexity that becomes more than social or moral. It refers to a willful fatality in the conditions of life, an enmity in nature or matter which can be met only by submission or recognition—if not, in characters too violent for such compromise, by acts of nihilism and self-destruction. The egotism of the resisting personality must either surrender or perish. Clennam and Pip surrender. They accept their humility. But Headstone and Jasper will destroy themselves because their natures have defied the laws of their fate. Headstone does so blindly and desperately, but in Jasper's case it is he himself who becomes his own accuser and condemner.

Carton surrenders and dies but he also saves—saves himself morally but also saves and redeems humanity in doing so. He "chooses" his death, but he is given the opportunity of making it a sacrifice, and to him is granted a faith in regeneration which the self-destroyer is otherwise denied. For the first time in his novels Dickens resorts to the explicit language of the religious hope: "I am the Resurrection and the Life." Dickens, whose religion was wholly personal, conventional, and undoctrinal when he talked about it, resorted for once to the phrases of supernatural faith and used them for prophetic purposes. As revolution in politics promises the rebirth of society, so resurrection in its Christian reference implies a spiritual rebirth gained through sacrifice: not an old life remade or rebegun, but an old life lost or destroyed in order that a new one may supervene.

The principle of revolution which Dickens feared in its political and social consequences, and on whose French manifestation he leveled a characteristic English rebuke, had deeper roots in his make-up than his moral sentiment could openly admit. It was rooted in the recalcitrant egotism of his personal morality. If, as V. S. Pritchett has recently said, the "emphasis on the self" in modern literature derives from the "intense feeling of being part of history in the making," the Dickensian egotism reveals itself as revolutionary in the radical sense. It sees the root of human evil and injustice as more than social or political. It sees it as humanly constitutional, and resists it by means of a personal defiance which usually ends in sacrifice. The self becomes at once a challenge and an agent of expiation. "Although Communist writers regard the enhancement of egotism as a sign of social disintegration, it is really revolutionary, and is the necessary civilizing force in mass society." [8]

The moral compromise in Dickens' later novels, their suspicion of political logic and the idea of historical necessity, was partly his tribute to the English tradition of empirical faith, partly his acquiescence in the doctrine of prudence in matters of social and moral success. Against it there works the force of his personal resistance, defiant and rebellious, a mode of personal integrity but also a sacrificial means of redeeming the deceived human condition. The non-conformism of Dickens' character finally shows itself to be both destructive and expiatory. He reserved for himself the fate of the dissentient and the redeemer, and by expressing it in Carton's death and redemption, he spoke for the revolutionary fate by which the rebel against convention and compromise justifies his office in society.

If the French Revolution in *A Tale of Two Cities* brings havoc with its justice, the heroism of Carton suggests a nobler, a more humane, hope. It is the hope of the regenerative capacity in the moral per-

----

[8] V. S. Pritchett, *The New Statesman and Nation* (London), Vol. LI, p. 601 (May 26, 1956).

sonality of humanity. Dickens, behind his outward sentiments and conventionality, shared it with his greater Nineteenth Century contemporaries—with Baudelaire, Dostoevsky, and Tolstoy. If his involvement in the Victorian situation kept him from expressing it with their logic in argument or self-exposure, his share in it still gave him the representative force of becoming the most eloquent voice of personal dissent and revolutionary challenge the English novel of his age can show.

1956

Hardy in Defense of His Art

THE AESTHETIC OF INCONGRUITY

The first artists, in any line, are doubtless not those whose general ideas about their art are most often on their lips—those who most abound in precept, apology, and formula and can best tell us the reasons and the philosophy of things. We know the first usually by their energetic practice, the constancy with which they apply their principles, and the serenity with which they leave us to hunt for their secret in the illustration, the concrete example. None the less it often happens that a valid artist utters his mystery, flashes upon us for a moment the light by which he works, shows us the rule by which he holds it just that he should be measured. This accident is happiest, I think, when it is soonest over; the shortest explanations of the products of genius are the best, and there is many a creator of living figures whose friends, however full of faith in his inspiration, will do well to pray for him when he sallies forth into the dim wilderness of theory. The doctrine is apt to be so much less inspired than the work, the work is often so much more intelligent than the doctrine.

—JAMES on MAUPASSANT

I

That Hardy's was a native and persistent order of genius; that he expressed it in a style and drama which he made unmistakably his own; that his work carries the stamp of a theme and vision which have impressed a large area of art and experience in the last eighty years; that he exists as a force in modern literature in spite of some of the severest critical reservation any notable writer has been subjected to—these we may take as facts which have survived excesses both of distaste and of eulogy and become part of the record of modern English literature. In Hardy's middle years the scorn of Henry James and George Moore joined with the scandalized protests of press and pulpit to deny him aesthetic as much as public respect. In his old age and after, a reckless apotheosis has proved almost as damaging. Hardy survives them both. Virginia Woolf, when she visited him at Max Gate in 1926, was sincere in recognizing a fact of history. "I wanted him to say one word about his writings before we left and could only ask which of his books he would have chosen if, like me, he had had to choose one to read in the train. I had taken *The Mayor of Casterbridge* . . . 'And did it hold your interest?' he asked. I stammered that I could not stop reading it, which was true, but sounded wrong." Few readers have missed the spell, and few have missed feeling in some sense confused about it.

Yet the radical quality is less likely to be mistaken in Hardy's work than in most writers of his rank. It can easily be simplified to a convenient fault or virtue, according to the prejudice of the critic. It often remains crudely defined in memory. The conflicting elements that shape it may be minimized by admirers who are anxious to forget the difficulties they met in salvaging his genius from the uneven and erratic body of his work. But it is a quality as unmistakable in his prose and verse as in his personality and thought; as prominent in his style as in that reading of life which he insisted on disclaiming as a "philosophy."

It derives from the conjunction, in his temperament, of conformist and skeptical tendencies; in his humanism, of stoic acquiescence with moral protest; in his response to human character, of a kinship with gifted, rebellious, or destructive aberrations from the human norm as against his sympathy with the rudimentary types and stable humors of the folk. In his thought it appears in his leaning toward cosmic simplifications so large and unwieldy that their grandeur becomes inflexible, an impediment to critical thinking and an oppression to the imagination, and conversely in his humble loyalty to the claims of life in all its elusive and stubborn deviations—its vital

struggles and appeals that protest and so make bearable the mindless negation of the universe. What this ambivalence of temper did
to Hardy's style is apparent on almost every one of his pages. Their
salt, tang, and sincerity are continuously accompanied by habits of
rhetoric, pretension, and straining eloquence, even by astonishing
repetitions and laborings of effect, that exceed those in most of the
writers in a century abnormally conscious of crisis and the "urge to
rhetoric."

To credit these divergences to Hardy with any special emphasis
is to say that the large schemes into which he cast his problems, and
the stormy dramas he made of them, make the central discordance
in his work insistent, the basic clue to his talent. Obviously this
discordance exists widely in modern art and thought. Hardy saw it
as a primary rift or dichotomy in man which post-rationalist Europe
had thrown into a new relief. His contemporaries were torn and
distraught by it; it is the frame and condition of the modern man's
typical agony. Nor does one distinguish Hardy particularly by saying
that his style and form are inordinately marked by rough contrasts
and antitheses. Such contrasts—of aesthetic logic and selection at
odds with the rough justice and violence of experience, or plots
shaped and contrived to the point of artifice against the disorder of
life, of characters reduced to the basic patterns of human nature
against the subtle divinations of modern psychologists—are apparent
throughout modern fiction; they swarm through that chaotic and
amorphous medium to which the courtesy title of novel is applied.
The same heterogeneity exists in modern poetry, where serious purposes are offset by startling levities, where the grand manner is de-
flated by vulgar intrusions, where moral earnestness is scoffed by the
scurrilities of cynicism, and where a sense of responsibility to the
traditional dignities of the human spirit became so violently re-
proached by the squalor of modern society that satirists like Laforgue
and Corbière wrought these jarring collisions into a critical medium
that has descended to Pound, Eliot, Joyce, Auden, and the satirists
and realists of contemporary poetry and fiction.

Hardy participated little in these developments and showed

small interest in the artistic results of the modern man's skeptical consciousness. But he was too much a child of his time to remain unmarked by the traits of Nineteenth Century art. He inherited the aesthetic disorder of the age, its unresolved antipathies, its sprawling appetite for life, and the instability that reflected the surrounding distraction. That instability is deeply imbedded in his books, and if popular reverence now tends to slight its prominence there, two other factors insist on emphasizing it. For one thing, Hardy wrote and matured during a period in which aesthetic reformers in fiction and poetry were grappling with the problem of reducing the elements of the arts to a new unity and integrity, of bringing them into a harmony that might enhance their value, force, and intelligence. He was the contemporary, in other words, of Baudelaire, Flaubert, and Turgenev, of James, Moore, Yeats, Proust, Pound, Valéry, and Eliot, but a colleague of none of them. He was, secondly, conscious throughout his life of the struggle in himself of a distressing opposition of faculties—of immediate personal sympathies and large intellectual ambitions—and in the face of the critical hostility that surrounded him through two-thirds of his literary career he struggled to formulate a defense of his talent and method. Thus he shaped a personal aesthetic for himself; and though it shows something of the amateur's pedantry that is evident in his early fiction and in his metaphysical excursions, it demands attention from anyone concerned with the artistic progress of the modern novel and with the interrelations of modern fiction and poetry.

He was no adept at critical or aesthetic reasoning; he felt a lifelong suspicion of its practitioners; his literary notes and prefaces sound a note of peremptory impatience toward them. Yet his methodical habit of mind exercised itself over many years in notations on structure, form, style, and aesthetic ideas, and in a continuous effort to generalize these into working principles. The craft of fiction had not come to him easily. Poetry was his first ambition, and until he was sixty he was in doubt whether his real vocation had been obstructed or merely painfully slow in maturing. "I was quick to bloom; late to ripen." "I was a child till I was 16; a youth till I was 25; a young man till I was 40 or 50." [1] The groping awkwardness he showed in mastering the business of fiction-writing is equaled by the step-by-step pains he took to come into some kind of conscious knowledge of his aesthetic purposes. One of the first things he discovered about himself was a natural lack of artistic sophistication. He knew he was unequipped for competition with the rising schools of Paris and London. He felt the pull of older traditions of romance and a brotherhood with the rough-and-ready masters of Victorian fiction, the dramatic and sensation novelists of the sixties from whom he learned his trade. The homeliness of his tastes is evident in "An Ancient to Ancients." In music his favorites, when not the hymns of Tate and Brady, were *The Bohemian Girl* and *Il Trovatore*. In painting, though he carefully studied the Dutch and Italian schools, he warmed to the Academy pictures of Etty, Mulready, and Maclise. In fiction the "throbbing romance" of Bulwer, Scott, Dumas, and Sand had made a golden age. His poetic loyalties, rooted in the romanticism of Keats, Shelley, and Tennyson, spent their last real enthusiasm on Browning and Swinburne. As early as 1873 we find him attempting to justify natural impulse and fancy as the basis of art:

> Read again Addison, Macaulay, Newman, Sterne, Defoe, Lamb, Gibbon, Burke, *Times* Leaders, in a study of style. Am more and more confirmed in an idea I have long held, as a matter of common sense, long before I thought of any old aphorism bearing on the subject:

----

[1] The passages quoted from Hardy in this essay are from the prefaces as they appear in the Mellstock Edition (London, 1921–1922), in *Late Lyrics and Earlier* (London, 1922), and in *Winter Words* (London, 1928); from Hardy's essays, notes, and letters as they appear in *Life and Art*, collected by Ernest Brennecke, Jr. (New York, 1925); from his notebooks and letters as quoted by Mrs. Hardy in *The Early Life of Thomas Hardy* (New York, 1928) and *The Later Years of Thomas Hardy* (New York, 1930): from several entries quoted by Carl J. Weber in *Hardy of Wessex* (New York, 1940) and in the studies of Lionel Johnson, H. C. Duffin, Arthur McDowell, and S. C. Chew; and from unpublished correspondence. The *Early Life* and *Later Years* published by Mrs. Hardy after Hardy's death now take on an increased importance since Richard Little Purdy, in his *Thomas Hardy. A Bibliographical Study* (1954), pp. 262–67 and 268–73, has shown them to be "in reality an autobiography," prepared for posthumous publication by Hardy himself.

"Ars est celare artem." The whole secret of a living style and the difference between it and a dead style, lies in not having too much style —being in fact, a little careless, or rather seeming to be, here and there. It brings wonderful life into the writing:

> A sweet disorder in the dress. . . .
> A careless shoe-string, in whose tie
> I see a wild civility,
> Do more bewitch me than when art
> Is too precise in every part.

Otherwise your style is like worn half-pence—all the fresh images rounded off by rubbing, and no crispness or movement at all.

It is, of course, simply a carrying into prose the knowledge I have acquired in poetry—that inexact rhymes and rhythms now and then are far more pleasing than correct ones.

He began to turn to nature for his justification of such defect and awkwardness:

So, then, if Nature's defects must be looked in the face and transcribed, whence arises the *art* in poetry and novel-writing? which must certainly show art, or it becomes merely mechanical reporting. I think the art lies in making these defects the basis of a hitherto unperceived beauty, by irradiating them with "the light that never was" on their surface, but is seen to be latent in them by the spiritual eye.

"Faultlessness," he once agreed with Browning, "avails neither a man nor book anything unless it can be surmounted by care and sympathy," and when he read Henry James's *Reverberator* on its appearance in 1888 he emphatically dissociated himself from the new motives in fiction:

After this kind of work one feels inclined to be purposely careless in detail. The great novels of the future will certainly not concern themselves with the minutiae of manners. . . . James's subjects are those one could be interested in at moments when there is nothing larger to think of.

This defense of casual vitality now appears inseparable from Hardy's emphasis on the significance of chance and accident in life. In his aesthetic morality it results in a defense of instinctive and emotional qualities above the intellectual. The purpose of great fiction is not basically critical, intellectual, dialectic, or minutely discriminative; it is to seize and embody the values of the heart, of instinct and intuitive sympathy, of the passions which Hardy shared with the Victorian moralists and humanitarians and which he saw exhausted and vitiated among the critical efforts of the modern schools. The "seemings" which he held, in the preface to *Jude* and elsewhere, to be the sum and substance of his work, as against the imputation of philosophical pessimism or negation (in 1917 he wrote: "I find I wrote in 1888 that 'Art is concerned with seemings only,' which is true"), are for him exactly those responses which are authorized by the heart as against the canceling judgments of the head. "I hold," he said late in life,

> that the mission of poetry is to record impressions, not convictions. Wordsworth in his later writings fell into the error of recording the latter. So also did Tennyson and so do many other poets when they grow old. Absit omen! . . . I believe it would be said by people who knew me well that I have a faculty (possibly not uncommon) for burying an emotion in my heart or brain for forty years, and exhuming it at the end of that time as fresh as when interred.

Hardy, recognizing the undeviating identity of his feeling and style over a space of seventy years, took that fact as a means of justifying the permanence of "impressions" above the instability of intellectual doctrines and convictions. "Poetry must feel," he maintained. "The Poet takes note of nothing that he cannot feel emotively." "There is a latent music in the sincere utterance of deep emotion, however expressed, which fills the place of the actual word-music in rhythmic phraseology on thinner emotive subjects, or on subjects with next to none at all." The translation of that emotion into style became his single assurance of success as a poet:

> Consider the Wordsworthian dictum (the more perfectly the natural object is reproduced, the more truly poetic the picture). This reproduction is achieved by seeing into the *heart of a thing* (as rain, wind, for instance), and is realism, in fact, though through being pursued by means of the imagination it is confounded with invention, which is pursued by the same means. It is, in short, reached by what M. Arnold calls "the imaginative reason."

Such a view of the matter made drudgery for Hardy of any intense technical discipline. When, in his earlier books, he was obliged to treat of modern artificial life, he particularly felt the strain. He had "mostly aimed at keeping his narratives close to natural life and as near to poetry in their subject as the conditions would allow, and had often regretted that those conditions would not let him keep them nearer still." When he reread Henry James in old age, he marveled and was perplexed that "a writer who has no grain of poetry, or humor, or spontaneity, in his productions, can yet be a good novelist. Meredith has some poetry, and yet I can read James when I cannot look at Meredith." He saw Meredith's failure in the fact "that he would not, or could not—at any rate did not—when aiming to represent the 'Comic Spirit,' let himself discover the tragedy that always underlies Comedy if you only scratch deeply enough." "If all hearts were open and all desires known—as they would be if people showed their souls—how many gapings, sighings, clenched fists, knotted brows, broad grins, and red eyes should we see in the market-place!"

The prejudice here is clear. Hardy saw the growth of sophistication and critical intellection in art as evils at its root. His scruples as a workman and his methodical seriousness as a student, even his systematic ambition for literary fame, were outbalanced by his sense of being an outsider to art's higher mysteries. It is no wonder that James and Stevenson, though compelled to admire, groaned over the flaws in *Tess*, or that George Moore spent his harshest invective on that book and its author, or that T. S. Eliot, in *After Strange Gods*, has set Hardy down as a "symptom of decadence," a victim of emotion run morbid, "a minor poet" whose matter of communication is not "particularly wholesome or edifying." The approach to Hardy through his artistic medium ("he was indifferent even to the prescripts of good writing," says Eliot, ". . . at times his style touches sublimity without ever having passed through the stage of being good") has often resulted in this inclusive contempt. This approach is inescapable; it is necessary; but in the case of

Hardy's sharply qualified and unstable talent, the approach must be made in unusually wide and comprehensive terms. His own anti-aesthetic position committed him to a search for the timeless qualities of life and destiny, to a sense of history that shares little of the critical scrutiny of time and experience that was soon to become a major prepossession of the modern artist. Hardy stood, indeed, in an honored English line. He felt that poetry and fiction, if they bowed to the critical faculty, would ultimately meet an enervation of their strength, their native daemon and validity. He held in this with Bacon, Goldsmith, and Macaulay; he anticipated some of the fears that I. A. Richards has voiced in *Science and Poetry*. Caught between the intimacy of his physical sensations and the enveloping grandeur of his imaginative and scientific visions, he based his faith as a poet on a magical conception of man and nature. This sympathy suffuses his literal-mindedness, his prosaic tedium, his almost mawkish dissection of passionate fact. And he proposed to defend and exemplify it in his work as long as he lived.

Accordingly we find Hardy arguing that fiction must share with poetry the task of relieving the oppression of life's fact and commonplace. He opposed the naturalists, whom he saw joining forces with aesthetic rationalists in making an unbearable oppression of the actual.

> The real, if unavowed, purpose of fiction is to give pleasure by gratifying the love of the uncommon in human experience, mental or corporeal.
> This is done all the more perfectly in proportion as the reader is illuded to believe the personages true and real like himself.
> Solely to this latter end a work of fiction should be a precise transcript of ordinary life: but,
> The uncommon would be absent and the interest lost. Hence,
> The writer's problem is, how to strike the balance between the uncommon and the ordinary so as on the one hand to give interest, on the other to give reality.
> In working out this problem, human nature must never be made abnormal, which is introducing incredibility. The uncommonness must be in the events, not in the characters; and the writer's art lies in shaping that uncommonness while disguising its unlikelihood, if it be unlikely.

He subscribed to Coleridge's view that the aim must be "at *illu-sion* in audience or readers—*i.e.*, the mental state when dreaming, intermediate between complete delusion (which the French mis-takenly aim at) and a clear perception of falsity." As late as 1919, long after he had abandoned fiction, he felt a weight on his con-science that he had led the novel too much toward positive realism, and had by that means aided in stultifying the suggestive and poetic force of modern novel-writing. He would, he said, write at the beginning of each new romance: "Understand that however true this book may be in essence, in fact it is utterly untrue." Two days after completing *The Mayor of Casterbridge* in 1885 he had written, "The business of the poet and novelist is to show the sorriness under-lying the grandest things, and the grandeur underlying the sorriest things." Nature, if left unprejudiced and uninterpreted, becomes a curse and burden to man, and this can be alleviated only by the imaginative penetration of her meaning which it is the function of art to supply. "Nature is an arch-dissembler. A child is deceived completely; the older members of society more or less according to their penetration; though even they seldom get to realize that *nothing* is as it appears." And again:

> Nature is played out as a Beauty, but not as a Mystery. . . . I don't want to see the original realities—as optical effects, that is. I want to see the deeper reality underlying the scenic, the expression of what are sometimes called abstract imaginings.
> The "simply natural" is interesting no longer. The much decried, mad, late-Turner rendering is now necessary to create my interest. The exact truth as to material fact ceases to be of importance in art— it is a student's style—the style of a period when the mind is serene and unawakened to the tragical mysteries of life; when it does not bring anything to the object that coalesces with and translates the qualities that are already there,—half hidden, it may be—, and the two are depicted as the All.

Thus he came to suspect any rationalization that pretended to account for the totality of life or reality, and any literary theory that maintained it is the purpose of art to convey a sense of such totality. "Since I discovered," he said in 1882, "that I was living in a world where nothing bears out in practice what it promises incipiently, I have troubled very little about theories. . . . Where development according to perfect reason is limited to the narrow region of pure mathematics, I am content with tentativeness from day to day." So it comes about that Hardy, whatever his connection with post-Darwinian fashions in determinism, resisted the formulation of a logic of experience or history.

> Is not the present quasi-scientific system of writing history mere charlatanism? Events and tendencies are traced as if they were rivers of voluntary activity, and courses reasoned out from the circumstances in which natures, religions, or what-not, have found themselves. But are they not in the main the outcome of *passivity*—acted upon by unconscious propensity?

Just before the War, viewing the rise of a new generation of documentary realists, he said that "they forget in their insistence on life, and nothing but life, in a plain slice, that a story *must be worth the telling*, that a good deal of life is not worth any such thing, and that they must not occupy a reader's time with what he can get at first hand anywhere around him."

What is "worth telling" is what recedes from the apparent, the external, the visible. It is the part of experience that withdraws into the private, the subjective, the subconscious, and hence into the mysterious energy of living matter.

> People who to one's-self are transient singularities are to themselves the permanent condition, the inevitable, the normal, the rest of mankind being to them the singularity. Think, that those (to us) strange phenomena, *their* personalities, are with them always, at their going to bed, at their uprising!
>
> Footsteps, cabs, etc., are continually passing our lodgings. And every echo, pit-pat, and rumble that makes up the general noise has behind it a motive, a prepossession, a hope, a fear, a fixed thought forward; perhaps more—a joy, a sorrow, a love, a revenge.
>
> London appears not to see *itself*. Each individual is conscious of *himself*, but nobody conscious of themselves collectively, except perhaps some poor gaper who stares round with a half-idiotic aspect.
>
> There is no consciousness here of where anything comes from or goes to—only that it is present.
>
> In the City. The fiendish precision or mechanism of town-life is

what makes it so intolerable to the sick and infirm. Like an acrobat performing on a succession of swinging trapezes, as long as you are at particular points at precise instants, everything glides as if afloat; but if you are not up to time—

When he transferred this sense of the endless dichotomy of life, its mysterious dualism of subject and object, to the problem of narrative, Hardy saw that the inherent animus of experience is something more than the double vision of which the blessed simple folk of the world are unconscious but by which the seeing intellects are eternally tormented. It is a matter of maintaining a precarious balance, in art as in intelligent life, between the necessities of personal, practical, and localized experience, and the knowledge of universals which transcend all individuality. "I do not expect much notice will be taken of these poems," he said when publishing *Moments of Vision* in 1917; "they mortify the human sense of self-importance by showing, or suggesting, that human beings are of no matter or appreciable value in this nonchalant universe." This was only an echo of what he had written during the stormy aftermath of *Tess* in 1893: "The whole secret of fiction and the drama—in the constructional part—lies in the adjustment of things unusual to things eternal and universal. The writer who knows exactly how exceptional, and how non-exceptional, his events should be made, possesses the key to the art." Upon that conviction he based his idea of tragedy. "The best tragedy—highest tragedy in short—is that of the WORTHY encompassed by the INEVITABLE. The tragedies of immoral and worthless people are not of the best." When *Jude* fell under the lash of the reviewers in 1895, he committed himself to his final patience and wrote in his notebook:

> Tragedy may be created by an opposing environment either of things inherent in the universe, or of human institutions. If the former be the means exhibited and deplored, the writer is regarded as impious; if the latter, as subversive and dangerous; when all the while he may never have questioned the necessity or urged the non-necessity of either.

Thus he made consoling generalizations on his creative plight. But he was also able to localize the tragic sense in himself. That he had reasons for doing so, especially during his first marriage, we have come to understand only lately (Mr. Carl Weber's biography makes them clear enough). Sometimes the twist of this pathos seized him with a pang almost as ludicrous as that which so frequently strikes his Clyms, Bathshebas, Judes, and Henchards. Once in middle life he found himself afflicted with toothache. "I look in the glass. Am conscious of the humiliating sorriness of my earthly tabernacle, and of the sad fact that the best of parents could do no better for me. . . . Why should a man's mind have been thrown into such close, sad, sensational, inexplicable relations with such a precarious object as his own body!"

II

Everyone has experienced certain tests of credulity and assent in reading Hardy. All lovers of his work, at one time or another, are caught up by the strain he places on belief and sympathy. Perhaps his own word best labels the pervading quality of his effects: they are "tentative." His appeal is cumulative, seldom concentrated; deliberate with a patient confidence in the latent meaning of life, not immediate and assumptive in its acceptance of cosmic justice. His reading of experience, whatever sense he conveys of implacable forces and blind principle, is groping, experimental, suspended, empirical. As is well known, he explicitly repudiated the imputation of pessimism in his thought, just as he implicitly broke with the monistic conception of life and matter. He practiced, "by the exploration of reality and [a] frank recognition stage by stage along the survey," the mode of thought which he called "evolutionary meliorism." At least three times he challenged directly the charge of his critics (Alfred Noyes on one notable occasion) that he argued from a position of dogmatic negation and that he reduced deity to nonentity and God to an "imbecile jester." The cosmic theatre in which the warring nations of *The Dynasts* are mixed shows them obeying "resistlessly the purposive, unmotivated dominant Thing," but Hardy requested his reader not to make too close an inspection of his phantoms or arguments since they "are but tentative, and are advanced with little eye to systematic philosophy." *Jude* was offered to the public in 1895 as "simply an endeavor to give shape and coherence to a series of seemings, or personal impressions, the question of their consistency or their discordance, of their permanence or their transitoriness, being regarded as not of the first moment." And for the general preface of the Mellstock Edition in 1921 he wrote:

Positive views on the Whence and the Wherefore of things have never been advanced by this pen as a consistent philosophy. Nor is it likely, indeed, that imaginative writings extending over more than forty years would exhibit a coherent scientific theory of the universe even if it had been attempted—of that universe concerning which Spencer owns to the "paralyzing thought" that possibly there exists no comprehension of it anywhere. . . . That these impressions have been condemned as "pessimistic"—as if that were a very wicked adjective—shows a curious muddle-mindedness. It must be obvious that there is a higher characteristic of philosophy than pessimism, or than meliorism, or even than the optimism of these critics—which is truth. Existence is either ordered in a certain way, or it is not so ordered, and conjectures which harmonize best with experience are removed above all comparison with other conjectures which do not so harmonize. . . . And there is another consideration. Differing natures find their tongue in the presence of differing spectacles. Some natures become vocal at tragedy, some are made vocal by comedy, and it seems to me that to whichever of these aspects of life a writer's instinct for expression the more readily responds, to that he should allow it to respond. That before a contrasting side of things he remains undemonstrative need not be assumed to mean that he remains unperceiving.

These statements of Hardy's reduce to several conclusions. He had no inclination to see science as absolute or final; its whole appeal to him lay in its dissolution of "counters and fixities" in both experience and universal law. He inclined, with the natural leaning of his post-Romantic generation, toward the validity of individual perception. His respect for scientific thought was a respect for the goal it set for itself—a liberal, unprejudiced, and cumulative mode of truth. He was an empiric but not, as he insisted, a pragmatic. He sympathized less with the pessimistic arguments of Schopenhauer than with the creative and evolutionary motives of English thinkers. Of *The Dynasts* he said, "My pages show harmony of view with

Darwin, Huxley, Spencer, Comte, Hume, Mill, and others, all of whom I used to read more than Schopenhauer." The year 1859 was always remembered as a red-letter date in his career: he was one of the first readers of *The Origin of Species* and at once sensed its epoch-making importance. It was the evolutionary or progressive principle, with its creative implications, that won his sympathy for the historical patterns defined by Comte, Spencer, and Eduard von Hartmann's *Philosophy of the Unconscious*. The closing lines of *The Dynasts* are often overworked by embarrassed apologists, but they express what Hardy repeatedly insists on; their gleam of promise and aspiration in the universal order redeems, as with a flicker of faith, the darkness that drops on Tess, Jude, and Henchard.

Hardy was, in fact, more than is generally assumed a pioneer defender, with Butler and Shaw, of the creative principle in evolution. The will to live, as he dramatizes it, persists through every apparent confusion of local and individual purposes. It is never without its consolations. Momentarily it instructs man in accepting nature as the refuge of his tormented spirit. Prophetically it lends him the hope that his life will be harmonized with the unconscious or instinctive energy of nature. It even advances to a higher plane and glimpses a victory of intelligence, a release of the higher Will from its cosmic condition of "immanence," so that it may become assimilated to the conscious energy and vision of human beings.

"The discovery of the law of evolution, which revealed that all organic creatures are of one family," he wrote to a New York correspondent in 1909, "shifted the center of altruism from humanity to the whole conscious world collectively." And he agreed with an Australian admirer that *The Dynasts* offered an idea harmonious with the principle of Christian revelation: the Immanent Will, far from showing fiendish malignance, may appear blind and irresponsible, but it implies a growth into self-consciousness. One recent critic, Mr. Amiya Chakravarty, has extended this possibility in Hardy's thought by drawing the analogy of Freud's categories: the Spirit of the Years (of conscious or calculated experience) is analogous to the Freudian Ego; the Spirit of the Pities (of human

purpose, identity, effort, frustration, tragedy) with the Super-
Ego; whereas the principle of unconscious and abiding energy, the
Id, is represented by "the continuum of blind forces which unites
the instincts with Nature and whose actions are the main theme of
the drama." [2] These forces, basic and anterior to consciousness,
may ultimately, with the arrival of a universal harmony, become
lifted and approximated to the purposes of human will and aspiration. Another student, Pierre d'Exideuil, has echoed Hardy's distress that his version of Will should be regarded as an aimless one
and that pessimism is the only adequate estimate of life, by going
behind the Freudian analogy into the thinking of Hardy's middle
years. He has proposed another affiliation: "the fundamental difference between Schopenhauer's and Hardy's outlook perhaps lies
in the fact that Schopenhauer is pre-Darwinian, whereas Hardy's
thought was definitely moulded by the conception of evolution."
D'Exideuil sees that "between Schopenhauer and Hardy, as between
Schopenhauer and Nietzsche, stands Darwin, the channel whereby
meliorism, the idea of the greatest possible enriching and perfecting
of life, reaches the poet of *The Dynasts* and the hero of *Zarathustra*.
Life, therefore, may become its own aim, whereas Schopenhauer
stopped short with the denial of any final aim." [3]

This oversimplifies Schopenhauer's thought and minimizes its contribution to the Freudian principle of energy. But it points to an
important fact. Hardy may have diverged from Schopenhauer but
he saw with him the dualistic character of man, his division between compulsive force, supremely embodied in sexual urge, and
his attraction toward the transcendence of idea—an aspiration of
intellect rendered pathetic or tragic by the warfare of passion. Sex
is for Hardy what it is for Schopenhauer—the focal point of Will,
the final sublimation of sincerity. Yet Hardy never advanced as far
as Schopenhauer did in "his insight into the overweening power of

---

[2] Amiya Chakravarty, *The Dynasts and the Post-War Age in Poetry* (Oxford,
1938), p. 22.
[3] Pierre d'Exideuil, *The Human Pair in the Work of Thomas Hardy* (London,
1929), p. 209.

instinct and the derogation of the one-time godlike reason, mind, and intellect to a mere tool with which to achieve security."

Hardy, as both poet and novelist, was prevented by his response to man's character and courage from a dualism so extreme. Accordingly, the opposition of will and idea, instinct and intellect, is never absolute and rigorous with him. The two spheres interpenetrate. He conveys, by the dramatic reality of his characters and the poetic truth of his finest verse, a promise of ultimate unity among the forces that harry and destroy men which Schopenhauer, working within the frames of theory and ratiocination, stopped short of. Hardy's modest and confident temper never suffered the German's exacerbation. Yet what Thomas Mann has said of Schopenhauer is enlightening at this point: there is a fundamental connection between his pessimism and his humanism, "this combined melancholy and pride in the human race which make up Schopenhauer's philosophy."

> His pessimism—that is his humanity. His interpretation of the world by the concept of the will, his insight into the overweening power of instinct and the derogation of the one-time godlike reason, mind, and intellect to a mere tool with which to achieve security— all this is anti-classic and in its essence inhumane. But it is precisely in the pessimistic hue of his philosophy that his humanity and spirituality lie; in the fact that this great artist . . . lifts man out of the biological sphere of nature, makes his own feeling and understanding soul the theatre where the will meets its reverse, and sees in the human being the savior of all creation.[4]

What Schopenhauer arrived at by something resembling a counsel of desperation, Hardy arrived at by the humane insight and compassion of a great artist. Where Schopenhauer rests on the latent form of such "artistry," Hardy succeeds by the imaginative immediacy of art. His Henchard, Tess, and Jude enter the sphere of "saviors of all creation" where Hamlet, Macbeth, and Lear stand in the ranks of the triumphant.

The transition in Hardy from doubt and negation to humanistic

----

[4] Thomas Mann, *The Living Thoughts of Schopenhauer* (New York, 1939), p. 29.

hope was encumbered by an amateur's crudity in handling philosophical machinery, and the clumsiness is evident in all his dramas. He contrives his defeats and frustrations as a means of reducing to its final and minimal condition the saving heroism, dignity, and integrity of his characters. His use of every known portent, accident, and coincidence of chance destinies is notoriously excessive. The impression that survives such buffetings of the reader's patience corresponds, no doubt intentionally, to the indestructible essence of human worth and dignity with which his characters manage to survive, Greek-like, their havoc of ruin and defeat. The role of man in the universe is, for Hardy, comparable to the role of will and intelligence themselves: it is a role of emergent exoneration and supremacy. The word *emergent* is important. Man's exoneration is not to be taken for granted. It is not to be rashly assumed by means of defiance, ambition, or egotism. It materializes slowly, out of blight and despair. It materializes so slowly and painfully, indeed, that one is inclined to think that Hardy saw an analogy for this painful vindication in the equally painful and agonized degrees by which modern man had suffered the loss of his traditional dignity in the teachings of Bacon, Montaigne, Galileo, Newton, Locke, Lyell, and Darwin, and yet survived to declare a new faith and worth for himself through a sublimation of his egoistic individuality into the instinctive wisdom and slowly maturing intelligence of the natural universe itself. Some such allegory is conveyed by the stories of Clym Yeobright, Michael Henchard, and Jude Fawley; it is implicit in Hardy's children of nature—Gabriel Oak, Giles Winterborne, Marty South, Diggory Venn, and John Loveday.

Hardy's "seemings" are rightly termed "a tentative metaphysic." His faith in nature and cosmic purpose is emergent. Correspondingly, the role of man—never demoted from his position of superiority to other parts of nature—must be emergent also. His dignity is arrived at by test, denial, humiliation, disillusion, and defeat—by every possible accident of fate, ironic mischance, and the apparently hostile action of nature. The vindication of man implies the vindication of purpose in the universe. It will appear by means of reserves that issue from the blind or instinctive life in order to become conscious and creative. This inspiration of personal will through violence and suffering corresponds to the gradualism whereby, in the closing chorus of *The Dynasts,*

the rages
Of the ages
Shall be cancelled, and deliverance offered from the darts that were,
Consciousness the Will informing, till It fashion all things fair!

III

Any reader of Hardy is continuously aware of difficulties exactly corresponding to Hardy's own slow, trial-and-error "impressions" of the meaning of man's place in nature and to the deliberate, trial-and-error way by which he built them into his tales. His novels, teeming with contrivance, show the cumbersome plotting, the exaggerated mountings, the devious complexity, which the whole craft of modern fiction, from Flaubert and Turgenev to James, Conrad, and Proust, has insisted on rejecting, and which even such prodigal contrivers as Dickens, Trollope, and Hugo had managed to subdue to their more relaxed and spacious versions of modern life.

Almost any tale by Hardy, on first reading at least, nettles the sympathy, offers stumbling-blocks to attention, and is likely to make the suspension of disbelief a resentful ordeal. The selling of Mrs. Henchard in the opening pages of *The Mayor of Casterbridge* is a violent instance of such assault on credulity, and others follow fast in the remainder of the book. It now takes persistence to move past these wrenchings of congruity, and one's faith in the novelist's seriousness must survive a good many tests before the gathering force of the local color, the Dorset speech, the richness of country customs, and the mounting grandeur of pathos slowly subsume the defects and crudities of Hardy's plots. The opening situation in *Tess* is relieved by the droll humor of its treatment, but minor tales like *Two on a Tower* are pitched at so violent an angle of improbability that they creak under the excesses of their romantic plots and the added burden of astronomical machinery that nearly crushes the lives out of the characters instead of rendering them tragically pitiable. Even the famous overture of *The Return of the Native* shows so exaggerated an air of portentous solemnity (and so much overwriting, dragging erudition, repetition of motives, and rhythmic orotundity) that it takes all the subsequent weight of the novel, all of its passions, rustic naïveté, and counterbalancing melodrama, to overcome the ponderous effect of the first chapters. Certainly *The Dynasts*, however it may impress many readers and however memorably it offers its flashes of historic synthesis and characterization, cannot survive as drama or history. The burden of its pretensions and the falseness they inflict on its style are too pervasive. Hardy admitted this to some degree; he told Henry Newbolt that "instead of saying to themselves 'Here is a performance hugely defective: is there anything in it notwithstanding the huge defects?' [the critics] have contented themselves with picking out bad lines, which any child could do, there are myriads of them, as I knew too well before they said so"; and he took consolation in Meredith's praise of the "panoramic" validity of the work. But even as a panoramic achievement *The Dynasts* puts our understanding of poetic integrity under a killing strain. The shorter poems are another matter; the finest are exquisite and superbly alive, and below the finest are three or four other levels of quality which one may richly enjoy; but even this leaves a considerable bulk that embarrasses Hardy's resources to a painful degree.

We are never permitted to forget the profound disparity in Hardy's taste and genius, a permanent division between his instinctive attraction toward life and his confusion by it, between his native feeling for words and character and his incurable tendency toward stiff erudition, toward ponderous generalizations on life and experience, toward grandiose symbolism and immensities of scale that wildly exceed the proportions necessary for maintaining his picture of man's atomic part in existence. There is an essential incongruity in Hardy's world. And he stretched the terms of the incongruity to such a degree that his tales often collapse under the test. It soon becomes apparent that the incongruity existed in his own temperament to a greater degree than most artists could ever hope to tolerate or justify. The imponderables of his thought and curiosity almost overwhelm the native and intimate resources of his personal character. "The machinery contrived by the Gods for reducing human possibilities of amelioration to a minimum" which he mentioned in *The Mayor of Casterbridge* often becomes a machinery contrived by Hardy for reducing the artistic possibilities of imaginative conviction to a vanishing point.

Yet in that incongruity, and in what he made of it, lies the secret of Hardy's success, and his success survives some of the severest criticism that has been made against an author of his rank. He was conscious of this hostility among critics; he never became thick-skinned enough, even in his final apotheosis, to disregard it. His prefaces, which are usually devoted to disclaiming charges made against his moral or philosophical ideas, are always mildly defensive and in the one prefixed to *Late Lyrics and Earlier* in 1922 he voiced a denunciation of contemporary reviewers as Isaiahan as anything one may find in the prose of Housman. (Charles Morgan, as an Oxford student in 1920, found in this querulous resentment the one "failure of balance" in Hardy's personality.) But even when criticism is something more than the moral indignation of journalists or the snobbery of rising talents, its severity usually permits Hardy to emerge with the stature of a master. Mr. Frank Chapman, in one of the best essays yet written on the novels, comes to the conclusion that "his greatness [may be seen] as the greatness of the Victorian age, in its solidity and its sureness of what it really valued, yet Hardy is above the Victorian ethos and did not share the limitations that made tragedy impossible." And Vernon Lee, in the severest analysis ever made of Hardy's style, concluded her merciless dissection by saying that superior stylists like "Stevenson, Meredith, or Henry James would scarcely be what is wanted for such subject-matter . . . the faults of Hardy are probably an expression of his solitary and matchless grandeur of attitude. He belongs to a universe transcending such trifles as Writers and Readers and their little logical ways." [5] But here we return to Hardy's own analysis of his problem.

In 1888, in his essay on "The Profitable Reading of Fiction," he defended the novelist's right to be inconsistent and unequal.

> However numerous the writer's excellencies, he is what is called unequal; he has a specialty. This especial gift being discovered, he fixes his regard more particularly thereupon. It is frequently not that feature in an author's work which common repute has given him credit for; more often it is, while co-existent with his popular attribute, overshadowed by it, lurking like a violet in the shade of the more obvious, possibly more vulgar, talent, but for which it might have received high attention. Behind the broad humor of one popular pen he discerns startling touches of weirdness; amid the colossal fancies of another he sees strokes of the most exquisite tenderness; and the unobtrusive quality may grow to have more charm for him than the palpable one.

This is sufficiently astonishing as self-examination and prophecy. It is exactly in his touches of weirdness and strokes of exquisite tenderness that we now see the qualities that redeem the broad humor and colossal fancies that are the bane of Hardy's work. He said something equally cogent in 1891, in the essay on "The Science of Fiction," when he maintained that "Art is science with an addition"; that while fiction must unquestionably show "that comprehensive and accurate knowledge of realities which must be sought for, or intuitively possessed, to some extent, before anything deserving the name of an artistic performance in narrative can be produced," it is in the addition that the vital and life-giving quality resides. Only when this "constructive stage is entered upon, Art—high or low— begins to exist." Accordingly Hardy takes issue with Zola's creed of the *roman expérimental* and repudiates the notion that fiction can ever be Truth, whole, consistent, and inclusive; that it can ever rely like science on the evidence of the outer senses; that it can ever rest on the logic and documentation of scientific naturalism; and that there is any possibility "of reproducing in its entirety the

---

[5] Frank Chapman, "Hardy the Novelist," in *Scrutiny* (Cambridge, England), Vol. III (June 1934), pp. 22–37. Vernon Lee, *The Handling of Words* (London, 1923), pp. 222–41.

phantasmagoria of experience with infinite and atomic truth, without shadow, relevancy, or subordination."

> The fallacy appears to owe its origin to the just perception that with our widened knowledge of the universe and its forces, and man's position therein, narrative, to be artistically convincing, must adjust itself to the new alignment, as would also artistic works in form and color, if further spectacles in their sphere could be presented. Nothing but the illusion of truth can permanently please, and when the old illusions begin to be penetrated, a more natural magic has to be supplied.

Here Hardy is not only aware of his instinctive use of the poetic method in fiction and of his impulse toward metaphorical values; he is arguing again along the line of Richards: that "the Neutralization of Nature, the transference from the Magical View of the world to the scientific," is robbing life of "a shape, a sharpness, and a coherence that no other means could so easily secure," and so deprives the artist of an "ease and adequacy with which the universe . . . could be emotionally handled, the scope offered for man's love and hatred, for his terror as well as for his hope and his despair." [6] (The proem of *The Return of the Native* sounds this same danger when it raises the question "if the exclusive reign of this orthodox beauty is not approaching its last quarter. The new Vale of Tempe may be a gaunt waste in Thule . . . and ultimately, to the commonest tourist, spots like Iceland may become what the vineyards and myrtle-gardens of South Europe are to him now.") What he is further arguing is that the meanness and inconsequence to which scientific realism is reducing human life are despoiling both poetry and fiction of their traditional moral and heroic values; that these must be maintained or substituted for; that

> what cannot be discerned by eye and ear, what may be apprehended only by the mental tactility that comes from a sympathetic appreciativeness of life in all its manifestations, this is the gift which renders

----

[6] I. A. Richards, *Science and Poetry* (New York, 1926), cf. pp. 53–65. The quotations in the last two paragraphs of the present essay are from Alice Meynell, *The Second Person Singular and Other Essays* (Oxford, 1922), p. 140; and from *Further Letters of Gerard Manley Hopkins,* edited by Claude Colleer Abbott (Oxford, 1938), pp. 222–23.

its possessor a more accurate delineator of human nature than many another with twice his powers and means of external observation, but without that sympathy.

Hardy was protesting here not only against realism—the confounding logic by which the naturalists were depriving art of meaning and power—but also against the aesthetic version of this discipline which Flaubert and Pater were advocating—the "minutiae of manners" and of stylistic detail which spelled for him nothing but a revulsion to the "purposely careless." When he wrote on "The Profitable Reading of Fiction" for *The Forum* in 1888, he told his readers:

> To distinguish truths which are temporary from truths which are eternal, the accidental from the essential, accuracies as to custom and ceremony from accuracies as to the perennial procedure of humanity, is of vital importance in our attempts to read for something more than amusement. There are certain novels, both among the works of living and the works of deceased writers, which give convincing proof of much exceptional fidelity, and yet they do not rank as great productions; for what they are faithful in is life garniture and not life. . . . A living French critic goes even further concerning the novelists of social minutiae. "They are far removed," says he, "from the great imaginations which create and transform. They renounce free invention; they narrow themselves to scrupulous exactness; they paint clothes and places with endless detail."

His own precepts were even simpler, in the end, than these. "A story should be an organism." "Style . . . can only be treatment, and treatment depends upon the mental attitude of the novelist." "Nothing but the illusion of truth can permanently please."

Hardy becomes in his poetics something very different from the victim of scientific determinism that the literal reading of his novels and key-phrases makes him. He never resists the limitations of materialism so eloquently as when he resents the modern effort to yoke the artist with mechanisms of technique or with the utilitarian purposes of economic or physical theory. His force as a stylist, dramatist, and allegorist is clarified by his refusal to fall in with the restrictions of naturalism, or with an aesthetic based on the rigid and obvious congruities of physical fact. He defended the salient quality of his art, and any intelligent reader must be compelled by it in the end, whether it is represented by startling properties like Stonehenge and Egdon and Knight's vision as he hangs from the cliff's edge in *A Pair of Blue Eyes,* by extreme characters like Arabelle, Sue, Eustacia Vye, Gabriel Oak, and Jude, by his use of obvious choral devices like the Shakespearean rustics and the Parcae of Casterbridge, or, best of all, by those brilliant strokes of dramatic incident which illuminate and suddenly justify the wildness of his plots—the door closed against Mrs. Yeobright, the tree-planting by Marty and Winterborne, Tess's seeing the blood-stained paper as she stands ringing the bell of the empty house of Clare's parents. He now appears to us as a realist developing toward allegory—as an imaginative artist who brought the Nineteenth Century novel out of its slavery to fact and its dangerous reaction against popularity, and so prepared the way for some of the most original talents of a new time. He stands in a succession of novelists that includes Melville, Emily Brontë, and Hawthorne, that takes in James and Flaubert in the wider reach of their faculties, and that has arrived at the achievements of Joyce, Proust, Gide, and Kafka.

When his novels falter in that demonstration, his poetry takes it up. The shorter poems are, in fact, the spiritual center of his production. He was right in calling them "the more individual part of my literary fruitage." They reveal his rich and sympathetic humanity, alive with recognitions of spirit, alert in sensitive invention, and always correcting the arguments of human ignominy and defeat by their respect for man's capacity for passion, endurance, and sacrifice. They show at their best an originality that springs from deeply felt and tested experience in the ways of human ordeal. Their devices of stanza and rhythm, of verbal oddity and surprise, begin to lose the inhibiting effect of a personal convention and to take on the qualities of a genuine contribution to English diction and meter. In their finest development ("The Darkling Thrush," "He Abjures Love," "Voices from Things Growing," "The Schreckhorn," "To

Meet or Otherwise," "The Something that Saved Him," "I Say I'll
Seek Her," the elegies of "Veteris Vestigia Flammae") they arrive at
an authentic poignance and wholeness of style. This is not only a
matter of their delicacy of suggestion and tone or their candor in
restoring personal appeal to poetry in the face of the impediments
which modern sophistication and experiment have set against that
appeal. It is a matter of Hardy's gradual mastery of effects: of
subtle turns and balances of phrasing, of the fine shadings he is
able to put on traditional emotions, of the sure hand with which he
succeeds in justifying, by the time a poem ends, its apparently fal-
tering progress from stanza to stanza. It is a matter also of Hardy's
skill in restoring to poetry some usages which had fallen into neglect since the Seventeenth Century: for one, his exquisite use of the
negative particle:

> By briefest meeting something sure is won;
>   It will have been:
> Nor God nor Demon can undo the done,
>   Unsight the seen,
> Make muted music be as unbegun,
>   Though things terrene
> Groan in their bondage till oblivion supervene.

This is "our profound and powerful particle, in our 'undone,' 'unloved,' 'unforgiven,'" which Mrs. Meynell once named in describing
the genius of English speech: "the 'un' that summons in order that it
may banish, and keeps the living word present to hear sentence
and denial, showing the word 'unloved' to be not less than arch-
angel ruined." And in its homely archaism it reminds us of another
description that suits Hardy's achievement in poetry almost exactly.
"It is his naturalness that strikes me most," said Gerard Hopkins of
Hardy's friend, the Dorset poet William Barnes, "he is like an
embodiment or incarnation or manmuse of the country, of Dorset, of
rustic life and humanity. He comes, like Homer and all poets of
native epic, provided with epithets and images and so on which seem
to have been tested and digested for a long age in their native air

and circumstances and to have a *keeping* which nothing else could give; but in fact they are rather all of his own finding and first throwing off."

Hardy never shared Barnes's privilege of writing poetry undistracted by the claims and disturbance of the outer world. He divided his life between Wessex and the tumult of his age. The two worlds gave him a dramatic stage on which to meet the conflicts of modern thought, to witness the tragic hostilities of life, to study the discord that marks the divided nature of man. But he mastered the "keeping" of his art and brought to it the force of his long intellectual and moral struggle. How he harmonized these in the poetry of his last thirty years is one of the notable personal achievements of literary history. It crystallizes for us the conflicts of a great age of distress; it makes evident Hardy's success in forging, out of the baffling incongruities and discords of experience, not only an aesthetic but an art. It also emphasizes that he succeeded because he was a "man of character," and it makes unmistakable that character's central quality: its resolving sincerity.

1940   [1956]

Samuel Butler

THE VICTORIAN INSOLVENCY

I

The Way of All Flesh is one of the milestones in the history of the English novel. The fact was recognized almost as soon as the book was published in 1903, but it is a fact that could have astonished no one more than its author. He was not a professional novelist. He wrote only one novel and never published it during his lifetime. To find it claiming a rank with the other books that set the dates and mark the progress of English fiction—*Robinson Crusoe, Pamela, Tom Jones, Tristram Shandy, Pride and Prejudice, Waverley, Pickwick, Vanity Fair, Adam Bede, Richard Feverel,* and their peers—could hardly have entered the calculations of his ironic mind. Yet this book, first issued two years after the death of Victoria, a year after Samuel Butler's own death, and about twenty after its completion, is not only the work by which Butler chiefly survives in literature but a book that marks as distinctly as any the point of division between the Victorian age and the Twentieth Century.

In its last pages its hero, Ernest Pontifex, having survived his ordeal to become a man of means and an author, says, in words that Butler certainly meant to apply to himself: "What can it matter to *me* whether people read my books or not? It may matter to *them*— but I have too much money to want more, and if the books have any stuff in them it will work by-and-by. I do not know nor greatly care whether they are good or not. What opinion can any sane man form about his own work?" And a moment later Ernest's publishers says that "Mr. Pontifex is a *homo unius libri*"—a man of one book. Butler appears to have believed that he himself might be remembered as a man of one book, but he thought the book would be *Erewhon,* his satirical fantasy of 1872, the only one of the seventeen volumes he published in his lifetime that had found any degree of popularity or touched the imagination of his contemporaries. Today *Erewhon* is still remembered as one of the most effective pieces of social criticism and prophecy the Nineteenth Century produced. And Butler is known and indexed in his age for a number of other reasons—for his notebooks and his advocacy of note-keeping as an indispensable habit of authorship; for his battle with Darwin and the theory of Natural Selection; for several eccentric theories of his own, such as his notion that the *Odyssey* was written by a woman in Sicily or his unorthodox interpretation of Shakespeare's sonnets; for his championship of then-neglected geniuses like Handel, Giovanni Bellini, Tabachetti, and Gaudenzio Ferrari, all of whom he used to challenge the father-images of their mightier contemporaries; for his promulgation of the ideas of "creative evolution," "life force," and "unconscious memory" that forecast the future thought of Shaw, Bergson, Freud, and Jung. But all these features of Butler's after-fame are known chiefly to specialists, to students of Victorian scientific controversy, to connoisseurs of English eccentricity, or to social and literary historians. It is as the author of *The Way of All Flesh* that he claims his place in the pantheon of English literature and among the forces that have shaped the modern novel and the Twentieth Century mind.

Its impact on the art and morality of our time has passed into common acceptance. One recent critic has epitomized its reputation by calling it "one of the time-bombs of literature":

> One thinks of it [says V. S. Pritchett] lying in Butler's desk at Clifford's Inn for thirty years, waiting to blow up the Victorian family and with it the whole great pillared and balustraded edifice of the Victorian novel. The book Thackeray failed to write in *Pen-*

dennis had at last been written. After Butler we look back upon a
scene of devastation. A spiritual slum has been cleared. . . . Yes,
says Samuel Butler, this was Heartbreak House.

Butler, he goes on to say, "opposed a system and its myth not with
another system but with the claims of the human personality. Against
Victorianism he placed himself; himself with both feet on the ground,
telescope to blind eye and in perverse self-possession, against people
whose dreary will to power—and whose hold on spiritual and material property as well—had dried the sap of sense and life." [1]

No moment could have been more timely than 1903 for the appearance of such an attack. Butler's strategy of delay was justified. His
hour of deferred posthumous celebrity had, however, been long prepared, anticipated as if by express plan and design. He had taken his
clue and much of his method from his great forerunners in Victorian
satire and criticism—from Dickens, Thackeray, and Gilbert, from
Mill, Spencer, and George Eliot. His lineage as a satirist reaches back
farther still: to Fielding, Sterne, Byron, perhaps even Jane Austen—
all the critics who had impaled the cant, hypocrisy, and sanctimony
that form the dross of English habit and character. Though he has
been regarded at different times as an eccentric, a pariah, an odd
fish, a gadfly, a biological or spiritual "sport" in the English moral
tradition, he is firmly a part of that tradition—part of its character
and mentality, part of its divided intelligence, part of the wit that
competes with its self-esteem and parochialism, never so effective as
when he shows himself to contain its full ambivalence of temperament and personality. Dickens, if a single name is to be emphasized,
is his direct ancestor—the Dickens who both loved and pilloried the
national character, who summed up in his lifework the riddled self-
delusion and spiritual dry rot at work in the social body of his century,
and whose families—Pecksniffs, Chuzzlewits, Chadbands, Smallweeds, Gradgrinds, Dorrits, Barnacles, Veneerings, Wilfers—anticipate the Pontifexes. But neither Dickens nor Gilbert nor Gissing, not
even the iconoclasts of the nineties, not Shaw in his early plays or

---

[1] V. S. Pritchett, "A Victorian Son" in *The Living Novel* (1946), pp. 102, 104.

Wells in his early novels, had so specifically fixed and isolated the virus of Victorian fatuity and the special organism of its most fruitful growth, the Victorian family, as Butler's novel did.

The Way of All Flesh classified this germ with the accuracy of a bacteriologist. The English social novel found the fresh impetus it was looking for. The Pontifexes became the case-history of a lingering malady, coldly, remorselessly, almost passionlessly diagnosed. The bourgeois ethos of the Victorian age had already died a dozen deaths, but it was still alive and persistent in the mentality of the English middle class. Not even the death of Queen Victoria herself in 1901 spelled its doom more decisively than Butler's novel did two years later. Slow at first to win a public hearing, the book soon began to stamp its imprint on the work of a new century—on Shaw, Wells, Bennett, Forster, Beresford, D. H. Lawrence. "It drives one almost to despair of English literature," said Shaw in 1905,[2] "when one sees so extraordinary a study of English life as Butler's posthumous *The Way of All Flesh* making so little impression that when, some years later, I produce plays in which Butler's extraordinarily fresh, free, and future-piercing suggestions have an obvious share, I am met with nothing but vague cacklings about Ibsen and Nietzsche. . . . Really, the English do not deserve to have great men." Bennett, youthfully eager to define a congenial paternity for his work, soon called the tale "one of the greatest novels of the world." Another young writer of the 1900s, then feeling his way toward authorship, was to recall years later why the author of *Erewhon* struck his mind so sharply. "For one thing," says E. M. Forster, "I have the sort of mind which likes to be taken unawares. The frontal full-dress presentation of an opinion often repels me, but if it be insidiously slipped in sidewise I may receive it, and Butler is a master of the oblique.

---

[2] For Shaw on Butler see his review of *Luck or Cunning?* in the *Pall Mall Gazette*, May 31, 1887; his review of Henry Festing Jones's *Samuel Butler: A Memoir* in *The Manchester Guardian*, November 1, 1919; "Mr. Gilbert Cannan on Samuel Butler" in his *Pen Portraits and Reviews* (1932), and the prefaces to *Man and Superman* (1903), *Major Barbara* (1907), *Androcles and the Lion* (1913), and *Back to Methuselah* (1921, but especially in its new edition with postscript, 1946).

Then, what he had to say was congenial, and I lapped it up. It was
the food for which I was waiting." [3] And when Shaw, at a later date,
attempted to explain why he considered Butler a man of genius, he
said:

> A man of genius is not a man who can do more things, or who
> knows more things, than ordinary men: there has never been a man
> of genius yet who has not been surpassed in both respects in his
> own generation by quite a large number of hopeless fools. He is
> simply a man who sees the importance of things. . . . Butler saw
> the importance of what he had hit on, and developed it into a mes-
> sage for his age.

What that message was has become, in the half-century since Butler's death, something perhaps simpler than Butler intended. This
is doubtless the one unmistakable evidence of the factor of genius
in a talent whose authority is elsewhere debatable, or greatly confused by erratic and perverse tendencies. One way of defining genius
is by its ability to make a certain idea or principle unmistakably its
own, impossible to think of or employ except in the special form it
has discovered for it. Butler's is a case of this order. He is celebrated
as the demolisher of Victorian moral sanctimony and the mentality
it produced. This reputation, based on his criticism of religion in *The
Fair Haven,* on his satire on society in *Erewhon,* on his attack on the
new orthodoxy of science in *Evolution Old and New, Life and Habit,*
and *Luck or Cunning?,* but mainly on *The Way of All Flesh,* is
valid up to a point. It derives from the radical antinomianism in his
make-up. It issues from a fundamental impulse in all his work. "I had
to steal my own birthright," he once said. "I stole it and was bitterly
punished. But I saved my soul alive." Yet the punishment, as Edmund
Wilson has pointed out, "affected him more permanently than he
knew. He had blasted Langar Rectory to eternity, but it had left
upon him its blight. His soul was alive; but, as Bernard Shaw says,

----

[3] E. M. Forster, "Books That Influenced Me: Samuel Butler's *Erewhon,*" under the title "Books in General" in *The New Statesman and Nation* (London),
July 15, 1944, now included in his *Two Cheers for Democracy* (1951), pp. 219–
23. See also his "Butler Approached," a review of P. N. Furbank's *Samuel
Butler,* in *The Spectator* (London), November 12, 1948.

he had been maimed by his early training. Having begun as the bad boy of a pious family, he was never to outgrow that state of mind." [4] Another recent writer on Butler, G. D. H. Cole, has corroborated this verdict:

> Acute critic as he was of many Victorian values, he was very much a Victorian himself. His perception seldom travelled far from the Victorian middle-class home and family; and when it did his view of things became superficial at once. Nothing could well be more thoroughly *bourgeois* than his picture of Erewhonian society; and it is not for being *bourgeois* that Butler mocks at it, for the way of living that he implicitly holds up beside it is not less *bourgeois*. No one ever insisted more firmly than Butler on the Victorian virtue of having enough money to live on securely in a comfortable *bourgeois* way; and no one ever upheld more strongly the importance of prudence—surely the most *bourgeois* of all the virtues. . . . Fiercely as he attacked the Victorian family, its spell was upon him, and he could not even try to throw it off. Nor could he ever stop worrying about God, even when he had become fully convinced that God was not worrying about him. He had most of the Victorian obsessions, though he had many of them upside down. [5]

This states Butler's predicament and the ambiguous cast of his legacy to his inheritors succinctly. It also indicates the complexity and saving virtue of his case—the virtue of writing from deep inside the Victorian ethos—that gives his work its authenticity. The greatest satirists have written thus and perhaps only thus, from a profound involvement in their material. None of them was ever more inextricably involved than Butler was. To see how and why, a glance at his life is necessary, the more so since he transcribed that life so closely in his novel.

II

Butler was born in 1835 in the rectory of Langar in Nottinghamshire, son of the Reverend Thomas Butler and his wife Fanny

---

[4] Edmund Wilson, "The Satire of Samuel Butler" in *The Triple Thinkers* (1938); reprinted in *The Shores of Light* (1953), pp. 556–65.

[5] G. D. H. Cole, preface to *The Essential Samuel Butler* (1949); see also his *Samuel Butler and The Way of All Flesh* (1947).

Worsley. Thomas Butler was the son of Dr. Samuel Butler, head-master of Shrewsbury School, later to become Bishop of Lichfield, one of the most formidable pedagogues and divines of his day and the subject of his grandson's one dull book, the biography the younger Samuel published in 1896 when, in an access of family conscience, he reversed the judgment on his grandfather that forms one of the most brilliant portraits in *The Way of All Flesh*, that of Ernest's grand-father George, the self-made, fatuously successful religious publisher. The family had advanced from the professional gentility of the Eight-eenth Century, so deftly drawn in the first chapters of the novel with their picture of old Mr. Pontifex of Paleham, into the clerical class of the Nineteenth Century, custodian of English morality and edu-cation. As Mr. Cole has pointed out, the Butlers' class "was not the new *bourgeoisie* which had been created by the Industrial Revolu-tion, but rather that middle class which had existed in the Eighteenth Century and had come through the Industrial Revolution almost unchanged, with a lively sense of its own gentility as contrasted with the vulgarity of many of the new rich, and with a steady allegiance to the Church of England as the church to which all really decent people belonged." This class prided itself on its associations with the liberal professions, with culture and religion in their official, class-vested character. It was not above making money: it made enough of it to provide the Butlers with substantial means and a reverence for means that remained one of Butler's own deepest convictions. "Money losses are the hardest to bear of any by those who are old enough to com-prehend them," says the narrator of the novel, and money is in the book not only a mode of access to the pleasantest things in life but a refuge from vulgarity and indignity, a shield against ugliness and squalor, a weapon of tyranny, no doubt, but also an armor for the spirit. No novel of modern moral repute is more expressly a defense of the principle of property.

But Langar Rectory was more than an abode of rank and respect-ability. It was a fortress of religious sanctimony, with the Reverend Thomas its vested agent, a man of self-conceit and a bully, with an adoring wife to support his bullying discipline of their four children,

Sam and Tom, Harriet and Mary. Of these Sam was the boy of sensitive nature, the child born to rebel. From the first he recognized his
father as his enemy. "He never liked me, nor I him," he said years
later; "from my earliest recollections I can call to mind no time when
I did not fear him and dislike him. . . . I have never passed a day
without thinking of him many times over as the man who was sure
to be against me, and who would see the bad side rather than the
good of everything I said and did." A regimen of lessons, hostile
authority, and almost daily beatings was intermitted only once, when
the family went on a carriage journey—how different from Ruskin's
cushioned progresses in the family chariot—through France, Germany, Switzerland, and Italy, where Sam's love of nature, art, and
the South found its first flowering. The rest of his childhood was a
thralldom that bred his earliest resolution—to escape.

At ten he was sent to school at Allesley, and in 1848 to Shrewsbury
School, where his grandfather's influence still prevailed and his shy,
distrustful nature found a new kind of unhappiness. In 1854 he went
on to Cambridge and knew happiness for the first time. But further
distresses awaited him there too. He came to grips with the orthodox
theology in which he had been bred and with the challenge of the
profession his family had conceived for him, the ministry of the
Church. He soon discovered that he was a natural skeptic, that he
could never follow his father and grandfather into the clergy, that
what he really wanted to be was a painter. He also discovered a will
of his own capable of resisting his parents' effort to get him to enter,
in default of the ministry, a respectable calling like the law or teach-
ing. The upshot of the struggle was that when he finished Cambridge
he decided, on the strength of a personal capital of two hundred
seventy pounds and a promise of funds from his father, to emigrate
to New Zealand and become a sheep farmer.

He sailed in 1859 at the age of twenty-three and stayed five years.
He became, perhaps to his own surprise as much as to his family's, an
efficient farmer. He made money. His health became robust. He de-
lighted in the wild splendors of the southern wilderness (later to become the landscape of *Erewhon*). He found his first freedom of mind

and spirit and returned to England a prosperous man, able at last to indulge his tastes and ambitions. But a new complication had entered his affairs and another confusion declared itself in his emotions. He returned with an incubus in the form of a friend, Charles Paine Pauli. Butler was fated to ill-advised or disappointing friendships all his life. They had their origins in his distracted and unresolved emotions, divided between romantic needs, uneasy suspicions, and a fear of giving himself freely that was dictated as much by social prohibitions as by the laming hostilities of his childhood. Pauli's was the most ill-fated of these. It clung to him, leechlike, money-draining, and nerve-sapping, for years.

In London Butler became a pupil at Heatherley's Art School, learned to paint, and before long was exhibiting at the Royal Academy. At Heatherley's he made another friendship, more tragic in its consequences even than Pauli's but the most fruitful of Butler's life. Eliza Mary Ann Savage, plain, lame, witty, one of the many pathetic wraiths of Victorian life and literature, was like himself a dissenter from Victorian smugness, and the one woman to whom Butler ever responded with a genuine spiritual sympathy. She may have loved him or she may not: her story is lost in silence and obscurity. Butler could never love her, but he also found it impossible to live without her lively response and encouragement. She became his modest Egeria. It was she who spurred him to write his novel, contributed much to its growth and detail, provided the model for its one bright spirit, Ernest's Aunt Alethea, and when she died in 1885 Butler was left with the remorse of having been unable to give her the love and marriage he came to realize she wanted. "The wrong I did in that I did no wrong": his sonnet to her memory speaks with the most intense poignance he ever permitted himself. The little lame lady who passed her courageous life between a depressing home and the various clubs or societies for emancipated women in which she served as secretary or manager remains the elusive sphinx of Butler's history. What is certain is that without her he would have missed the one creative relationship of his career and perhaps the stimulus for the writing of his novel.

He had made a tentative start in authorship with *A First Year in Canterbury Settlement,* put together by his father out of his letters from New Zealand in 1863. In New Zealand too he had begun to cultivate the literary talent he had first discovered in essays and exercises at Cambridge, contributing to a local newspaper the fanciful sketches that yielded the germ of the chapter of *Erewhon* called "The Book of the Machines." Now in London the germ developed, produced in 1872 the book of *Erewhon,* and brought Butler his first notice as a writer. The next year he published *The Fair Haven,* a satire on the historicity of the Scriptures and an argument for the legendary, non-miraculous nature of Christianity. Having settled for the moment his accounts with his inherited religion, he plunged into the next of his lifelong battles, that against the mechanistic spirit of Darwinism. The result was his first book on "creative evolution," *Life and Habit,* in 1878. Here he set Buffon and Lamarck against Darwin and Huxley, whose hypotheses he believed to have "banished Mind from the Universe," creating a "soulless Determinism" and "a vacuum which Nature abhors." Thus in three books he set himself against the three great shibboleths of his age—material progress, religious orthodoxy, and scientific determinism. He took on himself the task and odium of defying the gods of Victorian England, and systematically made himself a pariah of contemporary culture.

Meanwhile, living in rooms in Clifford's Inn and with the help of Pauli's cash-consuming parasitism, he was rapidly running through his capital. A banker friend, Henry Hoare, hastened this process by involving him in a series of wildcat promoting schemes that lost Butler most of his remaining fortune. He had to go to his father for help, the bitterest concession he ever experienced. These experiences left him with a dread of speculation and a passion for secure investments. His attempt to salvage what he could from Hoare's ventures took him to Canada on two trips in 1874 and 1875. There he recovered about two thousand pounds (though he felt obliged to buy up the defaulted shares of those whom he had influenced to invest), and it was in Montreal that he profited by the colonial species of British cant when he discovered that a plaster cast of the "Discobolus" had been relegated to the basement of the local museum by the city's prudes, thus inspiring the "Psalm of Montreal," his best-known piece of invective. His financial troubles were over by 1886 when the inheritance due from his grandfather's estate came to him. The final twenty years of his life were spent in Clifford's Inn, in frequent trips to France and Italy (his love of mountains and the South was recorded in *Alps and Sanctuaries* in 1882), in indulging his love of music and Handel, in watching out the deaths of Miss Savage and Pauli, in satisfying his sexual needs clandestinely through a Frenchwoman, Mme. Lucie Dumas, the seamstress who became his mistress, in finding a brief romantic friendship with a young Swiss called Hans Faesch and a new friend and Boswell in Henry Festing Jones, and in writing, composing music, translating Homer, and publishing a sequel to *Erewhon* called *Erewhon Revisited* in 1901, until death overtook him at sixty-six in June 1902.

It was a life that carried to its end the scars that had been stamped on it from birth and childhood. They show in its cautions and privations, in its perversities of intelligence and temperament, in its failure to love or give itself in love. In *The Way of All Flesh* Butler says that "accidents which happen to a man before he is born, in the persons of his ancestors, will, if he remembers them at all, leave an indelible impression on him; they will have moulded his character so that, do what he will, it is hardly possible for him to escape their consequences. If a man is to enter into the Kingdom of Heaven, he must do so, not only as a little child, but as a little embryo, or rather as a little zoosperm—and not only this, but as one that has come of zoosperms which have entered into the Kingdom of Heaven before him for many generations. Accidents which occur for the first time, and belong to the period since a man's last birth, are not, as a general rule, so permanent in their effects, though of course they may sometimes be so." The determinism he repudiated so violently in scientific theory claimed him in his personal fate. But against this belief his sense of justice enabled him to see also the plight of parents: that, as Edmund Wilson has pointed out, "parents have not chosen their children any more than their children have chosen them and that the

plight in which the situation places us may be equally cruel for both"
—thus the chapter called "The World of the Unborn" in *Erewhon*.
This double burden of hurt and guilt never eased its weight in Butler.
It came as close as it ever has among modern talents to inhibiting his
gifts and canceling the liberty and birthright he won for himself
through his harsh ordeal.

He has been accused by some critics—by Malcolm Muggeridge
for one, in the most scathing of the indictments drawn against him [6]
—of being a character essentially deformed who read his personal
liabilities back into the age and conditions that produced him, of
owning a nature dominated by defeatism and an egocentricity that
could only hate. A share of this indictment is true: Butler never carried his resentment into a full intellectual or creative maturity like
the greatest of the Victorian rebels. His books deny more effectively
than they affirm. The worm of rancor and frustration gnaws their
roots. Except in flashes he never won the vision of human suffering
that animates the greatest satirists, from Aristophanes and Juvenal to
Swift and Voltaire. The hurt he suffered was so much a part of himself that he could never disown it, never disengage himself from its
injuries. He prized his wound and nursed his grievance; held the
world at arm's length because he feared it; and protected himself
with that world's own weapons—money, self-conceit, a protective
suspicion of life. He knew himself a failure in compassion as much
as in love, and he knew too much of great art—of Homer, Shakespeare, Handel, Bellini—to believe he had realized himself fully as
an artist. He remained a Victorian—rebel and victim, agonist and
apologist, radical and reactionary—to the end.

So much is evident. Butler does not stand in the highest rank of

----

[6] Malcolm Muggeridge, *The Earnest Atheist: A Study of Samuel Butler*
(1936). ("A crosspatch of a book"—E. M. Forster.) This is the most inclusive
attack on Butler and Butlerism that has appeared; for a shorter one see Graham
Greene's in his *The Lost Childhood and Other Essays* (1951); and for three
French studies written from outside the English situation see Madeleine L.
Cazamian's in *Le Roman et les Idées en Angleterre* (Strasbourg, 1923), Valery
Larbaud's *Samuel Butler* in *Les Cahiers des Amis des Livres* (Paris, 1920), and
J. B. Fort's two-volume work, *Samuel Butler: 1835–1902* (Paris, 1935).

English or Victorian genius. He belongs to a radically limited order of English talent—it appears in such contemporaries as Beddoes, Lewis Carroll, Walter Pater, and Housman—that shows an ingrowth of imagination and spirit and that produces an art curtailed by doubt, self-indulgence, or eccentricity. His notebooks, with their flat cynicism, staled vituperation, and facile cheapness in deflationary witticism or crude raillery, show the sterility of emotion and moral insight that is betrayed when the mask of imagination is dropped. But such a talent can make its mark by a strategy of its own. It often appears on the scene of history at opportune moments to seize what more vigorous men may miss—the canker at the heart of human nature or society that inhibits the flowering of life. Its own defects become a clue to a prevalent malady of the human spirit. By recognizing that malady in itself, it sometimes gains its own definition of honor and justice. That, in the face of the endemic cant and confusion of his age, is what Butler won for himself, for the contemporaries who gave him a hearing, and for the followers who took and assessed the cue he gave them. He used those least popular of keys, common sense, imagination, and justice, to unlock certain important secrets of moral energy and to make them available to the thought and art of a new century.

III

The Way of All Flesh maintains its importance, if for no other reason, because it records the ordeal necessary to such liberation in himself and his generation. *Life and Habit* is probably, as Clara G. Stillman argues in her excellent book on Butler,[7] his "most important book from the point of view of his contribution to scientific and

----

[7] Clara G. Stillman, *Samuel Butler: A Mid-Victorian Modern* (1932). This is the best book on Butler produced in America and the best work to combine biography with a critical interpretation of Butler's work and ideas; it surpasses the earlier studies of Gilbert Cannan (1915), John F. Harris (1916), and C. E. M. Joad (1924) in this respect, as well as P. N. Furbank's later book (1948), and serves as a critical interpretation of the biographical material in the memoirs of Henry Festing Jones (1919) and Mrs. R. S. Garnett (1926).

philosophic thought," and for what it and its sequels, *Evolution Old and New* and *Luck or Cunning?*, gave to Shaw, Bergson, and a new age of moral and ethical values. *Erewhon* is his most original work and his real title to a place in the satirical tradition. His poetic gifts and aesthetic capacities are best seen in *Alps and Sanctuaries*. But *The Way of All Flesh* gives his conflict of spirit its substance of fact and human actuality, of a tonic quality of wit and disillusioned insight that will remain Butler's distinctive achievement in the art of words. This gives it its rank among modern examples of the novel of initiation and education in life, the *Bildungsroman,* where its companions, to name only English examples, are *Pendennis, Great Expectations, Feverel, Adam Bede, Jude the Obscure,* Forster's *The Longest Journey,* Wells's *Tono-Bungay,* Bennett's *Clayhanger,* Lawrence's *Sons and Lovers,* and Joyce's *Portrait of the Artist as a Young Man.* Among these it is and will remain a landmark.

Reading it today we are able to see it as something more than the pure polemic or indictment verging on caricature that its reputation for iconoclasm and irreverence once made it appear. Butler's failure to publish it in his lifetime is far from meaning that he did not write it with all the seriousness in his power. He wrote it slowly, revised it conscientiously, took to heart Miss Savage's acute criticisms, and kept it in his desk as a kind of investment or insurance against the impermanence he felt his other books might suffer. He seems also to have felt the difficulties under which a book that issued so intimately from his own history labored. These are quite visible in its pages. By dividing himself into two men—the callow victim and prig Ernest, and the seasoned and disillusioned narrator Overton—he distanced his ordeal but he also inhibited the imaginative reality of his hero. Ernest is unfortunately the weakest part of the story. Compare him with Dickens' Pip, with Forster's Rickie Elliott, with Lawrence's Paul Morel or Joyce's Dedalus, all of them drawn with equal intimacy from their authors' selves, and his blankness as a character is apparent. The agony of the boy is continuously attenuated by Overton's mature wisdom. He lives too much after the fact to live convincingly within the fact, and thus becomes one of the least impressive heroes of his kind. For Ernest, says Mr. Pritchett, "one cares very little. Unlike Butler he does not act; because of the necessities of the book he is acted upon. His indiscretions are passive. He has no sins; he has merely follies." But Pritchett's further argument that "the characters are dwarfed and burned dry by Butler's argument," that he "chose them for their mediocrity and then cursed them for it," and that he did not sufficiently listen to Miss Savage when "she pointed out the dangers of his special pleading," is not so convincing. A close reading of the book shows that this special pleading yielded to a sound imaginative instinct in the best parts of it and permitted Butler to create certain characters that are triumphs of their sort.

These are old Mr. Pontifex of Paleham and his wife, Butler's tribute to the soundness in the older stock of his breed that came to suffer so sorry a decline in later generations; the grandfather of Ernest, George Pontifex, a portrait of canting hypocrisy that competes with Dickens' Pecksniff; Ernest's Aunt Alethea, briefly drawn but convincing as Butler's portrayal of the life-giving sympathy and generous instincts from which he felt genuine goodness to derive; and of course Ernest's parents, Theobald and Christina. Here Butler's sense of justice was put to its severest test. He knew them in all their meanness, self-conceit, and fatuity, their jealous smallness and niggardly complacency; he had not lost his sense of their enmity to him and the kind of life he valued; but some instinct—perhaps the very link of family attachment and tribal identity he never succeeded in breaking—kept him in sufficient sympathy with their misguided natures to permit a wholeness and complexity in the portraiture. He makes palpable their smugness, their selfish stratagems, the insinuating craftiness of their cruelty, but he shows where, in parental influence and social deceit, these originated, and before he has finished with them he makes us pity them as much as we blame them.

If, as Shaw said, Butler "actually endeared himself by parricide and matricide long drawn out," it is as much because he drew his dissection of these two characters out to its inevitable conclusion of pathos and tragedy as because he avenged himself and his generation for the blight they had suffered at the hands of Victorian parent-

hood. By the time we see Christina dying or Theobald in his comfort-
less old age we know how just but also how pitiful Christina's
torturings of Ernest on the inquisitorial sofa or Theobald's fear of
marriage on his ludicrous honeymoon make these scenes of their final
despair. The lesser characters in the book—Ernest's sisters, the Cambridge evangelists, the Dickensian Mrs. Jupp, the sinister Pryer,
even the ill-fated, vigorously drawn Ellen—show the lively realism
of people taken directly from their moment in time. Here Butler's
task was easier, though he met it with remarkable accuracy in comic
invention. It was his more complex relations with his parents and
grandfather that made his dealings with them difficult, and that
saved him from facile caricature when he brought them to the bar
of comic justice. That he did not shirk these difficulties is shown in
the fact that he succeeded in lifting them to a level which makes
possible not only a sound moral realism but the elements of tragedy.

By the time the book ends Ernest is saved. He is honest at last, a
man of humanity and humor, a redeemed prig, a sane creature won
over from the powers of ignorance to the side of life. He is not, however, oppressively or heroically edifying. He is happy to be well off,
feels no scruples in leaving his children to be raised as wards of a
Thames bargee, and means to live a life of modest effort and intelligent selfishness. His will has never recovered, will never fully recover,
from its almost fatal testing. He will not impose or oppress, but he
is unlikely ever to command and create. He mirrors, in this, his inventor. Both he and Butler have known too well what it means to be
edifying in the wrong way to risk the dangers of becoming edifying
in the right way. The book ends on a sigh of relief, a note of caution,
an audible shudder of relaxation. The will has at last been cured of
mania and excess. A soul has been saved and claimed its birthright.

Butler succeeded in putting the whole of himself into the novel.
His shrewd if amateur scientific feeling is there; his sense of the conflict between conscious and unconscious forces in the human psyche
is everywhere implicit; his hatred of mechanistic doctrine and the
moral heartlessness it breeds is argued; his love of music and art is
voiced by Overton's taste and Ernest's devotion to the organ; his

contempt of the duplicity and inverted ethic of bourgeois morality suffuses the book, bringing the fantasy of *Erewhon* to terms with the realistic claims of fictional art. Overton's commentary, however intrusive and damaging to the imaginative freedom of the tale, nevertheless sums up the wisdom that Butler wrested from his personal history, and this is what makes the book, however short in the ultimate passion and vision of moral genius, a point of definition in the experience of its century. Osbert Sitwell has said that "the indictment against the Victorian age is not that it was not comfortable, or, in spite of its many cruelties, kindly; but that it left its debts, mental, moral, and physical, to be paid by a later generation." Butler, who missed in his age the greater vision and capacity for idealism that even critics as merciless and scathing, and as different, as Dickens and Baudelaire, Ibsen and Rimbaud, defined for it, was yet one man who determined to do his share in preventing that insolvency. It is for this reason—sufficient for his representative importance in modern experience and conflict—that the Twentieth Century has been grateful to him, has called *The Way of All Flesh* a classic among records of the human spirit in its struggle toward liberty and truth, and has granted him his honorable place among its benefactors.

1950   [1956]

Henry James

THE ACT OF LIFE

I

To recover "the continuity of an artist's endeavour, the growth of his whole operative consciousness": it was thus that Henry James set the problem he took upon himself when, in 1907 and at sixty-four, he faced the task—"immense," "formidable," an "extremity of labour" —of reviewing the work of his lifetime, confident that he would find, "under this backward view, his whole unfolding, his process of production, for a thrilling tale, almost for a wondrous adventure." "When vigorous writers have reached maturity," he had said thirty years earlier in writing of Turgenev, "we are at liberty to look in their works for some expression of a total view of the world they have been so actively observing. This is the most interesting thing their works offer us. Details are interesting in proportion as they contribute to make it clear." Now the same challenge confronted him in the long file and four decades of his own fiction.

"Everything counts, nothing is superfluous, in such a survey," he recognized. For "really, universally, relations stop nowhere, and the exquisite problem of the artist is eternally but to draw, by a geometry of his own, the circle within which they shall happily *appear* to do so. He is in the perpetual predicament that the continuity of things is the whole matter, for him, of comedy and tragedy; that this continuity is never, by the space of an instant or an inch, broken, and that, to do anything at all, he has at once intensely to consult and intensely to ignore it." But however much the progression of idea and purpose may be suspended when the book of a given moment is being written, its presence must still be felt as the very principle of the artist's existence: "experience has to organize, for convenience and cheer, some system of observation—for fear, in the admirable immensity, of losing its way."

When and how had such a system begun to operate for James himself? A notable fact about most serious writers is how early their prepossessing subject seizes them, and today as we look back over the half-century of James's work we feel that he was never unaware of the urgency of his own. Its signals begin to flash almost as soon as he began to write at all. One Sunday in November 1863 when he was twenty, and forty years before he started the prefaces for the New York Edition of his fiction, he wrote a letter to the bosom friend of his youth, Thomas Sergeant Perry, the "Dear Sargy" or "Mon cher vieux Thomas" of his earliest surviving correspondence. The subject of prejudice had come up for discussion. "I agree with you perfectly that 'prejudice is one of the worst evils which afflict humanity,'" he said in responding to Perry's earnest speculations. "Is not a prejudice a judgment formed on a subject upon *data* furnished, not by the subject itself, but by the mind which regards it?" "These *data*," he continued, "are the fruits of the subtlest influences—birth, education, association. Unless carefully watched they insinuate themselves into every opinion we form. They grow to be the substance of our very being. So far are they from being subjects of consciousness that they almost become vehicles thereof . . . They are so intimately connected with every mental process, that they insidiously pervert our opinions, discolour and distort the objects of our vision." But can a man ever free himself from them? "In his desire to believe nothing but what his reason showed him to be true, I think he would end by believing nothing at all. . . . We were certainly born to believe. The truth was certainly made to be believed. Life is a prolonged reconciliation of these two facts. As long as we squint at the truth instead of looking straight at it—*i.e.* as long as we are prejudiced instead of

fair, so long we are miserable sinners. . . . When by some concerted movement of humanity the air is purified then the film will
fall from our eyes and (to conclude gracefully) we shall gaze un-
dazzled at the sun!!!" The long preoccupation of the future is already emerging.

A few years later, in 1867, James had something more to say to
Perry about the career and "system of observation" he was charting
for himself. Now an additional confidence appears to reinforce his
"arrogant hope." "Deep in the timorous recesses of my being," he
confided, "is a vague desire to do for our dear old English letters and
writers *something* of what Sainte-Beuve and the best French critics
have done for theirs." "At the thought of a study of this kind, on a
serious scale, and of possibly having the health and time to pursue it,
my eyes fill with heavenly tears and my heart throbs with a divine
courage." It is "by this constant exchange and comparison, by the
wear and tear of living and talking and observing that works of art
shape themselves into completeness." And could he not boast of
possessing a special advantage for such a task?

> When I say that I should like to do as Sainte-Beuve has done, I
> don't mean that I should like to imitate him, or reproduce him in
> English: but only that I should like to acquire something of his in-
> telligence and his patience and vigour. One feels—I feel at least, that
> he is a man of the past, of a dead generation; and that we young
> Americans are (without cant) men of the future. I feel that my only
> chance for success as a critic is to let all the breezes of the west blow
> through me at their will. We are Americans born—*il faut en prendre
> son parti*. I look upon it as a great blessing; and I think that to be an
> American is an excellent preparation for culture. We have exquisite
> qualities as a race, and it seems to me that we are ahead of the Eu-
> ropean races in the fact that more than either of them we can deal
> freely with forms of civilization not our own, can pick and choose
> and assimilate and in short (aesthetically &c) claim our property
> wherever we find it. To have no national stamp has hitherto been a
> regret and a drawback, but I think it not unlikely that American
> writers may yet indicate that a vast intellectual fusion and synthesis
> of the various National tendencies of the world is the condition of
> more important achievements than any we have seen. We must of
> course have something of our own—something distinctive and homo-
> geneous—and I take it that we shall find it in our moral conscious-

ness, our unprecedented spiritual lightness and vigour. In this sense at least we shall have a national *cachet*.—I expect nothing great during your lifetime or mine perhaps: but my instincts quite agree with yours in looking to see something original and beautiful disengage itself from our ceaseless fermentation and turmoil.

"Everything counts, nothing is superfluous": it is not difficult to feel that when James began the inventory of his lifework in 1907 he was harking back, however dimly, to the program he had laid down for himself in the distant and confident years of the 1860s. "This is why," he said, "as one looks back, the private history of any sincere work, however modest its pretensions, looms with its own completeness in the rich, ambiguous aesthetic air, and seems at once to borrow a dignity and to mark, so to say, a station." This too is why he found himself, "all attentively, in presence of some such recording scroll or engraved commemorative table—from which the 'private' character, moreover, quite insist[ed] on dropping out." And this was doubtless also why, in the last decade of his life, "his whole unfolding, his process of production," took on the fascination of a "wondrous adventure." For, as he presently said in another preface, "the figures in any picture, the agents in any drama, are interesting only in proportion as they feel their respective situations. . . . Their being finely aware—as Hamlet and Lear, say, are finely aware—*makes* absolutely the intensity of their adventure, gives the maximum of sense to what befalls them."

That James here spoke with conscious reference to himself, to his own adventure in the eventful age he witnessed and to his own way of turning it to account, is evident not only in the prefaces but in the memoirs he was soon to add to them as an assessment of the events and forces that had shaped his mind and work. The world of readers and critics was slow to admit the intensity of his adventure or to recognize the "maximum of sense" he gave to it. His private history was not of the kind that "looms large" with the dramatic capacities in action or passion that have made a whole host of modern writers—from Goethe, Byron, and Dostoevsky to Rimbaud, Yeats, Lawrence, and Lorca—vivid figures in the mythology of the human spirit. Outwardly viewed, James's career was unspectacular. It was the art and vision by which he enriched it that made it momentous, and that continue to make James "an attesting witness" and one of the most significant figures in the drama of the past century.

It was a life which, apart from profound family affections, many devoted friendships, many travels, a few high moments of public celebrity and several of uncomfortable notoriety, was a record of little but incessant labor at the desk, many books read and many written, and finally a quiet death in the fulness of years. It was committed to a difficult and increasingly thankless kind of work, and in spite of James's unfaltering respect for his profession, his almost sacerdotal reverence for the literary vocation, he was repeatedly beset by fears that his efforts had come to nothing. More than once he felt that he had "entered upon evil days," that his finest work had "reduced the desire, and the demand, for [his] productions to zero," that he was "condemned apparently to eternal silence." What he called the "complete failure" of the sumptuous New York Edition of his fiction left him, toward the end of his life, "high and dry"—"at my age . . . and after my long career, utterly, insurmountably, unsaleable"—and he called that crowning monument of his labors "a sort of miniature Ozymandias of Egypt ('look on my *works*, ye mighty, and despair!')." He wrote his failure to win popular recognition into a series of ironic and searching tales—"The Author of Beltraffio," "The Lesson of the Master," "The Death of the Lion," "The Middle Years," "The Next Time," and a dozen others—which picture art as a tyrannical task-master who breaks his devotees when they are frail, tests them cruelly when they are strong, or grants them at best a secret victory which the world appears bound to condemn or ignore. ("Die Kunst ist im Glück eine Zier; im Unglück eine eiserne Tür": they all echo Rilke's maxim.) But the confidence with which he launched himself on his career in youth never seriously deserted him. It was with something like the defiance of a proud desperation that he told William Dean Howells, at one particularly bleak moment in his fortunes, that "some day all my buried prose will kick off its various tombstones at once."

We have seen his prophecy justified. When the hundredth anniversary of James's birth arrived in 1943 it saw his fame sweeping into the full tide of a revival that has raised him to a position of supremacy among the novelists of the English-speaking world and given him a rank in the highest company of modern writers. The decade of the 1940s and the years of crisis just preceding it witnessed a crowded procession of centenaries—anniversaries of artists and thinkers who helped to shape a momentous century in the life of Western man. Hardy, Zola, and Nietzsche; Swinburne, Pater, and Butler; Mallarmé, Verlaine, and Anatole France; Cézanne and Renoir; Americans like Mark Twain, Howells, Henry Adams, William James, Bierce, and Lanier—in a time of danger and catastrophe the date of each of them sounded its knell on a darkening age and provided its occasion for revaluing the legacy, heartening or dubious, they left to their inheritors. None of them met a more dramatic recognition than Henry James. As if by a stroke of ironic justice, his own worst fears for his future were dispelled at a time that brought ignominy to much of the civilization he had most valued. "During our current afflictions," said one English tribute, "he has found a greater body of readers than ever before, who discover in him a mirror of the civilized enjoyments now in abeyance, a guardian of the values that war repudiates."

It was an axiom of the aesthetes of the nineties that nature imitates art. James's work makes us believe that history does so also. A great share of the history of his age now appears to find its permanent image in his pages. His books have become a standing example of what he meant when he told H. G. Wells in 1915 that literature "*makes* life, makes interest, makes importance . . . and I know no substitute whatever for the force and beauty of its process." Our present interest in James derives partly, no doubt, from the distrust of history and action that has been bred by the political and moral disorder into which the world has fallen, by the prolonged crisis and sense of disintegrating traditions in which we have come to live. We see in him, by a species of retrospective logic, what men have always seen in their image-makers and heroes of form—what Santayana meant when he said, defining Proust's achievement, that "life as it flows is so much time wasted, and that nothing can ever be recovered or truly possessed save under the form of eternity, which is also . . . the form of art."

The revival of James has bred its excesses of cult and sanctimony. They come partly from a natural pride—notably an American pride —in reclaiming the books that were for many years disputed or rejected by critics of many schools and prejudices: by realists, by patriots, by skeptics of culture, by reformers of society, by proletarians, all of whom combined to make the public forget that James had his faithful if limited audience through fifty years; that his tales and novels were printed in magazines on a scale that has become incredible in our own boasted age of literary freedom and experiment; that he met positive defeat only once—in his efforts to become a successful dramatist—and turned even that drastic disappointment to the advantage of his real work in fiction; and that his fellow writers had granted him the title of "Master." His critics preferred to charge him with most of the sins in the literary and American calendars—with repudiating his birthright, with being a snob, with falling indecisively between two cultures and finding himself at home in neither, with evading a full commitment to life, with accepting only the values of privilege and aristocracy, with excluding a great share of human misery and injustice from serious consideration. He was accused of being the "culmination of the superficial type," a man who "doesn't find things out" and so produces "tales of nothingness"; of being "a fat, wistful remittance man with a passion for elegance"; of having "never succeeded in coming to grips with life"; of creating "the impassioned formalism of an art without content"; of "magnificent pretensions, petty performances!—the fruits of an irresponsible imagination, of a deranged sense of values, of a mind working in the void, uncorrected by any clear consciousness of human cause and effect"; even, finally, of being "simply not interesting: he is only intelligent; he has no mystery in him, no secret; no Figure in the Carpet." [1]

---

[1] The critics quoted are H. G. Wells (in *Boon*, 1915), Burton Rascoe, Somer-

This long bill of particulars includes some arguments with which every serious reader of James must eventually deal, but the verdict is now, on the whole, a very different one. As early as 1918 one of James's most perceptive followers had made bold to call him "the most intelligent man of his generation," and today critics of resolute astuteness and of radically different standards attest his distinction. "Henry James *is* a great artist, in spite of everything," says one of them; "his work is incomplete as his experience was; but it is in no respect second-rate and he can be judged only in the company of the greatest." Another, asking only that he be permitted to define the novel in a way "neither difficult nor illegitimate," has said he would "be inclined to consider James as the greatest novelist in English, as he is certainly one of the five or six greatest writers of any variety to be produced in North America." A third has called James "a man who if he had never written a novel, would be considered the first of short-story writers, and if he had never written a short story, the noblest of letter writers, and if he had never written anything would by his talk alone be known as a great man." A fourth has flatly asked, "What achievement in the art of fiction—fiction as a completely serious art addressed to the adult mind—can we point to in English as surpassing his?" [2]

When controversy, enthusiasm, personal legend, and historic occasion combine in the rediscovery of a writer and make of it a significant episode in the history of taste, it is clear that he constitutes what James himself would have called a "special type"—that he was marked by circumstances as well as genius to play a significant role in the drama of culture. James held a high opinion of the artist's right to such a role. "To do something *great*" of which "the world shall hear" was one of his earliest ambitions. Once, in the earlier days of his conquest of England, he was a guest of Lord Rosebery

---

set Maugham, J. Middleton Murry, Van Wyck Brooks (in *The Pilgrimage of Henry James*, 1925), and André Gide.

[2] The critics quoted here are T. S. Eliot in *The Little Review*, August 1918; Edmund Wilson in *The Triple Thinkers* (1938); Yvor Winters in *Maule's Curse* (1938); Cyril Connolly in *Horizon*, May 1943; F. R. Leavis in *The Great Tradition* (1948).

and his Rothschild wife amid the splendors of Mentmore. "I have retired from the glittering scene, to meditate by my bedroom fire on the fleeting character of earthly possessions," he wrote home to his mother in America. "Tomorrow I return to London and to my personal occupation, always doubly valued after 48 hours among *ces gens-ci,* whose chief effect upon me is to sharpen my desire to distinguish myself by personal achievement, of however limited a character." The desire for fame and power, that "sense of glory" which had struck him in boyhood like a revelation in the Galerie d'Apollon in the Louvre, possessed him even though he felt the peril it entailed. He would certainly have agreed with what one of his contemporaries, Gerard Hopkins, then wholly unknown to fame, once wrote in a letter to Robert Bridges: that "fame, the being known, though in itself one of the most dangerous things to man, is nevertheless the true and appointed air, element, and setting of genius and its works"; that works of art are designed "to educate, to be standards"; that to produce "is of little use unless what we produce is known," for "it is by being known it works, it influences, it does its duty, it does good."

What James took to be the duty and good of his art, what means he employed to provide a standard for the use and education of society, what tests and scruples he met in the effort, and how his purpose was finally proved and justified—all this makes his career one of the dramatic chapters in modern literature and permits it to loom in a way that has become a major instance of the persistence and integrity of the writer's vocation. But because James was a man who, contrary to a still-surviving derogation, did not live or work unaware of his situation and office in the culture of his age, it has become something more.

II

James published his first signed tale in 1865, when he was twenty-two years old.[3] That date, in the career of an American, serves as an

---

[3] "The Story of a Year" in *The Atlantic Monthly,* March 1865. Although, following the policy of the *Atlantic* at that time, James's name was not attached to

initial signal. The Civil War was at the point of ending. The American nation, and James and his generation with it, stood at the threshold of a new age. The native literature had already passed through its formative phases, and each of them had found a man, some of them several men, to give voice to its deciding impulse. Bradford, Mather, Edwards, and Franklin; Jefferson, Irving, Cooper, Emerson, and Whitman, had brought the republic by clearly defined stages—colonial, religious, revolutionary; frontier, pioneer, and nationalist—to the moment when several talents possessed of a vision more original and searching than any of these crowned the progress of the American spirit with what serious maturity in any ordained course inevitably entails: a moral challenge, a check of self-esteem, a warning to the will, a vision of the tragedy implicit in pride and success. The American mind, rooted in its hereditary conscience, had never escaped its hauntings by darker powers, its stirrings of ancestral guilt, what Howells was presently to call "the slavery implicated in our liberty." Poe had recently imaged them unmistakably. But an enormous confidence in the American destiny allayed them until Hawthorne, Melville, and, in her Amherst seclusion, Emily Dickinson gave them their classic and prophetic definition. The Civil War came as if to certify their presence. An hour of judgment sounded. It called for a new order of intelligence in American life, a critical intelligence; and neither the victory of 1865 nor the prosperity that followed it in the North could disguise the summons.

No writer more than the novelist is so likely to prove, once his work is finished, that he was born at precisely the right moment to become the artist he was intended to be. Stendhal, Balzac, and Dickens, Tolstoy, Proust, and Thomas Mann, all illustrate the opportunity with which history favors the prose chronicler beyond any other type

----

his contribution, this was identified as by "Henry James, Jr." in the table of contents of the magazine. It has now been discovered by Mr. Leon Edel, in his *Henry James: The Untried Years* (1953), that this story, long identified as James's first, had been preceded by another, "A Tragedy of Error," unsigned, in *The Continental Monthly* of New York for February 1864, eight months before James published his first unsigned critical review, of Nassau W. Senior's *Essays on Fiction*, in *The North American Review* for October 1864.

of artist. The literary novice of 1865 could hardly remain unaware of his special opportunity, particularly when, as in Henry James's case, he saw the end—both triumphant and tragic—of a great national conflict in which a mischance of health had prevented him from taking an active part and whose meaning he was made to feel with a special personal intensity. Already in 1865 James had declared his opposition to Walt Whitman's kind of visionary emotion, but he shared with Whitman the non-participant's sense of the crisis that befell the American nation in the spring of that year.

This is to say that several distinct tasks—two great tasks especially—presented themselves to the young writer of 1865 who was able to see their urgency. One was the problem of defining the point at which America had arrived in her venture of nationhood and of determining her relation to the rival civilization of Europe—a problem which, in spite of the fact that almost every serious American writer had already addressed himself to it, still remained unsettled in the balance-books of history. The other was the re-creation of the art of fiction as a form of critical intelligence by rescuing it from the debris of tradition and the compromises of popularity, thus raising it to the dignity of moral power which novelists like Balzac, Turgenev, and Flaubert had already won for it in Europe, but which only Hawthorne and George Eliot (as James assessed the situation) had reached in the novel of the English-speaking world. James saw, with the full insight of his youthful acumen, these two great opportunities at his disposal. He saw he had a major theme to treat, and he saw that a new kind of art was needed to treat it adequately; and he took these as the special tokens of his vocation in literature.

His subject was made inescapable by the family into which he was born. His Irish grandfather had provided the wealth that endowed his heirs with the privileges of comfort, travel, and social affluence. His father, another adventurer but in religion and philosophic speculation instead of trade, had converted those assets to the service of thought and imagination. The James home was a breeding place of curiosity, ideas, and bookish pleasures. Emerson was a familiar guest there—"the divinely pompous rose of the philosophic garden," the elder James called him—and the air was a stir of enthusiasms. Idealism, transcendentalism, and democratic emancipation bred the new faith in humanity whose guides were Emerson and Fourier, and a creative freedom in religion whose prophets were Sandeman and Swedenborg. What a later American,[4] echoing Emerson, has ascribed to the American character as "a heightened sensitivity to the promises of life" was the native emotion of the James home. Man was to be redeemed by society. Society was to be redeemed by a rebirth of moral confidence and a faith in "possibilities." Such ideas implanted in both William and Henry James a religious conviction which, persisting beyond rationality or agnosticism, was to fix its stamp on their ultimate conceptions of science and of art.

But another emotion, balancing and complicating the ardor of emancipation, dominated the family. It was the spell of the past, the call of Europe. "I saw my parents homesick, as I conceived, for the ancient order," Henry James said many years later, "and distressed and inconvenienced by many of the more immediate features of the modern, as the modern pressed about us, and since their theory of our better living was from an early time that we should renew the question of the ancient on the very first possibility I simply grew greater in the faith that somehow to manage that would constitute success in life. I never found myself deterred from this fond view, which was implied in every question I asked, every answer I got, and every plan I formed." In her early essay on James, Rebecca West said that the essential thing about him was that "he was an American; and that meant, for his type and generation, that he could never feel at home until he was in exile." James himself said it better when he wrote, "It's a complex fate, being an American, and one of the responsibilities it entails is fighting against a superstitious valuation of Europe," and better still when he declared it was his function as an artist to be a man "on whom nothing is lost." It was the decree of the Jameses' father that his children should experience their fate as Americans by knowing the share Europe played in their destinies.

----

[4] F. Scott Fitzgerald.

By taking his family abroad at decisive junctures of their childhood he enforced the instinct of tradition and cultural complexity in his sons, and he prepared Henry James for the subject that was to tax him throughout his life.

James's Europe, first in boyhood but presently in early manhood, was what Europe is bound to be at some point in the life of every American with any of the emotion or imagination of history in his constitution. It was "the threshold of expectation," the "gate of admirations," a "scene for the reverential spirit." It was "that dear old Europe," a world "immemorial, complex, accumulated"; and he came to it with his spiritual responses fully exposed and every antenna of his sensibility aquiver—a "passionate pilgrim," an "heir of all the ages." There he feasted on his "banquet of initiation," experienced "the sense of glory," "looked at history as a still-felt past and a complacently personal future, at society, manners, types, characters, possibilities, and prodigies and mysteries of fifty sorts." There he was to learn that glory meant "ever so many things at once, not only beauty and art and supreme design, but history and fame and power, the world in fine raised to the richest and noblest expression." But though he brought to Europe a good share of his traditional American innocence—in fact, he combined in himself two classic American characters, the "passionate pilgrim" and the "innocent abroad"—he also brought a shrewd curiosity and a divided sympathy. "I still love my country," he wrote his mother in 1869 from his "wondrous England," and that love, tough-rooted and ineradicable, soon defined an attitude that was to assert itself as radical. It set in motion a debate, a drama of contrasts and oppositions, that was never to subside wholly, either in his mind or in the tales he created.

What he really had carried to Europe, along with his native exhilaration and the reverence he had been bred in in his father's house, was another emotion of which the Jameses—father, William, Henry, Alice—were all to become aware in their lives. Henry named it many years later, in 1896, in a letter to a friend. "I have the imagination of disaster—and see life indeed as ferocious and sinister." It was a presentiment that had already visited his father, as it was to visit his brother and sister, in the form of panic seizure and crises of emotional illness. In Henry himself it remained controlled by a strong and vigorous imagination, but it remained none the less radical to his nature; and it soon added the force of a tragic vision to his excited responses to the scene of Europe.

We hear much about the dialectic intelligence in modern literature. It has come to be regarded as a primary clue to all serious art, a symptom of radical morality. It is a kind of intelligence of which James is a major exponent in our literature. He was schooled in it by his earliest experiences and education. It suffuses all of his work, serves as fulcrum to his insights and judgments, and plays its part continuously in the oppositions—America and Europe, innocence and experience, glory and disaster, illusion and reality—which are the basic terms of his drama of morality and culture.

Its workings in his fiction have been variously defined. One critic, Yvor Winters, has defined them with particular relevance: James's fiction argues that "there is a moral sense, a sense of decency, inherent in human character at its best; that this sense of decency, being only a sense, exists precariously, and may become confused and even hysterical in a crisis; that it may be enriched and cultivated through association with certain environments; that such association may, also, be carried so far as to extinguish the moral sense." And further: that "the moral sense as James conceives it is essentially or at least appears to James most clearly in American character; that it can be cultivated by association with European civilization and manners; that it may be weakened or in some other manner betrayed by an excess of such association." [5]

This is not to say that the American character supplies the invariable norm of virtue or decency in James's tales. The American he pictures in Europe may be innocent, worshipful, honest, or idealistic —may be Daisy Miller, Isabel Archer, Christopher Newman, Milly Theale, Maggie Verver—and thus fall victim through the very fault of his innocence to duplicity or intrigue in the older culture. He may

----

[5] Yvor Winters, "Maule's Well, or Henry James and the Relation of Morals to Manners," in *Maule's Curse* (1938), p. 169.

also become perverted by some moral weakness, or by wealth, self-indulgence, and the corruption of cynicism, and thus a doer of evil —Roderick Hudson, Madame Merle, Gilbert Osmond, Charlotte Stant. He may save himself there like Lambert Strether or lose himself like Hudson and Osmond. He will in any case be tested by a complexity he is never likely to have known in his native element; and the test will measure not only his own capacities for intelligence and moral dignity but also the America he came from.

Equally he will act as a test of the culture he encounters, for James's Europe shows a hostility of forces equal to that shown by America or by the two worlds when they meet in conflict. If the America James knew in youth gave him a standard of soundness and honesty (*The American, The Europeans, Washington Square*), it could also be crude, simple-minded, predatory, and half-barbaric (*Watch and Ward, Confidence, The Bostonians*); and if the America he redis-covered late in life revealed unsuspected capacities of energy, in-ventiveness, and social amenity (*The American Scene*), it also warned him of a corruption through wealth and power that could debase its victims and make Europe in turn assume the virtues of spiritual dignity and maturity ("The Jolly Corner," "A Round of Visits," *The Ivory Tower*). But when the Jamesian drama shifts to England and offers a drama exclusively European, as it does in *The Princess Casamassima, The Tragic Muse, What Maisie Knew, The Awkward Age, The Spoils of Poynton,* and *The Sacred Fount,* it may depict the forces of morality and culture not as stabilized by tradition but as even more dangerous in their workings, their pregnancy of evil and treachery, than in the younger and simpler society. There the idealist, the artist, the innocent, or the child may encounter an immanence of disaster even more "ferocious and sinister" than Amer-ica offers, by reason of the cynicism which time and privilege have bred.

Henry James was incapable of his sister Alice's scathing criticism of European society and politics, as he was incapable of his brother William's robust confidence in the American future. But he fully sensed the evil in what he called "the increasing dehumanization of society"; he knew what threat existed in the "black depths" and "enormous misery" of "the people"; he dreaded the advance of the "grossly materialistic"; and he spoke partly for himself when he made the heroine of *The Princess Casamassima,* his most ambitious drama of modern politics, describe English society as "the old regime again, bristling with every iniquity and every abuse, over which the French Revolution passed like a whirlwind; or perhaps even more a reproduction of Roman society in its decadence, gouty, apoplectic, depraved, gorged and clogged with wealth and spoils, selfishness and scepticism, and waiting for the onset of the barbarians."

James's argument, however rooted in the antithetical values of America and Europe, was never capable of simplicity. He was too deeply implicated in his own divided loyalties to permit it to become so. He was " 'between' countries," as Edna Kenton has rightly said: "There lay his subject and his relation to it, and there was his home," and "life is a struggle, wherever we are." But another loyalty claimed him too, another law of moral justice that forbade the rigidities of bias or the simplifications of prejudice. It was the principle of his art, with its standards of detachment, critical lucidity, and mind—that "quality of mind" which he defined as art's crowning virtue because it embodies the fullest possible measure of critical and moral sympathy, "unprejudiced and imperative," and thus insures a value higher than either passion or dogmatism. "I have not the least hesitation," he wrote his brother William in 1888, "in saying that I aspire to write in such a way that it would be impossible to an outsider to say whether I am at a given moment an American writing about England or an Englishman writing about America (dealing as I do with both countries), and so far from being ashamed of such an ambiguity I should be exceedingly proud of it, for it would be highly civilized."

III

The worth of an art "civilized" in James's sense was not a matter of common acceptance when James wrote those sentences, and it is ceasing to be so in various quarters today. Literature, like life it-self, is again being reclaimed by prejudice and force. Having passed through a great period of experiment and sophistication, it is once more called upon to declare positions, judgments, decisions; to revert to crudity or didacticism in order to serve the uses of social justice; to become prejudiced, partisan, political, or *engagé*. That demand continues to support the argument that James's work is a symptom of the casuistry, ambiguity, and equivocation that have undermined society and incurred its disasters. Thus the long-standing complaints about "a mind working in the void, uncorrected by any clear consciousness of human cause and effect," "an art without content," an inability "to come to grips with life."

They are complaints which, lodged against a minor part of his work, have a certain relevance, but they cannot stand against the weight and solidity of his whole achievement. James must be read, and read in his entirety; read not with the demand that he be another Tolstoy, Dostoevsky, or Melville, or even a Balzac or Dickens, but because he had his own unique contribution to make to the art of fiction and made it in a way that proves him as much a moral historian as any of these, even when he fell short of their final range and eloquence.

It may be allowed that the lengths of subtlety, analysis, and density to which James carried his craft can, if we do not follow him far enough, obscure the laws on which he based it. A factor of contrivance or calculation does figure in his workmanship. The ideas or "germs" for his tales which he compiled in his notebooks—those germs which illustrate the "odd law which somehow always makes the minimum of valid suggestion serve the man of imagination better than the maximum"—sometimes take on the appearance of theorems in moral algebra or exercises in an abstruse dramatic calculus. Occasionally his stories—slighter tales like "The Solution," "The Great Condition," "The Real Right Thing," "The Friends of the Friends"; intricate parables like "The Figure in the Carpet"; elaborate studies in social morality like *The Tragic Muse* and *The Awkward Age;* dramas of obsession or hallucination like *The Other House* and *The*

Sacred Fount—will show a virtuosity that results in a sheer excess of intellection or a disembodiment of sensibility. James's plays for the theatre, deprived of his narrative and stylistic body, almost invariably expose their skeletons of contrivance and lapse into theatrical formulae and hollow *tours de force*. H. G. Wells, hostile as a social and scientific realist to James's art, charged that James's exhaustive analysis of motives becomes "psychologizing" rather than genuine psychology, but even some of James's greatest admirers have found in the novels of his final period—*The Ambassadors, The Golden Bowl,* and *The Sense of the Past* notably—an "unhealthy vitality of undernourishment and etiolation," a failure in the "sense of human solidarity," an "excess of expression" over "what is actually felt." Is *The Ambassadors,* for instance, what James himself and a large body of his readers consider it, "the best 'all round'" of his novels, or is F. R. Leavis justified in thinking it "to be not only *not* one of his great books, but to be a bad one"? Is *The Awkward Age,* as Leavis claims, "one of James's major achievements," its dialogue "marvellously good, an amazing exhibition of genius," or does it, as Edmund Wilson believes, combine "a lifeless trickery of logic with the equivocal subjectivity of a nightmare"? [6] James was always fascinated by the difference between "a given appearance and a taken meaning," and obviously this hiatus, pushed far enough, can produce a disproportion between fact and illusion, substance and ratiocination, manners and moral truth, which is likely to end in casuistry and moral enigma.

These are the serious grounds, the necessary questions and disputes, of Jamesian criticism and of the problems his work imposes on its serious investigators. What seems clear is that James established his certain mastery, his essential subject, style, and relationship to his age, in the books of his so-called "middle period." That sequence, extraordinary in rapid invention and the exhilaration of powers suddenly come to maturity out of their early gropings and tentative excursions, begins with the concise perfection of *Washington Square*

----

[6] F. R. Leavis in *The Great Tradition* (1948), pp. 126, 169–70; Edmund Wilson in *The Triple Thinkers* (new edition, 1948), p. 111.

in 1880, continues through *The Portrait of a Lady* (possibly the touchstone of his entire achievement, with its shapeliness and movement as of fine music and its superbly controlled sympathy and justice) and his two masterly studies in social drama, *The Bostonians* and *The Princess Casamassima,* and is rounded out by the brilliant *nouvelles* of the nineties, to reach its climax in such searching studies of human and ethical values as *What Maisie Knew* and *The Spoils of Poynton.*

Yet given James's gifts and purpose, it is impossible to see him as resting with the achievements of those astonishing twenty years. The momentum of his vision was incapable of stopping short at that point. He had earned his right to carry his art into the poetic and metaphysical risks of his final period, particularly when that period produced the rich results and tragic quality of *The Wings of the Dove* (whatever the dramatic frailty of its nebulous heroine, certainly his highest point in subtle delicacy of moral criticism), the profound ethical reverberation of *The Golden Bowl,* and that phenomenal revival of his powers as a critic of society, *The Ivory Tower.* *The Ambassadors* may show too arbitrary a schematization to permit its formal mastery the full strength it calls for; *The Awkward Age,* *The Outcry,* and *The Sense of the Past* may err in the direction of abstraction; but the final phase of James's work brought the modern novel into a greater sense of its moral and imaginative capacities than any other work of the early Twentieth Century. And in spite of his increasing addiction to obsessive themes and subjective method, the vigorous recuperation of realism in *The Ivory Tower* shows how genuinely he was sustained to the end of his life by the principles he adopted in early maturity and how these yielded him a creative longevity, a persistence in imaginative invention, that is virtually unique in the history of fiction.

Those principles animate his work as a critic. They are brought to focus in his most famous essay, "The Art of Fiction." James was not a formal critic, and it is possible to recognize that he wrote brilliant criticism without being a "great" critic. He never formulated a comprehensive or organic aesthetic; he did not investigate classical literature, not even English or French; he had little skill in the theory or appreciation of poetry. It has been said of him that he never arrived at "a relation to the whole body of literature" such as we find in Johnson, Coleridge, Sainte-Beuve, Arnold, and Eliot. Instead he worked empirically, pursuing consistently only his personal interests in fiction and drama. But within these limits he showed an integrity of interest that was tireless, and he produced the most coherent study of a chosen craft by a practicing craftsman to be found in English. His essays rival Baudelaire's in their continuous relevance to actual creation and to the origins of creation in the artist's mind and sensibility.

His emphasis is primarily on devices—on what he called "doing," at that time a major problem in his craft. Thus the attention he gave to the "grammar" of fiction—to such matters as "the point of view," "scene," and "dramatizing" ("Dramatize! dramatize!"), plotting and motivation, *ficelles* and *disponibles;* to problems of inclusion and exclusion, form and structure, distancing and perspective. This may often appear to be an exaggeration of method for method's sake. But James's practice always proves more than his theory, and it is in his practice that he succeeds in proving that technique of any valid kind is, if it justifies itself, always an instrument of values. He saw, from the vantage point of a lifetime's discipline and responsibility, the disintegrating and cheapening tendencies at work in the entire body of literature. He saw further, by the clairvoyance of his resolute artist's intelligence, that these tendencies, in the closing decades of the Nineteenth Century, were entering on their most productive and demoralizing phase. When he made his "plea for Criticism, for Discrimination, for Appreciation on other than infantile lines—as against the so almost universal Anglo-Saxon absence of these things, which tends so, in our general trade, it seems to me, to break the heart," he was calling on his art to serve as a warning against license and the deceptive privileges of a free age for authorship.

The generation to which he addressed himself, between 1870 and 1914, was the enthusiastic inheritor of creative freedom and of the dazzling possibilities of naturalism. The zest for experience had not yet been curbed by the terrors or the surfeit of realism; the feast of detail had gone largely undisciplined by selective taste and form. France, the country of James's early aesthetic affinity and apprenticeship, had set up standards in both—the discipline of fact in Balzac, Zola, and the Goncourts, the rigor of design in Flaubert. England and America had for the most part missed these correctives. The Victorian masters had receded; the traditions of romance and moral omniscience were in decline. The new generation of storytellers who appeared in the nineties—Kipling, Wells, Bennett, Galsworthy, Dreiser —were in most cases products of a higher journalism, rescued for periods by the finer conscience of their material but descending too readily to tract-writing and the manufacture of popular entertainment.

James viewed this hazardous passage in the fortunes of the novel with uneasiness and distress. He was no exponent of restrictive or arbitrary principles—his manifesto on "The Art of Fiction" in 1884 offered the modern novelist the "freedom" of "a splendid privilege," the "magnificence of the form that is open to him, which offers to sight so few restrictions and such innumerable opportunities." ("The other arts, in comparison, appear confined and hampered; the various conditions under which they are exercised are so rigid and definite.") But he saw the novelists of a new age as declining from a great tradition, as standing in a precarious position where they no longer commanded the vigor of that tradition's energy but still too immature in critical acumen to find in true perception or formal maturity the antidote that might rescue them from the "sickness of popularity." He was aware that this situation offered its opening to new modes of originality or sincerity; his praise of Conrad shows that he saw how, for the resolute craftsman, a dangerous transition might be bridged. But he was also aware that between the deterioration of romantic sentiment (as Reade or Stevenson had represented it) and the new license of realism (as Wells and Bennett were to show it) there offered itself one certain mediator—the proving discipline of technique. He was intimately aware of this because he himself had been rescued by just such a discipline from his early taste for the fabulous, the romantic, the ingenuities of fancy and the rival lure of pure phenomena. He, in his earlier generation, had been obliged to work out of the fertility of moralistic invention and social curiosity (*Roderick Hudson, Watch and Ward, Confidence, The American*) toward a critical authority which would permit him to bring under control not only the abundant novelties of the American scene but the larger problems of the European heritage. For him the age of discovery was past, but the age of values had just begun. The age of Dickens, Melville, and Tolstoy, as of Hugo, Whitman, and Swinburne, was one of inventive fertility but not of discrimination. He knew its privileges; he was also one of the few to be fully aware of its perils.

But James's famous stylistic subtlety and formal refinement have more to justify them than their aim to perfect the techniques of his craft. They are inseparable from his conception of the artist's intelligence. The principle of omniscience was for him a matter not of scope but of insight, not of inclusion but of penetration. Craft became for him an index of the creative intelligence, the one concrete evidence of the fact that in serious art "the moral sense and the artistic sense lie very near together," and of "the very obvious truth that the deepest quality of a work of art will always be the quality of the mind of the producer." "In proportion as that intelligence is fine will the novel, the picture, the statue partake of the substance of beauty and truth." R. P. Blackmur has rightly said that

> James had in his style and perhaps in the life which it reflected an idiosyncrasy so powerful, so overweening, that to many it seemed a stultifying vice, or at least an inexcusable heresy. . . . He enjoyed an excess of intelligence and he suffered, both in life and art, from an excessive effort to communicate it, to represent it in all its fulness. His style grew elaborate in the degree that he rendered shades and refinements of meaning and feeling not usually rendered at all. . . . His intention and all his labor was to represent dramatically intelligence at its most difficult, its most lucid, its most beautiful point. This is the sum of his idiosyncrasy.

In other words, it ceased to be an idiosyncrasy and became a test of character and moral vitality, a mode of realizing what an artist's specific and inescapable function in the experience of life finally is. And it is by that test that he brought more than his craft—he brought his moral sensibility itself—to serve as an instrument of values. He never lets us forget what his primary values are, for they emerge from his books—from their complex craftsmanship, their subtleties and ironies, their wit and ambiguities—bearing the short and simple names he insisted on giving them. One is "truth"; the other is "life."

Truth was simply, for James, the basic law of realism. It means honesty, first of all, but it also means justice to the writer's material. It takes precedence over conscious morality. It is the single test of all genuinely valid morality. He defined it in an early essay: "When once a work of fiction may be classed as a novel, its foremost claim to merit, and indeed the measure of its merit, is its *truth*—its truth to something, however questionable that thing may be in point of morals or of taste." The something to which it refers is wide, various, and illimitable; it is, in fact, life itself—not Whitman's life of enraptured abstraction; not Zola's life in its raw and "unprejudiced identity," a phenomenon for scientific dissection; not the life lyrically idealized by Emerson and the naturalistic mystics. It is life "felt," "realized," "penetrated," "understood." In one of his prefaces James said that there is "no more nutritive or suggestive truth" than that of "the perfect dependence of the 'moral' sense of a work of art on the amount of felt life concerned in producing it." And when he said that "just in proportion as he is sentient and restless, just in proportion as he reacts and reciprocates and penetrates, is the critic a valuable instrument," he formulated a law that applies as much to the novelist as to the critic:

> To lend himself, to project himself and steep himself, to feel and feel till he understands, and to understand so well that he can say, to have perception at the pitch of passion and expression as embracing as the air, to be infinitely curious and incorrigibly patient, and yet plastic and inflammable and determinable, stooping to conquer and serving to direct—these are fine chances for an active mind, chances to add the idea of independent beauty to the conception of success.

For of the novelist it is no less true than of the critic, that "there is something sacrificial in his function, inasmuch as he offers himself as a general touchstone." And the elements that qualify him as a touchstone are the elements that must be counted on to make the art he produces a mode of truth. They are his feeling, his passion, his curiosity, his patience; above all, his understanding and the sincerity that animates it ("the only condition that I can think of as attaching to the composition of the novel is . . . that it be sincere."). These are the one basis of a valid realism. They tell us why James, in Paris in the seventies, came to believe that *l'art pour l'art* was an "absurdity" and naturalism a "treacherous ideal." They alone, incorruptibly exercised, can make of the novel "a living thing, all one and continuous, like any other organism"; give it the "air of reality," "solidity of specification," "illusion of life." They are "the beginning and the end of the art of the novelist"—"his inspiration, his despair, his reward, his torment, his delight."

When, in the summer of 1889, James was asked to participate in a summer school on the novel in Massachusetts, he sent his doctrine from England to "the nymphs and swains who propose to converse about it under the great trees at Deerfield," and he put it on that occasion in his most generous and inspired terms:

> Oh, do something from your point of view; an ounce of example is worth a ton of generalities; do something with the great art and the great form; do something with life. Any point of view is interesting that is a direct impression of life. You each have an impression coloured by your individual conditions; make that into a picture, a picture framed by your own personal wisdom, your glimpse of the American world. The field is vast for freedom, for study, for observation, for satire, for truth. . . . I have only two little words for the matter remotely approaching to rule or doctrine; one is life and the other freedom.

The two words are our best clues to everything James stood for as a critic or achieved as an artist. He made them imperative as principles among his disciples and fellow craftsmen. Conrad, for one, was only speaking the Jamesian language when he said that the artist

"cannot be faithful to any one of the temporary formulas of his craft."
All of these will "abandon him—even on the very threshold of the
temple—to the stammerings of his conscience and to the outspoken
consciousness of the difficulties of his work," so leaving him to descend "within himself, and in that lonely region of stress and strife,
if he be deserving and fortunate, [to find] the terms of his appeal."

IV

James staked his appeal on the quality of mind he sought to make
his art embody, but quality of mind is only another name for the
quality of the life art yields when it achieves its essential purpose.
Merely to live—the cult of experience and sensibility—is not enough.
Strether's words to little Bilham in *The Ambassadors*—"Live all you
can; it's a mistake not to. It doesn't so much matter what you do in
particular, so long as you have your life. . . . Live!"—can, if taken
too literally or in isolation, be mistaken for the whole moral principle
of James's work. The exhortation strikes one of his deepest convictions, but it was not intended as an argument for self-sufficient living
or for the creeds of personality and egotism which, whether among
aesthetes or pragmatic optimists, became popular doctrines of
James's age. Strether himself qualified his counsel when he said,
"What it comes to is that it's not, that it's never, a happiness at all,
to *take*. The only safe thing is to give. It's what plays you least false."

The essence of mediocrity for James was selfishness, as the essence
of baseness was treachery, and the essence of failure a denial of the
spiritual capacity of life—of the wisdom that comes through suffering
or privation, the fulfillment that comes through generosity and love.
To deny these is to face at last the real "beast in the jungle" and to
meet the worst of damnations, which is negation. Isabel Archer, in
The Portrait of a Lady, voiced another of James's deepest convictions.
She first came to Europe with the theory that one "should move in a
realm of light, of natural wisdom, of happy impulse, of inspiration
fully chronic," and with "a fixed determination to regard the world
as a place of brightness, of free expansion, of irresistible action." Yet

she also brought a bolder sense of the human fate. One of her suitors, Lord Warburton, on being rejected by her, views her assertion that she "can't escape unhappiness" with skepticism and accuses her of fostering a romantic view of misery. "I'm not bent on a life of misery," Isabel answers. "I've always been intensely determined to be happy, and I've often believed I should be. . . . But it comes over me every now and then that I can never be happy in any extraordinary way; not by turning away, by separating myself." "By separating yourself from what?" he asks. "From life," she answers. "From the usual chances and dangers, from what most people know and suffer."

The ideal of consciousness she implies was the basis of James's morality as an artist. It has been called his religion. He refused to make it a means merely of spiritual luxury or happy self-extension. He shows it to be a much harder thing than that. It is a principle of realization, of self-knowledge, of moral limitation and recognition. And this is what permitted him to make it a principle of sanity and of tragedy. When he named Hamlet and Lear as examples of the kind of living that endows life with intensity and gives it a maximum of sense, he took his examples from tragic drama. By doing so he assented to the classic doctrine that it is the denials and privations of life that must be made to enrich it; its capacity for tragedy that gives it its final value. Yeats was one poet who agreed with him: "Hamlet and Lear are gay."

When James, in 1910, wrote his essay "Is There a Life After Death?" he gave his belief in "the unlimited vision of being" the appealing accents of a Platonic idea. Death offers the possibility of "a renewal of the interest, the appreciation, the passion, the large and consecrated consciousness" of life itself. But when he wrote closer to the actual conditions of living he found a stricter language. He used it in the magnificent letter he sent his old Cambridge friend Grace Norton in 1883, at a time when she was passing through an ordeal of suffering:

> I am determined not to speak to you except with the voice of stoicism. I don't know *why* we live—the gift of life comes to us from I don't know what source or for what purpose; but I believe we can

go on living for the reason that (always of course up to a certain
point) life is the most valuable thing we know anything about, and
it is therefore presumptively a great mistake to surrender it while
there is any yet left in the cup. In other words consciousness is an
illimitable power, and though at times it may seem to be all consciousness of misery, yet in the way it propagates itself from wave to wave,
so that we never cease to feel, and though at moments we appear to,
try to, pray to, there is something that holds one in one's place,
makes it a standpoint in the universe which it is probably good not
to forsake. . . . Only don't, I beseech you, *generalize* too much in
these sympathies and tendernesses—remember that every life is a
special problem which is not yours but another's, and content yourself with the terrible algebra of your own. Don't melt too much into
the universe, but be as solid and dense and fixed as you can. We all
live together, and those of us who love and know, live so most. We
help each other—even unconsciously, each in our own effort, we
lighten the effort of others, we contribute to the sum of success,
make it possible for others to live. Sorrow comes in great waves. . . .
It wears us, uses us, but we wear it and use it in return; and it is
blind, whereas we after a manner see.

What James here phrased as a precept of experience he made the
guiding principle of his vision as an artist. He had already recognized
it as such early in his career, in 1874, when he first discovered the
wisdom of Turgenev. Turgenev crystallized a reading of life James
had already traced in his chosen models of seriousness in the craft
of fiction—Hawthorne, Balzac, George Eliot—but he gave it a force
of "charm," of spiritual lucidity, which lent a particular intensity to
James's statement of it:

> Life *is*, in fact, a battle. On this point optimists and pessimists
> agree. Evil is insolent and strong; beauty enchanting but rare; good-
> ness very apt to be weak; folly very apt to be defiant; wickedness to
> carry the day; imbeciles to be in great places, people of sense in small,
> and mankind generally unhappy. But the world as it stands is no
> illusion, no phantasm, no evil dream of a night; we wake up to it
> again for ever and ever; we can neither forget it nor deny it nor
> dispense with it. We can welcome experience as it comes, and give it
> what it demands, in exchange for something which it is idle to pause
> to call much or little so long as it contributes to swell the volume of
> consciousness. In this there is mingled pain and delight, but over the
> mysterious mixture there hovers a visible rule, that bids us learn to
> will and seek to understand.

James carried his conviction of that rule into the great scene of his age—carried it out of the simpler world of his youth in America into the *Imperium* of pride and vanity which he made the stage of his complex drama of cultures and moralities. There he traced the rule in all its workings of humor and pathos, success and hardship, virtue and evil; and to the drama it offered him he brought a wit, compassion, and moral curiosity which not only give his work its depth and richness of imagination but establish its authority as a historical document. He refused to see that drama as anything but riddled and confused—pregnant of "disaster": "ferocious and sinister"—by the forces of vanity, selfishness, and moral anarchy abroad in the world. The salvation he grants his heroes and heroines—Isabel Archer, Hyacinth Robinson, Strether, Milly Theale, Maggie Verver —whether it comes to grief or to success, rests on the conquest of moral identity which he made the supreme adventure of their lives. These people, living lives of emotional or social conformity, embody the modern sensibility beset by the conditions of modern sophistication and privilege; they recognize the splendors of tradition, the pressure of inherited instinct and decorum, but also the license of moral liberalism. It is from this confusion that each must retreat, through ordeal, agony, or betrayal, to the final authority of selfhood. They embody James's definition of the modern problem. The validity he gave that definition derives equally from his undiscouraged response to the capacities of life for energy and fulfillment and from his sense of its limits, "the virtue in necessity, the vision which tragedy comes to crown."

The tragic principle competes to the end with the principles of consciousness and possibility, but it was never permitted to disable them. The James who, in one of his last testaments, defined the " 'taste' of the poet" ("a blessed comprehensive name for many of the things deepest in us") as "at bottom and so far as the poet in him prevails over everything else, his active sense of life," the "silver clue to the whole labyrinth of consciousness," was also the writer who, at the age of seventy, declared himself to Henry Adams as "an obstinate finality, an inexhaustible sensibility"—"that queer monster, the artist," upon whom "appearances, memories, many things, go on playing . . . with consequences that I note and 'enjoy' (grim word!) noting"—and who showed himself, in his letters as much as in his books, to be a mind and personality in continuous process of realization, a seeker less obstinate in finality than in curiosity and moral research, a sensibility as "inexhaustible" in enthusiasm and response as it was in the creative energy that kept it active until it ceased in its seventies. "*Of course*," he told Adams in his effort to rally his melancholy friend from the "unmitigated blackness" of old age: "*Of course* we are lone survivors, of course the past that was our lives is at the bottom of an abyss—if the abyss *has* any bottom; of course, too, there's no use talking unless one particularly *wants* to." But "it all takes doing—and I *do*," he concluded. "I believe I shall do yet again —it is still an act of life."

No one who reads James seriously today is likely to miss the bearing of his insight and prophetic vision on the present circumstances of our lives. As much as Balzac or Stendhal, Tolstoy or Proust, he saw his age and its crisis in the perspective of the future. He seized his special privilege as a citizen of two worlds to create a classic drama of their rivalries and oppositions, but before he had finished his work he also achieved an art that transcends the international drama and becomes capable of analyzing the forces in men or societies that yield, in comedy or tragedy, the vision which is more than moral or critical: it is the vision of human and moral truth.

To his task James brought a large fund of the faith, idealism, and confidence that were instinctive in his American generation, but the realism that accompanied these, while it denied him the comfort of the idealist, enforced in his character something of much greater importance to a novelist—a sense of the inescapable value of life and a responsibility, equally inescapable, to its principles of necessity and justice. It was these instincts that permitted him to show what T. S. Eliot, in one of the most famous remarks ever made about James, once called "his mastery over, his baffling escape from, Ideas; a mastery and an escape which are perhaps the last test of a superior intelligence"—"a mind so fine that no idea could violate it." His personal character as we come to know it in his work, exemplifies what his art embodies as a standard. His last secretary, Theodora Bosanquet, speaking as an intimate witness, has said that it became a passion with James "not to exercise any tyrannical power over other people"; that his "Utopia was an anarchy where nobody would be responsible for any other human being but only for his own civilized character."

That passion is what finally gives James the terms of his appeal. It ensured both his authority as an artist and his responsible seriousness as an intelligence. In taking as his supreme ambition the achievement of an art "fully civilized," he assumed the task of reconciling knowledge with beauty: of holding, in Yeats's great phrase, "in a single thought reality and justice." That is what permitted him to realize his youthful ambition of making his work, like his life, a "prolonged reconciliation" of prejudice and truth. That is also why his work has reasserted its value in the tragic and ominous crisis of the Twentieth Century and why, the prospects for justice and intelligence being what they are in our time, it will continue to do so. James, whose respect for truth freed him from the abstraction of ideas, also freed himself by the same means from the age that surrounded and conditioned him. He became what only the resolute artist has any hope of becoming: a "contemporary of the future."

1951 [1956]

PART II

The Terms

of the Response:

Twentieth Century

"What, after all [said Goethe], is the beginning and end of writing, this reproduction of the outer world by the inner, this seizing upon everything, com-
bining, re-creating, kneading, remoulding after its own form and in its own
way?—this, God be praised, is and remains a perennial mystery . . ." But
this business of reproducing the outer world through the inner, which it re-
creates after its own form and in its own way, never does, however much
charm and fascination may emanate from it, quite satisfy or please the outer
world. The reason is that the author's real attitude always has something of
opposition in it, which is quite inseparable from his character. . . . For what
are the factors that condition the life of the writer? They are twofold: perception and a feeling for form; both of these simultaneously. The strange
thing is that for the artist they are one organic unity, in which the one implies,
challenges, and draws out the other. This unity is, for him, mind, beauty,
freedom—everything.

—THOMAS MANN

If there is on earth a house with many mansions, it is the house of words. . . .

To forget its Creator is one of the functions of a Creation. . . . Just as words
have two functions—information and creation—so each human mind has two
personalities, one on the surface, one deeper down. . . . What is so wonderful about great literature is that it transforms the man who reads it towards
the condition of the man who wrote, and brings to birth in us also the creative
impulse. . . .

The personality of a writer does become important after we have read his book
and begin to study it. When the glamour of creation ceases, when the leaves
of the divine tree are silent, when the co-partnership is over, then a book
changes its nature, and we ask ourselves questions about it. . . . Then we
are no longer reading the book, we are studying it. . . .

Imagination is our only guide into the world created by words. Whether those
words are signed or unsigned becomes, as soon as the imagination redeems
us, a matter of no importance, because we have approximated to the state
in which they were written, and there are no names down there, no personality as we understand personality, no marrying or giving in marriage. . . .

—E. M. FORSTER,
Anonymity: An Enquiry

Conrad

I. CHANCE AND RECOGNITION

Conrad's title pages always taxed his scruples as severely as any part of his manuscripts, not always to his own satisfaction or to ours in the titles he arrived at, but with notable success in the epigraphs he placed below them. These he used consistently. Mrs. Conrad has said that they were always chosen with extreme care, Conrad taking pains that these "quotations had always a close and direct relation to the contents of the book itself" and that they should express "the mood in which the work was written." Sometimes it is the mood, whether of memory, pathos, irony, or tragic conviction, that is emphasized. More often the epigraph hints of the motive or attitude that directed Conrad's shaping of his material and the conception of experience it dramatizes.

The quotation he fixed below the title of *Lord Jim* is a clue not only to the narrative method which, in his long recitatives, monologues, and self-inquisitions, Conrad made his special instrument for the achieving of realism and form, but to the psychological compulsion under which his characters, caught in the moral or circumstantial prisons of their lives, are forced to speak, and by which Conrad himself, if we trace his nature in his tales and personal writings, was compelled toward his special kind of art and revelation. "It is certain my conviction gains infinitely, the moment another soul will believe in it": Novalis's aphorism is a key to the necessity that is a source both of Conrad's imaginative method and of his appeal to psychological realists.

Sometimes the complex of fate requires solution by something more violent than an ordeal of personal exoneration. Shakespeare's "So foul a sky clears not without a storm" at the head of *Nostromo* suggests a prevailing symbol. When the novel is of a more exotic or melodramatic tendency, it sustains a sense of the marvelous or miraculous, of a thrilled response to the incredible turns and hazards of fate, of "marvels and mysteries acting upon our emotions and intelligence in ways so inexplicable that it would almost justify the conception of life as an enchanted state"—so reflecting the romantic tendency in Conrad's temperament that involved him in the fortunes of his career and that took a lifetime of discipline to bring to terms with the critical force of his moral intelligence. A French nursery rhyme sets the tone for *A Set of Six:* "Les petites marionnettes / Font, font, font, / Trois petits tours / Et puis s'en vont." A phrase from Boethius—". . . for this miracle or this wonder troubleth me right gretly"—stands at the head of the autobiographical *Mirror of the Sea. Victory* begins under the spell of three lines from Milton's "Comus":

> Calling shapes and beckoning shadows dire
> And airy tongues that syllable men's names
> On sands and shores and desert wildernesses.

But there is another series of these quotations that indicates even more clearly the idea that possessed Conrad in his reading of experience. It was an idea that doubtless originated in a profoundly significant root-experience of his own temperament and history. He was to employ it as the incentive of his greatest tales. It is suggested repeatedly in his epigraphs from his first book to his last. The quotation on *Almayer's Folly* in 1895 is from Amiel: "Qui de nous n'a eu sa terre promise, son jour d'extase, et sa fin en exil?" Baudelaire's "D'autres fois, calme plat, grand miroir/ De mon désespoir" serves as heading to *The Shadow Line* in 1917. An aphorism from La Bruyère acts as a clue to *The Arrow of Gold* in 1918: "Celui qui n'a

connu que des hommes polis et raisonnables, ou ne connaît pas
l'homme, ou ne le connaît qu'à demi." The motto for *The Rescue* in
1920 is from Chaucer's "Frankeleyn's Tale":

> "Alas!" quod she, "that ever this sholde happe!
> For wende I never, by possibilitee,
> That swich a monstre or merveille mighte be!"

Most specific of all, the quotation below the title of *Chance*, in 1913,
is from Sir Thomas Browne: "Those that hold that all things are
governed by Fortune had not erred, had they not persisted there."

The meaning and consistency of these passages is clear. They
permit us to summarize briefly, if too simply, the basic theme of
Conrad's fiction. His work dramatizes a hostility of forces that exists
both in the conditions of practical life and in the moral constitution of
man himself. Men who show any fundamental vitality of nature, will,
or imagination are not initially men of caution, tact, or prudence,
"polis et raisonnables," and they are certainly unlikely to remain so.
They are possessed by an enthusiasm that makes them approach life
as an adventure. They attack the struggle with all the impulsive
force of their illusion, their pride, their idealism, their desire for fame
and power, their confidence that Chance is a friend and Fortune a
guide who will lead them to a promised goal of happiness or success, wealth or authority. Chance, under this aspect of youthful
illusion, is the ideal of expectation and generosity. She is the goddess
of the ignorance we prize as sincerity before we learn that sincerity
is a virtue which, like James's cipher in arithmetic, depends for its
value on the number to which it is attached. She takes the color of
her benevolence from youth's impetuosity and ardor, before those
qualities have revealed their full cost in experience and disillusionment. It sometimes happens that the illusion we impose on our lives
at their outset is not enthusiastic but cynical or pessimistic. The cost
then proves all the greater. The hero of "Youth," *The Arrow of Gold*,
and *The Shadow-Line* is at times supplanted by a man like Heyst
in *Victory* or Razumov in *Under Western Eyes*, whose untested
misanthropy is as fatally romantic a presumption on the conditions
of the responsible life or the obligations of character as an untested

optimism. ("Woe to the man whose heart has not learned while young to hope, to love—and to put its trust in life!") An equal enemy lies in wait for both. That enemy—"our common enemy"—leaps from unknown coverts: sometimes from the hiding-places that fate or accident has prepared, but more often and seriously, like the beast in the jungle, from the unfathomed depths of our secret natures, our ignorance, our subconscious or unconscious selves.

When the moment comes the victim is forced to commit himself to it. It is the signal of his destiny, and there is no escape for the one who meets it unprepared. The terms of life are reversed by it. It is the stroke by which fate compels recognition—of one's self, of reality, of illusion, error, mistaken expectation, and defeat. At that moment, if a man can measure up to it, his conscious moral existence begins, an existence for which previous intellectual or theoretical anticipation can never fully prepare. "We begin to live when we have conceived life as tragedy." Chance is no longer beneficent. She is a setter of traps and snares. Her opportunities have become the measure of risk and peril, and her favorites are no longer adventurers or idealists but those who can say, in another sentence of Yeats's that is an explicit phrasing of Conrad's idea: "When I think of life as a struggle with the Daemon who would ever set us to the hardest work among those not impossible, I understand why there is a deep enmity between a man and his destiny, and why a man loves nothing but his destiny."

The crisis in almost every one of Conrad's novels—many of which form a prolonged and exhaustive analysis or sublimation of crisis—arrives when, by a stroke of accident, or by an act of decision or error rising from the secret necessities of temperament, a man finds himself abruptly committed to his destiny. It is a commitment to which all men of morally significant quality are bound. It is the test and opportunity of fundamental selfhood, and there is no escape from it. Its necessity is variously stated in Conrad's books—most memorably perhaps in "Typhoon":

> The sea . . . had never put itself out to startle the silent man, who seldom looked up, and wandered innocently over the waters with the

only visible purpose of getting food, raiment, and house-room for three people ashore. Dirty weather he had known, of course. He had been made wet, uncomfortable, tired in the usual way, felt at the time and presently forgotten. So that upon the whole he had been justified in reporting fine weather at home. But he had never been given a glimpse of immeasurable strength and of immoderate wrath, the wrath that passes exhausted but never appeased—the wrath and fury of the passionate sea. He knew it existed, as we know that crime and abominations exist; he had heard of it as a peaceable citizen in a town hears of battles, famines, and floods, and yet knows nothing of what these things mean—though, indeed, he may have been mixed up in a street row, have gone without his dinner once, or been soaked to the skin in a shower. Captain MacWhirr had sailed over the surface of the oceans as some men go skimming over the years of existence to sink gently into a placid grave, ignorant of life to the last, without ever having been made to see all it may contain of perfidy, of violence, and of terror. There are on sea and land such men thus fortunate—or thus disdained by destiny or by the sea.

The full implications of this final sentence extend beyond Conrad's tales and even his life; they give us his judgment on a world lapsed into the anarchy that results from a morality of casuistry and opportunism. It was not only in political and commercial society that he saw that violence at work, with the ramifying evil he depicted in *The Secret Agent* and *Under Western Eyes*—novels whose wholly European or English settings give little occasion for an occluding exoticism, and so bring out the full force of Conrad's critical powers. He saw it in the crisis of civilization which he witnessed in Europe, and he saw it there in terms of a question whose import he felt with personal intensity and even with guilt—the question of the fate of Poland. A few of his essays suggest his long scrutiny of this problem, but explicitly he rarely, if ever, elucidated it. It remains involved in the complex of his tales, which is what makes it memorable and dynamic. To grasp the larger significance of Conrad's vision of the violence in his age requires a special attention to what the tales contain and convey.

Conrad's temperament, like that of his characteristic heroes, was rooted in an impulse, an impetuosity, that involves the poet, as much as the man of action, in a presumption on the laws of moral responsibility. He was initially, by his emotional disposition—and perhaps inevitably, by the dramatic circumstances of his Polish youth and revolutionary heritage—an idealist whose passions were early set at a pitch of heroic resolution, committed to a struggle that called on the fullest indomitability of will and spirit. The stoic sentiment of contemporary romantics—"Nothing ever happens to the brave"—could never be the principle of such a tradition. The fiery hopes of Polish nationalism and the cause of Poland's freedom had already exacted the fullest share of bravery, suffering, and ignominy from Conrad's people, and from his own family. Yet even here the illusion of Providence was not missing. Conrad's father was a nationalist of Shelleyan tendencies, translator of Vigny's *Chatterton* and Hugo's *Hernani* and *La Légende des Siècles*. In his note to *A Personal Record* Conrad protested that his father should not be called revolutionist since "no epithet could be more inapplicable to a man with such a strong sense of responsibility in the region of ideas and action and so indifferent to the promptings of personal ambition," and that he was "simply a patriot in the sense of a man who, believing in the spirituality of a national existence, could not bear to see that spirit enslaved." But Danilowsky, the Polish historian, describes this father as "an honorable but too ardent patriot," who was known to the Tzarist police as an "agitator," author of the seditious mandate that brought about his arrest in October 1861, his imprisonment in Warsaw, and his subsequent deportation to the Government Vologda for a four-year exile which brought on the death of his wife and eventually his own death as well. Apollo Korzeniowski's verse is passionate in its defiance of misfortune:

> Ready is your boat, and in the outspread sails
> Blows the wind, lighthearted,
> Some of us life may deceive,
> You will choose the right way.

> May cowards tremble at lofty waves,
> To you they bring good fortune!
> You know the hidden reefs,
> And are familiar with the tempest!

Your eager boat, with eagle's wings,
Will make a rapid passage,
And, steered by reason, governed with strength,
Will reach the shores of fame!

But, resting from your journey,
In the golden lands of fortune,
Remember, O remember with a sigh
Those who perished in the tempest!

This "Korzeniowski strain," as his wife's relatives called it, with
its devotion to Utopian ideals and revolutionary hazards—impulsive,
sarcastic, impatient—seems to have served as a warning to the members of the Bobrowski family, whose daughter he courted and who
considered him "an undesirable pretender." The Bobrowskis, who
were, like the Korzeniowskis, of the land-owning gentry and had a
brilliant record as soldiers and patriots, were of more conservative,
reformist leanings. They were agricultural, closely devoted as a
family, apparently more realistic and cautious in their view of the
nationalist cause than the young poet whom they knew as a "red"
and who, despite his sensitive character and human sympathies,
was famed for his recklessness and scurrilous impatience with
temporizers. The hazardous conditions of Conrad's youth (he was
only five when his father was arrested and deported), the unsettled
fortunes of the family, and his knowledge of his father's courage,
must have fostered his early ambitions about his own career. When
he turned from the East of Europe which he always feared and dis-
liked, since it represented the national enemy Russia as well as those
unfathomed conflicts that reflected his own severe doubt of himself,
he looked toward the countries that promised a career of greater certainty. He looked toward France, with her marine service and political opportunities, and more particularly, in these earliest years of
his travels, toward Spain of the Carlist cause, in whose service he
was to take his first great chance, as a gun-runner and agitator. Conrad's celebrations of the hope and illusion of youth, of innocence,
of courage and the bravery it supports in the untested nature of the
immature man, of the sincerity which blesses this primitive kind of

emotion—these are too evident in his work to be doubted as revivals, in his later memory, of the excitement with which he launched himself on life when he left Poland behind in 1874, at the age of seventeen, and boarded the west-bound Vienna express for Venice and Marseilles, "as a man might get into a dream."

Once Conrad had embarked on that adventure, however, a rival strain of his inheritance asserted itself. How early we cannot tell, for the documents on this part of his life, from 1873 until the middle eighties, are few. Apparently it did not appear during his first years in Marseilles, when he frequented the conservative *légitimiste* circle of the banker Delestang and his wife, or during his first two sea-voyages that ensued from this acquaintance—that in 1875 on the *Mont-Blanc* to Martinique and Le Havre, and that in 1876 on the *Saint-Antoine* to St. Pierre, Port-au-Prince, and the Gulf of Mexico. It apparently did not deter him during the romantic episode among the Spanish legitimists of Don Carlos's cause which involved him between October 1877, and February 1878, in the exploits of the gun-running tartane *Tremolino*, his love affair with the prototype of Rita de Lastaola, his duel with the American J. M. K. Blunt, and the other escapades (later to be recorded in *The Arrow of Gold*) that caused so much alarm among his relatives in Poland that his guardian uncle, Tadeusz Bobrowski, threatened to stop his allowance and compel him to come home. These experiences terminated in fiasco. Wounded in the duel, Conrad was barely on his legs when his alarmed uncle arrived in Marseilles from Kiev to find his nephew deserted by his Carlist friends, embittered by humiliation, and ready to throw up all adventurous political schemes in favor of a job on an English coaster, the *Mavis*, carrying coal and linseed-oil cargoes between Lowestoft and Constantinople.

When Conrad arrived in Lowestoft on June 18, 1878, he stepped for the first time on English soil, knowing only as much English as he had picked up on the voyage, practically without money, without acquaintances in England, and, as his biographer tells us, "alone in the world." This is the first of two decisive dates in Conrad's life. (The other was to come in 1895.) Poland, Marseilles, Carlism, and

youth were behind him. Poverty and the rigorous routine of a merchant vessel descended on him and fixed his life for the next seventeen years.

What now rose in Conrad's personality was a force more familiar
to us in his books than the ecstatic emotion of youth which he often
celebrates but which he was able to recapture only in moments of
lyrical memory and which, as a consequence, never rings as authen-
tically as the darker emotions which now announced themselves and
persisted in his nature to the end of his life. His benevolent uncle
Tadeusz began to write him in response to the letters which Conrad
was sending back to Poland. Conrad's shift from youth, Poland, and
France to the unsparing exactions of sea-life was one great transition
in his fortunes. He was to submit another, of even severer conditions,
in 1895, when he threw up the sea and ventured on a career in literature. He did this not with convinced determination, for he tried repeatedly to get a new command even as late as 1900, when his first
five books had been published. These breaks or changes have, as we
now observe them, the appearance of having been undertaken with
a kind of compulsion of inherent vocation, to test his strength and
fortitude in the face of a long-delayed creative necessity; but conscious intention as yet played little part in his actions. Troubled, in the
early eighties, by the growing melancholy and passionate introspection induced by long sea-watches, by solitary duties, and by the rack-
ing boredom which in later life he confessed to be the one sensation
he remembered from his sailing days, he found welling up within
him symptoms of the tragic inheritance of his race and family.

His life had begun in disturbance, danger, and a great ascendant
hope. It had become vividly adventurous in France, Spain, and the
West Indies. Now, abruptly, it became confined, ruthlessly vigilant,
curtailed to the most tyrannous necessities, calculated to the hour
and moment by the charts on the captain's table, the needle in the
binnacle, the movements of the stars. His voyages to African coasts,
the Americas, and the Malay and China seas brought contrasts of
novelty and exotic discovery, but by the time Conrad took his journey
to the Congo in 1890, reality had become unconditional. The con-

tinent of Africa and his voyage up its coiled, snakelike river figured as his descent into Hell. His journal of the trip still conveys the agony of that palpable damnation. He returned ravaged by the illness and mental disruption which undermined his health for the remaining thirty years of his life.

Between 1891 and 1895 his voyages were broken by intervals spent alone and homeless in London, with only his uncle remaining of his immediate family (and he was to die in 1894) and a distant cousin by marriage, the Polish-Belgian novelist Marguerite Poradowska, of Brussels, to serve as his confidante in Western Europe. When Conrad lay ill in London in 1891 he received a letter from his uncle Tadeusz which we may take as an account of his predicament written from the point of view of a privileged observer:

My dear boy:
  I begin as I always do, but I ought to address you as "my dear pessimist"; for judging from your letters that description would fit you best. I cannot say that I am pleased by your state of mind, or that I am without apprehension about your future. . . . Thinking over the causes of your melancholy most carefully I cannot attribute it either to youth or to age. In the case of one who is thirty-four and has had as full a life as you have had, I am forced to attribute it to ill-health, to your wretched sufferings on the African adventure, to your illness which resulted from them, and to the fact that you have had lately plenty of time to give yourself up to the habit of reverie which I have observed to be part of your character. It is inherited; it has always been there, in spite of your active life.
  I may be mistaken, but I think this tendency to pessimism was already in you as long ago as the days when you were at Marseilles, but it was then part of youth. I am sure that with your melancholy temperament you ought to avoid all meditations which lead to pessimistic conclusions. I advise you to lead a more active life than ever and to cultivate cheerful habits.
  Our country, as Slowacki well says (although he himself was not free from the reproach), is the "pan" of the nations, which in plain prose means that we are a nation who consider ourselves great and misunderstood, the possessors of a greatness which others do not recognize and will never recognize. If individuals and nations would set duty before themselves as an aim, instead of grandiose ideals, the world would be a happier place. . . . Perhaps you will reply that these are the sentiments of one who has always had "a place in the

sun." Not at all. I have endured many ups and downs; I have suffered in my private life, in my family life, and as a Pole; and it is thanks to these mortifications that I have arrived at a calm and modest estimate of life and its duties, and that I have taken as my motto *"usque ad finem";* as my guide, the love of the duty which circumstances define.

It is not to be argued that Conrad's life explains his art in its fullest dimensions, any more than his "ideas" explain his novels, or that we can use his personal documents and letters as a substitute for that explanation. Indeed, his defensive nature made it unlikely that he should write these as such an explanation. The reproofs he expressed to several students of his career indicate that he would have endorsed Eliot's sentence which his own preface to *The Nigger of the "Narcissus"* to some degree anticipated: "The more perfect the artist, the more completely separate in him will be the man who suffers and the mind which creates." Conrad was a dramatic genius and an artist in character; his creations are always more than the sum of his conscious motives and critical intelligence. Any comparison of his personal writings with his novels shows that he found his full voice only when writing imaginatively. Only then does he resist the charge made against him by E. M. Forster when he said that "the secret casket of his genius contains a vapor rather than a jewel." At the same time it is impossible to neglect the value which the events of Conrad's life and the testimony of his intimate correspondence contribute toward the interpretation of his fiction. At the least, these provide us with a comment on the problem he dramatized in a language which almost perfectly coincides with the spirit of his plots and situations. We know, in addition, how strongly he protested against the purely impersonal order of art advocated by the naturalists; how he considered their novels a perpetuation of the worst vices of the old convention of arbitrary omniscience in fiction; how lifeless he found the critical objectivity of his friend Galsworthy; how he disagreed as vigorously as Yeats did with Stendhal's conception of art as "un miroir qui se promène sur la grande route." Five of his narratives were never denied as autobiographies. He said that all his characters were "at one time or the other known by me." And although it is inevitable that we can never prove the personal basis of his greater novels, we cannot read them without sensing the existence of such a basis, or observing that Conrad's repeated hints of such relevance were expanded and explored from one end of his production to the other.

The letters he wrote Mme. Poradowska between 1890 and 1900 reveal that almost every fundamental problem of his later fiction was sketched or suggested in that correspondence and applied there with remorseless intimacy not to fictitious characters but to his own plight and state of mind. They also reveal that during those critical years of his life, when he was making a harassed transition from maritime service to the profession of novelist, he was already groping for the means and courage to translate these experiences into fictional form, to objectify them dramatically, and thus to come into an intelligent realization of their meaning: to save himself, as he once expressed it, "from the madness which, after a certain point in life is reached, awaits those who refuse to master their sensations and bring into coherent form the mysteries of their lives."

Conrad's sense of the crisis of moral isolation and responsibility in which the individual meets his first full test of character is repeatedly emphasized in his tales, to a degree which has put a special stamp on his heroes. These are men marked by a number of conditions which have become much more familiar during the past half-century than they were when Conrad began to write. Even then, however, they had been established by serious novelists and dramatists. James and Ibsen, to name only two, had dramatized the plight of the man or woman on whom life closes down. By divesting him or her of the familiar supports and illusory protection of friendship, social privilege, or love; by throwing the individual violently out of an accepted relationship with family or society, this crisis suddenly makes him aware of a hostile or unknown world which must be learned anew, conquered or mastered, before survival is possible. Obviously this order of drama has a classic ancestry. It is the oldest mode of tragedy. But the social and psychological emphasis of modern times has given it a substance, a basis of practical moral conditions, not always apparent even in Shakespeare. It is this drama of alienation and spiritual recognition which appears in the characteristic novels of Mann, Gide, and Kafka, in Robinson's poems, in Joyce and Hemingway. It is carried to lengths of symbolic extension in *Death in Venice, The Trial, Nightwood*, and ultimately in *Finnegans Wake*. One of its latest appearances is in the novels of the French existentialists, who have given tragedy a new dimension in the irrationality or absurdity of the universe. But it is doubtful if any of these writers has achieved a more successful *dramatic* version of the problem than Conrad did—a more complete coincidence of the processes of psychic recognition and recovery with the dramatic necessities of the plot; and this for a reason which distinguishes Conrad's contribution to modern fictional method: his imposition of the processes of psychological experience, notably the experience of recognition, on the structure of the plot. Even in James, as later in Thomas Mann and André Gide, whose moral drama also took this direction, the ratiocinative element and structural manipulation of the action did not permit an equal immersion in the "destructive element" of psychic reality, an equal coincidence of moral sensibility with form.

The conditions that mark the plight of a Conrad character who is caught in the grip of circumstances that enforce self-discovery and its cognate, the discovery of reality or truth, are remarkably consistent in his books. The condition of moral solitude is the first of them —the isolation of Razumov in *Under Western Eyes*, of Heyst in *Victory*, of Flora de Barral in *Chance*, of Jim himself in *Lord Jim*, and of a large number of other outcasts, exiles, or estranged souls— Willems, Lingard, Mrs. Travers, Mrs. Verloc, Peyrol; even men whom age or accident has suddenly bereft of the solid ground of security or confidence—Captain Whalley, Captain MacWhirr, the young captain on his first command in *The Shadow-Line*, or Kurtz of "Heart of Darkness" in his last abandonment of soul. The isolation varies in its nature. Willems is alone because he is a banished wastrel who has made life a law to himself; Mr. George is alone because he is young and irresponsible; Lingard and Captain Whalley have accepted stoically their estrangement from the ties of normal life; Jim and

Flora feel themselves excommunicated from society by disgrace and by the false confidence or idealism that has betrayed them; Razumov is isolated by an impenetrable mystery of birth and social alienation; Heyst by the disgust, induced by a fatal vein of skepticism in his nature and so tending toward a nihilism of all values, which follows a misplaced trust in his fellow men. In all these more serious cases, isolation tends to become so absolute that it can be bridged again only by some irresistible compulsion that rises out of the psychic and ethical necessities of character. Life demands justification by love or honor, as with Flora and Razumov; it exacts justice from the disillusioned, as with Mrs. Verloc; it demands, in the case of Heyst, the last and absolute testimony of honor which only suicide can give. Conrad leaves no doubt of the extreme to which he pushed this condition. Of Heyst we hear that "Not a single soul belonging to him lived anywhere on earth . . . he was alone on the bank of the stream. In his pride he determined not to enter it." And of Razumov: "He was as lonely in the world as a man swimming in the deep sea. . . . He had nothing. He had not even a moral refuge—the refuge of confidence."

But if isolation is the first condition of these lives, it is never an isolation that brings independence or liberty. Freed by choice from normal human ties and obligations, Conrad's men find themselves in the inescapable presence of conscience. "I am being crushed—and I can't even run away," cries Razumov. The solitary may take to debauchery and self-law like Willems: even that does not permit him to escape. He may rise to power and fame like Kurtz: that permits escape least of all. He may believe he has formed a world of his own like Heyst:

> Heyst was not conscious of either friends or enemies. It was the very essence of his life to be a solitary achievement, accomplished not by hermit-like withdrawal with its silence and immobility, but by a system of restless wandering, by the detachment of an impermanent dweller amongst changing scenes. In this scheme he had perceived the means of passing through life without suffering and almost without a care in the world—invulnerable because elusive.

But the world allows no such independence. "No decent feeling was ever scorned by Heyst," and that fact proves his undoing and finally his moral salvation. These men are all brought to discover what the oldest religious systems of the world have advocated: that the more liberty we have, the less we can use. The man who is alone in the world can never escape, for he is always with himself. Unless he is morally abandoned beyond the point of significance through profligacy or irresponsibility, he lives in the company of a ruthless inquisitor, a watcher who never sleeps, a perpetually vigilant judge: with his instinct of identity, the moral imperative of his existence. A novelist who proposes to explore the full experience of the justice imposed on our faculties by conscience will be impelled, like Conrad, to penetrate a world that lies below the appearances of conduct. The explorations made by Conrad in that dimension have advanced, in our time, to the farthest reaches of the unconscious self. If Conrad did not reach those depths he pointed the way to them. *Lord Jim, Chance,* and *Under Western Eyes* join the experiments of Melville, Dostoevsky, James, and Joyce in charting the experience of the unconscious, and the means by which it is to be explored.

It is here that Conrad's work enters a dimension which is ostensibly psychological and which, for purposes of drama and characterization, must appear validly so. But it goes farther. It encounters the problem of appearance and reality, of bringing into single focus the processes of subjective intuition and the conditions of social and moral necessity—the values of egotism and those of ethical fact. It may treat these in terms of the relativity of appearances and sentiments as Proust defined it, but it will also insist on relating the psychic and moral ambiguity of human nature to the ambivalence of reality as art embodies and struggles with it, and finally to the metaphysical condition of value itself. When Conrad enters that dimension fully he leaves his sentimental limitations and prejudices behind him and takes his place as one of the authentic creative imaginations of our time—one who certainly outdistances the other English novelists of his generation.

The order of art to which Conrad addressed himself, less apparently by conscious intention than by instinct and personal necessity, is one that has become paramount in the literature of the Twentieth

Century. The ambiguity of truth, the conflict of appearance and reality, the rival claims of the secret and the social self—these are now integral to modern fiction in its major manifestations, whether in Proust or Mann, James or Kafka, Gide or Sartre. They arrive at something like the condition of paradigm in Pirandello's *Six Characters in Search of an Author.*

The six characters emerge from their half-created, unrealized lives and make their claim for the reality of their existence. The play they see being devised on the stage shocks and appals them by its failure to do justice to the truth of their experience. They plead that their agony be given the truth it had in life itself; that their passions and motives be understood; that reality be brought to terms not only with art but with moral insight and compassion. The actors and director who grapple with their plea can make nothing but a travesty of the tragedy they attempt to enact. Their struggle to render it justice produces, in Pirandello's hands, a metaphysical dilemma. It is not only art that is at odds with life; it is human comprehension itself. But the question insists: can life ever do justice to its own reality? Are suffering, agony, tragedy comprehensible in their own condition? Is it possible for them to achieve comprehension until consciousness, moral sympathy, or art intervene to interpret and define them? Can man, or life, be said to exist in terms of significance until these modes of definition and justice succeed in embodying them? The dilemma, driven to the extreme lengths of suspense and contradiction, ends finally in enigma and fiasco. The question remains unresolved. It collapses under the test of resolution. Conrad's problem in *Lord Jim* was this same problem. There too, in spite of driving Jim's fate to the logic of catastrophe, the question of the reality of his moral identity ends in enigma. But the problem of resolving it had become an obsession with Conrad. It taxed him continuously to the end of his life. At times he resorted to desperate measures of heroism, suicide, or moral compromise to resolve it; sometimes he fell back on the arbitrary formulas of ethical duplicity or stoicism. But it remained to the end the essential theme and animus of his drama.

It is instructive to turn again to Conrad's letters for confirmation of his sense of the crisis which induces the test of selfhood to which he subjects his heroes. When Conrad passed, around 1895, out of the perfectly controlled and adjusted mechanism of sea-life, with its accurate regimen of human relations and balances, he entered into a freedom which he soon discovered to be no liberation but a prison. For him, in those middle years of the nineties, the self was doubly trapped. He found himself alone not only with his poverty and rigorous self-discipline but with his creative conscience, now struggling to express itself.

His dramatizations of the trapped sensibility were preceded by that harrowing period in London in which he decided to face a kind of labor that meant daily and yearly solitude, with no give-and-take of human approval or disagreement, with no one to judge his principles or results but himself, and with a brutal aesthetic judgment— soon divested of the amateur excitement with which he wrote *Almayer's Folly*—ruling his waking and sleeping life. It is small wonder that Conrad, who was to make the trapped man the object of his special study, should have always remembered this period of his life, for it marked the beginning of an anxiety and a discipline that were not to end until his death. We find him recurring to the idea of the convict with an insistence, and with none of the defiance, that marks Rimbaud's salutations to that form of fate in the *Saison en Enfer*. Tormented all his life by the "stérilités des écrivains nerveux" which he shared with Baudelaire, Conrad began the grinding labor of his books. Years later, in 1909, he wrote to Norman Douglas that "there's neither inspiration nor hope in my work. It's mere hard labor for life —with this difference, that the life convict is at any rate out of harm's way—and may consider the account with his conscience closed: and this is not the case with me. I envy the serene fate and the comparative honesty of the gentlemen in gray who live in Dartmoor. I do really. I am not half as decent or half as useful." But earlier, in the nineties, he was already acknowledging that fate to his "cousin" in Brussels, Mme. Poradowska:

I am not so happy to be working as you seem to think. There is nothing very exhilarating in doing disagreeable work. It is too much like penal servitude, with the difference that while rolling the stone of Sisyphus you lack the consolation of thinking of what pleasure you had in committing the crime. It is here that convicts have the advantage over your humble servant.

Again:

I astonish and perhaps scandalize you by my joking about criminals, while you think me capable of accepting or even admitting the doctrine (or theory) of expiation through suffering . . . there is no expiation. Each act of life is final and inevitably produces its consequences in spite of all the weeping and gnashing of teeth and the sorrow of weak souls who suffer as fright grips them when confronted with the results of their own actions. As for myself, I shall never need to be consoled for any act of my life, and this because I am strong enough to judge my conscience rather than be its slave, as the orthodox would like to persuade us to be.

And again:

Remember, though, that one is never entirely alone. Why are you afraid? And of what? Is it of solitude or of death? O strange fear! The only two things that make life bearable! But cast fear aside. Solitude never comes—and death must often be waited for during long years of bitterness and anger. Do you prefer that?

But you are afraid of yourself; of the inseparable being forever at your side—master and slave, victim and executioner—who suffers and causes suffering. That's how it is! One must drag the ball and chain of one's selfhood to the end. It is the price one pays for the devilish and divine privilege of thought; so that in this life it is only the elect who are convicts—a glorious band which comprehends and groans but which treads the earth amidst a multitude of phantoms with maniacal gestures, with idiotic grimaces. Which would you be: idiot or convict?

The alter ego of the conscience was an inevitable corollary—as Conrad here indicates—of his conception of inescapable selfhood. The *Doppelgänger* becomes part of the drama of character and self-determination. When Jim delivers his long monologues to Marlow; when Flora bares her soul to Marlow, Mrs. Fyne, or Captain Anthony; when Razumov writes his passionate entries in his diary and disburdens his soul to the old language-teacher and finally to Nathalie Haldin herself; when Decoud or Gould ruminate their secret histories, these people are really carrying out the drama of their divided natures, objectifying under the compulsion which psychoanalysts have seized upon as therapeutic necessity their souls' dilemmas and thus trying to save themselves from madness. But the divided man— the face and its mask, the soul and its shadow—figures even more concretely than this in Conrad's dramatic method (though rumination and monologue were usually his own means of giving genuine substance to his realism). The rival character—sometimes a villain, sometimes a friend or lover, sometimes a fellow-fugitive like the "secret sharer" in the story of that name—serves the hero as a transferred embodiment of his other self.

Thus love, or the sense of honor, or the obligation of duty, or even the social instinct itself, enters the novels as a means by which the individual is lifted out of his isolation and morbid surrender. The inward-driving, center-fathoming obsession of the tale becomes reversed and takes a centrifugal direction toward external standards of value. It is finally the world which saves us—the world of human necessities and duty. It may be the world of a ship and its crew, as in *The Shadow-Line;* it may be the world of an island and a single fellow-soul, as in *Victory;* it may be that wider world of social and political relationships which Conrad seldom explored fully but which he did build in solid form in *Nostromo* and *Chance.* In one of the most perfect of Conrad's tales, "The Secret Sharer," the allegory of the alter ego is achieved within the narrowest possible limits. In one of the finest of his novels, *Under Western Eyes,* the conception is made to embody the whole complex of Russian history. "The Secret Sharer," as Miss M. C. Bradbrook has pointed out, is the microcosm of the basic concept in Conrad's fiction. Leggatt, the swimmer, has committed murder and so, by a moment's blind action, has ruined his life. He escapes, but finds refuge, naked, under cover of night on a strange ship—"a fugitive and a vagabond on the earth, with no brand of the curse on his sane forehead to stay a slaying hand." The captain hides him in his cabin, learns his guilt, and thus becomes allied to that guilt, the refugee's secret becoming an embodiment of the captain's own secret life. The hidden self of the captain is "exactly the same" as that of the fugitive, who is of necessity concealed from the world, is dressed in a sleeping suit, the garb of the unconscious life, and appears out of and again disappears into the sea, naked again, under cover of darkness. But before he disappears at last, "a free man, a proud swimmer striking out for a new destiny," the captain has come to know the secret self he lives with. His life is changed. He too must address himself to a "new destiny." A new vision of humanity has broken in upon the impersonal regimen of his days—upon the "ideal conception of one's own personality," abstract, illusory, and therefore insecure and perilous, which "every man sets up for himself secretly." The "sharing" has recreated him, stirred him to a sense of his latent moral insecurity, and so enforced in him the necessity of human community—that "unavoidable solidarity" which Conrad persistently invokes as the inescapable commitment of men: "the solidarity in mysterious origin, in toil, in joy, in uncertain fate, which binds men to each other and all mankind to the visible earth."

For Conrad, however existential he may have been by inclination, the commitment could never remain arbitrary. It is a necessity which defines man as human, his moral consciousness as imperative, and his persistence in that consciousness as the fundamental law of life. From this germinal presentation of the case Conrad's drama of the self widens until, in his most ambitious books, it comes to include the larger workings of that law in society and politics, even in the destiny of nations and of races. The growth in his thought from an idealistic conception of life to a critical one, from his temperamental romanticism to his later realism of values, is the drama of his genius in its difficult emergence, its strenuous self-discipline, and its eventual successes. That growth appears most typically in the three novels that show his dramatic method most explicitly—*Lord Jim, Under Western Eyes,* and *Chance,* but it is extended to more sheerly creative feats of dramatization in three other books—*Nostromo,* his most complex historical and political drama, a comprehensive matrix of his moral and ethical sensibility, resonant of a profoundly riddled debate of moralities and creeds of conduct; *The Secret Agent,* his highest achievement in tragic irony; and *Victory,* his most concentrated symbolic narrative.

The romantic element in his work, like the romantic impulse in his nature, was never effaced. It persisted as the basis of his popularity and of the excesses of style and treatment which appear in his evocative tendency in language, in his treatment of the sea, of woman, and of fortune as inscrutable entities, in his exotic and rhetorical effects, in his sentimental emphasis on the heroic and the miraculous in human fate and character, in the fatigued naïveté of fatalism that reasserts itself in his last three novels. But if it was not effaced, it was recognized. Conrad himself admitted an inherent romanticism as a component of his imagination and of his ordeal in moral and creative responsibility. He referred to it late in life in a passage of apology:

> The romantic feeling of reality was in me an inborn faculty. This in itself may be a curse, but when disciplined by a sense of personal responsibility and a recognition of the hard facts of existence shared with the rest of mankind becomes but a point of view from which the very shadows of life appear endowed with an internal glow. And such romanticism is not a sin. It is none the worse for the knowledge of truth. It only tries to make the best of it, hard as it may be; and in this hardness discovers a certain aspect of beauty.

His success came when responsibility and discipline opposed the self-indulgence which a romantic impulse had encouraged in his early emotions and sensibility. When these correctives assert themselves in his pages, they produce the rigor of style and feeling which stiffens and gives structure to the natural extravagance of his emotions, his impulsiveness in sentiment, the untested enthusiasm of his responses to scene, character, and experience. Conrad's development as an artist—with due allowance made for the weakening powers of his later novels—reproduces the ordeal of self-mastery and moral exoneration which he repeatedly dramatized in the lives of his characteristic heroes. "All a man can betray is his conscience," his Razumov says in *Under Western Eyes*. The measure of Conrad's character and his artistry may be taken from the fact that neither his sense of honor nor his sense of realism permitted him to betray the conscience which it took him half his life to discover in himself, and the other half to test and dramatize in his books.

1945 [1956]

II. THE EAST AND THE SEA

The Nigger of the "Narcissus"

I

When Conrad wrote *The Nigger of the "Narcissus"* he was still working under the force and urgency of his first impulse in author-ship. He was, it is true, already a man of forty. His entrance into liter-ature had come only two years before, in 1895, when *Almayer's Folly*, the book he had begun "by a sudden and incomprehensible impulse" six years earlier and written in the ships and ports of his voyages, was published in London, and he found, to his "perpetual surprise," his first novel printed and bound in his hands and a new life opening to him. The prospect was no less formidable than compelling. He paused, doubted, groped for a new opening; and only on the sug-gestion of his first literary friend and editor, Edward Garnett—"Why not write another?"—did he receive the impetus that led him to at-tempt a second book, *An Outcast of the Islands*.

Those first two novels issued from a realm of experience that Con-rad had encountered and explored during the fifteen years of voyag-ing that had preceded his first determination to set words to paper and test his skill in art. It was the world of the East—a scene of alien people and tragic life in which the exiled Pole had met a race of men that appealed to his homeless condition and gave him the elements of a drama into which he could project his personal and racial plight: a drama by means of which, as V. S. Pritchett has said, he could turn "the Polish exile's natural preoccupation with nationality, history, defeat, and unavailing struggle from his own country to these East-ern islands." But there was another realm, more elemental even than the subtle and barbaric East, that Conrad had come to know during his years as a mariner in the British Merchant Service. It, too, was a world that appealed to the inmost forces of his nature and it gave him an even more radical medium and symbol for the exercise of his moral imagination. It was the Sea; and now, in *The Nigger of the "Narcissus,"* he dramatized it for the first time in the splendor, violence, and intimacy by which he had known it.

His account with the Sea, like his account with the East, was never to be fully closed. It preoccupied him throughout his career. It led him to write further tales of ships and seamen—*Lord Jim,* "Youth," "Typhoon," "The End of the Tether," "The Brute," "The Secret Sharer," *The Shadow-Line*—as well as tales or novels in which the ocean plays a more incidental part—"Amy Foster," "Freya of the Seven Isles," "The Partner," "The Planter of Malata," *Chance, Victory, The Rescue, The Rover.* It inspired, in *The Mirror of the Sea,* his most sustained work in nonfiction and autobiography. But here, in *The Nigger of the "Narcissus,"* he wrote not only in the full freshness and immediacy of his material but with a personal passion and vividness of memory that kindled his imagination to its first full powers of poetic vision. When Henry James said of the book in 1902 that it "is in my opinion the very finest and strongest picture of the sea and sea-life that our language possesses—the masterpiece of a whole great class," he recognized that vision and paid the work a tribute which many readers have since seconded. And when Conrad himself called it "the book by which, not as a novelist perhaps, but as an artist striving for the utmost sincerity of expression, I am willing to stand or fall," and said that "its pages are the tribute of my unalterable and profound affection for the ships, the seamen, the winds and the great sea—the moulders of my youth, the companions of the best years of my life," he testified to the intense emotion with which he wrote it and to the ineradicable impression made upon him by the experiences it records.

However short the tale may fall in revealing Conrad's highest powers—the complex artistry and moral insight that were to be given their richer opportunity in books like *Lord Jim, Nostromo, Under Western Eyes,* and *Victory*—it still shows Conrad in command of powers of language and evocation that were more tentatively suggested in his first two books. The Conrad who spoke in *The Nigger of the "Narcissus"* was no translated self like Almayer and Willems. He was a man who felt himself still allied to the life of ships and seafaring, and who was far from sure that his active share in that life was over.

The East and the Sea: it is not often that a novelist finds himself endowed by practical experience with two subjects of such rich and suggestive possibilities, subjects which enter his life from outside the conditions of his race and birth, striking his senses and imagination during his years of keenest impressionability, and offering themselves to so rich a dramatic and symbolic use. The exotic novel—by Morier, Melville, Stevenson, Loti, Huysmans, Ebers, Kipling, and many lesser men—boasted a special cachet in Nineteenth Century fiction. Whatever its degeneration into facile modes of romance and sensationalism, it played its part in relieving the prose imagination of the age of its addiction to fact, science, and social realism, and in reasserting the kinship of fiction with poetry. It has a long ancestry, reaching back into fable, parable, and legend. But the reasons for the suspicion and contempt under which it has fallen in modern times are obvious. It encourages artifice. It easily trades in mere shock and extravagance. It invites fancy and allegory at the risk of divorcing a writer from his native roots and ties in actual life. Despite the liberation it promises the fact-shackled spirit or the opportunities it gives the imagination, it also encourages irresponsibility and triviality, an irresponsibility to the tests of moral realism from which even the best of modern virtuosi in myth and allegory—Gide, Kafka, Mann, and Joyce—have not wholly redeemed it. Kipling, with his deep-seated knowledge of India to draw on, was not able to make *Kim* a successful novel. It took the Stevenson of *Treasure Island, The Wrecker,* and *The Ebb Tide* a long time to arrive at the power of *Weir of Hermiston.* Melville alone, among earlier novelists, was able to convert his barbaric and maritime adventures into books of authentic power, but he achieved these—*White Jacket, Moby Dick,* "The Encantadas," "Benito Cereno," "Billy Budd"—only after he had worked himself, through harrowing ordeal and conflict, out of the footloose exhilaration and sensory indulgence of *Typee, Omoo,* and *Mardi.* A serious tale of either the exotic or the adventurous is, in spite of its imaginative privileges, one of the hardest kinds of book to write. Its numbers in modern literature are few.

Conrad was, on one side of his nature, a self-confessed romantic. He probably felt the attraction of the remote and the unreal as strongly as any modern author. But two factors operated to save him from the risks of his material. One was a ruthless moral instinct that forced him to identify himself, sympathetically and morally, with even the most extravagant of his adventures. The other was the practical condition of his case—of his life as an exile and seaman.

His moral sense was made acute by his solitude, his deracination, his estrangement from family and homeland. His practical sense was made rigorous by his need to keep himself alive, to earn his living, to assert his skill and personality among strangers, to redeem the family honor and patriotic trust he had wronged by leaving Poland through achieving success in the harsh life of ships and alien countries. It was to the first of these conditions that Scott Fitzgerald referred when he once wrote in a letter: "So many writers, Conrad for instance, have been aided by being brought up in a métier utterly unrelated to literature. It gives an abundance of material and, more important, an attitude from which to view the world. So much writing nowadays suffers both from lack of an attitude and from sheer lack of any material, save what is accumulated in a purely social life." [1] To achieve such an attitude, whatever the abundance of material an author may draw on, is of course no simple task; but given Conrad's propensity toward moral commitment, his material came to test and prove it as no immersion in the familiar or taken-for-granted ever could. And it was to the second condition of Conrad's work—its schooling in a practical necessity—that T. S. Eliot referred when he said, writing of Mark Twain (whom he instanced as an example of the first "way" of experience):

---

[1] F. Scott Fitzgerald, *The Crack-Up,* edited by Edmund Wilson (New York, 1945), p. 301.

There are, perhaps, only two ways in which a writer can acquire the understanding of environment which he can later turn to account: by having spent his childhood in that environment—that is, living in it at a period of life in which one experiences much more than one is aware of; and by having had to struggle for a livelihood in that environment—a livelihood bearing no direct relation to any intention of writing about it, of *using* it as literary material. Most of Joseph Conrad's understanding came to him in the latter way.[2]

Conrad's material, whether that of the East or of the Sea, first came to him in terms the reverse of aesthetic. It came to him as fact, as the data of serious and responsible experience. However romantic or adventurous the emotion he took with him as a young man into the Merchant Service or the Orient, he knew those worlds first as worlds to be met and conquered by dint of hard labor, scrupulous industry, skill in the technique of his trade and cunning in his dealings with men. Almost twenty years were to pass before he gave rein to his creative need, and even when he finally indulged it he worked in a language foreign to him which still exacted the utmost discipline, tact, and shrewdness. His books issued from conditions as different as possible from those that produced the tales of Loti, Stevenson, or Maugham, all of them authors by profession, travelers by design, men who reconnoitered the exotic with express literary intention. Conrad is closer to such recent cases as those of Malraux, Saint-Exupéry, and George Orwell. He had to learn, know, and accept his subject matter on its own terms before he could see it in terms of art. When, years later, he came to make fiction of it, the integrity of the material acted as a discipline for the artist.

That kind of discipline was particularly important to Conrad in his early books. It acted as a curb to the extravagance of his imagination, the melodrama of his action, the flamboyance of his language and rhetoric. These are all apparent in his first tales and novels. But something else is apparent too—something Eliot alluded to on an earlier occasion when he said that the language that is important to us in modern literature is "that which is struggling to digest and ex-

---

[2] T. S. Eliot, "Introduction" to *The Adventures of Huckleberry Finn* by Mark Twain (London and New York, 1950), p. xiv.

press new objects, new groups of objects, new feelings, new aspects, as for instance, the prose of Mr. James Joyce or the earlier Conrad." [3]

Such struggle is evident through the first half at least of Conrad's career. It was not until he had spent fifteen years at writing that he arrived at the verbal spareness, aphoristic concentration, and stylistic security he can show in works like "The Secret Sharer," *Under Western Eyes, Victory, The Shadow-Line*. Even then his style is not a matter of studied control and finish. He could still lapse into the verbal excess of *The Arrow of Gold* or the diluting evocations of *The Rescue*. He is notable among modern novelists of his rank in never arriving at fluent ease or assurance in his craft. The fact that he did not makes a continuous test of his powers as an artist. When he wrote *The Nigger of the "Narcissus"* he was in the first phase of his problem. But here, more than in his first two books, his romantic impulse joined with the strictest realism he had yet attempted. The book clearly demonstrates what he once said in an important passage about his work—it comes in the preface he wrote for *Within the Tides*:

I have not sought for special imaginative freedom or a larger play of fancy in my choice of characters and subjects. The nature of the knowledge, suggestions, or hints used in my imaginative work has depended directly on the conditions of my active life. It depended more on contacts, and very slight contacts at that, than on actual experience; because my life as a matter of fact was far from being adventurous in itself. Even now, when I look back on it with a certain regret (who would not regret his youth?) and positive affection, its coloring wears the sober hue of hard work and exacting calls of duty, things which in themselves are not much charged with a feeling of romance. If these things appeal strongly to me even in retrospect, it is, I suppose, because the romantic feeling of reality was in me an inborn faculty. . . . My subjects are not medieval, and I have a natural right to them because my past is very much my own. . . . the mere fact of dealing with matters outside the general run of everyday experience laid me under the obligation of a more scrupulous fidelity to the truth of my own sensations. The problem was to make unfamiliar things credible. . . . This was the hardest task of all and the most important, in view of that conscientious rendering of truth in thought and fact which has always been my aim.

[3] T. S. Eliot, "Swinburne as Poet," in *The Sacred Wood* (London, 1920; third edition, 1932), p. 150.

II

The truth of fact served Conrad when he wrote *The Nigger of the "Narcissus,"* as it did to some degree in most of his tales. The story, as he testified, was "founded on an actual voyage from Bombay to England made by the author in a ship of that name." The *Narcissus* was a sailing ship of the old Merchant Service. Conrad signed on her as second officer at Bombay late in April 1884, after resigning from a berth on a steamer of the British India Line because he was charmed by the beauty of the *Narcissus*. His love of sailing ships was strong; he never reconciled himself to the age of steam. "A sea-bird's slender body . . . like a bird indeed, skimming rather than sailing the seas," could charm him as no engine-driven vessel could.

He had by this time spent almost ten years on French and English ships. His initiation had come in 1875 when he served his apprenticeship on the *Mont-Blanc* from Marseilles to Martinique and back to Le Havre and followed that voyage in 1876–77 with a trip on the French schooner *St.-Antoine* from France to the West Indies. Those were the years of his first foreign venture; the Polish homeland of his youth had already become, at the age of seventeen, a tragic memory to him.[4]

The Polish cause had been ineradicably rooted in his nature, but the bleak prospects of the country and her ancient fear of Russia impelled Conrad, like other Poles of "Westernizing" sympathies in that age when the Slavic world was divided between East and West, toward Western Europe—toward France with her cultural and political tradition, and toward England with her "sanity and method." During the four years he lingered in Marseilles, a protégé of the banker and shipper Delestang and his circle of *légitimiste* sympa-

----

[4] Conrad's early life in Poland, France, England, and at sea is detailed in G. Jean-Aubry's *Joseph Conrad: Life and Letters* (New York, 1927) and his *Vie de Conrad* (Paris, 1947); in Gustav Morf's *The Polish Heritage of Joseph Conrad* (London and New York, n.d.); and in John Dozier Gordan's authoritative study *Joseph Conrad: The Making of a Novelist* (Cambridge, Massachusetts, 1940).

thizers, he had sailed twice on French ships to America, had bought
with three of his younger friends a share in the tartane *Tremolino*
to smuggle illegal arms to the supporters of Don Carlos in Spain, had
had his love affair with a woman of the Carlist circle in Marseilles,
wooed her unsuccessfully, and was left seriously wounded after a
duel with one of his rivals for her favors. When these affairs, later
to be used in *The Arrow of Gold,* ended in fiasco, the young Conrad
faced a crisis.

He had caught his first sight of the sea from the Lido at Venice in
the summer of 1873 on a vacation trip with his English tutor at
Cracow, Mr. Pulman. The determination to become one day a sailor
had come to him on the spot, but the resolution remained a youth's
romantic impulse even during his voyages on French ships. Now,
defeated in Marseilles in the spring of 1878—he was not yet twenty-
one—he got up from his bed and accepted the mandate his uncle,
who had come to his rescue from Poland, gave him: "You wanted
to be a sailor, and you must be responsible for the consequences; you
have forfeited my confidence. Work now to regain it; you will win
it back if you apply yourself steadily and pull yourself together." In
the harbor of Marseilles he found a berth on a British ship, the *Mavis.*
"If I was to be a seaman then I would be a British seaman and no
other." On June 18 he landed in England, at Lowestoft. "I was,"
he recalled later, "pursuing a clear aim, I was carrying out a deliberate plan of making out of myself, in the first place, a seaman
worthy of the service, good enough to work by the side of the men
with whom I was to live; and in the second place, I had to justify my
existence to myself, to redeem a tacit moral pledge."

For more than a year he sailed as an ordinary seaman on English
boats—on *The Skimmer of the Seas* along the English coast, on the
Duke of Sutherland to Australia, on the *Europa* to the Mediterranean.
In 1880 he became third mate in the Merchant Service. The *Loch-
Etive* took him again to Australia; the *Riverdale* to Madras; the old
barque *Palestine* carried him in 1882 as second mate from Falmouth
toward Bangkok but caught fire in the Indian Ocean, exploded, was
abandoned by her crew for open boats, and thus opened to Conrad

for the first time "the portals of the East"—a memory he was to transcribe in the story of the ship *Judea* in "Youth": "the first sight of the East on my face. That I can never forget. It was impalpable and enslaving like a charm, like a whispered promise of mysterious delight . . . for me all the East is contained in that vision of my youth."

Thus Conrad had already weathered a series of signal initiations by the time he embarked on the *Narcissus* at Bombay in April 1884. That voyage of six months impressed another on his mind. Several factors combined to make it do so—the beauty of the ship, the affection he and the crew felt for her, "an awful gale in the vicinity of the Needles, south of the Cape," the death of a Negro member of the crew. The alchemy of Conrad's imagination was already working, though it took another twelve years to express itself in his tale.

By the time he came to write his tribute to the *Narcissus* the facts of the original voyage were distant enough to yield to selection and reshaping. "Most of the personages," Conrad told his biographer, G. Jean-Aubry, "actually belonged to the crew of the real *Narcissus*, including the admirable Singleton (whose real name was Sullivan), Archie, Belfast, and Donkin. I got the two Scandinavians from associations with another ship." The Negro was also a member: "He was in my watch. A Negro in a British forecastle is a lonely being. He has no chums. Yet James Wait, afraid of death and making her his accomplice, was an impostor of some character—mastering our compassion, scornful of our sentimentalism, triumphing over our suspicions." Forgetting the man's name, Conrad took it from another Negro who had been with him on the *Duke of Sutherland* six years earlier. That Negro's arrival on board, singing out his name to the Captain during the mustering of the crew, gave him the striking opening scene of the novel. But he never forgot the actual Negro on the *Narcissus*:

> All this is now old, but it was quite present before my mind when I wrote this book. I remember, as if it had occurred but yesterday, the last occasion I saw the Nigger. That morning I was quarter-officer, and about five o'clock, I entered the double-bedded cabin where he was lying full length. On the lower bunk, ropes, fids, and pieces of cloth had been deposited, so as not to have to take them down into the sail-room if they should be wanted at once. I asked

him how he felt, but he hardly made me any answer. A little later a
man brought him some coffee in a cup provided with a hook to suspend it on the edge of the bunk. At about six o'clock the officer-in-
charge came to tell me that he was dead.

The *Narcissus* docked at Dunkirk, on the north coast of France,
but "from other voyages which I made under similar circumstances"
Conrad fashioned the flight of the ship on its home stretch up the
chops of the Channel and into the port of London, to her berth near
the Board of Trade Office on Tower Hill. There, in the novel, he
leaves his mates, blinking, hesitating clumsily, "as if blinded by the
strange quality of the hazy light, as if discomposed by the view of
so many men; and they who could hear one another in the howl of
gales seemed deafened and distracted by the dull roar of the busy
earth."

That homeward voyage and landfall in London's great port was
also a vivid memory to Conrad. He gives another description of it in
The Mirror of the Sea—"the oldest and greatest of river ports," re-
calling a "jungle by the confused, varied and impenetrable aspect
of the buildings that line the shore" and "hide the depths of London's
infinitely varied, vigorous, seething life." "It is the waterside of water-
sides, where only one aspect of the world's life can be seen, and only
one kind of men toils on the edge of the stream." There "the crew of
the *Narcissus* drifted out of sight. I never saw them again. The sea
took some, the steamers took others, the graveyards of the earth will
account for the rest. . . . A gone shipmate, like any other man, is
gone for ever; and I never met one of them again. But at times the
spring-flood of memory sets with force up the dark River of the Nine
Bends. Then on the waters of the forlorn stream drifts a ship—a
shadowy ship manned by a crew of Shades."

When Conrad wrote his tale in 1897 it was that ship and memory
he commemorated. The *Narcissus* was rivaled by only three other
ships in his affections—the *Tremolino* of his Carlist adventure in
1877; the *Palestine* whose foundering in 1883 opened the East to
him; and the *Otago* on which, in 1888–89 during her voyage from
Bangkok to Australia, he held his first command. Each of these vessels

marked a stage in his career at sea, his progress through the hazards of early manhood. He records them in *The Mirror of the Sea* and *A Personal Record*. Each ship received her tribute in a tale—the *Tremolino* in *The Arrow of Gold*, the *Palestine* in "Youth," the *Otago* in *The Shadow-Line*. The *Narcissus* received the most eloquent tribute of them all. She herself becomes an actor in the drama, more so than the ships in "Typhoon" and *The Shadow-Line*. She and her crew join their forces against the fury of the storm. To save themselves the crew must save her. She is, so to speak, the heroine of the tale, as the crew is its collective hero. When they leave her at last in the port of London, she has become an inseparable part of their lives, as she had become part of Conrad's.

III

The tale begins in the harbor of Bombay. Night is coming on; the double stroke of nine has just rung. The decks have been swept, the windlass oiled and made ready, the hatches battened down: "the ship was ready for the sea." In the tropical darkness Mr. Baker, chief mate, is mustering the crew. They have come from the ends of the earth: Craik—"Belfast"—the North Irishman; Wamibo, the Russian Finn; two young Scandinavian giants "with smooth baby faces"; Archie, Campbell, Smith, young Charley, and the rest. They are what Conrad called them in the title used for the first American edition of the novel—children of the sea: tough, weathered, profane, hardbitten, at once cynical and immature, a medley of human types, with the austere officers of the Merchant Service, impersonal, never known as intimates, over them—Baker, Creighton, Captain Allistoun. Among them we find the two members who are to enact the antagonism of forces that works in any crew or company of men.

One is Donkin the Cockney, with his shifty eyes and yellow hatchet face, looking "as if he had known all the degradations and all the furies," inefficient, cadging, whining, wheedling, treacherous. "They all knew him":

Is there a spot on earth where such a man is unknown, an ominous survival testifying to the eternal fitness of lies and impudence? . . . They all knew him! He was the man that cannot steer, that cannot splice, that dodges the work on dark nights; that, aloft, holds on frantically with both arms and legs, and swears at the wind, the sleet, the darkness; the man who curses the sea while others work. The man who is the last out and the first in when all hands are called. The man who can't do most things and won't do the rest. The pet of philanthropists and self-seeking landlubbers. The sympathetic and deserving creature that knows all about his rights, but knows nothing of courage, of endurance, and of the unexpressed faith, of the unspoken loyalty that knits together a ship's company. The independent offspring of the ignoble freedom of the slums full of disdain and hate for the austere servitude of the sea.

The other is old Singleton, silent, selfless, intensely absorbed as he reads *Pelham,* "unmoved in the clash of voices and cries"; he who had "sailed to the southward since the age of twelve" and who "in the last forty-five years had lived (as we had calculated from his papers) no more than forty months ashore."

. . . he appeared bigger, colossal, very old; old as Father Time himself. . . . Yet he was only a child of time, a lonely relic of a devoured and forgotten generation. He stood, still strong, as ever unthinking; a ready man with a vast empty past and with no future, with his childlike impulses and his man's passions already dead within his tattooed breast. The men who could understand his silence were gone—those men who knew how to exist beyond the pale of life and within sight of eternity. They had been strong, as those are strong who know neither doubts nor hopes. They had been impatient and enduring, turbulent and devoted, unruly and faithful. Well-meaning people had tried to represent those men as whining over every mouthful of their food; as going about their work in fear of their lives. But in truth they had been men who knew toil, privation, violence, debauchery—but knew not fear, and had no desire of spite in their hearts. . . . They were the everlasting children of the mysterious sea. Their successors are the grown-up children of a discontented earth. . . . They are gone now—and it does not matter. The sea and the earth are unfaithful to their children: a truth, a faith, a generation of men goes—and is forgotten, and it does not matter! Except, perhaps, to the few of those who believed the truth, confessed the faith—or loved the men.

Conrad is doing more than writing a tribute to his old brothers of the days of sail. He is doing what all tellers of the tales of ships have done, from Homer in the *Odyssey* or the satirists of the *Narrenschiff* and *Ship of Fools* to Cooper, Dana, and Melville. He is making of the *Narcissus* and her crew a world, an image of humanity on its hazardous voyage into the elements, the future, the unknown. That world will hold what Conrad always dreaded—its "plague spots," its falsehood, meanness, and evil, its Donkin. It will also hold the steadfast faith of a Singleton and, somewhere above, its code-ruled, self-effacing, steady captains, its Allistouns. Yet what these are worth may not be apparent until the test is imposed on them, and in *The Nigger of the "Narcissus"* two such tests are imposed.

One suddenly arrives on deck just as the mustering is completed. "Wait!" cries a man in a deep, ringing voice. The crew, the chief mate, ready to begin the routine business of the voyage, stop agape in consternation. "What's this? Who said 'Wait'? What . . ." Mr. Baker advances intrepidly. "Who are you? How dare you . . . ?" "My name is Wait—James Wait," says the newcomer, the last man on board. The Negro is "calm, cool, towering, superb." He is black, his "head vigorously modelled into deep shadows and shining lights —a head powerful and misshapen with a tormented and flattened face—a face pathetic and brutal: the tragic, the mysterious, the repulsive mask of a nigger's soul." He coughs: "metallic, hollow, and tremendously loud, it resounded like two explosions in a vault; the dome of the sky rang to it, and the iron plates of the ship's bulwarks seemed to vibrate in unison . . ." He brings into the ship his lonely pride, his fear, his ailing body, his intimation of death.

The next morning the ship weighs anchor and starts on its voyage.

> Round her the abysses of sky and sea met in an unattainable frontier. A great circular solitude moved with her, ever changing and ever the same, always monotonous and always imposing. . . . She had her own future; she was alive with the lives of those beings who trod her decks; like that earth which had given her up to the sea, she had an intolerable load of regrets and hopes. On her lived timid truth and audacious lies; and, like the earth, she was unconscious,

fair to see—and condemned by men to an ignoble fate. The august loneliness of her path lent dignity to the sordid inspiration of her pilgrimage. She drove foaming to the southward, as if guided by the courage of a high endeavor.

The drama into which Conrad has by this time initiated us is one that holds more in common with old chronicles and epics than with the arts of the modern novel. His ship and crew are a microcosm of mankind. His plot is shaped less by human motives and conflicts than by a strife of elements. These elements lie outside man and oblige him to pit his strength against them, but they also lie within him. "Both men and ships live in an unstable element," Conrad said in *The Mirror of the Sea.* When the crew man their ship, obey her impersonal regimen, submit their wills to the will of their Captain, they identify themselves with her and with the craft she exacts of her manipulators. When she advances out of fair weather into foul, and thus into the fury of the storm, they become one with her life. They must bend every ounce of their strength to save her from the concerted fury of natural forces—water, wind, cold, rain—that appears intent on destroying the tiny barque and her frail load of humanity. But another instability threatens them: their disunity as men, their secret fears and cowardice, the insecurity that competes with their tough and almost mindless tenacity as sailors who are closer to brutes than to civilized beings.

That insecurity lives among them in the Negro. He has come from no one knows where. He belongs to another world than Europe's. He becomes their charge and their child as illness overtakes him and makes him the object of their pity and dread. The fear, hatred, and love they feel for him as he fights his battle are the dread and reverence they feel in their own lives as they hang frailly between the anger of the storm and the doom of the sea.

What comes forward in the book, what makes it important as the work in which Conrad first defined the central motives of his art, are several of the primary conceptions that were to be developed and given their full complexity of realization in his future novels. There is first the sea itself, now for the first time imaged by Conrad as a symbol of unconscious nature—a nature which woos man into its mindlessness but which proves, once he faces its reality, to test his capacity to save and declare himself against its nihilism. The sea is thus a cognate of the East. It is a realm of elemental nature in which the conscious personality and egotism of man dissolve on encountering a force unbroken to the reason and assertive will of civilized life. At grips with it, life resumes the terms of a primary hostility and danger. It symbolizes for Conrad the anti-human—cleansing, purging, primitive, but destructive too, what Stein in Lord Jim calls "the destructive element," and with the simplest condition of man's fate implicit in it.

There is, too, that drama of man's destiny which Conrad repeatedly emphasized: the conflict between his isolation as an individual, the incommunicable secrecy of the self which begins and ends in loneliness, and his need to share his life with others, the force of that "solidarity" which Conrad insistently invoked as a human necessity, a mode of salvation from the nihilism of the isolated temperament. An "unavoidable solidarity," he called it, "the solidarity in mysterious origin, in toil, in joy, in hope, in uncertain fate, which binds men to each other and all mankind to the visible world." What we get in The Nigger of the "Narcissus" is a forecast, under the primitive conditions of sea life, of the complex versions of this drama which were to come in Lord Jim, Nostromo, and "Typhoon," and, among Conrad's later works, in Under Western Eyes and Victory.

A third factor in the drama appears in the role played by James Wait. He plays it, it first seems, unconsciously, though perhaps he is never wholly unconscious of it. It is the role which Marlow plays in Lord Jim, "Heart of Darkness," and Chance with intent purpose; the role also which Leggatt, of "The Secret Sharer," enacts in the life of the young captain on whose ship he finds refuge. Leggatt, like Wait, like Marlow, and like Nostromo, becomes the secret sharer of the weakness, guilt, and fear all men carry within themselves. He is the man they fear to be but who they find they must be and are—the man alone in life and death, at last unable to rescue himself from his fate by the subterfuges of life—the man all men must finally know and whose secret they must share if they are to prove themselves worthy not only of life but of death. So Wait, weakening, protesting, torn by self-pity, silently accusing the fate that has condemned him, at last dying, shares his secret with the men who curse him and try in vain to help him. When his body is committed to the sea, he leaves his secret with his survivors. It will destroy or strengthen them according to their natures.

Thus the drama of the Negro joins with the drama of the sea. Conrad strove, as his work progressed, to bring the fact of human isolation out of its confinement in egotism into the "hard facts" of man's life and condition on earth. His greater novels all move in the direction of a larger social morality, even a political morality, which exacts its price in every man's life. That morality is present here in the concentrated form of the community and regimen of the ship. Yet whatever community of purpose a ship requires of its crew, the sea will also have its special test for every single man aboard. He may conceal his ordeal. He may never confide the knowledge it has yielded him to another man. But that knowledge will be born in him and he will emerge from peril, if he measures up to the test, as a man worthy of his fate as a man. For Conrad the ordeal is a measure of the individual's fitness for his destiny as a human being. There are, of course, those who fail the measure, like Captain MacWhirr of the *Nan-Shan* in "Typhoon," before he enters on his cataclysmic voyage across the China Sea, the stolid Scot who has never in a lifetime's service met the full fury of the sea: "ignorant of life to the last, without ever having been made to see all it may contain of perfidy, of violence, and of terror. There are on sea and on land such men thus fortunate—or thus disdained by destiny or by the sea."

As the storm is the test and symbol of life, so James Wait becomes for the crew a test of their ability to face another, an equally inevitable, imperative of destiny—death. Conrad meant him to act as such: "In the book he is nothing; he is merely the center of the ship's collective psychology and the pivot of the action." When, after Wait dies and his body, about to be lowered into the sea, clings reluctantly to the planks, Belfast shrieks passionately, "Jimmy, be a man!" He speaks for the crew and the wisdom they have wrested from their agony. To be men worthy of a man's destiny, it is not only life that must be faced and mastered. It is also death.

The reader is bound to feel that in this book Conrad was testing himself and his powers more intimately than he had yet succeeded in doing. In Almayer and Willems he portrayed the vagrant, renegade, illusion-fed tendencies he could trace in his own complex nature, and both *Almayer's Folly* and *An Outcast of the Islands* gave him the training in dramatic construction he needed to begin his work as a novelist. In both those books the East gave him the scene of his drama—the semi-barbaric Oriental world where men live under a more primitive justice than Europe permits. But in *The Nigger* the exotic yields to another and even more salient simplicity —that of nature and her elements as the seaman knows them. Almayer, Willems, and the men of the East show an impressive moral and psychological truth, but it is a truth attenuated by distance, strangeness, barbarism, and by what Conrad instilled into these—a romanticized primitivism of good and evil. *The Nigger of the "Narcissus,"* though suffused by its own kind of sentiment, gains from the conditions of practical reality it works in. Here, long before he became vexed by "that infernal tail of ships and that obsession of my sea life" which had led him, unjustly he felt, to become classified by critics as a "'spinner of sea yarns—master mariner—seaman writer' and so forth" rather than as a serious novelist, Conrad was writing out of the direct immediacy of his maritime experience and memory. The rudimentary conditions of life on a ship gave him a special advantage: "in that condition of life, the elementary feelings exist in a stage of greater simplicity and consequently may be more accurately contemplated and more forcibly communicated." And because he transcribed faithfully what he himself had seen, "this limitation," as Miss Bradbrook has said, "increases and concentrates his power of suggestion and implication." [5]

It also permitted him to arrive at the truth of effect which by this time he had defined as his special purpose as a novelist and which he fashioned, in the "Preface" he wrote when the tale was finished, into his credo as an artist: that "a work of art that aspires, however humbly, to the condition of art, should carry its justification in every line"; that "art itself may be defined as a single-minded attempt to render the highest kind of justice to the visible universe"; that "the artist descends within himself, and in that lonely region of stress and strife, if he be deserving and fortunate, he finds the terms of his appeal"; and that, for himself, "my task, which I am trying to achieve, is by the power of the written word to make you hear, to make you feel—it is, before all, to make you *see*. That—and no more, and it is everything."

The Nigger of the "Narcissus" was dedicated to this task—to a rendering of life in terms of specific conditions, and to making the reader see them. Here Conrad for the first time came close to the principle of Flaubert, one of his chosen masters. And he addressed his book also to another task he defined for himself: the task of invoking the "invincible conviction" of moral community in men. When the crew of the *Narcissus* gathers for the last time on Tower Hill in London before life blows them apart again, they stand "a dark knot of seamen," like "castaways making merry in the storm and upon an insecure ledge of a treacherous rock," while "the roar

---

[5] M. C. Bradbrook, *Joseph Conrad: Poland's English Genius* (1941), pp. 15–20: "The storm, the death of the Nigger, and his burial at sea, can all be given in direct statement. The exactitude of the rendering depends on the fine detail; and the detail depends very often on simile. Conrad maintains the exterior method, that is, he describes only what can be *seen*, but because he describes what is seen by means of simile, this limitation increases and concentrates his power of suggestion and implication. The whole scene is dramatized; it is removed from 'realism' by the richness of the similes and it is tied down to realism by the consistent concreteness of the writing; whilst this special kind of matter of fact treatment is both limited and intensified to a further degree by the very noticeable absence of comment. . . . The whole tale depends for its richness upon its limitations" (p. 18).

of the town resembled the roar of topping breakers, merciless and strong." Before they drift away, "the sunshine of heaven" falls "like a gift of grace on the mud of the earth, on the remembering and mute stones, on greed, selfishness; on the anxious faces of forgetful men."

But these men—except for Donkin, whom destiny disdains—will not forget the voyage they have made. "Haven't we, together and upon the immortal sea, wrung out a meaning from our sinful lives?" Nor is the reader, any more than Conrad himself, likely to forget "a shadowy ship manned by a crew of Shades." What he has just read will remain for him, if not the richest experience Conrad can give him in some of his other books, a memory of descriptive powers and suggestive writing at one of their highest points of artistry in English fiction. Here and in "Typhoon" Conrad made his drama of the sea in storm, as in "The Secret Sharer" and *The Shadow-Line* he made it of the sea in its other aspect of danger—calm. And he made it with a power that is rivaled only in the mightier pages of Melville's *Moby Dick*. Unified as is the impression the tale leaves, poetic as are its conception and rendering from first to last, it unquestionably arrives at its fullest strength in its powerful third chapter—the great scene of the storm. There Conrad not only reaches the height of his descriptive art; he also brings the whole complexity of his theme into brilliant fusion—the ship, the men, the doomed Negro, the thundering seas, the deadly contest between the crew and the elements; and in their midst, "swaying upon the din and tumult of the seas, with the whole battered length of the ship launched forward in a rolling rush before his attentive face," Singleton at the wheel: he who knew from the first the truth about Wait—"Why, of course he must die"—and who also knows that the ship must survive the storm and that its crew will live. "In front of his erect figure only the two arms moved crosswise with a swift and sudden readiness, to check or urge again the rapid stir of circling spokes. He steered with care."

1950 [1956]

III. THE THREAT TO THE WEST

Under Western Eyes

I

"Books have their fate," said Conrad in one of his essays: "they share with us the great incertitude of ignominy or glory—of severe justice and senseless persecution—of calumny and misunderstanding—the shame of undeserved success." Nor can they rely on "the formulas of art" for assurance against these hazards of chance or fortune, for these too "are dependent on things variable, unstable, and untrustworthy; on human sympathies, on prejudices, on likes and dislikes, on the sense of virtue and the sense of propriety, on beliefs and theories that, indestructible in themselves, always change their form—often in the lifetime of one fleeting generation."

The fate of Conrad's own books supports his contention. From early neglect to later success; from public admiration for the romantic glamour of his exotic tales and settings to popular indifference to the serious values that were masked by these; from the impatience of careless readers to a gradually insistent critical esteem, the fortunes of his art during the past half-century fairly describe the chosen destiny of his resolutely individual talent. Some of his works have now become recognized as classics, but certain others—among them some of his mature achievements—still await the turn of taste or of events that must be counted on to do them an adequate justice. Perhaps such a turn of events has now arrived for *Under Western Eyes*, a failure when it was first published in 1911 and still one of his least-read novels, but without question one of the books that must be examined by anyone concerned to know his art in its full dimensions and resonance.

The tales of Conrad still most widely read happen to be those he wrote early or late in his career. *Almayer's Folly, The Nigger of the "Narcissus," Lord Jim,* "Youth," and "Heart of Darkness" were all completed by 1900, in his first six years as a professional writer. *Victory, The Shadow-Line, The Rescue,* and *The Rover*—the novels that won him public success in the last decade of his life—came after 1914. But between these two groups of tales he produced a series of novels that may be called the works of his middle period— books that deviated from the maritime or exotic subjects of his most popular fiction by addressing themselves to the drama of modern society and politics. These novels—*Nostromo, The Secret Agent, Under Western Eyes,* and *Chance*—show not only some of his most serious subjects but some of his most ambitious art; and if their value was little recognized at the time of their publication, it has been made unmistakable by the events and crises that have followed them in the Twentieth Century. *Under Western Eyes* perhaps profits by this irony of circumstance more than any of the others.

Nostromo (1904), variously rated by critics as his most difficult book and as "one of the great novels of the language," and called by Conrad himself "an intense creative effort on what, I suppose, will always remain my largest canvas," gave him, in its complex drama of civil war and rival moralities in the South American state of Costaguana, his first full test as a dramatist of politics and state-craft. *The Secret Agent* (1907) is now recognizable as a pioneer classic in a genre—the tale of political intrigue, espionage, and moral anarchism in modern Europe—which has become a typical mode of fiction in our sinister age of *Machtpolitik,* scientific violence, and "international evil." *Chance,* the book that turned the tide of Conrad's fortunes when it ran serially in the *New York Herald* in 1912, combines its maritime theme with a drama of modern finance and social persecution in which Marlow, the narrator of *Lord Jim,* "Youth," and "Heart of Darkness," reappears to manipulate, in the history of Flora de Barral, one of Conrad's most intricate tales of moral conflict and alienation. *Under Western Eyes* has, as Conrad himself admitted, a personal relevance that gives it a special interest among his books. Its subject—Russian character, despotism, and revolution—is one with which, as a Pole whose race and family had suffered under the heel of Russian occupation, he was bound sooner or later to come to terms in his art. But beyond this it forms, along with *The Secret Agent,* his most serious effort to describe the forces at work in the body politic of modern Europe. It also serves as his closest link with the Dostoevskian tradition in Russian fiction—a tradition which, however persistently he might repudiate it, indicates a special problem of temperamental sympathy and influence in his work. And lastly the book employs a theme which, however remote from the public interests of forty years ago, has become of absorbing concern to the West during the past three decades, and never more so than at the present moment.

The novel fell flat in England and America on its first publication, but not in Russia. There it found a remarkable success. Numerous editions were issued before 1914 in Moscow and St. Petersburg; it was serialized in the popular magazine *The European Messenger* (*Wiestnik Evropy*); its popularity continued after 1917; and while its recent fate is unknown to me, it must still be the book by which Conrad is best known to Russian readers. The present crisis in history provides a specific occasion for its rediscovery by English and American readers. An age which has been bred on classics like *Crime and Punishment* and *The Possessed,* and which has found images of its ordeal in books like Kafka's *Trial,* Koestler's *Darkness at Noon,* Orwell's *1984,* the tales of Graham Greene, Sartre, and Camus, not to mention those of Aldanov, Victor Serge, and a host of other recent novelists of crisis and terror, must encounter *The Secret Agent* and *Under Western Eyes* with the shock of discovering novels which, written well in advance of their time, have been appallingly corroborated by events that have become an ominous reality in modern history.

The present writer has found himself returning to *Under Western Eyes* over a space of a quarter-century as often as to any of Conrad's books. This may be a matter of personal taste, but it has been supported by several of Conrad's distinguished readers. Ford Madox Ford once said that for himself the novel was "the greatest of [Conrad's] books"; and André Gide, who on first making its acquaintance in 1917 admired its "prophetic reflections about the Russian soul," continued to read and ponder it, saying of the theme it shares with *Lord Jim* that "there is no more pathetic subject for a novel," and finding in it a reflection of his own lifelong concern with "that *irresponsible act* of the hero, to redeem which his whole life is subsequently engaged." More recently V. S. Pritchett has said that the book has become "more and more suggestive to the contemporary reader," and F. R. Leavis has rated it among Conrad's best—"a most distinguished work" which "must be counted among those upon which Conrad's status as one of the great English masters securely rests." And Conrad himself had a strong feeling for his effort "to capture the very soul of things Russian," and one of the last plans of his life was to make a play out of the novel under the title *Razumov*.[1]

To these opinions there has been a certain amount of critical dissent, and it is possible that the casual reader will find, at least at first glance, that the novel shows Conrad for pages on end at his

----

[1] The play, apparently sketched and partly written, was never finished. Conrad's most serious ambitions as a playwright concerned his tales of political subject. He dramatized *The Secret Agent* in 1919–20 and it was produced for a short run in London in 1922. In 1920 he wrote a film scenario based on his short tale of South American warfare, "Gaspar Ruiz," and in 1914, under the stimulus of the Huerta revolution in Mexico, he planned to make a dramatic version of *Nostromo* with his Polish friend J. H. Retinger. *Under Western Eyes* eventually reached dramatic form in a film version, perhaps the most serious attempt thus far to put Conrad on the screen. It was produced as *Razumov* in France in 1936 by André Daven and directed by Marc Allegret. The cast was distinguished: Razumov was played by Pierre Fresnay, Haldin by Jean-Louis Barrault, Mikulin by Jacques Copeau, Mikulin's agent by Pierre Renoir, Laspara by Michel Simon, Nikita by Gabris, Razumov's father by Roger Karl. These parts were well played but the film—surprisingly so in view of Gide's possible hand in it—was largely a fiasco. The assassination was changed from a bombing to a shooting, the motive of Razumov's betrayal of Haldin was pointlessly altered, the part of Nathalie Haldin was atrociously misinterpreted (by Danielle Parola), and after the action moved to Geneva Conrad's plot was reduced to complete ineptitude and distortion and its dénouement became wholly unrecognizable.

densest and least encouraging. Anyone is likely to admit that there
is little in modern fiction more powerful than its first or its last hundred pages, but while, between these parts, it repeatedly rises to
points of extraordinary intensity and penetration, it may be allowed
that there are stretches of dramatic indirection, delay, psychic and
moral dissection, which are likely to put the reader's patience to a
test. Yet even these offer less of a strain on attention or credulity
than many distinguished modern books do; it remains for the reader
to stay with the book, to keep his patience on the stretch, and to wait
to see what comes of the novel's long-drawn tensions. He is likely
to find himself rewarded with a memorable experience in fiction,
and to discover a reason in Conrad's method—here applied in one
of its most characteristic forms—which, though it may not be as
directly compelling as in some of his other tales, will have much to
say about the kind of art Conrad here practised at its maturity and
about the difficult theme of justice and retribution with which the
novel deals.

II

The writing of the book, as so often with Conrad, gave him severe
difficulties. The finishing of *The Secret Agent* in 1907, like the writing of *Nostromo* four years earlier, had left him exhausted and with
the now-familiar sensation that "there was nothing more in the
world to write about." He had already started *Chance*, but that tale
also proved intractable, was pushed aside, and remained unfinished
for another five years. At this distracted juncture he remembered
"something told [him] by a man in Geneva many years ago"—as
long ago as 1895, during his first year as a published author, when
he had gone to Switzerland in search of health and inspiration. Now,
having recently revisited the Swiss city, he recaptured the earlier
memory, and by January 1908 he was at work on the novel that
became *Under Western Eyes*. At that point he called it *Razumov*
and his conception of it differed radically from the book completed
five years later and published on October 5, 1911, with its dedica-

tion to his American friend Agnes Tobin, of San Francisco, "who brought to our door her genius for friendship from the uttermost shore of the West."

The strands of suggestion and memory that combined in Conrad's shaping of his tale were both immediate and remote, and they included some of the profoundest emotions of his life. There was first the atmosphere of Geneva itself, "the respectable town of dreary hotels, tendering the same indifferent hospitality to tourists of all nations and to international conspirators of every shade": Voltaire's

> ville froide et fade, où tout est entamé,
> Où l'on calcule toujours, et ne sent jamais—

the city of Calvinist rectitude which from the time of Herzen, Bakunin, and Kropotkin to that of Lenin and Trotsky had offered its impervious sanctuary to the exiles of Tzarist autocracy.[2] There, perhaps in the quarter which, "on account of many Russians residing there, is called *La Petite Russie*," Conrad heard from his unknown acquaintance the story which served as his germ. (He was as avid as Henry James for those chance suggestions that illustrate what James called the "odd law which somehow always makes the minimum of valid suggestion serve the man of imagination better than the maximum"; though, as Graham Greene has pointed out, there is a striking difference between the germs Conrad seized upon,

----

[2] The reader of *Under Western Eyes* will find interest in the literature of the Russian revolutionary exiles, notably the memoirs of Alexander Herzen (*My Past and Thoughts*) and of Prince Peter Kropotkin (*Memoirs of a Revolutionist*), as well as accounts of the careers of Ogarev and Bakunin. Especially relevant among books in English are Edward Hallet Carr's *The Romantic Exiles* (1933) and his *Michael Bakunin* (1937), Edmund Wilson's *To the Finland Station* (1940), and George Woodcock's and Ivan Avakumovic's *The Anarchist Prince*, a biography of *Kropotkin* (1950). The possibility of comparing certain characters in the novel—Laspara, Peter Ivanovitch, Madame de S——, Tekla— with Herzen, Ogarev, Bakunin, and the members of their circle will not be missed by those interested in such likenesses. Another side of the background of the novel is illuminated by the literature of Russian anarchism and terrorism, activities of which a particularly relevant account is given in Boris Nikolajewsky's *Azeff the Spy: Russian Terrorist and Police Stool* (1934), which contains, among much interesting matter, a photograph of the wreckage of Plehve's carriage in the streets of St. Petersburg after the throwing of Sasonov's bomb.

"remarkable as a rule for their anarchy or their ambiguity," and "those neat little dinner-table stories which set James off construct-ing his more intricate and deeper fictions.")

Whatever Conrad remembered of the stranger's tale in Geneva in 1895 must have fallen in with the mood that still possessed him after the writing of *The Secret Agent*. That tale of intrigue, anarchism, and treachery in the London of the early 1900s, with its plot of terrorists, bomb-makers, and *agents provocateurs* manipulated by an unnamed foreign power (obviously Tzarist Russia) in the inter-ests of inciting the Western European nations to suppress the alien revolutionary groups they harbored, was Conrad's first description of two of the evils he feared most profoundly in his age—the "plague spots" of anarchy that undermined the solidarity of Euro-pean society, and the "ferocity and imbecility of an autocratic rule" that bred them. The shadow of Russian tyranny and violence was already falling heavily across Europe. The year 1905 saw the aborted revolution that foreshadowed 1917; nihilism, anarchism, and revolutionary socialism had spread westward through five or six decades; the First International at the Hague in 1872 had brought to a head the conflict between the scientific socialism of Marx and the anarchist policy of Bakunin, resulting in the expulsion of the anarchists; and from the time of Turgenev's *Smoke* and *Virgin Soil* or the novels of Dostoevsky, the modern novel had become increas-ingly concerned with themes of despotism, protest, and revolt. Twenty years before Conrad wrote his novel, Henry James had dealt with the subject of revolutionary anarchism in Europe in *The Princess Casamassima*. That book, inspired by the radical activities of the 1880s, was the first notable novel in English on its theme; and Lionel Trilling has shown in his essay on the book how closely its material tallies with such events as the Lyons riots of 1882, with a series of attempts to assassinate the rulers of Germany, Spain, Italy, and Russia, with the Phoenix Park murders in Ireland and the Hay-market Riots in Chicago, with dynamite conspiracies in England and Germany, and with the activities of such anti-scientific socialist rivals of Marx as Bakunin and Johann Most. In Russia the "Socialist Revolutionary" Party and its terrorist Battle Organization was augmented by the student revolutionary groups that sprang up in the nineties. And against them stood the organized forces of Tzarist officialdom and the political secret police, the Okhrana. All these provided Conrad with his situation and background and from their activities he chose the episode of recent history with which his novel opens—"an event characteristic of modern Russia in the actual fact"—"the successful attempt on the life of Mr. de P——, the President of the notorious Repressive Commission of some years ago, the Minister of State invested with extraordinary powers."

The novel thus hinges on an occurrence which had only recently shaken Europe and figured in the world's news. De P—— was the celebrated Viatscheslav Konstantinovitch Plehve, whose assassination took place in July 1904. Born in 1846 of Lithuanian stock, educated in Warsaw and the University of St. Petersburg, he had ascended by careful stages from assistant solicitor-general to become director of the Russian state police, secretary of state, member of the council of the Empire, and eventually in 1902 minister of the interior. He had attracted the favor of Alexander III for his work in investigating the assassination of Alexander II; had earned the hatred of Poland, Lithuania, and Finland by his ruthless "Russification" of those alien provinces; had manipulated pogroms against the Jews and persecutions of Armenians in the Caucasus; was credited with being accessory to the Kishinev massacres; opposed Witte's policy of commercial development in Russia along European lines because it furthered both a dangerous proletariat and a prosperous middle class; and became the fanatical archetype of the autocratic principle and an arch-villain in revolutionary history. Long plotted by the Battle Organization, his murder was finally brought off as he was driving on his way to the Petershof to make his regular report to the Tzar, and it made an enormous impression on all strata of Russian society and throughout Europe. The assassin indicted for the murder, Sasonov, enacted the role which Victor Haldin plays in Conrad's story.

Plehve's assassination involved another person who became notorious in Russian revolutionary history. This was Azev, or Azeff, one of the most famous of the police-spies who, double-dealing as revolutionary conspirators and as tools of the Tzarist police, became a familiar product of the politics of despotism. From the time of Vidocq and Balzac's Vautrin they had figured in modern European political life, but Azeff achieved a special notoriety. Born of poor parents in 1869, he absconded from Russia with some stolen money at the age of twenty-three, went to Karlsruhe (like Stuttgart, Baden, and Geneva, one of the centers of Russian conspiracy abroad), joined there a band of Russian student-revolutionists among whom he appeared as a student of engineering, and at the same time offered his services as a spy to the Russian state police.

Thus while, as a member of the Socialist Revolutionary Party and head of its terrorist section, Azeff was chiefly instrumental in plotting the assassination not only of Plehve in 1904 but of the Grand Duke Sergei in 1905 and of Dubasov, governor-general of Moscow, in 1906, he simultaneously remained the best-paid and most valued secret agent of the Okhrana. His double life was symptomatic of the fantastic world he inhabited. The drawn battle between the Tzarist state and the revolutionary anarchists was hardly less deadly than the rivalries within each of these bodies. State officials were willing to see their rivals assassinated and their policies discredited by terrorist outrages; frequent atrocities increased the importance of the Okhrana; a police spy against whom suspicion might be directed by one set of officials could find patronage in another set. And against these tangled lines of officialdom stood the equally tangled loyalties and divisions within the revolutionary circles themselves, riddled by sectarian rivalries through which a traitor like Azeff might pick his way if he possessed a sufficient genius for duplicity. The situation was typical of the crazy world of Tzarist politics; and it took the exhaustive persistence of V. L. Burtzev, editor of the revolutionary historical review *The Past* (*Byloye*), to track Azeff's treachery down by extracting the truth about it from a disappointed ex-director of the Police Department, Lopuhin, and exposing the sordid case in the pages of his journal. Whereupon Azeff, his dual standing as terrorist and spy shattered, had to flee Russia and go into hiding in Germany, where he lived on a false passport as an apparently respectable citizen and member of the Berlin Stock Exchange in the company of his mistress Madame N—— (known also as "La Bella Heddy de Hero") until, to his horror, he was arrested in 1914 by the German authorities as "a dangerous revolutionary, anarchist, and terrorist, who, according to the international police conventions, was to be handed over to the Russian authorities at the end of the War." He was thrown into the Moabit Prison, but was released on the outbreak of the Bolshevist Revolution in 1917, given a minor post in the German Ministry of Foreign Affairs, and died in Berlin in 1918.

It is not to be assumed that Conrad took the career of Azeff as a model for his story of Razumov. The two characters are quite different. But there is a possibility that Conrad followed Burtzev's exposure of Azeff while he was writing his novel—it took place in 1908 while *Under Western Eyes* was in its first stages. And Conrad had already fixed upon the police spy and *agent provocateur* as a radical symptom of the whole sinister machinery of European and Russian corruption. The hero of *The Secret Agent,* Mr. Verloc, was precisely such a character on the squalid level of London anarchist life, simultaneously employed by a foreign embassy (i.e., by Russia) and accepted as a fellow-conspirator by the gang he harbored in the back room of his shop in Soho. As Henry James, in *The Princess Casamassima,* shows his hero Hyacinth Robinson becoming fatally involved in the anarchist machinations of Paul Muniment, the ambiguous Princess, and the great Hoffendahl, so Conrad shows his squalid Verloc and his high-minded Razumov both trapped by the treacheries and furtive guilt into which the dupe or the unwilling victim falls when he traffics with the evil genius of despotism or anarchy.

But Conrad, in treating this subject, felt the force of it, more intimately than James could have felt it. Conrad was a Pole, born in Russian-occupied Poland in 1857 as the son of one of the most energetic participants in the Polish National Committee, and with a

tradition of Polish insurrection and a profound fear of Russian autocratic power in his blood. Three of his uncles had been killed or
exiled during the Polish rising against Russia in the 1860s, and his
own father, Apollo Nalecz Korzeniowski, had been arrested by the
Russian authorities in 1861 for his part in the illegal National Committee and sentenced to deportation in a remote province of Russia,
where his wife and five-year-old son accompanied him. Both of
Conrad's parents died as a result of the hardships of exile soon after
they returned to Poland, and their son found himself, at the age of
twelve, bereft of his immediate family by the repressive hostility
of Tzarist autocracy. The stamp of that tragedy was never effaced
from his mind or memory.

Thus Conrad brought into his early manhood two strains of his
native inheritance—the patriotic revolutionary ardor of his father's
nature and the more conservative "land-tilling gentry" temper of his
mother's people, the Bobrowskis. And while he was later to become
confirmed in the conservative leanings of his mother's family, he
carried into his mature life a divided allegiance. One side of his
nature was ardent, excitable, strenuous, radical, adventurous, guiltily
haunted by the memory of his father's and his country's courage—it
was the side that led to his first youthful ventures of bravado, Carlist
gun-running, and amateur seamanship in France and Spain. But
the other side of his character was incurably committed to sombre
doubts and pessimism, hating violence, anarchy, fanaticism, and
Slavic instability, all of them symptoms of the autocratic or revolutionary extremism Russia had come to represent in his mind, and
which led him eventually to seek his future in the "sanity and
method" of England and her Merchant Service.

When Razumov, in *Under Western Eyes*, finds himself caught
in the trap of his betrayal of Haldin and attempts to justify his
treachery to himself, he writes certain lines on a sheet of paper and
impales them on his bedroom wall with his pen-knife. They describe the antagonism of forces which Conrad had known in his
personal history and define the reaction to which his deep-seated
historical pessimism had finally compelled him:

History not Theory.
Patriotism not Internationalism.
Evolution not Revolution.
Direction not Destruction.
Unity not Disruption.

When he came to write his "Author's Note" to the novel in 1920, Conrad confessed that his "greatest anxiety" in writing it had been "to strike and sustain the note of scrupulous impartiality." "I had never been called before to a greater effort of detachment: detachment from all passions, prejudices and even from personal memories," he said, insisting that "the obligation of absolute fairness was imposed on me historically and hereditarily, by the peculiar experience of race and family, in addition to my primary conviction that truth alone is the justification of any fiction which makes the least claim to the quality of art or may hope to take its place in the culture of men and women of its time." But his final judgment on the book and on the modern Russian history to which it refers—he is now writing three years after the Bolshevist revolution of 1917—is emphatic:

> The ferocity and imbecility of an autocratic rule rejecting all legality and in fact basing itself upon complete moral anarchism provokes the no less imbecile and atrocious answer of a purely Utopian revolutionism encompassing destruction by the first means to hand, in the strange conviction that a fundamental change of hearts must follow the downfall of any given human institutions. These people are unable to see that all they can effect is merely a change of names. The oppressors and the oppressed are all Russians together; and the world is brought once more face to face with the truth of the saying that the tiger cannot change his stripes nor the leopard his spots.

As for the charge that Conrad harbored an unbalanced "Russophobia," a comment E. M. Forster made on him in 1920 is to the point: Conrad's "passions are intelligible and frank: having lived thus, thus he feels, and it is as idle to regret his account of Russians as it would be to regret Dostoevsky's account of Poles in *The Brothers Karamazov*. A philosopher would moderate his transports, or attempt to correlate them. Conrad isn't that type: he claims the right to be unreasonable when he or those whom he respects have suffered." Miss Bradbrook, writing in 1941, said of *Under Western Eyes:* "No wonder the book was unpopular in 1911, but at the moment its premises are familiar." It scarcely needs emphasizing that the premises of the novel have if anything increased in familiarity and tragic relevance today.

What Conrad called a "senseless desperation provoked by senseless tyranny" epitomized the Russian danger that led him to desert Poland in 1874 and to identify his personal fate with the West. Yet his divided allegiance between East and West remains basic to his novel and was referred to explicitly when he decided on what he called its "awkward title," *Under Western Eyes.* It became his special purpose to hold in double focus two views of the Russian fate— that of Russians themselves (and the book's success in Russia perhaps testifies sufficiently to his success on this score) and that of their alien observers who represent the standards of Western culture and character. This alone, quite apart from its difficult moral theme, gives the novel its characteristic Conradian complexity. A distinguished critic to whom I once gave the book remarked of its handling of Russians—"about whom," he admitted, Conrad "says many things that seem to me true and penetrating"—that "deeply intelligent as it is, it has a little the second-hand quality of most sketching of national types by foreigners." "Isn't it," he asked, "much more satisfactory to read *The Possessed* or *Crime and Punishment?*" Doubtless on this score it is. Conrad, as Thomas Mann once said, may be "far from being the size of Dostoevsky," but Mann also went on to say that though "Conrad's objectivity may seem cool" it is "a passion—a passion for freedom," the "refusal of a very much engaged intelligence to hang miserably in the air between contraries." And a foreigner may have a contribution of value to make in writing about another nationality. Stendhal made one in writing about Italians, James in writing about the English, Forster in writing about India, Lawrence in writing about Mexico, Koestler and Orwell in writing about the Russians and the Burmese. Conrad, divided between a profound and justified fear of violence and tyranny and the rigors of the impartial justice to which his art committed him, achieved in *Under Western Eyes* what is probably the most searching analysis of Russian character and history that has yet been arrived at in an English novel. Its justice is more than a matter of detachment or impartiality. It is a matter of the charity and compassion that have their origins in sympathy and suffering.

III

But the book he wrote is, of course, more than a document on Russian character or history; more than exemplum of his conviction that "the old despotism and the new Utopianism are complementary forms of moral anarchy." It is a novel whose subject and artistry are continuous with his other work, and the reader of *Lord Jim*, *Nostromo*, "Heart of Darkness," "The Secret Sharer," and *Victory* will soon realize that *Under Western Eyes* offers yet another version of the hero and the moral drama that Conrad made unmistakably his own. Indeed, the book shows his theme and method in essence, as well as the ordeal of doubt and creative intensity that had, by the time he wrote it, become habitual with him.

On January 6, 1908, Conrad wrote a letter to his old friend Galsworthy in which he described his first steps in the writing of the novel:

> *Et le misérable écrivait toujours.*
> He is writing now a story the title of which is *Razumov*. Isn't it expressive? I think that I am trying to capture the very soul of things Russian—*Cosas de Russia*. It is not an easy work but it may be rather good when it's done.
> Listen to the theme. The Student Razumov (a natural son of a Prince K.) gives up secretly to the police his fellow student, Haldin, who seeks refuge in his rooms after committing a political crime (supposed to be the murder of de Plehve). First movement in St. Petersburg. (Haldin is hanged, of course.)
> Second in Genève. The Student Razumov meeting abroad the mother and sister of Haldin falls in love with that last, marries her, and, after a time, confesses to her the part he played in the arrest of her brother.

The psychological developments leading to Razumov's betrayal of Haldin, to the confession of the fact to his wife and to the death of these people (brought about mainly by the resemblance of their child to the late Haldin), form the real subject of the story.

And perhaps no magazine will touch it . . . Ah! my dear, you don't know what an inspiration-killing anxiety it is to think: "Is it saleable?" There's nothing more cruel than to be caught between one's impulse, one's act, and that question, which for me simply is a question of life and death. There are moments when the mere fear sweeps my head clean of every thought. It is agonizing,—no less. And,—you know,—that pressure grows from day to day instead of getting less.

But I had to write it. I had to get away from *Chance*, with which I was making no serious progress.

Two years later, on December 23, 1909, we find him still laboring at the book and writing to Norman Douglas:

The novel hangs on the last 12,000 words, but there's neither inspiration nor hope in my work. It's mere hard labour for life—with this difference, that the life convict is at any rate out of harm's way —and may consider the account with his conscience closed; and this is not the case with me. I envy the serene fate and the comparative honesty of the gentlemen in gray who live in Dartmoor. I do really, I am not half as decent or half as useful . . . All the same, don't give me up in your thoughts entirely. In the light of a "tormented spirit" I am not to be altogether despised.

It was almost two years more before the novel finally appeared, not under the title Conrad gave to Galsworthy but as *Under Western Eyes*—a change which, in indicating a shift in the post of observation from the hero to a disinterested spectator (the old English teacher of languages in Geneva who tells the story) and to a critical attitude alien and largely incomprehensible to the Russian, tells much about the narrative method Conrad had by this time made his own and outside of which he rarely trusted himself to work. It was, of course, more than a method. It was a temperamental necessity and compulsion. When Henry James described Conrad as "a votary of the way to do a thing that shall make it undergo most doing," and his method as "a prolonged hovering flight of the subjective over the outstretched ground of the case exposed," he put his finger on the radical factors that operate throughout Conrad's art—its exhaustively empirical workmanship, its intensity of scrutiny and analysis, and its origins in personal conditions of temperamental sympathy and moral intimacy that stamp it from beginning to end.

Conrad's letter to Galsworthy shows that he first conceived the story in strongly active terms, embodied in physical encounters and external conflict of an almost melodramatic tendency. But what had already happened in the writing of *An Outcast of the Islands, Lord Jim,* and *Nostromo,* and what was to happen again in *The Rescue* and *The Rover,* happened in this case. The title was not the only thing that was changed: the plot was also transformed. Razumov and Nathalie Haldin never marry; they never have a child who resembles the dead Haldin and thus "brings about" the "death of these people"; and the "psychological developments" which Conrad planned as leading to the marriage and these deaths were altered to take a different direction. As in so many of his books, the more Conrad pondered his idea, the more he came to grips with the shaping of it, the less he was able to adhere to an objective dramatization of it. What remained was his initial episode—the assassination of Plehve by Haldin, Haldin's seeking refuge with Razumov, Razumov's betrayal of that confidence, Haldin's arrest and execution—and then the trap of official suspicion snapping shut on Razumov when, resolving "to retire" into his solitude and win the University's prize that will rescue his life from its lonely nonentity, he finds his illusion of safety suddenly shattered by Councillor Mikulin's quiet question: "Where to?"

By the time Razumov reappears in Book II among the exiles of Geneva, we see what that question means. "Isolation and conscience are the dominant motifs in the novels of Conrad," says Mr. Pritchett; and Razumov is to enact a drama that has already been enacted by Tuan Jim, by Kurtz and Marlow in "Heart of Darkness," by Decoud, Dr. Monygham, and Nostromo himself in *Nostromo,* by the young ship captain in "The Secret Sharer"; it will be enacted again by Flora de Barral in *Chance,* by Axel Heyst in *Victory,* and by Tom Lingard in *The Rescue.* Geneva, where, unknown to the Russians among whom he is accepted as a fellow-conspirator and

dedicated spirit, Razumov comes as a spy for Mikulin, is to become
the stage of his test of conscience, his ordeal of self-condemnation
and expiation which, by driving him finally to confession—first to
Nathalie Haldin herself and then publicly to the revolutionists—
and to the virtually suicidal disclosure of his guilt, will save him
from the damnation of living his lie and his treachery. In that drama
of conscience all the exiles will partake. The fatuous philosophical
pretensions of Peter Ivanovitch, the seedy egotism of Madame de
S——, the devoted ardors of Sophia Antonovna, the dedicated labors of Laspara, the cowed humility of Tekla, the anthropoid brutality of Nikita—all these lenses of delusion, cruelty, and devotion
will turn and refract the light of truth or falsehood upon Razumov's
agony of mind and conscience. All of them will serve to objectify
or "transfer" the lie his treachery toward Haldin and the unsuspected
egotism that motivated it have trapped him into living. They will
define for him the "everlasting black hole of his life" into which,
like Jim, his failure in moral courage forced him to jump. They will
take him on his downward journey into that "destructive element"
of reality which, by destroying him, may finally save him. But most
of all he will be damned and saved by Nathalie herself. Her pure
and ardent spirit—one of Conrad's exceptional successes among his
portrayals of women—will condemn him to self-contempt and self-
betrayal, to the test of honor that at last breaks and redeems him.

Razumov is what the Conradian hero invariably is: a solitary. He
is the man designed by nature or circumstance to live not by the law
of his kind but by self-law. Like Jim, Kurtz, Willems, Nostromo, and
Heyst, he is Conrad's version of the man—descendant of the heroes
of Balzac, Stendhal, Turgenev, and Melville, and brother to those of
Mann or Gide—who chooses or is compelled to live a life of egotistic
self-regard or compulsive self-assertion. So we are told of Razumov
that "he was as lonely in the world as a man swimming in the deep
sea . . . He had nothing. He had not even a moral refuge—the
refuge of conscience." And on the heels of that statement comes
another no less terrifying: "Who knows what true loneliness is—not
the conventional word but the naked terror? To the lonely them-

selves it wears a mask. The most miserable outcast hugs some memory or some illusion . . . No human being could bear a steady view
of moral solitude without going mad."

When, in one of the novel's greatest scenes, Razumov walks the
wintry night streets of St. Petersburg, furious that Haldin has suddenly erupted into his lonely life of high resolve and secret ambition with his crime and his appeal for help, he stamps his foot in
rage upon the snow-sheeted ground, suddenly to discover that he
has stamped the earth of Russia herself, "inanimate, cold, inert, like
a sullen and tragic mother hiding her face under a winding-sheet"
beneath "the clear black sky of the northern winter, decorated with
the sumptuous fires of the stars." Without warning he finds himself
standing "on the point of conversion." His pathetic and desperate
egotism finds refuge in the "sacred inertia" of the Russian earth, with
its "guarantee of duration, of safety, while the travail of maturing
destiny went on—a work not of revolutions with their passionate
levity of action and their shifting impulses—but of peace." "Don't
touch it," a voice cries within him; and another says "Haldin
means disruption." And "like other Russians before him, Razumov, in conflict with himself, felt the touch of grace upon his
forehead." But cutting across that sudden benediction comes one of
Conrad's most acute comments: "a train of thought is never false.
The falsehood lies deep in the necessities of existence, in secret fears
and half-formed ambitions, in the secret confidence combined with
a secret mistrust of ourselves, in the love of hope and the dread of
uncertain days." And in the struggle to rationalize his confused impulse of treachery and selfishness, Razumov presently articulates another and even deadlier recognition: "All a man can betray is his
conscience."

Though he does not yet know it, his existence has become committed to that implacable truth—committed to what Gide has called
those fatal or unconscious acts, typical of Conrad's heroes, for which
"a whole lifetime, afterward, is not enough to give them the lie and
to efface their mark." The novel becomes the drama of their consequences. There is no escape from them. And as we watch the

unfolding of Razumov's fate in Geneva—watch it through the shifting focus of the Russian eyes and the Western; follow it through Razumov's encounters with all the varieties of human delusion, conceit, sincerity, or honor in the characters who surround him; trace it through the splendidly imaged scenes that shift from the Haldin apartment to the Château Borel, from the alleys of the Bastions to Rousseau's island in the lake, from Razumov's tormented colloquies with Nathalie and the other exiles to his bitter vigils in the Rue de Carouge or on the bridge beneath which the water, "violent and deep," rushes headlong in "its vertiginous rapidity, its terrible force" —we see where that fate is leading him. It is leading him remorselessly to the moment his confession breaks through his torment in the white boxed glare of the Haldin vestibule, thence into the storm-lashed streets of Geneva where the rain "washes him clean," and thus to Laspara's house where his guilt is made public and Nikita's brutal fist deafens him forever.

The prolonged attenuation and indirection of Conrad's narrative seem as if designed to put the reader's senses on the rack as much as Razumov's. The method of Conrad's work had by this time arrived at this almost excruciating development of the *progression d'effet*, this extreme elaboration of sensory and moral impressionism. But the process is repeatedly relieved and condensed in superb passages of imagery and action—moments that mount toward the novel's shattering climax and its final, bitter conclusion, suspended between pathos and irony. The humanity of Conrad's pessimism insists on both. Razumov, crippled and deafened, lies at last in Russia, tended by the faithful Tekla, broken to the law of "unavoidable solidarity" which all of Conrad's significant heroes must finally recognize. Nathalie too has returned to Russia, carrying her faith into the ominous future of her country. The truth that wrecked his life and the hope that sustains hers both offer the coldest of comforts to those who persist in asking "from men faith, honour, fidelity to truth in themselves and others." But there is no other comfort certain— perhaps no comfort at all except in that "resignation, not mystic, not detached, but . . . open-eyed, conscious, and informed by love" which Conrad believed to be "the only one of our feelings for which it is impossible to become a sham." The moral community he insistently invoked, exemplified as much by his personal tenacity as by the art he practiced against all but defeating obstacles of doubt and insecurity, offered little but this grim consolation to his skepticism; but that much it did offer, and on that principle of trust and sincerity he staked his faith; staked, moreover, whatever hope for Europe he was able to salvage from the anarchy of conduct and the casuistry of morals he saw as a threat to the West with which he had allied himself. A more certain confidence lies with Sophia Antonovna and Peter Ivanovitch; it is for her stubborn principle and his triumphant self-conceit that the novel's final touch of irony is reserved: "for such men thus fortunate—or thus disdained by destiny or by the sea."

Under Western Eyes shows Conrad working in the radical strength of his sincerity and despair, his passionate irony and his austere humanism. If it lacks the stronger intimacy of *Lord Jim* and "Heart of Darkness," the richer reverberations and comprehensive moral dialectic of *Nostromo*, the ironic tautness of *The Secret Agent* or the symbolic concentration of *Victory*, it still shows his powers to memorable effect and ends by making its impression of assured authority and justice. The justice with which it is concerned is unsparing and elusive, but his treatment of it, despite its complexity of sympathy, is not evasive, and the workings in it of truth and conscience are not shirked. Perhaps, as Mr. Pritchett surmises, Conrad wrote the book "to bring a harder Western focus upon a theme of Dostoevsky." The book has at any rate something of the effect of translating the Dostoevskian vision and ethos into terms of a moral necessity which the West, whatever its compromises or failures of principle, can never forget, and which it will betray now only at its peril.

That Conrad should have been able to illuminate that necessity by means of a subject so deeply involved in his personal history, and to achieve in so doing a sympathy for the Russian fate that invites comparison with the art of the Russian masters themselves, testifies to the risks he was willing to take in his art and to the insight that rewarded his courage. The novel, as strenuous in its craftsmanship as in the drama it describes, carries its remorseless reading of the modern fate to a pitch of sometimes unendurable intensity, and the judgment at which it arrives is as severe as any we are likely to find in modern fiction. Yet it leaves its question open and its tragedy pending the moral decision of Europe and the West. Though the moral law it dramatizes is unsparing, what we make of that law in our lives and society today is left to us to determine. The book thus becomes more than an experience in the craft of one of the most serious of modern novelists. It also becomes a parable and a portent for an age whose crisis Conrad, by the virtue of his own experience and severity of vision, was able with a remarkable prophetic vision to foresee.

1951 [1956]

IV. CONRAD IN HIS AGE

Great claims for the novel have become commonplaces of literary argument during the past hundred years. It has been defined and defended as the dominant art form of the century, the medium destined to assimilate the values and substance of the others, the only literary mode fully equal to the task of embodying the complexity and conflicts of modern life. Yet skepticism persists in asserting itself. The privileges and license of fiction seem bent on confounding its opportunities. No art is so unstable in purpose, so treacherous in its processes of growth and experiment, so free and thus so uncertain in its conditions. And none has been so much the vehicle and the victim of specialized principles. A poet, if he arrives at any degree of maturity, is expected to outgrow his eccentricity and master his personality. The novelist, once he refuses the safety or routine of popular convention, is encouraged to cultivate both and to become the exponent of a manner, idiosyncrasy, or theory. Is this because the novel's freedom from tradition encourages subjective impulses and so is likely to end in the tenuity and personal emphasis that have restricted the art of writers like Meredith, George Moore, Gide, and Virginia Woolf? Or is it because fiction is so receptive to limiting techniques—naturalism, impressionism, stream of consciousness, satirical or symbolic method—that it is denied its larger energy and so makes our age notable for *petits maîtres,* one-book authors, men without métier? These factors may account for the situation as much as the more obvious demoralization that comes from popular claims and uses, or from the demand for prophecy and "reform" that came to distract the generation of Howells, Wells, Bennett, and Galsworthy, and has later tested the courage even of men like Lawrence, Fitzgerald, and Hemingway. Whatever the answers, it appears that the very richness of the novelist's opportunities are the measure of his dilemma. His profession arrives at an impasse of exhaustion or demoralization every quarter-century or so. A crisis of this kind has been apparent during the past decade.

Another was visible sixty years ago when Conrad began to publish his novels, and the situation he faced, and his way of meeting it, still has its lesson for writers and students of fiction. The English novel, in spite of its enormous popularity and the fecundity of its average practitioners, had arrived at a point of emergency which Henry James alone seems to have recognized and which his manifesto on "The Art of Fiction," as well as his own rigor of discipline and experimentation, virtually admitted. Hardy's abandonment of novel-writing in 1895 was symptomatic of the situation. The old order of free invention had reached its exhaustion in Reade, Bagehot, and De Morgan. The high seriousness of George Eliot had arrived at the solemn end-stop of *Robert Elsmere.* "Throbbing romance had waned and wanned" in Stevenson. The aesthetes cultivated the trivia of exquisite myths, with only Kipling (for the moment) to offer the corrective censure of his high-pressure vitality. Meredith had driven the values of intellection and sensibility to

the brink of what Henley called "spiritual suicide"—a resolute individualism capable of brilliant feats of satire and lyricism but in
the end a celebration, as V. S. Pritchett had said, of Energy in its purest nihilistic essence, "the subject of the Nineteenth Century, the
problem that is never solved."

Conrad, amateur though he was, and despite the uncertainty of his
approach to literary professionalism, sensed the predicament of his
art at the outset. Though he was soon enlisted by James, Crane, and
Hueffer in the cause of form, style, and the *mot juste*, he seems to
have held these principles in considerable distrust. The new aesthetic
of the novel competed in his sympathies with his lifelong devotion
to older masters like Cooper, Marryat, and Dickens. He felt a temperamental suspicion of the specialized theories that were sponsoring the novel of arbitrary limits and schematized content. When he
arrived on the scene, the formal discipline sponsored by Flaubert
was being challenged by the experimental license of the young
aesthetic schools, but Conrad claimed the privileges of neither. Nor
were the rising forces of social naturalism which new friends like
Wells and Galsworthy joined to win his enthusiasm. The great
problem of his art he sensed unmistakably. It lay in the failure of its
makers to become personally and responsibly implicated in what
they were doing. They were too easily satisfied with fragments.
They defined their task not in terms of the moral wholeness of art
but of arguments, practical programs of social and public action,
subjective or documentary techniques. They failed to make an
effective union of principle and substance. They wrote too readily
under "the infirmity of an ideal."

Conrad, as much as Ibsen, Shaw, or James, was a critic of the
ideal. He struggled all his life with the problem of "illusion" and
the romantic tendencies in his nature that fostered it. His critical
sense of their danger to imaginative truth became the basis of his
personal literary doctrine when he wrote it into his preface to *The
Nigger of the "Narcissus"* in 1897. "A work that aspires, however
humbly, to the condition of art should carry its justification in every
line." "The artist descends within himself, and in that lonely region

of stress and strife, if he be deserving and fortunate, he finds the terms of his appeal." "Temperament, whether individual or collective, is not amenable to persuasion." To the serious artist "the temporary formulas of his craft" must always appear deceptive. "The enduring part of them—the truth which each only imperfectly veils—should abide with him as the most precious of his possessions, but they all—Realism, Romanticism, Naturalism, even the unofficial Sentimentalism . . . all these gods must, after a short period of fellowship, abandon him—even on the very threshold of the temple—to the stammerings of his conscience and to the outspoken consciousness of the difficulties of his work." He must reveal "the stress and passion within the core of each convincing moment"; must stir in men a "feeling of unavoidable solidarity"; and fiction itself "must be, like painting, like music, like all art, the appeal of one temperament to all the other innumerable temperaments whose subtle and resistless power endows passing events with their true meaning, and creates the moral, the emotional atmosphere of the place and time." Like all art it "appeals primarily to the senses . . . if its high desire is to reach the secret spring of responsive emotions." By thus assuming a "complete, unswerving devotion to the perfect blending of form and substance," and by making a principle of the "plasticity" which arrives when form is animated by the living reality of experience, Conrad arrived at his declaration of aims and the sentence which embodies his most famous contribution to modern fictional aesthetic: "My task which I am trying to achieve is, by the power of the written word, to make you hear, to make you feel— it is, before all, to make you *see*. That—and no more, and it is everything."

This credo at which Conrad arrived in his first years of authorship in the nineties was obviously born of something more than a purely aesthetic or literary intention. However closely it joins with James's "Art of Fiction" twelve years earlier, it is the expression less of a professional than a personal necessity. Conrad wrote it in the distracted middle years of his life when he was making his harassed transition from his Polish youth, French exploits, and twenty-year maritime service to reluctant and anxious professionalism as an author. Mr. John D. Gordan, in his closely documented study of this phase of Conrad's career,[1] says that the two parts of Conrad's life were halved as by a knife, but the cut was anything but clean. It was made in a mental state bordering on desperation, if not at times on actual derangement. Conrad had made no clear decision about giving up the sea. He tried repeatedly to get a new command, even as late as 1900, when his first five books were already published. To the sense of guilt which his profoundly susceptible nature already carried as a result of his youthful desertion of Poland and the nationalist tradition of his family there were now added his fears on entering on a career of risk and uncertainty in art.

His physical health had been undermined in Orient and Congo; his mental health also became painfully disorganized. He took up a precarious literary career in what became, once the amateur excitement of writing and finishing *Almayer's Folly* was over, the most distraught and irresolute state of mind possible, and this continued to plague him for years to come. He was perpetually tormented by exhausted inspiration and morbid crises. He was never free from what he remembered in his reading of Baudelaire—the "*stérilités des écrivains nerveux* . . . that anguished suspension of all power of thought that comes to one often in the midst of a very revel of production, like the slave with his *memento mori* at a feast." His letters to his "aunt" in Brussels, Mme. Marguerite Poradowska,[2] during the early and middle nineties, sound with the suicidal gloom induced in him by his Congo voyage, the homeless desolation of London, the terrifying blankness of the unwritten page, his fear of solitude and death ("the only two things that make life bearable"), his bewildered anxieties about publishers and reviewers, his "attacks of melancholy that paralyze my mind and will," his confessions of despair, of boredom, of nervous exhaustion, of the fact that

[1] John Dozier Gordan, *Joseph Conrad: The Making of a Novelist* (Cambridge, Massachusetts, 1940).

[2] *Letters of Joseph Conrad to Marguerite Poradowska: 1890–1920*, translated from the French and edited by John A. Gee and Paul J. Sturm (New Haven, 1940).

"it is my nature to be a miserable creature,—a moral pauper, bank-
rupt of courage." Obviously these years brought to a crisis the
natural irresolution, excitement, and self-absorption of Conrad's
temper. His veerings between indolence and despair, his sense of
guilt and indecision, his fretting suspicions and trussed-up sense of
honor, his tranced compulsion to write in the face of forbidding
handicaps of scruple, language, and mental insecurity, all describe
the state of mind out of which, by an appalling exertion of will-
power, his books were wrought, their style and matter determined,
their characters and psychological method conjured, their actual
themes and substance evoked.

His tales, with their repeated patterns of conduct, ordeal, and
conscience, their tenacious fixity of impulse, their deviously incremental sincerity and exhaustive penetration of static or trance-
bound situations, their centripetal mode of moral and dramatic
analysis, had their source in a creative necessity of a peculiar kind.
Conrad's talent was agonized but persistent, not instinctively dramatic, not natively inventive, not naturally precocious or boldly inspired. It succeeded in making powerful fiction out of desperate
obstacles, in dramatizing the *idées fixes* of the obsessed conscience,
in analyzing the classic moral situations and the pathos of modern
skepticism to the last detail; in devising a personal method and style
out of a profound condition of introversion and thus in adding to
English fiction, during a period of triumphant journalism and commercial banalities, an exotic force of language and a power of moral
insight that today appear as two of its few redeeming assets.
(Henry James made a perceptive statement on what these qualities
meant to the novel of that time when he supported the appeal for
a Royal Literary Fund grant for Conrad in 1902: "He has been to
me, the last few years, one of the most interesting and striking of
the novelists of the new generation. His production . . . has all
been fine, rare, and valid, of the sort greeted more by the expert
and the critic than (as people say), by the man in the street. . . .
When I think moreover that such completeness, such intensity of
expression has been arrived at by a man not born to our speech, but

who took it up, with singular courage, from necessity and sympathy, and has laboured at it heroically and devotedly, I am equally impressed with the fine persistence and the intrinsic success.") [3]

Conrad's subjects seem to have come to him usually in the form of specific physical actions or external dramatic conflict of a melodramatic tendency. His original conception of *Under Western Eyes*, described in his letter to Galsworthy in 1908 which I have already quoted, gives one example of this; others figure in the cases of *Lord Jim, Nostromo, The Secret Agent,* and *The Rescue.* But the more he pondered them, and the more he came to grips with the actual writing of them, the less he was able to adhere to an objective dramatization of his ideas. Once the writing of a book began, his originally vigorous conception of it seemed to dissolve. His ponderous imaginative processes were forced from their doubt or inertia by a haphazard, precipitous mode of composition. We can see what Ford Madox Ford meant when he said that Conrad could write a book only by beginning with the first word of the story and proceeding, word by word, until he reached the end. Conrad himself gives repeated evidence of the prolonged ordeal of immersion in the idea and mood of a story that preceded the setting of words to paper, and of the almost frenzied compulsion he found necessary to transfer that modal saturation to paper. At one point in the nineties, while struggling with *Almayer's Folly,* he wrote Mme. Poradowska: "I must go out sometimes, alas! I begrudge each minute I spend away from paper. I do not say 'from pen,' because I write very little, but inspiration comes to me in looking at the paper. Then there are soaring flights; my thought goes wandering through vast spaces filled with shadowy forms. All is yet chaos, but, slowly, the apparitions change into living flesh, the shimmering mists take shape, and— who knows?—something may be born of the clash of nebulous ideas." And again: "You know that when I am not well I have attacks of melancholy which paralyze my mind and will. I have often thought, though, of you and your book—*the book* to be. Once the

[3] British Museum, Ashley MS. 4792: Letter to Edmund Gosse, June 26, 1902.

general idea is settled on, you must let yourself be led by the inspiration of the moment. You are too much of an artist to go astray. *You* may be afraid of groping about in a blind alley, but *I*, who judge you 'from without,' am entirely unfearful of seeing you take a wrong turn. I have the utmost confidence in your inspiration, while I nevertheless realize that your doubts, your hesitation, are quite natural. How well I know them. . . ."

He was obliged to submit himself to an almost purely empirical mode of imaginative realization. Every new book was begun as if he "had never written a book before." The frightening drop of his inspiration that followed the completion of a manuscript could make him believe (as when he had finished *Typhoon* and not yet begun *Nostromo*) "that there was nothing more in the world to write about." These crises of exhaustion, corresponding closely to the depressive phases of his emotional life, seem to have recurred repeatedly. When he took up a new theme, he often did so because he stumbled on it accidentally or recalled it from some buried recess of memory, and the suggestion appears usually to have been of minute scope as compared with the complex book that finally resulted. To that suggestion he subjected himself for a long period of gestation that must have been, from his own accounts of it, of an almost willless or trance-like passivity. He made himself the registering medium of what in *Chance* he speaks of as "the irresistible pressure of imaginary griefs, crushing conscience, scruples, prudence, under their ever-expanding volume," and of "the sombre and venomous irony in the obsession." He surrendered to "that complete mastery of one fixed idea, not a reasonable but an emotional mastery, a sort of concentrated exaltation. Under its empire men rush blindly through fire and water and opposing violence, and nothing can stop them— unless, sometimes, a grain of sand." At one point in *Chance* Marlow pauses to ask his listener, "You understand?" and the listener answers: "Perfectly. . . . You are the expert in the psychological wilderness. This is like one of those Redskin stories where the noble savages carry off a girl and the honest backwoodsman with his incomparable knowledge follows the track and reads the signs of her fate in a footprint here, a broken twig there, a trinket dropped by the way. I have always liked such stories. Go on!"

Conrad's state of mind combined the responsive curiosity of his seamen with their practiced disillusionment. (He combined the traits in his narrator Marlow.) "A turn of mind composed of innocence and skepticism is common to them all," he once said, "with the addition of an unexpected insight into motives, as of disinterested lookers-on at a game." As a novelist he submitted to the fascination of his dramatic ideas at the same moment that he was tormented by the labor of translating them into the reality of words. He repeatedly shared with young Powell (again in *Chance*) that "moment of incredulity as to the truth of his own conviction because it had failed to affect the safe aspect of familiar things. He doubted his eyes too. He must have dreamt it all! 'I am dreaming now,' he said to himself. And very likely for a few seconds he must have looked like a man in a trance or profoundly asleep on his feet, and with a glass of brandy-and-water in his hand." Conrad confessed himself continually fascinated by the dreamlike unreality of experience, by the shock of the awakenings which personal crises bring into a man's life, by the power of the dream to appal and defeat a man's conscious efforts to control or understand it. His life was pitched between the world of fantasy and romantic desire and the world of brutal facts—the fact of his isolation, of his poverty, of his family responsibilities, of the next book that had to be written to keep the wolf from the door. Three proverbs seem to have haunted him all his life; his wife and friends have told how he murmured them habitually. One was "Life is a dream" (Calderón's *La Vida es sueño* was a favorite motto); another, "All things belong to the young"; the third, "Tout passe, tout lasse." They condense the temperamental, the moral, perhaps even the aesthetic attitudes of his nature.

Elizabeth Bowen once said that Conrad's way of projecting a dramatic subject was not by means of a development but by means of a "soaking," and this suggests a quality in his work that no attentive reader is likely to overlook—the verbal, modal, and atmospheric saturation to which the narrative idea is subjected and the equally exhaustive wringing out or draining out of the whole content of motive and consciousness that has been induced into the idea. The act of composition in Conrad took place between two contradictory impulses—the one instinctive, tentative, unmethodical, and yet intensely and violently absorbed; the other analytical, cautious, scrupulously calculating, with checkings in delayings of action, regressions of impulse, a retracing and challenging of motives, and with a complicated use of the averted suspense which the Renaissance rhetoricians called *occupatio*. But the devious, peripheral exploration of a situation—an exploration often heightened in realism by the use of narration put into the mouth of a speaker, Conrad's most typical method of oral and dramatic *vraisemblance*—was corrected by his rigorous sense of form, by his detestation of the mechanics of crude chronology, perhaps chief of all by his obsessional curiosity about the sources of action in the moral scruples, the psychic forces, and the expiatory or recriminative processes of the human conscience. Conrad tells us too much about himself in his letters to keep us from ascribing this curiosity to the ordeal of his own conscience, profoundly susceptible at best but intensified and made acute by the events and conflicts of his life. His congenital impulsiveness in action and enthusiasm was habitually and brutally checked by acute principles of honor and sincerity. Gustav Morf certainly simplifies when he ascribes the test of honor in Conrad's tales to his own sense of guilt in deserting Poland and his family's part in the nationalist cause there,[4] but there is no question that such a sense is made to operate repeatedly in the characters of his novels. The collision in them of impulsive action or the romantic delusions of an untested idealism with the agony of moral recognition and sincerity gives them their distinguishing mark among the characters of modern fiction.

They are men who enact Conrad's central moral argument: that

----

[4] Gustav Morf, *The Polish Heritage of Joseph Conrad,* n.d. (c. 1929).

the personal illusion of values must be compelled out of vanity, conceit, or the nihilism of the closed personality by the human necessity of action and commitment. By that law they meet the crises in their lives. Conrad's tales invariably center their dramatic and moral situations in a crisis of this order. If an epic regression to origins or causes is needed, it is retraced after the crisis is introduced or rapidly precipitated. This crisis, being by nature a fixed or static moment, is held under exhaustive scrutiny while every element in it—moral, social, conscious or unconscious, essential or peripheral—is wrung out of it by a series of checks, interrogations, challenges, pathetic searchings, recoveries of concealed, forgotten, or unconscious motives. To make this arrestment or diagnosis credible two things were usually needed: a central character of acutely self-conscious or morbidly activated faculties comparable to Conrad's own—Jim, Decoud, Mrs. Gould, Flora de Barral, Razumov, Heyst—and an extra-dramatic point of vantage or scrutiny—thus Marlow, or the old professor in *Under Western Eyes*, or the novelist himself in his role of inquisitor or interrogator. It must be noted, moreover, that the central characters usually exist in a condition of psychic obsession or vulnerability particularly conducive to the dissections of conscience. In Jim and Razumov the pathology is that of remorse; in Flora and Heyst it is the horrified shame or disgust, tending toward nihilism, that follows a mistaken idealistic confidence in life; in Almayer, Willems, and Kurtz, it is defeat; in Lingard and Mrs. Travers (*The Rescue*) it is a condition of psychic acedia, the plight of dispossessed middle age "standing alone, at the end of time, on the brink of days." In the hero of *The Shadow-Line* it is the moment of crucial transition from youthful illusion when it is "the privilege" of a man "to live in advance of [his] days in all the beautiful continuity of hope which knows no pauses and no introspection" to the abrupt realization of his isolation as an individual, his conscious and responsible selfhood. What precipitates these states of crisis may vary from the taking of one's first command to the falling upon life of a mortal blow to security or reputation; from the making of an unpremeditated but inescapable mistake (the "necessary error") to the secret or public violation of one's good name.

Once the crisis is defined there are certain conditions necessary to rendering it available to a treatment that opposes dramatic to anti-dramatic effects, action to analysis. They appear in some form in almost all of Conrad's longer tales and novels. The character is likely to be alone in the world. His plight must, however, have public reference or consequences: no man is finally alone. And there must exist in his character and in the world he lives in a recognized and operative principle of honor. It is the principle of honor that binds the private agony of the Conrad hero to the outer world of proofs and values. It brings to the focus and unity of the individual life the ramifications of truth and ethical justice. The idea of honor, operating within the acute confines of a morbid conflict, psychic trance, or trapped sensibility, thus provides the moral and dramatic leverage of Conrad's plots. And what is illuminated widens as the tales succeed one another: the fate of a ship, of a Malay tribe, of an island, of South American politics, of commercial society, of Russia, of Europe, of "international evil" in the modern world itself.

"We have this illusion of being one person for all," says the Father in Pirandello's *Six Characters in Search of an Author*, "of having a personality that is unique in all our acts. But it isn't true. We perceive this when, tragically perhaps, in something we do, we are, as it were, suspended, caught up in the air on a kind of hook. Then we perceive that all of us was not in that act, and that it would be an atrocious injustice to judge us by that action alone, as if all our existence were summed up in that one deed." He is defining the clue and problem in Conrad's characteristic heroes. He defines them further when he says: "Each one of us has within him a world of things, each man of us his own special world. And how can we ever come to an understanding if I put in the words I utter the sense and value of things as I see them, while you who listen to me must inevitably translate them according to the conception of things each one of you has within himself."

What an American student of Donne, James M. Cline, has said of his elaborately rhetorical sermons—that "there is no advance in thought, only a refinement of it, a deepening and gathering intensity of realization; until finally the great period crashes to a close, still reiterating, still sustaining, an incremental movement of passion and of mind"—has its relevance to Conrad's art and the principles it rests on. Once the rationale of his method is seized and its reflection of his personal history is reasonably allowed, the technical devices in his books take on a new significance, as likewise do his defects and mannerisms. The time-shift, the use of narrators, the recurrent motif or incident, the obsessive analysis of events, become instruments of consciousness, modes of sympathy and justice. The recurring incident (Jim's jump from the ship into "the everlasting black hole of his life," Flora's suicidal appearance at the edge of the cliff, Councillor Mikulin's "Where to?" to Razumov) goes beyond the ordinary mechanics of leitmotif by making each of its repetitions serve to mark an expanding realization, an advancing penetration of the event and all the causes and consequences involved in it. What has seemed to be a tied plot, gyrating aimlessly around a static point of crisis or obsession, is actually increasing in content and moral import, taking on a greater increment of value, gaining a wider periphery of meaning, until it comes to include not only the personal fate of the character but the fate of the society, world, or moral universe he inhabits.

The analytical principle has developed rapidly in the fiction of the past century. It produced in the Nineteenth Century the tale of detection, where a shrouded mystery, false appearance, or inscrutable condition of circumstance, baffling to the eye by reason of deception or accident, was methodically uncovered. From the fables of Poe this device advanced toward social analysis and criticism in Dickens, and thus toward the analysis of moral or ethical concepts as we find it in our own time in books like Gide's *Counterfeiters* or

Kafka's *The Trial* where, by methods varying from the dialectic to the legalistic, the successive husks of intention or consciousness are stripped from actions and personal relationships until the primary cell of origin is bared. The method is applied to psychological divination in the later plays of Ibsen, the later novels of James, the ruminative dramas of Robinson, where the exploration of a fixed moral, marital, or illusory relationship is made to reveal the ethical complex of a society. Browning used personal variations on a dramatic idea to dissect a historical situation in *The Ring and the Book*. The device has advanced to the scale of epic analysis and elaboration in the novels of Proust and Joyce.

The method finds a further dimension when, by carrying psychic dissection beyond the point of social or moral analysis, it concerns the conflict of appearance and reality and becomes in its implications metaphysical. It may deal with the relativity of appearances and sentiments as Proust defined it. It may go farther still by relating psychic and moral contradiction to the ambivalence of reality as art embodies or struggles with it, and thus to the metaphysical condition of values itself. When the novel arrives at this degree of complexity it works in dialectic terms and achieves metaphysical status. The *discordia concors* becomes more than psychological or dramatic; it becomes moral. James worked in the consciousness of this possibility in his art. *The Sacred Fount* may be a fable on the theme; *The Wings of the Dove* and *The Golden Bowl* achieve their resonance by what they define of this fundamental ambiguity of moral values. The quality was deliberately induced through speculative analysis by Proust and Pirandello. The condition works in Conrad's greater novels, sympathetically in *Lord Jim*, ironically in *The Secret Agent* and *Under Western Eyes*, in the full dimensions of moral and political dialectic in *Nostromo*.

We are in any case concerned in Conrad with a novelist in whom the devices of arrested action, thematic repetition, and incremental veracity were driven to the limits of their utility. By the analysis thus induced the nature of illusion is probed, the workings of truth are sublimated, the operations of intelligence and conscience are

tested, until finally, out of the deceptions of skepticism and the im-
posture of values which were threats to Conrad's own personal and
artistic security, a basis of moral certitude and actionable human
conviction is arrived at. When Stein in *Lord Jim* advises men to
submit to the "destructive element" and "with the exertions of your
hands and feet in the water make the deep, deep sea keep you up,"
he was not talking about the loss or surrender of personality. He
was talking about the salvation of personality by the test of experience and the necessary recognition of selfhood. What Conrad implies in the scene is the means of redemption allowed to modern
man when he finds himself faced with the necessity of rescuing himself from the willing impersonality, the irresponsibly abstract faiths,
and the moral nihilism to which the world encourages him to surrender himself. "Il n'arrive peut-être pas d'évènements inutiles." If
the Baudelaire he salutes in the epigraph of *The Shadow-Line* reinforced Conrad in any conviction, it was in his belief that it is as
futile as it is impossible for a man to escape his moral destiny, and
that no man can know or save mankind before he has first learned
to know and save himself.

It is only in his greatest novels—those that appeared in the fourteen years between *The Nigger of the "Narcissus"* in 1897 and *Under
Western Eyes* in 1911, with *Victory* and *The Shadow-Line* coming
as final allegories of his central subject—that Conrad achieved a
full and convincing drama for that truth. The pitch at which he
held the opposing claims of idea and reality always threatened and
sometimes betrayed him. It appears in what F. R. Leavis (in *The
Great Tradition*) has called the "adjectival insistence upon inexpres-
sible and incomprehensible mystery," a "thrilled sense of the un-
speakable potentialities of the human soul," which can become
oppressive in even so powerful a tale as "Heart of Darkness." It
shows in the exaggerated emphasis on stoic virtue and moral sympathy that too much betrays the secret of radical stories like "The
Secret Sharer" and *The Shadow-Line*. His treatment of the sea, of
life, of chance, and of woman as inscrutable entities, forces of mystery, cosmic confidence, or enigma, can pall with an insistence that

is a threat to his realism, his sincerity, and his truth. The conflict of pity and honor in *Chance* weakens toward the violence and catharsis of melodrama. In the works that came after 1917—*The Arrow of Gold, The Rescue, The Rover,* the unfinished *Suspense*—both drama and language resort to the fallacy of abstract or atmospheric evocation, with results evident not only in dramatic contrivance but in a radical deterioration of style.

It was doubtless the very intensity of his personal participation in his creation, as well as his laboriously empirical, trial-and-error workmanship, that permitted Conrad to work at full strength over the comparatively short period of two decades. He was denied the sustained power and capacity for renewal that kept James and Yeats active into their seventies. He had entered literature a mature man, at thirty-seven. Fatigue, illness, and the depletion of his intellectual powers account for his decline in his later years, but so must the fact that he had already worked his essential subject to the point of exhaustion and was left with little but echoes and attenuations of it in his final books. In such circumstances he was able to do little more than invoke the nobler ideals that appear in his personal statements and apologies—Sincerity, Honor, Fortitude, Fidelity. These, however they may have served him in his personal faith and ethic, were not the sources of his tragic power, his instinct for moral truth, or his strength in pessimistic realism, the basis of his radical humanism. Yet even when he invoked them as clues to his meaning and intention he could sometimes indicate what they had contributed to his art and moral vision. "Those who read me know my conviction that the world, the temporal world, rests on a few very simple ideas," he said in one of his most-quoted passages of apology: "so simple that they must be as old as the hills. It rests notably, amongst others, on the idea of Fidelity. At a time when nothing which is not revolutionary in some way or other can expect to attract much attention, I have not been revolutionary in my writings. The revolutionary spirit is mighty convenient in this, that it frees one from all scruples as regards ideas. Its hard, absolute optimism is repulsive to my mind by the menace of fanaticism and intolerance it contains. No doubt one should smile at these things; but, imperfect Esthete, I am no better Philosopher. All claim to special righteousness awakens in me that scorn and anger from which a philosophic mind should be free."

Conrad's avowed dislike of Dostoevsky ("I don't know what Dostoevsky stands for or reveals, but I do know that he is too Russian for me. It sounds to me like some fierce mouthings from prehistoric ages") has usually been taken as a symptom of his Polish hostility to Russia or as a refusal to recognize his true father in art (for there is no question that Conrad alone among English novelists shares the Dostoevskian vision and moral drama, rather than those of the Flaubert or Turgenev he professed to admire). It may have another import, one that is perhaps illuminated by the French dramatist Lenormand's report that when once he lent Conrad two books of Freud's, Conrad regarded them "avec une ironic méprisante," took them to his room, and later returned them unopened. ("Ainsi m'était révélée la pudeur de l'artiste devant son oeuvre et la sagesse du créateur qui se résout finalement à ne pas forcer le secret de ses créatures.") The tendency of Dostoevsky toward mystical illuminism seems to have been for Conrad as great a danger to the creative will and integrity as the scientific sublimation of conflict. To such a temperament the ideal of consciousness, as exemplified by James and Mann, was as inimical to creative sincerity as the idea of l'art pour l'art itself. Each threatens the responsibility to which the artist dedicates himself. "All these gods must, after a short period of fellowship, abandon him—even on the very threshold of the temple—to the stammerings of his conscience and to the outspoken consciousness of the difficulties of his work." That consciousness is enough, and it is inescapable. It is the only one that can bring art and life into vital apposition, the single way of knowledge that permits no exemption from experience or endurance. The retreat of the moral conscience into science or into the mystic's refuge of vision is as great a presumption on the laws of the moral nature as it is on the demands of art.

When Thomas Mann introduced Conrad to German readers in a preface to *The Secret Agent,* he noted "the refusal of a very much engaged intelligence to hang miserably in the air between contraries." Something stronger than division worked in him: "a passion for freedom" which knew what freedom cost its defender. Once it was possible to look for literary masters in men who had the security of a stable tradition behind them. Today, with that stability broken and the human condition in crisis, we are more likely to look for masters in artists who are put to the test of recovering courage and moral authority in their own persons. The hero in modern fiction may be the man marked by apartness and alienation, but it is he who must serve as a focus of worth and honor when the world forgets what these mean.

Here Conrad's position in modern fiction, as well as in the crisis of his age, becomes clear. Though he still figures in some accounts as a kind of aesthetic and moral impressionist, the arrested moment, the test of isolation, was "only the beginning of the task." To suspend existence in sensation or abstract idealism spelled for him the threat of moral impotence and nihilism. He knew what these evils meant because they haunted him in his own life and personality; and he made his art the battleground of his resistance to them. For in his finest work Conrad exonerates the tormenting ambivalence of his temperament and moral distractions through a powerful and dynamic drama of forces: of sensibility against action, of analysis against plot, of the isolated soul with its illusions and obsessions against the demands of human sympathy and sacrifice. The anarchy of personality becomes controlled by the law of life. It is in this suspense and tension of forces that Conrad's essential art lies. He found a dramatic equivalent for the law that operates in both psyche and society. For him the greatest drama of which man is capable comes when the soul is compelled out of vanity or isolation into the whole organism of human experience: into that moral organism and coherence of humanity—"solidarity" was his word for it—which must be the novel's supreme theme and subject. It may appear naïve today, now that we have made all the necessary critical detractions of faults, excesses, and weakening powers from his achievement, to call Conrad what Mencken called him forty years ago, the "Beethoven of the English novel," but this much of J. W. N. Sullivan's characterization of Beethoven has its bearing on Conrad's quality: that he conveys the sense of "a man who experienced all that we can experience, who suffered all that we can suffer"; and "if, in the end, he seems to reach a state 'above the battle' we also know that no man ever knew more bitterly what the battle is." [5] A recent English estimate—Douglas Hewitt's in his short study called *Conrad: A Reassessment* in 1952—is closer to the language of modern critical discrimination. "The hero" in Conrad "is a hero, not because of any personal qualities which place him above other men, but because he is a *typical* figure in a central and responsible situation, so that he may be said to crystallize the problems of good and evil into precise and significant situations. In his fate is worked out the implications of the moral and spiritual order"; and "a consideration of the protagonists' plight, judged within the framework of values enforced by Conrad's 'unconventional groupings and perspective,' compels us to see inexorable laws which make for a progressively clearer sight of an evil or negative basis to human emotions or ideals and for physical and moral disaster. In the complexity and unity of this vision and in the integrity of its presentation his best works stand well-nigh alone among English novels and there are very few which, beside them, do not look superficial."

T. S. Eliot once grouped Conrad's work with that of Joyce in speaking of a language that is important to us because it "is struggling to digest and express new objects, new groups of objects, new feelings, new aspects" of experience. Conrad's importance in

-----

[5] Compare what Bertrand Russell says in his *Portraits from Memory* (1956) of his first meeting with Conrad: "We seemed to sink through layer after layer of what was superficial, till gradually both reached the central fire. It was an experience unlike any other that I have known. We looked into each other's eyes, half appalled and half intoxicated to find ourselves in such a region. The emotion was as intense as passionate love, and at the same time all-embracing. I came away bewildered, and hardly able to find my way among ordinary affairs."

modern fiction derives largely from that struggle. It gave his words, as they advanced out of their earlier opulence and before they declined into his later evasions, their keenness in specification, their firmness in realism and aphorism. Though his words like his plots fell short of the conscious control and powers of James's, at their best they breathe with immediacy, strike with a physical impact. His mastery of sensibility was coeval with the personal and structural maturity his themes required. He had no choice in the matter. What he had to say was indissociable from his way of learning to say it. The conventional division of form and content could not exist for him. Words and form themselves—and in no arbitrary aesthetic sense—made him the artist and the man he became.

The man who suffers and the mind which creates may be, ideally, separate, but once their ordeal is joined, they merge once more. The mind has created more than a book. It has created the man who wrote the book, in the only sense in which we can genuinely know him. It is not the Conrad who left Poland, sailed seas, saw strange men and places, who finally concerns us. It is the man who used those experiences as an artist, and who re-created himself in his mastery of them. When Conrad takes us on occasion into what Forster calls "the severe little apartment that must, for want of a better word, be called his confidence," and from which he can so curtly dismiss us, he is virtually a stranger, and what he says in his defensive or ceremonious way may have little practical bearing on the tragic truth his books embody. But when he comes to us as Wait, Singleton, Jim, Decoud or Nostromo, Razumov or Heyst, we know him as a man who has escaped the confines of his single person and perpetuated his mind and emotion in the human spirit.

On none of his truest work can the judgment be passed that it "isn't written." (His minor stories and sketches in *Tales of Unrest*, *A Set of Six*, and *Within the Tides* dissociate themselves, by their "romance," sentimentalism, or lip-service to popular standards, as emphatically from the three narratives of the *Youth* volume or "Amy Foster," "Falk," "The Secret Sharer," and *The Shadow-Line*, as his last four novels stand below the novels of his maturity.) Conrad's greater pages are so deeply scored, so passionately inscribed, that he can become for us a classic instance of the reality, complete, wholly absorbed, all-consuming, of the life in art. Few writers take us so forcibly into the agony of the creative act as he does, or illustrate so explicitly what the artist's quarrel with himself and his destiny can give to literature. He tried to be other things but his fate claimed him. None of the events of his career finally proved useless. He pushed the stone, dragged "the ball and chain of one's selfhood to the end." The task was less exhilarating than brutal, but its fascination compelled him none the less. It made him a stranger to his family and friends for months on end. The black fit beset him; disgust and desperation shattered him. But he knew in his deepest need that only one liberty was permitted him—the liberation that would come when the page was written, the book finished, the story told. Few novelists have known harsher conditions in their art and few a more eloquent result. It enabled him to become, like the man he once saw in the East—"appealing—significant—under a cloud" —permanently and securely "one of us."

1940–42   [1956]

E. M. Forster

THE TROPHIES OF THE MIND *

E. M. Forster lends himself no more easily to superficial recognition today than he did half a century ago when his first novel
was published. His books came into their first general popularity
early in the 1940s, when the war spurred the anxious recovery of so
much writing which suddenly appeared to defend a threatened
tradition or to embody the civilized values that war endangers. During the past fifteen years they have been read, reprinted, and discussed on a scale which no one, least of all perhaps their author,
would have had the daring to prophesy in the days of their first appearance. They have become firmly established as Twentieth Century classics. Yet even now Forster offers few of the appeals that
qualify a novelist for urgent "importance" or timely respect: no dogmatic beliefs in politics or religion, no radical stylistic novelty or
aesthetic oddity, no yearly appeal to his public with a new book.
For an author generally described, with admissible justice, as "the
most distinguished living English novelist," he suggests few tags of
easy distinction; perhaps only one—that he has practiced the difficult strategy of writing little but making it count for much; of keep-

----

* This essay, incorporating material from a series of writings on Forster over
the past twenty years, was written for the Buenos Aires magazine *Sur* in 1955,
as an "introduction" to Forster's work and a projected Spanish translation of his
novels by Editorial Sur.

ing his readers unsatisfied and asking for more. It is now more than thirty years since he published a novel, yet if he were to publish one tomorrow no book—certainly in the English-speaking world—would be more eagerly or expectantly read.

This attraction has been strong in his work from its beginnings. He published his first novel in 1905, his fourth in 1910 when he was just over thirty, his fifth and latest in 1924. To these he has on occasion added two collections of tales, three of essays and criticism, a life of Lowes Dickinson, a guide and book of studies on Alexandria, by-products of service in Egypt during the First World War, a chronicle (*The Hill of Devi*) of his two sojourns in Dewas State Senior in India, and a "domestic biography" of his great-aunt Marianne Thornton and her remarkable English family. He has contributed for almost six decades to the English liberal reviews and he has written a sizeable number of broadcasts for the BBC. None of his fictions came announced by the fanfares of innovation or technical experiment. If popularly read, as two of them were, they could be taken as witty and topical comedies in late-Victorian line of Meredith, brisk in language and insight, agreeably diverting in romantic interest. They showed plots of lithe and shapely movement, as insinuating in their darting charm as Jane Austen's, barbed with wit and comment, populated by characters who had the art of springing into quick and recognizable life with their first speeches. Whatever dissent, perplexity, or irritation they might arouse to tease the mind, they did little to disturb the literary conventions. Yet as time has gone on, these books have persisted and cut deeper into the memory and consciousness of the age. Of the new English novelists who made their mark between Hardy's retirement from fiction in 1895 and the war of 1914, Forster is the only one, except for Conrad and Lawrence, who survives as an intimate force among the younger talents of the present day. His books deal with events and circumstances which have now receded to historic distance, yet in effect, style, and meaning they seem as dateless as any novels of the century. His energy has issued from a firm center of moral and intellectual realism. If one were to define the ancestry of Auden's generation, Forster's name—whatever the claims of James, Conrad, Lawrence, or Eliot—would suggest the most accurate combination of critical and temperamental forces, the one most clearly stamped by the peculiarly English skeptical sensibility and moral passion that has survived two wars with sanity and made possible the reassessment of the tradition and delusion that made those wars and their consequences possible in the Twentieth Century. Today as much as thirty years ago, his special position is contested by no other talent. It is still useful to go back to his beginnings to see what qualities and temperament he brought into modern English fiction, and by what means he impressed these on the intelligence of his time.

In 1905 there appeared quietly in England a short novel by a new writer. It was called *Where Angels Fear to Tread;* its author was then twenty-six years old and had thus far published only a few stories in magazines of small circulation. It carried none of the marks that indicate a bold or unusual originality. The qualities of the masters then dominating the scene in England—the tragic vision of Hardy, the intellectual comedy of Meredith, the complex moral analysis and stylistic density of Henry James—were none of them obviously present in the deceptively modest tale. Nor was it a piece of solid social documentation in the vein of the younger naturalists and social radicals then rising to prominence—Bennett, Wells, Galsworthy, Beresford. The book was brief, lucid, apparently spontaneous and effortless in manner. It told the story of an international marriage, but it was cut along lines markedly different from the established "international theme" as it had for thirty years operated so intricately in the novels and tales of Henry James. Here the reader met, at the outset, a situation making for charming comedy and an absurd collision between cultures—middle-class English folk among the scenes and shrines of Italy.

He found himself first in the midst of the discreet and sheltered life of upper middle-class England, and among a family of the name of Herriton, who live a genteel suburban life in a London suburb called Sawston. This family—the widowed mother, a strong-minded dowager, Mrs. Herriton; her obtusely dogmatic, obstinately provincial spinster daughter, Harriet; her humorously sensitive, sanely intelligent younger son, Philip—find themselves burdened with an embarrassment in the form of a daughter-in-law, Lilia Herriton, the country wife, but now the widow, of an older son of the family who has died. Poor Lilia is vulgar. She has never become subdued to the well-behaved proprieties of Sawston and the Herriton family. She cannot be trusted to raise her fatherless young daughter according to the laws of the clan and its caste. Something must be done about her. And she herself, chafing in the bondage of her disapproving relatives, also yearns for an escape. Perhaps travel will help her. Perhaps Italy will civilize her. The Herritons hold a family council. Philip, who loves Italy as much as his fanatical Low Church sister Harriet hates it, urges that Lilia be given a year in that culturally enriching country as a means of curing her vulgarity and bringing her a little closer to the Sawston and Herriton standard. So off she goes, accompanied by an old friend of the family, Caroline Abbott, to become acquainted with Florence and the Uffizi, with Giotto and the Renaissance, and the land that Dante, Michelangelo, Petrarch, and such-like standard-bearers of respectable culture made great and famous.

The journey prospers. Lilia's and Caroline's letters to the family in Sawston are full of reassurances. Italy is being imbibed in great deep draughts. The paintings, the palaces, the cathedrals, the schools of art, the moral guidance of Ruskin, are all being studied with attentive docility by the two traveling ladies; and when news comes that they have at last left the beaten path and English-catering *pensions* of the larger cities and ventured to visit the smaller towns in the hills and valleys around Florence, Philip, whose last word had been advice along precisely such lines, is jubilant. Lilia is learning. She may become a fit member of the Herriton family after all.

But one day a letter comes that abruptly shatters these high hopes. It is from Miss Abbott, and what she has to confess is appalling. Lilia has fallen in love, in a little hill-town called Monteriano—fallen in love, moreover, with an Italian. The Herritons are thunderstruck. Such a calamity had never figured in their most desperate calculations concerning Lilia. The letter says that Lilia's fiancé is a member of the nobility—but what can that possibly mean? Philip, whose youthful pilgrimages to Italy had been the great romances of his life, suddenly finds himself commandeered by his masterful mother, equipped with money, and sent off on a raw, rainy spring night, out of England, across the Channel, across Europe, to hunt up his derelict sister-in-law and determine how far she has gone in disgracing her relatives.

He arrives in Italy at the height of the southern spring. The country is flooded with the purple of violets. The bursting landscape is rich with colors. And in a ramshackle hotel in the ancient Tuscan hill-town of Monteriano he corners Caroline Abbott and demands to know the worst. The worst is soon told. Lilia is indeed in love. What is more, she is engaged. Her fiancé, alas, is no member of the nobility. That lie was a desperate ruse on Caroline's part to ward off the wrath of the Herritons. His name is Gino Carella. He is twelve years younger than Lilia. And far from being noble, he is not even genteel. He is the son of a dentist.

> Philip gave a cry of personal disgust and pain. He shuddered all over . . . A dentist! A dentist at Monteriano! . . . False teeth and laughing gas and the tilting chair at a place which knew the Etruscan League and the Pax Romana and Alaric himself, and the Countess Matilda, and the Middle Ages, all fighting and holiness, and the Renaissance, all fighting and beauty! He thought of Lilia no longer. He was anxious for himself: he feared that Romance might die.

He who "for three years had sung the praises of Italians, but had never contemplated having one as a relative," instantly reverts from whatever love he once professed for Italy to the law of his kind. He accuses Caroline Abbott of treachery—treachery to himself, to his mother, to Sawston, to England, above all to the sacred honor and solid body of middle-class respectability. Caroline must decide. She is either with the Herritons or she is against them. She must help Philip rescue Lilia from this appalling situation or be their friend no longer.

Caroline too belongs to Sawston. She surrenders. She, like Philip, realizes that there is a difference between loving Italy as a work of art and capitulating to the greasy charms of the son of a provincial Italian dentist. So the two belligerents go off to confront Lilia and her lover. But then comes the greatest shock of all. Lilia and Gino are not merely engaged. They are already married! Philip, cut to the quick of his inherited instincts and summoning up all the rage he can muster, denounces and disowns his vagrant sister-in-law, brings the hapless Caroline to heel, and takes the next train out of Italy and back to England, to face his embattled mother and enraged sister. He is unaware that something momentous has happened to him. In that moment of defeat and absurd humiliation when he faced the laughter of the married pair, he had unconsciously achieved the first step in his spiritual education.

But the story is not yet over. A year or so later, letters begin to arrive in Sawston from Italy. Their news is disturbing, even to the Herritons who have been living in the assumption that Lilia is permanently disowned by them. She is unhappy. Then she is to have a child. And then she has died in giving the child birth. The Herritons suddenly find themselves facing a new problem. The child must be saved—saved from Gino, from evil, from corruption and impropriety and vulgarity, from damnation itself (for after all, it has never been baptized in the Church of England). It must be reclaimed for the Herriton way of life. So once more the rescuers go off to Italy—this time Philip accompanied by his sister Harriet, of whom we are told that "she was curiously virulent about Italy, which she had never visited, her only experience of the Continent being an occasional six weeks in the Protestant parts of Switzerland." Lilia had come to grief and death through her own fault. She had not been able to see that the glamour of Gino was only a passing summons to her flesh and that Italy would bring her to ruin. But her child remains, and England must reclaim it.

The rescue party arrive in Monteriano and begin their campaign. But they have not correctly estimated their adversary, Gino. Gino is indeed lazy, good-for-nothing, boastful, lustful, conceited. He has

lost his wife but he has gained what he really wanted. He has become "the father of a man like himself, and it held him with a grip
he only partially understood, for it was the first great desire, the
first great passion of his life. Falling in love was a mere physical
triviality, like warm sun or cool water, beside this divine hope of
immortality: 'I continue.'"

Caroline Abbott's conscience has been stricken too. She knows
that, on that earlier trip, it was really she who, secretly hating the
smugness, intolerance, and airless respectability of Sawston, had
encouraged Lilia to welcome the advances of Gino and literally
thrown her into his arms. Now she is filled with remorse. She feels
that she was the cause of Lilia's unhappiness and death. The child
must be brought to England and properly reared. She too has gone
back to Monteriano and joins forces with the rescuers.

But then again something happens to the rescuers—to Philip and
Caroline, since Harriet is adamant and unconvertible in her hatred
of Italy and everything it stands for. The beautiful country surrounds them. The full, abundant, vulgar life of it engulfs them.
While preparing their campaign, they go one night to the opera.
The uproarious passions and luscious melodies of *Lucia di Lam-
mermoor* sweep them off their moorings. They encounter Gino
there. He embraces Philip like a brother, and Philip's defenses begin
to crack. And the next day, in Gino's untidy house, they find him
with his child, giving it a bath, fondling its crowing flesh, exulting
in his fatherhood, preening himself in the pride of his sexual achievement:

> It was in a shocking mess. Food, bedclothes, patent-leather boots,
> dirty plates and knives lay strewn over a large table and on the floor.
> But it was the mess that comes of life, not of desolation. It was
> preferable to the charnel-chamber . . . and the light in it was soft
> and large, as from some gracious, noble opening.

Gino brushes aside Philip's absurd offer to take the baby away
from him—buy it from him if necessary; and both Philip and Caroline know that they are defeated by Gino's primitive love for his
child. But Harriet recognizes no such defeat. Inflamed by the grim

spirit of her Low Church religion, and seeing that her two accom-
plices will betray her, she plots alone. She goes secretly to Gino's
house on the night when the English party plan to leave. She steals
the baby, and with the sleeping child in her arms she catches at the
last moment the coach that is to drive them down the valley to the
train. It is dark; a storm rises; the coach lurches and overturns; the
baby is killed. Philip, his arm broken in the accident, must go back
to Monteriano to break the news to Gino. "And now," as Lionel
Trilling says in his book on Forster, "occurs the scene of horror which
matches and balances the scene of joy at the opera. It is the crucial
scene in the book. . . . Gino receives the news in terrible silence,
then hurls the lamp out of the window, and in the darkened room
obscenely stalks Philip. When he catches him, he methodically tor-
tures his broken arm and then carefully and slowly begins to choke
him to death." Only the entrance of Caroline Abbott, suddenly em-
powered by a strength she never knew she possessed, saves Philip
and converts Gino's hatred into broken-hearted despair. For Gino's
kind of hatred and violence, unlike the hatred and cruelty of Mrs.
Herriton and Harriet, can learn to break and surrender, and so to
love. "Gino may become temporarily a devil because he is a man;
but Harriet is permanently a devil because she is not really a
woman. . . . Gino's deviltry is the result of passion, not of principle and will, and it passes."

So the three ambassadors leave Italy and go back to England,
leaving ruin and death in their wake. But because two of them know
they have been defeated by something greater than themselves, they
have won a glimpse of salvation, a gleam of illumination. Philip,
who was too proud of his intelligence to realize that he was also a
man, becomes a man for a moment, even if he will never become
a complete one. The mark of his family and of Sawston is too in-
delibly stamped upon him. In the train that carries them over the
Alps, back to the North from the South, he tries to propose marriage
to Caroline. He knows how little he has to offer her. I know at last,
he had said, that "some people are born not to do things. I'm one
of them. . . . I don't die—I don't fall in love. And if other people

die or fall in love, they always do it when I'm just not there. You are quite right; life to me is just a spectacle, which—thank God, and thank Italy, and thank you—is now more beautiful and heartening than it has ever been before." Caroline answers him solemnly: "I wish something would happen to you, my dear friend; I wish something would happen to you." Gently she refuses to marry him. She likes him but she knows that he is, and will remain, an uncommitted man. What she really loves is Gino—loves him grossly, sexually, physically—loves him "because he's handsome." "I mean it crudely," she says. "Get over supposing I'm refined. That's what puzzles you. Get over that." She will go back to dull, correct, safe and proper Sawston, to a life just barely endurable but one she has at last learned to endure. Both she and Philip will live condemned to that life, but it will never quite defeat or imprison them again, for they have learned the truth about it. The novel ends with their train climbing northward over the Alps, carrying them to a life which their newly discovered knowledge has relieved of the implacability of a doom, freed by what they have learned about themselves from complacency and fear. They will live there presumably until they die. But they will live in a manner saved.

This first novel of Forster's established the subject and direction of all his future work. That direction had already been indicated in several short tales he had written soon after his university years at Cambridge, and a number of others were presently to amplify it— his two collections of stories, *The Celestial Omnibus* in 1911 and *The Eternal Moment* in 1928, were assembled in his book of *Collected Short Stories* (1947). It was to arrive at fuller expression in the three novels that now followed in quick succession—*The Longest Journey* in 1907, *A Room with a View* in 1908, *Howards End* in 1910. His theme was finally to arrive at its richest embodiment fourteen years later, in *A Passage to India* of 1924. The titles of these books are themselves indicative of a continuous and unifying preoccupation. All of them are tales which venture out of the solid framework of English social and moral convention, out of the received values and established securities of a complacent tradition, into regions "where angels fear to tread." Their heroes or heroines are people who, by some instinct or compulsion, are impelled to take the way of Shelley and so leave

> the code
> Of modern morals, and the beaten road
> Which those poor slaves with weary footsteps tread,
> Who travel to their home among the dead
> By the broad highway of the world, and so
> With one chained friend, perhaps a jealous foe,
> The dreariest and the longest journey go.

They are people who live in rooms, but the rooms may have a view which they may learn to look at. Sometimes they are men or women who, by some grace of vision, are permitted a sight of that farther goal of the human spirit which lies beyond the rational and aggressive principles of western life, its logic and moral fixities, in the realm of spiritual fulfillment and self-surrender which lies in the South or in the East—and to attain which the western soul must embark upon what Walt Whitman, who gave Forster the title for his fifth novel, called a "passage to India." In pursuing this theme, Forster anticipated a fundamental impulse in the fiction of the Twentieth Century—the fiction of, among others, Virginia Woolf and D. H. Lawrence.

A *Room with a View* was another comedy of English travelers in the old pre-1914 Italy. Here it is a young girl, Lucy Honeychurch, who faces marriage with an aesthetic prig and model of educated self-righteousness, Cecil Vyse, only to be rescued by the spell of Italy for true love and marriage with the honest young outsider, George Emerson. The world to which Lucy belongs is cracked and shaken by her rebellion against its code, but once she rebels, nothing can ever again reclaim her to the sin of denying her spirit and her emotions. In *The Longest Journey* we have another kind of conflict, which this time leads to tragedy. Here the hero is Rickie Elliott, the orphan son of a despicably civilized, bigotedly selfish father, and of a mother whose greatness of nature was enslaved to her husband's hatred and self-conceit. Rickie too is caught in a world of genteel discretion, of masked lives and stultified spirit. But he has gone to college at Cambridge, and Cambridge has nursed and consoled him, told him that life can be beautiful if dedicated to intelligence, spirit, and friendship. Yet once he leaves Cambridge, the forces of fear and duplicity reclaim him. He finds himself trapped in a loveless and barren marriage by a selfish woman, Agnes Pembroke, an old family friend. He slowly becomes part of that world. He allows his brother-in-law, Herbert Pembroke, to convert him into a schoolmaster at Sawston School, which is an incarnation of the denials and vices of the Sawston world. So, with his one chained friend, who is really his jealous foe—his wife Agnes—Rickie is bound over to the life of falsehood. But forces outside that life protest. Though Rickie himself has surrendered and sunk into moral apathy, there erupts into his prison of self-treachery an unconquerable man of nature, Stephen Wonham, who proves to be his own half-brother, a love-child of his mother by the honest farmer who tried to rescue her from her cruel marriage to Rickie's father. Stephen, seeing the dishonor and falsehood that have submerged his brother, strikes out at the forces of evil—at Rickie's wife and her brother, even at Rickie himself; and he brings their plans to ruin, with Rickie at last killed, a victim of his sin against himself. The Pembrokes survive and prosper, it is true. Their kind always does. But Stephen also survives and is the only victor in the end.

In *Howards End,* which came in 1910, the stage is larger. We are in London, the busy, prosperous London before 1914, and in the home of two brilliant sisters, Margaret and Helen Schlegel. Their mother was English but their father was a German professor, a philosopher of the old idealistic German lineage, so despite their well-furnished lives of privilege and comfort, the sisters are not quite "English to the backbone." They are modern, advanced, liberal, intelligent, lovers of music and art, busy students of social and political ideas. Inadvertently they admit into their lives two hostile forces: on the one side, the rich, pushing, prosperous family of the Wilcoxes, epitomes of everything that spells efficiency, success, and power in modern life; and on the other side, a young, seedy, feeble fellow of the London underworld that just barely belongs to respectable society—a pallid insurance clerk called Leonard Bast, whom they have made acquaintance with at a concert when Helen Schlegel accidentally walked away with his umbrella. Leonard is married to a slovenly, slatternly, brainless woman of empty beauty. He has his feeble vision of the larger life of beauty and success, but it is only a glimpse, for the abyss of meanness and poverty is sucking him down. He becomes for the brilliant Schlegel sisters a pawn in their game of wits and intelligence. They will "do something for him." They will pit him and his misery against the coarse mastery of the Wilcox clan, and demand that justice be done. But the sisters soon find that they cannot play this game without themselves becoming involved in it. Margaret finds herself proposed to by the rich widower, Mr. Wilcox, whose first wife has suddenly died. She finds something in her womanhood that responds to this powerful, aggressive masculinity, and she accepts him. But her sister Helen sees this as treachery to their ideals, a betrayal of their standards. It is the Mr. Wilcoxes who have damned the Leonard Basts to mediocrity and despair; and when Helen finds that she must choose sides, it is Leonard that she chooses. In that choice the Schlegels and the Wilcoxes—the forces of intelligence and the forces of power —become tragically involved. The collision is fatal. Before it ends, Leonard goes down to his death, Helen becomes a social outcast, and the Wilcoxes themselves are broken, their pride humiliated, their ruthless ethic blown apart and their secret weakness betrayed.

It was fourteen years before Forster produced *A Passage to India,* but when it came, it carried the problem that had taxed him in Cambridge, in Italy, and in London into a deeper and more complex world than any of these—to India and the East, which had always fascinated him and where, by this time, he had made two long sojourns. Here the scene is Chandrapore, a small city on the upper Ganges, tense with antagonisms of class and race. The life of the town is divided between the swarming native populace and the small circle of English officials who form the local outpost of Empire. This is the India already made familiar to English readers in

the tales of Kipling, but it no longer has the attributes of romance
and reckless adventure of Kipling's military and war-stirred im-
perial scene. The age of conquest and bravado is past. So too is
Kipling's world of aggressive, vulgar action, though not his suggestion of uneasy conscience and morbid hauntings—even if Forster's
treatment of these is miles removed from Kipling's style and drama.
We are now in the early Twentieth Century. Imperialism has become a thing of hardened routine and of guilty uneasiness. The
townsfolk of Chandrapore, part though they are of the teeming sea
of Indian life, are dominated by Oxford or Cambridge-trained na-
tives whose inherited loyalties are mixed with the enlightened yet
defensive sensibility bred by their western contacts.

Into this restless situation come two visitors from England—Adela
Quested, who has come out to India to get re-acquainted with one
of the local officials, Ronny Heaslop, with a view to marrying him;
and Mrs. Moore, Ronny's mother, who accompanies Adela as
chaperon. The two ladies are products again of well-bred English
gentility, but they exasperate the English colony, smugly locked in
its code of club life and official superiority, by their earnest desire
to see "the real India." Adela is serious, sober, plain-natured, ear-
nestly dull, but Mrs. Moore is something more. Mrs. Moore is a
character who appears sooner or later in every Forster novel. She
is anticipated by Caroline Abbott in *Where Angels Fear to Tread;*
by Charlotte Bartlett, Lucy Honeychurch's family friend and chaperon in Italy, in *A Room with a View;* by Rickie Elliott's mother in
The Longest Journey; by the first Mrs. Wilcox in *Howards End.*
Mrs. Moore also belongs to the English moral tradition, to middle-
class life with its guarded, self-protective mores, to the orbit of
discreet and defensive ethic which makes her class and nation
strong; but she is also gifted—or perhaps damned—by having a
secret and inner life of her own, a spirit that protests the complacent
confines of her kind and that rebels against the closed mind of a
dominant world, the hardened mentality of privilege, the smugness,
cant, and intolerance that are bred by power and authority.

These two ladies make contact with two members of the Chandrapore community who are regarded with distrust by the English officials. One is Mr. Fielding, the principal of the Government College, an Englishman but a disillusioned one: a man of middle age and rough experience whose imagination has penetrated the Indian world and made friends there, and who has become a standing threat to the local English solidarity. The other is the Indian physician, Dr. Aziz, educated in England, a small, wiry, witty, half-absurd man, partly a poet, partly a careerist, a widower with three small children, desperately anxious to ingratiate himself with his English superiors, yet nervously defensive of his own intelligence too, and of his race and his loyalties to it. Adela gropes toward the friendship of Aziz and Fielding with a liberal, well-disposed woman's eager decency. But Mrs. Moore has no need to grope or yearn. Old age has dissolved her ambitions and illusions. Like Mrs. Wilcox in *Howards End*, she knows herself to be approaching the mystery of death. The vast inchoate mystery of India around her is something both to fear and to love: something that means death's horror but also its rewarding release. She has responded instantly to the charms of Dr. Aziz and has become his friend. So it comes about that Aziz, always eager to make alliance with the English, arranges a picnic excursion to the Marabar caves in the mountains that lie across the hot plain beyond Chandrapore. These caves have dominated the landscape from the first page of the novel. Now they become the scene of crisis. Adela is anxious to see the caves out of her alert tourist's curiosity. Mrs. Moore the caves attract but they also repel. They are entrances to the kingdom of death that makes all things alike—life and death, good and evil—and their famous echo spells for her the dissolution of the life and faith she was bred to back in England:

> . . . the echo began in some indescribable way to undermine her hold on life. . . . it had managed to murmur: "Pathos, piety, courage—they exist, but are identical, and so is filth. Everything exists, nothing has value." If one had spoken vileness in that place, or quoted lofty poetry, the comment would have been the same—"ou-boum." If one had spoken with the tongues of angels and pleaded for all the unhappiness and misunderstanding of the world, past, present, and

to come, for all the misery men must undergo whatever their opinion
and position, and however much they dodge or bluff—it would
amount to the same. . . . Devils are of the North, and poems can
be written about them, but no one could romanticize the Marabar
because it robbed infinity and eternity of their vastness, the only
quality that accommodates them to mankind. . . . But suddenly at
the edge of her mind, Religion reappeared, poor little talkative
Christianity, and she knew that all its divine words from "Let there
be Light" to "It is finished" only amounted to "boum."

So the fatal picnic party stands at the edge of the Indian mystery.
And then at last the long-drawn tension and secret hostilities of
Chandrapore snap. Abandoning Mrs. Moore to her fatigue and
exhaustion, Adela and Dr. Aziz visit the caves. Something happens
there—we never learn exactly what—but Adela, her moral and
sexual defenses breached by the strange influences working on her
that day, believes she has been assaulted by Dr. Aziz and that he
has attempted to rape her. She rushes out; she makes her way back
to Chandrapore; the news spreads like wild-fire. Aziz is jailed. Every
Englishman believes him guilty except Fielding and Mrs. Moore.
His trial is set, and its verdict of guilty is assured. Fielding is ostra-
cized by his compatriots for asserting his belief in Aziz's innocence,
and Mrs. Moore, since she cannot be trusted to run with her pack,
is shipped by her son to England only to die en route and be buried
at sea in the tropic depths of the Indian Ocean. Then, at the trial,
with the populace of Chandrapore seething with fury and the
English colony desperately beleaguered but triumphant in the justice of their cause, the long arm of uncertainty once more reaches
out and flaws the defenses of the West. Adela, at her nerve's edge
in the witness-box, is suddenly touched by something akin to Mrs.
Moore's lucidity and intuition. Her conviction deserts her. She
recants her accusation. With the court and city at their highest
pitch of suspense, the whole case collapses. Aziz is exonerated. The
town bursts into frenzy and triumph for the Indians. Adela is
spurned and cast out by her tribe.

Some years later, Fielding, who has left India to return to England, comes back, now married to Mrs. Moore's daughter Stella. He

finds his old friend Aziz living far up-country with his children, a medical officer in a remote Moslem state. The old scars have healed, but they can still throb with remembered pains and unsettled racial scores. Aziz has reverted to his Moslem kind. England nearly ruined his life. He has never forgiven her. But the friends—Aziz and Fielding—know themselves to be brothers beyond any division of race or breed. Yet can they really live as brothers, forget the worlds that divide them, and unite in brotherhood and love? Never, cries Aziz, until "we shall drive every blasted Englishman into the sea." Then, and only then, shall "you and I be friends." "Why can't we be friends now?" asks Fielding. "It's what I want. It's what you want."

> But the horses didn't want it—they swerved apart; the earth didn't want it, sending up rocks through which riders must pass single file; the temples, the tank, the jail, the palace, the birds, the carrion, the Guest House, that came into view as they issued from the gap and saw Mau beneath: they didn't want it, they said in their hundred voices, "No, not yet," and the sky said, "No, not there."

In this book, so masterfully shaped, so keenly written, so symbolically suggestive, so nearly miraculous in condensing the huge dimensions of its theme and drama to concise terms, Forster has carried the riddle of human relations and society to its farthest boundary. Here he has driven the tragic evil of human division, of alienation, of hostilities and barriers—man against man, race against race, sex against sex, culture against culture—to its most complex and baffling condition. (England has now withdrawn and restored self-rule to India, but the problem of human and racial alienation remains as basic as it was before 1947. The political situation is only an external aspect of the deep-seated moral situation which is Forster's real concern. *A Passage to India* remains as much of a classic as ever to its Indian readers, as it does to English readers. Even those who challenge the accuracy of Forster's details or historical acumen—like, for instance, Nirad C. Chaudhuri in his article "Passage to and from India" in the June 1954 issue of the London magazine *Encounter*—miss the point, for Forster was writing about something incidental to India but actually applicable to the larger world of human and moral relations in our time.) Here, going beyond his earlier conflicts of England against Italy, of civilized life against the claims of nature, of North against South, of intelligence against instinct, of the business morality of the Wilcoxes against the spiritual morality of the Schlegels, of Cambridge against Sawston, he has placed his characters in a profounder element than he ever fathomed before. It is the element of India, in which the rationality of western man encounters the spiritual mystery and absolutes of the East; but it is also the essential element or realm of the spirit, the final court of human instinct and aspiration. And the argument he poses is the argument, so riddling and elusive, which he proposed at the beginning of his career. It is an argument for integration: a plea for mankind to save itself from defeat or disaster by surmounting its denials of spirit, its refusals of natural instinct, in order to arrive at the wholeness of life and spirit which must always be the final and hardest goal of all endeavor—a goal tragically obscured by the selfish delusions and treacheries that seem to be inevitable in so much of what is called civilized life.

Forster's character was initially fixed by pre-1914 Cambridge, the university pictured in *The Longest Journey* as a saving refuge of spirit, of detachment and humanism, a lonely defender of the article of faith that he was to profess throughout the dislocations and betrayals he has witnessed in his lifetime: "To see life steadily and to see it whole." The weary evangelism of Matthew Arnold's phrase may not do justice to the wit and acuteness of Forster's temperament, but no better label for his particular dedication of spirit in a confusing century can be named. And its accent reminds us also of the other source of his idealism—the humanism of Greece. To these sources of stability he soon added fertilizing enthusiasms: for Italy and the Mediterranean, that "exquisite lake" which he calls "the human norm"; for Dante, whom he resisted intellectually only to find him one of modern man's severest spiritual guides, the great master of the truth that the Lost Way may be found again; for Egypt and Asia Minor with their lessons in decadence; and finally for India, with its image of man's supreme division between matter and essence, mortality and spirit. These influences tested and enriched a nature that was diffident and bifocal, conditioned on one side by the cant and intolerance of middle-class "culture," with its fear of feeling and its muddled energies, and on the other side by a critical attraction toward the mystic impulse in human nature, the vital health of the South or the metaphysical absolutes of the East. Out of that opposition was bred Forster's strongest asset. It has given him first his liberal skepticism, morally uncompromising and rigorous, with its dialectic of refusing to simplify opposites by dogma or mandate, whether studied in men, in nations, or in books. What plays everywhere in Forster's work is what plays in another form in the only contemporary writing with which it closely compares—the work of André Gide. It is a restless disquiet of moral sensibility, a continuous empiricism of sympathy and sincerity—the impulse, *ondoyant et divers*, of the skepticism of Socrates and Montaigne, which takes as its duty the quickening to consciousness of moral values and necessities which are eternally betrayed to the intolerance or brutality of prejudice and force.

Gide's idea of the novel is also Forster's: it is "a crossroads—a meeting-place of problems." And so is another article of the Frenchman's faith: "Whatever your station or country, you should believe only what is true, and what you would be disposed to believe if you were of another country, another station, another religion." The dialectic intelligence of Forster's art escapes casuistry by rooting itself in the facts of politics, of economy, and of passion. Once the Cambridge philosopher and friend of Forster, G. Lowes Dickinson, said that "Forster's kind of double vision squints." So it may, or so it may seem to do—but we should compare what a microscope or the lens of art demands of our eyes with what has been produced in this age of the fish by the smug eye of sanctimony, the glazed stare of obsession, or the lidless gaze of brutal fatuity before we credit that squint to myopia or a tic of nerves. For it has rightly been said of Forster's work, by Lionel Trilling, that it reverses the familiar paradox of the hard-boiled writer of the Hemingway type, whose surface hardness may disguise a softness of mind or feeling. Forster's work may look soft but inside it is as hard as nails. It is based on a stubborn and unfaltering moral realism.

The second thing that Forster's "double vision" gave him was the basic theme of all his books. For like most responsible novelists and poets—like Conrad and Lawrence, Hardy and Gide—he has a single theme. Conrad made his theme the human illusion of values, compelled out of vanity, nihilism, or despair, by the human necessity of commitment and moral action. Lawrence took for his the vital principle of sexual energy, redeeming the modern man's enervation of mind and spirit. Forster sees this same dichotomy. It is a common inheritance from the Nineteenth Century. He made his object the search for the *wholeness* of truth and of life—the synthesis of matter and essence; of civilization with its inhibitions and nature with its crude energy; of the fragments and denials on which life is commonly founded and the total vision of reality which man's sloth or cowardice forbids him to acknowledge. The central statement of his argument comes in *Howards End,* whose title-page carries the phrase "Only connect":

> Only connect the prose and the passion, and both will be exalted, and human love will be seen at its height. Live in fragments no longer. Only connect, and the beast and the monk, robbed of the isolation that is life to either, will die.

This union can be neither the formal unity of moral logicians nor the tepid synthesis of academic humanists. It must be a vital tension of elements. Its secret is proportion—the proportion that comes only through a passionate experience of both life and idea.

> The business man who assumes that this life is everything, and the mystic who asserts that it is nothing, fail, on this side and on that, to hit the truth. . . . Truth, being alive, is not halfway between anything. It is only to be found by continuous excursions into either realm, and though proportion is the final secret, to espouse it at the outset is to insure sterility.

Such an argument may fall flatly on the ears of modern believers, on muddled and insecure men who today take refuge in revived dogmatisms and absolutes, on those who argue that liberalism and intelligence have shown their inadequacy to decision and action, and who disregard the fact that we are not in a position to know whether reason and tolerance are bad for humanity for the simple reason that they have never been given a full chance to prove their worth against the violence, brutality, and vindictiveness which dogmas or superstitions have sanctioned in human history. It is Forster's belief that no dogma has ever succeeded in respecting the full complexity of human nature; that our psychic and moral natures refuse to be compelled by the simplifying codes of social and political action. Mankind may be stricken by a curse, but it is important to know what that curse really is. Forster calls it the Primal Curse, which is not the "knowledge of good and evil, but the knowledge of good-and-evil," in their baffling and inextricable complexity. Such knowledge allows no easy formulation. It resists the simplism of force. It permits no access except through incessant struggle and inevitable grief. Yet in the face of its stupendous challenge, Forster recommends neither cynicism nor resignation, neither facile optimism nor tragic submission. Mankind refuses to resign itself to the ambiguity of truth. It survives by accepting the ambiguity, the conflict, the torment. Only then can it possess even a small part of the truth, and know freedom through it.

What Forster's novels show is the sense of such truth, and the liberation it permits. Whether laid in Italy, England, or India, they oppose the "prose" of life to its "passion." The prose lies in the falsity, cant, and philistinism of middle-class prejudice, in suburban "culture," in the racial and sexual snobbery of Florentine *pensions*, in big business with "its outer world of telegrams and anger," in the brutal officialdom of Chandrapore. It comes from people who are afraid of their inner natures and who dare not say "I" for fear of facing or recognizing themselves: not only Napoleon and Cecil Rhodes and Pierpont Morgan and the modern despots, but Cecil Vyse, Mr. Wilcox, the Callendars, the Pembrokes, the Reverend Cuthbert Eager, and that ugly embodiment of twisted bigotry, Mrs. Failing, Rickie Elliott's aunt in *The Longest Journey*. The "passion" lies in the life of vital grace and sincerity, of instinctive truth and natural emotion, whether in Cambridge, Tuscany, or India: in vivacious natures like Margaret Schlegel, Lucy Honeychurch, and Dr. Aziz; in sensibilities sometimes driven to tragedy by their crippled emotions, like Rickie Elliott, Helen Schlegel, and Leonard Bast; above all, in children of invincible nature like Gino Carella and Stephen Wonham. Between these opposites exist the mediators, the troubled searchers for the connection that will resolve the tragic antitheses of humanity: disillusioned intelligences like Fielding and Stewart Ansell, or unconscious mystics like Mrs. Wilcox and Mrs. Moore, who, usually in old age, touch the hem of the mystery, and, shuddering at the tragedy of life, "the horrors of the universe and its smallness," see in "the twilight of the double vision" a redemption through some other-worldly revelation that snatches them from the abyss where they have caught a glimpse of the horror of nothingness, "the serpent of eternity made of maggots."

In some of Forster's books it is love which comes as a solvent (*A Room with a View*). In some, it is brotherly affection, or human relations, that desperately survive racial hates (*A Passage to India*). Once it is social calamity that breaks down hostility (*Howards End*). Once, in *The Longest Journey*, which is Forster's most strenuous but also his most personal and passionate novel, tragedy destroys without saving, and only the unconscious life of nature is left to endure in its unconscious strength. But mostly Forster leaves his plots and characters as complex and unresolved as he found them. The truth has been glimpsed, though the glimpse may have blinded. Or the novel may close with the effect of having revealed a crisis in human relations, a titanic collision of shrouded forces, a way of life clutching the brink of ruin, and with nothing solved. But we have *seen*—seen what starvation and wreckage the life lived in fragments can cause; seen what havoc the "undeveloped heart" can create; seen how truth and honesty are constantly betrayed to meanness and duplicity; how sincerity is sacrificed to force and how honesty is betrayed to the sanctioned cruelties of civilized behavior. No modern English writer—not even those whose creative gifts and energies greatly surpass Forster's—has made the sight of such facts firmer and clearer than he has. And if it may be argued that his kind of intelligence poses problems rather than solves them, the insight and honesty of his work have given him the right to use the answer that Ibsen once gave his critics: "It is not my business to give you the right answers. My business is to ask you the right questions."

Like the modern Greek poet C. P. Cavafy, on whom he has written sympathetically, Forster stands "at a slight angle to the universe." And like André Gide, whom he respected, he is one of the "free minds" which "are as rare as great [ones], and even more valuable at the present moment." He too makes it his task to transmit not "life's greatness," which he has called "a Nineteenth Century perquisite, a Goethean job," but "life's complexity, and the delight, the difficulty, the duty of registering that complexity and conveying it." He honors Freedom, Democracy, Humanity, and Culture—the grand capitalized ideals of liberal civilization—but he rejects the abstractions or mandates by which these have been brutalized and made impotent. Therefore he believes even more in the realities that work better without capital letters—in tolerance, in harmony, in personal relations, and in art. He also believes in an aristocracy "not of power based upon rank and influence, but an aristocracy of the sensitive, the considerate, and the plucky." That is why, even in 1939 and on the brink of world disaster, he thought that two cheers for democracy were "quite enough"—"one because it admits variety, and two because it permits criticism . . . there is no occasion to give three. Only Love the Beloved Republic deserves that."

Forster has his limitations, his decided curtailment of creative capacity and action. He himself virtually admits and urges them. They exist not only in his sometimes skittish mannerism and elusive decision of sympathy, in his condescension to adroit idiosyncrasy in his literary tastes, in what was once called (no doubt in frank resentment) the "demurely bloodless gaiety" of his essays and shorter tales, in the refusals of recognition that can shrink his critical perceptions (his judgments on James and Joyce descend to an impatience which no creative prejudice can excuse), in his abrupt check to the

demands of political commitment and responsibility. Our feeling
about him fluctuates, as Mr. Trilling says, "between disapproval of
a dereliction from duty and a sense of relief that a fine artist has
not seen art as a grim imperative." He often appears to push his
suspicion of action to passivity and of beliefs to something close to
a defeatism of will. But all this is the result of measuring by Forster's
own standards the wholeness of his moral vision and his absolutely
honest search for the means by which that vision may be applied to
the life of muddle, evasion, and fear, of masked or stupefied purpose, at which his contemporaries have arrived. He is the historian
of the fatal estrangements that underlie the defeats and humiliations of his age. And he has never offered it the easy cures and pallia-
tives that are the stock in trade of the professional prophet or reformer.

So in his two collections of essays—*Abinger Harvest* in 1936, *Two
Cheers for Democracy* in 1951—he ranges over the problems and
commitments of his lifetime: from England, Germany, America,
India, and South Africa to Shakespeare, Tolstoy, Ibsen, Eliot, Gide,
and Auden; from the pleasures of music and literature to the demands of the historic moment, the 1930s and 1940s, which imposed
on a faith in sanity the tests of politics, tyranny, and war. What
operated in Forster's novels also operates in his commentaries. The
novels too, long before the arrival of world crisis, were aware of
confusion and treachery, the intolerances of temperament, caste, and
race, the errors of the heart that remains "undeveloped" and the will
that works inflexibly. In that perception lay their tough and resilient
strength, and that strength, however supplely exercised or humorously modulated, remains the spring that has kept Forster's intelligence unstiffened by conformity, alert in energy, uncompromising
only when mind is threatened by brutality or love and art by the
sanctimony which is their death.

"We must love one another or die." Forster admits that he is
"commanded" by Auden's precept. But he insists on a qualifica-
tion. "We can only love what we know personally." When the idea

is promoted that "nations should love one another, or that business concerns or marketing boards should love one another, or that a man in Portugal should love a man in Peru of whom he has never heard, it is absurd, unreal, dangerous." Then love must yield to a "very dull virtue," tolerance, which, however "boring," "negative," or misrepresented by "a bad press," permits the humbler but more useful virtue of "putting up with people, being able to stand things," the "sound state of mind we are looking for."

So also, in the face of believers in Art who advocate the "perilous and vague sentimentalism" that "only art matters," or talk about "The Life of Art," "Living for Art," or "Art's High Mission," he emphatically asserts "an unfashionable belief" in all its "eternal importance." "I believe in art for art's sake." It exists for its own sake and no other because it remains one of the two categories of experience (religion, "on the evidence of the mystics," is the other) which "possess internal order," testify to "the internal harmony," and which, like "lighthouses [that] have never ceased sweeping the thankless seas," do "in fact concern people who do not care for art at all."

Forster thus declares himself the kind of artist who conceives of his work as a mediator between art's rightful superiority to use and the humanity that does not care about art at all. He is an individualist who recognizes the claims of society, a believer in liberty who knows that liberty must be responsible if it is to escape anarchism, a liberal who admits the law of necessity. ("We live in freedom by necessity.") It has always been his effort to reconcile the two tendencies which he sees in the writing of our century: the "popular, which absorbs what is passing, and the esoteric, which rejects it, and tries to create through art something more valuable than monotony and bloodshed." When he says that he does not "believe in Belief"; when he rejects inflexibility and praises curiosity; when he defines honesty in Tolstoy, Proust, Gide, Crabbe, or Samuel Butler, he reminds us of another standard which he has applied throughout his work and which he uses as a heading for certain of his essays

—the principle of "art in action." It is the principle that has brought him his success as artist and intelligence, and it wins for the row of his books the tribute he accords those of Virginia Woolf: "These trophies were won by the mind from matter, its enemy and its friend."

1938–51 [1955]

Ford Madox Ford

YESTERDAY AND AFTER

1932: *Return to Yesterday*

What he liked to call "the dubious pleasure of remembering analytically" was an indulgence Ford Madox Ford was never able to deny himself. His *Return to Yesterday* continued the chronicle of his adventures in art and literature which had formed a kind of serial production or random autobiography among his books almost from his beginnings in authorship.[1] Critics may question the worth of his facts and analysis, but no one can deny the pleasure he took in creating and patronizing literature or in writing its annals. He had, in fact, returned to yesterday too often to permit great novelty or surprise in the series of compendious installments on his career. They must be read with respect, however, by anyone conscious of his services to modern writers and of the two unflagging resources that made them possible—enthusiasm and a "sense of the past."

-----

[1] The chronicle, begun in 1911 with *Ancient Lights* and resumed in 1921 with *Thus to Revisit*, as again in 1932 in *Return to Yesterday*, filters also through Ford's books on *Ford Madox Brown* (1896), *The Pre-Raphaelite Brotherhood* (1907), *Henry James* (1913), *Joseph Conrad* (1924), to which could be further added *The Soul of London* (1905), *New York Is Not America* (1927), *Provence* (1935), *Great Trade Route* (1937). It was to be continued in further volumes before Ford died in 1939: *It Was the Nightingale* (1933), *Portraits from Life* (1937), *The March of Literature* (1939).

Even the skeptic is likely to marvel that in his eagerness to cultivate new friends and talents and to participate in a long succession of aesthetic and literary movements, Ford had the luck to play so many winning hands. Yet "luck" is a poor word for the perspicacity that took its lessons at the feet of veteran Pre-Raphaelites and Henry James, accepted on petition the collaboration of Conrad, befriended Stephen Crane, Norman Douglas, D. H. Lawrence, and any number of unrecognized talents, set *The English Review* in 1908 and later the *Transatlantic* in Paris afloat with their brilliant crews, and kept abreast of creative experiment during many years of journalistic distraction and war service until the Tietjens tetralogy was produced. Throughout his life in writing, Ford was conscious at every point of the program of events. He succeeded as did no other contemporary in reconciling his loyalty to the Victorian era which bred him, and of which he remained an isolated veteran, with a tireless avidity for novelty and insurgence.

The past was the lodestar of his career from its beginnings. He started life as the legatee of a circle of famous artists and writers who had weathered the heroic rigors of Victorian fame. His literary ambitions were supervised by a sponsoring host of distinguished relatives and near-relatives whom he was later to pay the tribute of acting as their grateful historian. The friendships and distractions of his crowded later years never succeeded in persuading him to relinquish his projects in discipleship and reminiscence. Whether in volumes of criticism and biography like *Ford Madox Brown, Rossetti, Henry James,* and *Joseph Conrad;* in books of historical or documentary character like the Katherine Howard trilogy (1906–08) and the series on *England and the English* (1905–07); in the Tietjens novels (1924–28); or in the long list of reminiscences to which *Return to Yesterday* came as a sequel, his work was spurred by a consciousness of temporal perspectives and of his own privileged existence among them. Disappointments in his public career were accompanied by disorders in his domestic (he spared his readers the latter but Miss Violet Hunt did not); yet through all the excitement, through all the collisions between external convention and personal independence, and in spite of a love of "making things grow" which frequently led him to desert literature for spasmodic excursions into agriculture, he was intent on staying young and contemporary.

By his own admission he always had to struggle against the fatigue of setting words to paper, a confession which his more than sixty books and unnumbered works of journalism would make difficult to credit were it not for his insistent and unquestionably sincere belief that the making of novels and poetry is the noblest occupation of man, worth the last ounce of his spiritual and physical energy. This same article of faith is the clue to his unbounded generosity for young talent. His books will have their value as "mémoires pour servir à l'histoire de son temps" chiefly because of the courageous, and sometimes costly, support he gave to a succession of poorly appreciated authors. From Crane, Hudson, and Conrad, through Pound, Lawrence, and the Imagists, down to Hemingway and the postwar generation of novelists and poets, these beneficiaries of his editorial acumen and personal loyalty offer a testimony to friendship which might pardon an even more repetitious and self-congratulatory record than Ford has written.

Generosity and enthusiasm are not, however, proofs of creative authority and they can contribute only marginally to Ford's claim to distinction among Twentieth Century novelists. In the nineties he was hailed, so he frequently reminded us, as "the most-boomed author in England" and "the foremost English stylist." With this beginning, his subsequent aimless and uninspired course must have come with the pain of distinct anti-climax. For about twenty years he wrote books which he could later call no better than "worthless." Admitting the pressure of financial necessity that kept him in journalism and potboiling, one is reminded by the lives of Conrad and Hudson, and by the portrait of his own Tietjens, that another course was open to him and that some failure in purpose or confusion of integrity kept him from following it. The clue to this is perhaps discoverable in *Return to Yesterday*.

Facts are probably not in any ultimate sense of great spiritual significance, but the discipline required to master them is. Ford's happy unconcern about dates, sources, and authenticity in his anecdotes stands in no greater contrast to Conrad's tortuous search for words and detail in writing a novel than do the "worthless" fictions of Ford's middle years to novels like *Lord Jim* and *Nostromo*. The self-esteem which could sometimes be as ingratiating as Yeats's or (more often) as tedious as Sisley Huddleston's, and which could condone in his later books wholesale repetitions from earlier volumes as easily as it could tempt disaster for the Tietjens chronicle by yielding to a New York lady-editor's plea for a fourth volume, stood in sharp contrast to the rigorous self-effacement of W. H. Hudson or Stephen Crane. And the uncertainty of motive in Ford's projects may be traced at least partly to his inability to resolve and localize his aesthetic and civil morals.

He was hospitable to revolt and insurgence in the creative order, yet confessed himself "a sentimental Tory," loving "pomp, banners, divine rights, unreasonable ceremonies, and ceremoniousness." Pitched less precariously than Henry James or Conrad between several cultural allegiances, he tacked fitfully from English traditions to German sympathies and ultimately to French enthusiasms. He was in turn an heir of the Victorians, an arbiter among the Georgians, and a postwar *révolté*. His creative impulses were fitful, his style in all but four or five books heavily damaged by erratic temporization and exhibitionism, and his attention susceptible to almost every literary breeze in the air. His patronage was spent wisely but far too eclectically for his own good. One of his critics wished for him "less facility and more self-restraint." It would be equally possible to regret the irresolution that denied his work conviction and a center. Given a cast of personal acquaintances intimately observed and the incentive of acute personal ordeal, he produced novels of extraordinary perception and technical truth like *The Good Soldier* and *Some Do Not*. Left to his less disciplined devices, he wrote books whose shrewd wit and engaging anecdotes did not annul a sense of frustrated intelligence and misspent energies. On a life of such generosity and on books of such charm as

Ford Madox Ford's, this is an ungrateful reflection; but in his chapters on James, Conrad, and Hudson, no less than in his accounts of desultory literary adventure in London, New York, and Paris, he himself provided examples of integrity and resolution that make such a reflection irresistible.

1949: *The Last Pre-Raphaelite*

The rough justice and grim fortune that dealt unsparingly with Ford Madox Ford during his more than forty years of authorship pursued him down to the time of his death in France in 1939, and seem intent on pursuing him even yet. Today all, or nearly all, of his eighty or more books are out of print.[2] He still figures rarely, if at all, among the century's ranking novelists. Ignored or slighted in later years in his own country, he received there, on dying, the official obloquy and grudging sarcasm of the obituarists of what in his day he had stubbornly resisted, "the Establishment." (The only decent memorial notice that seems to have appeared in London was a tribute by Graham Greene in *The Spectator*.) France and America gave him such success as he finally came by in the last twenty years of his long career, but after serving literature for half a century in three countries, his only official honor was a degree from Olivet College, Michigan, of which he was gratefully proud. The irony of this curiously baffled career persists even in the memoir and single book-length study of Ford which has thus far appeared—that of his one-time assistant on *The English Review*, Douglas Goldring,

---

[2] An attempt was made in 1951 and 1952 by a New York publisher (Alfred A. Knopf) to revive Ford's work; a collective one-volume edition of the Tietjens novels was published under the title *Parade's End*, followed by a reissue of *The Good Soldier*. These editions called for some serious reappraisal of Ford's achievement as a novelist and did something to re-establish him as a text for students of writing, but the "revival" can hardly be called an impressive success and the books soon appeared in sales of remainders.

which was called *The Last Pre-Raphaelite* when it appeared in
London in 1948 and which was titled, with a similar accent of ironic
pathos, *Trained for Genius* when it was published in New York a
year later.

Much as he exploited his Pre-Raphaelite ancestry and apprenticeship, Ford knew the liability that glamorous inheritance had laid
on him. He was "trained for genius" all too overpoweringly. It took
him a large part of his life to find his real work and bearings as a
writer. A sense of insecurity in his revered vocation never wholly
left him. But it will be unfortunate if these titles mislead Mr.
Goldring's readers. He was Ford's staunchest English friend; he
writes with a mixture of amused realism and stubborn respect about
the man he has always considered his literary guide and master; and
he has never forgotten the debt he owed Ford for being taken on,
at twenty-one in 1908, as sub-editor of *The English Review,* thus
gaining privileged access to the highest conclaves of modern English authorship. The book is, in fact, the second of Mr. Goldring's
tributes to Ford. In 1943 he published in London a memoir called
South Lodge. Its pages are not incorporated in the later volume,
which is a pity, for *South Lodge* is a better book than *Trained for
Genius*—a vivid evocation of the part of Ford's history Mr. Goldring
knew at first hand, with a brilliant picture of literary and social London on the eve of 1914, a sound account of Ford's successes and
miseries in that remote era, and a haunting portrait of Violet Hunt,
that embattled "woman who did," from her disastrous entry into
Ford's life until she died at eighty, alone, unforgetting, deranged,
among her houseful of trophies, while the bombs of 1942 provided
"the orchestral thunder of a dying age."

Mr. Goldring's will not be the last word on Ford. His biography
is without exact scholarship, and his criticism, while roughly valid,
yields to defensive polemic. Ford made a deathbed request against
biographies. His American legatee honored this wish by refusing
to cooperate. The Paris years are merely sketched, and the chapter
on Ford's American career is completely inadequate, since none of

his important friends here were consulted. It is, moreover, a bold
biographer who would venture on this task at all. Ford's own
accounts of himself were, for all their richness of content, always
unreliable and often fantastic: "impressions of truth" according to
their author, congenital lying according to his enemies, incredibly
embarrassing, wheezily garrulous even to his friends, with their
quagmires of yarn-spinning and stories that never quite agreed twice.
Had he really been dandled by Turgenev, had his chair stolen at a
concert by Liszt, modeled for Densher in *The Wings of the Dove,*
gone to Eton, attended the Sorbonne? The reader could never be
sure. And beyond these erratic records lies a muddle of gossip and
legend and what a host of ladies had to say about their parts in it—
Violet Hunt's *I Have This to Say: The Story of My Flurried Years,*
Jean Rhys's *After Leaving Mr. McKenzie,* Stella Bowen's *Drawn
from Life,* and a cloud of other documents in scandal, defense, and
litigation. Ford had a genius for making messes. Even his strokes of
fortune—friendship with James, collaboration with Conrad, contacts with Wells, Bennett, and other Edwardian talents, brilliant
editorships of *The English Review* and the *Transatlantic*—were
riddled by misunderstanding or mismanagement. His ventures in
and out of marriage became a minor epic of error and tactlessness.
Nor does the case become simpler when his file of eighty books and
massive journalism are tackled. Novels, verse, essays, criticism, memoirs, biographies, travels, histories, sociology, they range from potboiling meretriciousness to distinction, the incessant outpourings of
a polygraph who apparently wrote something every day of his life
from fifteen to sixty-six. Criticism, for understandable reasons, has
hardly begun to make something of this vast bulk of print. (Mr.
Robie Macaulay's perceptive essay in the *Kenyon Review,* Spring
1949, and Mr. Mark Schorer's introduction to the 1952 reprint of
The Good Soldier, though they both idealize rather drastically, will
perhaps serve as points of departure for the serious assessment of
Ford's achievement that may eventually arrive.)
The fact is that Ford's aesthetic origins and associations served

him both well and badly. They made it impossible for him to live any other life than that of literature, and to live it whole-souledly and passionately. They also made it impossible for him ever quite to sell himself to journalism, propaganda, or profitably slick mass-production like such comparable polygraphs as Wells and Maugham. They kept him through five decades a lover of good writing, original talent, authentic invention. But his dedication to form, style, and the *mot juste,* coupled with his habit of pontificating, desire to *faire école* at all costs, and compulsive addiction to paper ("an old man mad about writing"), likewise kept him writing, prosing, repeating himself, when there was, very often, little actual substance to work on. Style, technique, manner, and method were kept grinding away, half the time saying little and producing what can be, for long and desperate stretches, a garrulously tiresome parody of his intentions.

The better Ford was not a man spinning literature spiderwise out of his own entrails. For all his social, political, religious, and personal inconsistencies, he was a man who lived through and in his age. He never betrayed what Mr. Goldring rightly calls his 'highest merit, his unswerving loyalty to "the Standard of Values" and to the art that supported that standard when, in a demoralized and violent time, every other support was likely to fail. He was also a man who, though often mistaken, pretentious, foolish, or deluded, was never essentially self-deceived. He knew in his own life the risks, ignominy, and treacheries of his period. Whenever he drew on his two soundest resources—his instinct of honor, his generous sense of justice—he wrote out of a saving reserve of character. He could locate the trace the problem of honor in history—the Katherine Howard trilogy or *Ladies Whose Bright Eyes*—and find an original means to define it there. He could define it even better in his own age—in *The Good Soldier* and the Tietjens series—the first, as Graham Greene says, "a study of an averagely good man of a conventional class driven, divided, and destroyed by unconventional passion," the second an "appalling examination of how private malice goes on during public disaster," both of them to be counted among "the novels which stand as high as any fiction written since the death of

James." [3] This estimate is high, perhaps, like Mr. Goldring's, finally too high, but if it errs it does so on the side of justice.

Traditionalist, *révolté;* Catholic, skeptic; agrarian and internationalist; "small producer" and restless migrant; democrat, rituallover, and iconoclast; fond father, erring husband, harassed lover; loyal to England, to Germany, and to France—he was all these by turns and never fully succeeded in stabilizing or centering his personal or artistic loyalties. He came to reject half his work as "worthless," wrote remorselessly day after day, found joy elusive and trouble sure, died at last in poverty (though with two hundred manuscripts by young writers in his keeping, recipients of his unflagging care and encouragement), was written off as "dated" in England, soon forgotten in France, unread even in America. "But," says Graham Greene, "I don't suppose failure disturbed him much: he had never really believed in human happiness, his middle life had been made miserable by passion, and he had come through, with his humor intact, his stock of unreliable anecdotes, the kind of enemies a man ought to have, and a half-belief in a posterity which would care for good writing." Twice this life of avid human and aesthetic charity, un-self-protective impulse, and serious artistic dedication found the subject that could express its baffled generosity, once in *The Good Soldier,* again in the bitter fortunes of Christopher Tietjens; and in those two books—in the first of them with subtle poignance and studied craftsmanship, in the second with a more acute moral ferocity if, eventually, with a damaging distention of its material—he found the art he had groped toward with such dutiful understudy and painful search, so at last justifying himself as the artist he had always wanted to be, in a craft he held to be "the noblest to which a man can dedicate himself."

Mr. Goldring presents Ford complete with all his errors and faults, but with his honor intact too, and with what D. H. Lawrence, who owed his debut to Ford and *The English Review* and who could understand Ford's kind of ordeal, called the "dove-grey

---

[3] Greene's tribute to Ford, originally in the London *Spectator* in 1939, has now been included in his volume *The Lost Childhood and Other Essays* (1951).

kindliness" by which he served literature. "There was none too much of it left in the world after Ford's departure," adds Mr. Goldring, "which is no doubt one of the reasons why some of us, who knew him, cherish his memory." For those who didn't know him, Ford left other, less elusive evidence.

He left a record of creative sympathy that refused to rely on vested interests and prejudices but kept itself alert to the risk and independence that ensure the truth of moral insight. He carried over from the aesthetic radicalism of his Victorian sponsors a respect for the nonconformism that enlarges the boundaries of the imagination and of the arts that embody it. He allied himself consistently with the kind of energy that resists stultification by habit or easy success by compromise with standardized taste. He never lost his confidence that the methods of fiction and poetry were still open to new possibilities of invention, style, and discipline. And with this openness to novelty and experiment he joined, with an authority few men of his generation could so effectively define, a sense of the continuity and integrity of a literary tradition: of what Romantic and Victorian art had to offer as a basis of poetic discovery, and of what the novel of Joyce, Hemingway, and their contemporaries had to rely on in the disciplines established by the classic line of Stendhal, Flaubert, Turgenev, James, and Conrad.

The distractions of his personal life, the fitful and erratic impulses of his writing, justified themselves at last in this: that his zeal for innovation was never without its respect for the continuities of craft and discipline; that his susceptibility to untried talent had schooled itself in the discoveries that had proved their worth in the past and had demonstrated there how the tests of art form a constant mediation between past and future in the living ordeal of present truth and sincerity. Ford thus made himself, as novelist and teacher of novelists, a force of balance and compromise between two traditions whose necessary collision in the Twentieth Century he was one of the few to see, as he was one of the few to show, not only in his two real achievements in fiction but in the personal discomfort that made them possible, what their reconciliation imposed on the modern writer as a test of his courage and intelligence. It was logical that Ezra Pound, when he found Ford in the London of 1910, should have singled him out for tribute: "In a country in love with amateurs, in a country where the incompetent have such beautiful manners, and personalities so fragile and charming, that one cannot bear to injure their feelings by the introduction of competent criticism, it is well that one man should have a vision of perfection and that he should be sick to death and disconsolate because he cannot attain it."

Ford was never sufficiently blessed to lose either the vision or the dissatisfaction that accompanied it. Among so many books that seem to compromise his commitment and among the private misadventures that continually harassed it, he left two solid achievements and a lifetime's example of unprofitable generosity to testify to his refusal of complacency. It remains the task of his followers to recognize the evidence he left of what that refusal entailed, and, now that the necessary interval of posthumous probation has passed, to respect him for it.

1932-49 [1956]

Willa Cather

THE TONE OF TIME

In 1927, at fifty-four, Willa Cather, after three decades of steady and patient labor in her craft, stood at the height of her career, with fifteen years of her best work behind her and her most popular book, *Death Comes for the Archbishop*, claiming an unstinted admiration. When she died twenty years later,[1] she had already come to appear as the survivor of a distant generation, remote from the talents and problems of the past two anxious decades. This estrangement was no surprise to her. It was of her own choice and election. In 1936, in prefacing her collection of essays then called *Not Under Forty*, she admitted that her writing could have "little interest for people under forty years of age." "The world broke in two in 1922 or thereabouts," she said, and it was to "the backward, and by one of their number," that she addressed her later books. She had, in fact, so addressed her work ever since she first found her real bearings in authorship with *O Pioneers!* in 1913. Backwardness was with her not only a matter of her material and temperament. It was the condition of her existence as an artist.

She was one of the last in a long line of commemorators and

----

[1] On April 24, 1947. The date of Willa Cather's birth, long recorded as 1876, was discovered by E. K. Brown and Leon Edel in their biography of her (1953) to have been December 7, 1873. Her book of essays, *Not Under Forty*, was retitled *Literary Encounters* when she included it in her collected edition in 1937.

elegists of American innocence and romantic heroism that virtually dates from the beginnings of a conscious native artistry in American literature. Her books, once she found her natural voice and métier, and once she had put aside her Eastern subjects and earlier themes of rebellious protest, had become elegies, and Irving, Cooper, Hawthorne, Mark Twain, and Sarah Orne Jewett figure in their ancestry. When, on rare occasions, she praised her fellow-craftsmen, from Miss Jewett to Katherine Mansfield, Thornton Wilder, or Thomas Mann (who "belongs immensely to the forward-goers. . . . But he also goes back a long way, and his backwardness is more gratifying to the backward"), it was usually because they also turned to the past and rooted their values there.[2]

She was quite aware of the false and bogus uses to which the historic sentiment had been put in American fiction. Its products surrounded her in the early 1900s when she was feeling her way toward her career: "machine-made historical novels," "dreary dialect stories," "very dull and heavy as clay"—books by John Fox, Jr., James Lane Allen, Mary Johnston, and their successful competitors, the memory of which today she likened to "taking a stroll through a World's Fair grounds some years after the show is over." She knew Miss Jewett shone like a star in that lustreless company; that Henry James's "was surely the keenest mind any American had ever devoted to the art of fiction"; that Stephen Crane "had done something real." She also had to learn the secret of their distinction the

----

[2] This sympathy in Willa Cather was confirmed in the last years of her life in a project she did not live to complete: "to place the setting of a story straight across the world, quite far into the past—leaving America entirely—in the setting of medieval Avignon." She was "no longer at any pains to conceal her disillusion and aversion to most of the life about her." An account of this project has recently been given by George N. Kates in "Willa Cather's Unfinished Avignon Story," in *Five Stories* by Willa Cather (New York: Vintage Books, 1956). Mr. Kates says further of this story, whose title was to be *Hard Punishments:* "Willa Cather reached first for the stars over the pure air of Nebraska, and then, when their light became obscured, would accept nothing less beautiful in their place simply because it was American." Also: "Like many people of plain origins, her first great need had been to be reassured, to still the youthful panic of seeming to possess only an inferior brand of everything that her more fortunate brothers and sisters took as naturally theirs. This was a prime need; but she had conquered it in her own way, which was the way of genius."

hard way: she came out of the West attracted by the prairie girl's mirage of the East—its cities, salons, opera houses, studios, Beacon Hill sanctities, the fever and excitement of New York, the lure of Atlantic liners, with the shrines of Europe beyond. Her early stories, many never collected in her books, are full of this worshipful glamour, and she was past thirty-five when she tried to make something of it in her first novel, which combined a problem out of Edith Wharton, a setting and something of a manner out of Henry James, and an outsider's clumsiness in handling them, with inevitable results in self-conscious stiffness and crudity of tone.

Only then did she remember the advice Sarah Orne Jewett had once given her: "The thing that teases the mind over and over for years, and at last gets itself put down on paper—whether little or great, it belongs to Literature." "Otherwise," as Miss Jewett had also said, "what might be strength in a writer is only crudeness, and what might be insight is only observation; sentiment falls to sentimentality—you can write about life, but never life itself." Willa Cather put Beacon Hill and Bohemia behind her. She returned to Nebraska, to a prairie town trying hard not to be blown away in the blast of a winter wind. She found the local habitation of her talent, and her serious career in art began.

From that point she began her journey into lost time, going back beyond Nebraska, Colorado, and Kansas to colonial New Mexico, to eighteenth-century Quebec, and finally to the pre-Civil War Virginia of her family, every step taking her deeper into the values and securities she set most store by. She had, to help her, her rediscovered devotion to the scenes of her early youth, the Western fields and skies she called "the grand passion of my life," her brilliant gift for rendering landscape and weather in the closest approximation to the poetic art of Turgenev and Gogol our fiction has seen, her retentive sympathy with the life of farms, small towns, prairie settlements, immigrant colonies, and Southwestern outposts and missions. In all the tales of regional America that have been produced in the past forty years nothing has exceeded her skill in evoking the place-spirit of rural America in her finest books—*My Antonia, A Lost*

Lady, The Professor's House, and *Death Comes for the Archbishop.*

The pathos of distance by which she induced her special poetry into these scenes was, of course, stimulated by her feeling that the inspiring landscape of the prairies, deserts, and mountains, no less than the gracious charms of colonial Virginia or old New York, had been obliterated by a vulgar and cheapening modernity. The garage that now stands on Charles Street in Boston on the site of the house where Mrs. James T. Fields had once held court to "Learning and Talent" was symptomatic for Willa Cather of a general and humiliating degradation. So the old wagon roads of the West, "roads of Destiny" that "used to run like a wild thing across the open prairie," had been resurveyed and obliterated to make highways for tourist and motor traffic. The railways once "dreamed across the mountains" by a race of Titans, highways in the heroic conquest of the West, were streamlined for commuters between New York and California. Wooden houses and piazza'd mansions, once landmarks of pioneer fortitude and hospitality, came down and suburban Tudor or sham Château went up in their place. The frontier universities that had once fostered a scholarship of vision and historical passion yielded to academic power plants thick with politics and careerism. She despised such a world, whose literature itself she saw as mere statistics and "sensory stimuli," and apparently she preferred to be despised by it.

The interesting thing about Miss Cather's career is that it started in protest against and flight from the very world she ended by idealizing and mourning. It recapitulates a characteristic American pattern of rebellion and return, censure and surrender. The prairie and small town, the Western hinterland and the neighborly community, as she presented them in her best early stories—"A Wagner Matinee," "Paul's Case," "The Sculptor's Funeral," "A Death in the Desert"—were objects of a moral reproach and castigation as severe as anything she later directed against the vulgarizing influences of the modern world. She was, indeed, a pioneer in the Twentieth Century "revolt from the village," and she spared no scorn in describing the provincial spirit. It had created the life of a "dunghill," of petty existences, of "little people" and a small humanity, of stingy hates and warping avarice that made generous spirits shrivel and ardent natures die. The savagery of her indictment was perhaps the strongest passion she ever summoned in any of her works. Her frontier in those days was not the West; it was the East and the world of art, with desire the goad of her heroes and heroines and the running theme of her stories, as much as it was of Dreiser's.

It was in young artists—the dreaming, headstrong, fractious, or unstable young, fated to defeat or bad ends by the materialism and ugliness of their surroundings—that she first envisaged the heroic ideal. Paul, Katharine Gaylord, Harvey Merrick, and Don Hedger are the defeated or dishonored "cases" that foreshadow the triumphant lives of Alexandra Bergson, Thea Kronborg, Antonia Shimerda, Archbishop Machebeuf, and Nancy Till, and that lend their note of desire or vision to the middle terms of Miss Cather's argument—the inspired spirits who do not succeed but who, by some force of character or apartness of nature, lend significance to the faceless anonymity around them. These characters—the "lost lady" Marian Forrester, Myra Henshawe, Tom Outland, Professor St. Peter, even the slighter Lucy Gayheart in a later novel—are the most persuasive of Miss Cather's creations, her nearest claims to skill in a field where she was admittedly and obviously incompetent —complex and credible psychology. But somehow she could never bring her opposites into full play in a novel. They remained irreconcilably differentiated, dramatically hostile, morally and socially incapable of true complexity.

The full-bodied and heavily documented novel was never congenial to Miss Cather; she rightly understood her art to be one of elimination and selection, which eventually meant that it was an art of simplification and didactic idealization. *The Song of the Lark* and *One of Ours* drag with detail. *My Antonia* and *A Lost Lady* are her finest successes because there her selection defines, suggests, and evokes without falsely idealizing. When she seized a theme of genuine social and moral potentiality in *The Professor's House* or *My Mortal Enemy*, she pared away its substance until she produced what must always be, to her admirers, disappointingly frugal and bodiless sketches of two of the most interesting subjects in the America of her time. And when she decided to model *Death Comes for the Archbishop* on the pallid two-dimensional murals of Puvis de Chavannes, she prepared the way for the disembodied idealization, making for inertness and passivity, that overtook her in *Shadows on the Rock,* weakest of her books and portent of the thinness of her final volumes.

What overtook her plots and characters is the same thing that overtook her version of American life and history. She could not bring her early criticism into effective combination with her later nostalgic sentiment. She represents a case analogous to that of Van Wyck Brooks, who started by vigorously but disproportionately castigating American literature, and has ended in a sentimentalization equally unbalanced and simplistic. So Miss Cather, having never mastered the problem of desire in its full social and moral conditioning, passed from her tales of ambitious artists and defeated dreamers, worsted by provincial mediocrity or careerism, to versions of American idealism and its defeat that never come to satisfactory grips with the conditions of society and personal morality. As her lovers, her artists, her pioneers, and her visionary Titans become disembodied of complex emotion or thought, so her America itself became disembodied of its principles of growth, conflict, and historical maturity. There obviously worked in her nature that "poetic romanticism" to which Lionel Trilling has referred her case: what Parrington called "the inferiority complex of the frontier mind before the old and established"; the pioneer's fear of failure but greater fear of the success which comes "when an idea becomes an actuality"; the doctrine of American individualism to which F. J. Turner credited the pioneer's failure to "understand the richness and complexity of life as a whole." So to Willa Cather's early veneration for the distant goals and shining trophies of desire, ambition, and art, there succeeded a veneration for lost or distant sanctities which gradually spelled her diminution as a dramatic and poetic craftsman. The village, the prairie, the West, the New Mexican missions thus became in time abstractions as unworkable, in any critical or moral sense, as her simplified understanding of Mann's Joseph cycle. Art itself, in her versions of Flaubert, Gogol, Mann, or Katherine Mansfield, took on a remote ideality and aesthetic pathos that do much to explain her distaste for Dostoevsky or Chekhov. And the Church, to which she finally appealed as a human and historical constant, became in her unimplicated and inexperienced view of it the most abstract of all her conceptions, a cultural symbol, not a human or historical actuality, and the least real of any of the standards she invoked in her judgments and criticism of the modern world.

She defended her art in an essay, "The Novel Démeublé," in 1922, which belongs among the theorizings by artists which constituted for Henry James an "accident" which is "happiest, I think, when it is soonest over." At best, it shows Miss Cather's temerity in venturing into "the dim wilderness of theory"; at its worst it must be taken as one of those ventures which justify themselves only because they tell what a restricted view of art some writers must impose on themselves in order to get their own kind of work done. In 1922 it had some value as a warning against the excesses of realism and documentation in fiction, as a preference for feeling and insight over "observation" and "description." But when it went on to assert that Balzac's material—not merely Paris and its houses but "the game of pleasure, the game of business, the game of finance"—is "unworthy of an artist," that the banking system and Stock Exchange are scarcely "worth being written about at all," and that "the higher processes of art are all processes of simplification," it set Miss Cather down as an aesthetic fundamentalist whose achievement was bound, by the nature of her beliefs, to be sharply curtailed and inhibited. She stood by the essay; she reprinted it unmodified in her later editions. And there it shows, *post factum*, how little a principle of deliberate simplification can serve its believer if he is also an artist. Willa Cather set up a standard directly opposed to Zola's program of naturalism—and similarly deluding and disabling in its literalness and crudity. For both sensibility and naturalism arrive at the same impasse when they deny art its right to richness of thought and complexity. What such principles limit is not merely craftsmanship; it is subject-matter itself. Miss Cather saw as little as Zola did that to inhibit craftsmanship or content is to inhibit or starve the sensibility and insight that nourish them, and to arrive at the sterility of high-mindedness and the infirmity of an ideal. It is artists who have denied their art and theory no possible risk, challenge, or complexity who have arrived at the surer lease on creative life; it is to James and Conrad, to Yeats, Eliot, and Valéry, that we turn, in their theory no less than in their practice, for the more responsible clues to endurance and authority in modern literature.

Yet it was by such means of simplification, discipline, curtailment, that Willa Cather made her achievement possible and wrote the books of her best years—books which, if essentially minor in substance, are wholly her own, and if elegiac in their version of American history, revive a past that was once, whatever its innocence, a reality, and that required, in its own delusions as much as in the versions of it she created, the correction and resistance of a later realism. The boy who told the story of *My Antonia*, finding himself transported from Virginia to the prairies of Nebraska, said: "I had the feeling that the world was left behind, that we had got over the edge of it, and were outside man's jurisdiction. I have never before looked up at the sky when there was not a familiar mountain ridge against it." For thirty years Willa Cather found her clue to the heroic values of life in that Western world of open plains and pioneer struggle, lying, with its raw earth, untested possibilities, and summons to heroic endeavor, beyond the familiar jurisdiction of codes and laws. But when, in her last novel, *Sapphira and the Slave Girl* in 1940, she at last turned back, for the first time in her literary career, from Nebraska to the Virginia of her birth and earliest memories, to a country of older laws and severer customs—to Back Creek Valley west of the Blue Ridge and to the house of Henry Colbert, the miller, and his wife Sapphira, a Dodderidge of Loudon County—she brought the air of the more primitive Western world into it, the insistence on primary or primitive emotion.

The story offered the familiar features of her Western books—there is the retreat to the past, now 1856, when human dignity and honor were not yet outlawed by the confused motives and vulgar comforts of modern times; there is the idealizing pathos of distance and lost beauty; there is an epilogue that brings the story twenty-five years nearer—but only to 1881—when time has dissolved old conflicts, relaxed old tensions, and healed old wounds by its touch of grace and humility. There is a stoic husband, asking no questions of an unkind destiny. There is an imperious wife who finds herself exiled in the rough country over the Blue Ridge as earlier heroines like Marian Forrester and Myra Henshawe were exiled in the rough country of the West, self-confounded by her pride and fear of truth, defeating herself rather than allow victory or happiness to others. There is also a young girl, the Negro slave Nancy, on whom Sapphira vents her defeat and jealousy, another embodiment of the spirit of youth and natural grace which had already appeared in Alexandra, Thea, Antonia, Tom Outland, and Lucy Gayheart—the pure in heart whom no evil can defeat wholly and on whom Miss Cather fixed for her faith in character in an age of warring egotisms and debasing ambition.

Willa Cather thus risked not only a repetition of characters and effects in which her expertness had already passed from mastery to formulation. She duplicated her matter and her pathos so narrowly as to make unavoidable the sensation that what was once a sincere and valid theme had been subjected to a further attenuation of sentimental argument and special pleading. This effect was emphasized by the insistent plainness and simplicity of manner to which she adhered—that conscious simplicity, fiction most decidedly and stubbornly *démeublé*, which at times (in *My Antonia* and *A Lost Lady* particularly) she raised to a point of conviction and lyric poignance that must remain her one indisputable achievement as an artist, but which on other occasions (*One of Ours*, *Shadows on the Rock*) she permitted to lapse either into a kind of didactic dullness of sobriety or into a sentimentality that begs the whole question of creating and substantiating character by means of words, sensation, and observed detail.

Her devotion to the past and its perished beauty was sincere but inevitably limited by a didactic principle and threatened by the inflexibility of an idealistic convention. Only when her sentiment was toughened by personal or atmospheric realism did she bring off her pathos successfully, and only when her idealism was grounded in a hard sense of physical and regional fact was she able to avoid banality and abstraction. To reread the whole of her work is to realize how deliberately she accepted her risks and limitations in order to win her prizes. It is to see that the subtlety and scope of her themes—*The Professor's House* remains the most significant case—could readily fail to find the structure and substance that might have given them life or redeemed them from the tenuity of a sketch. It is to realize that her novels reduce to a single motive and pattern whose sincerity is undeniable but rudimentary and which eventually becomes threadbare. But it is also to admit, finally, that in her best work Willa Cather brought to a kind of climax and genuine epic vision the work of the American women who preceded her—Rose Terry Cooke, Sarah Jewett, Mrs. Freeman—and that she sublimated to its elements a conception of pioneer life and native energy which in other hands has generally lapsed into vulgar romanticism and the more blatant kinds of American eloquence.

It was her honesty and persistence in rendering this quality that made possible her real contribution to contemporary, and to American, writing. She defined, like Dreiser, Scott Fitzgerald, and a few other of her contemporaries between 1910 and 1930, a sense of proportion in American experience. She knew what it meant to be raised in the hinterland of privation and harsh necessities; knew what it meant to look for escape to Chicago and the world beyond; knew how much has to be fought in one's youth and origins, what the privileges of the richer world mean when they are approached from the outposts of life, what has to be broken away from and what has to be returned to for later nourishment, and how little the world appears when its romantic distances and remote promise are curtailed to the dimensions of the individual destiny. This sense of tragic limitation forms the saving leaven of realism and moral necessity in Dreiser's novels; Scott Fitzgerald gave superb expression to the experience in the last eight pages of *The Great Gatsby* and in *Tender Is the Night;* Katherine Anne Porter has given another and classic version of it in her work. Willa Cather unquestionably had something to do with preserving for such artists that proportion and perspective in American experience.

The space of seventy years is too short in human history, even in modern history, to permit anyone to claim that he saw the world break in two during it. The measure of the human fate is not to be calculated so conveniently, even in a century of disturbance like the Twentieth, and least of all in the moral perspective to which the artist or serious moralist must address himself. To do so is to impose a personal sentiment on something too large to contain it. It was to such sentiment, with its attendant didacticism and inflexibility, that Willa Cather came to submit. But it must also be granted that she lived through a cleavage and a crisis in something more than American life; that she saw "the end of an era, the sunset of the pioneer"; that it "was already gone, that age; nothing could ever bring it back"; and she defined the pathos, if not the challenge and moral imperative, its passing imposed on every survivor and writer concerned with it. She did not succeed in surmounting the confines of her special transition and the resentment it induced in her, and she did not write the kind of books that assure the future or the energy of a literature. That opportunity she consciously rejected. Talents who came after her have written books that surpass hers in conflict and comprehension, as in difficulty and courage—*The Enormous Room, The Sun Also Rises, Tender Is the Night, None Shall Look Back, All The King's Men, A Curtain of Green* and *Delta Wedding, Flowering Judas* and *Pale Horse, Pale Rider, The Sound and the Fury* and *Light in August.* Yet she did something in a time of distraction and cultural inflation to make the way clear for them, as much by the end she defined for one tradition as by the example of tenacity and personal scruple she set for herself. No one who read her books between 1915 and 1930 can forget their poetry of evocation and retrospective beauty—no sensitive reader can miss it today—particularly if he shared, as most Americans have shared, whether intimately or by inheritance, any part of the experience that went into their making. And Willa Cather also did something the aspirant to permanent quality rarely achieves: she wrote a few books—*My Antonia* and *A Lost Lady* chief among them—that are not only American elegies but American classics, and that can still tell us, in a time of sanctified journalism and irresponsible sophistication, how much of a lifetime it costs to make that rare and expensive article.

1940–47   [1956]

Graham Greene

THE BEST AND THE WORST

I

"There was something about a fête which drew Arthur Rowe irre-
sistibly, bound him a helpless victim to the distant blare of a band
. . . called him like innocence: it was entangled in childhood, with
vicarage gardens, and girls in white summer frocks, and the smell of
herbaceous borders, and security." We meet him—in one of those
opening pages we have come to recognize as seizing the attention
with the immediate spell of the born conjuror—in the blitzed and
gutted London of the early 1940s, stumbling on a charity bazaar in
a Bloomsbury square: a man alone and a murderer but fearless because he has made a friend of his guilt. When he gave his wife the
poison that released her from the suffering he pitied he had not asked
her consent; "he could never tell whether she might not have preferred any sort of life to death." A fortune-teller slips him, mistakenly,
the password by which he wins a cake in the raffle. But there are
others who want it and the thing concealed in its heart. Visited that
night in his shabby room by a cripple, Rowe has barely tasted the
hyoscine in his tea when out of a droning sky a bomb drops, explodes
the house, and blows him and us into a dream of horrors—man-hunt,
spies, sabotage, amnesia, murders, and suicide: an "entertainment"
by Graham Greene.

Again we enter the familiar spectre of our age—years of fear and mounting premonition in the 1930s, war and its disasters in the forties, its aftermath of treachery and anarchy still around us in the fifties: no matter what the decade, Greene's evocation of it through fourteen novels (of which *The Ministry of Fear* may be taken as typical of those he calls "entertainments") invariably brings with it an effect that he has made classic of its time and that has justly won him the title "the Auden of the modern thriller." Here once more is the haunted England of the Twentieth Century, the European nightmare of corruption and doom, a *Blick ins Chaos* where

> taut with apprehensive dreads
> The sleepless guests of Europe lay
> Wishing the centuries away,
> And the low mutter of their vows
> Went echoing through her haunted house,
> As on the verge of happening
> There crouched the presence of The Thing.
> All formulas were tried to still
> The scratching on the window-sill,
> All bolts of custom made secure
> Against the pressure on the door,
> But up the staircase of events
> Carrying his special instruments,
> To every bedside all the same
> The dreadful figure swiftly came.[1]

The fustian stage-sets of Oppenheim, Bram Stoker, and Edgar Wallace are gone with their earlier innocent day. We are in a world whose fabulous realities have materialized appallingly out of contemporary legend and prophecy—the portentous journalism of Tabouis, Sheean, Thompson, Gunther, and the apotheosis of the foreign correspondent; the films of Lang, Murnau, Renoir, and Hitchcock; the Gothic fables of Ambler, Hammett, and Simenon; the putsches, pogroms, marches, and mobilizations that have mounted to catastrophe in the present moment of our lives. Its synthetic thrills and anarchic savagery are ruses of melodrama no longer. Guilt pervades all life. All of us are trying to discover how we entered the nightmare,

---

[1] W. H. Auden, "New Year Letter" (1940), ll. 15–29, in *The Double Man* (1941).

by what treachery we were betrayed to the storm of history. "Mother, please listen to me," cries Rowe.—"My little boy couldn't kill anyone":

> His mother smiled at him in a scared way but let him talk: he was the master of the dream now. He said, "I'm wanted for a murder I didn't do. People want to kill me because I know too much. I'm hiding underground, and up above the Germans are methodically smashing London to bits all round me. You remember St. Clements— the bells of St. Clements. They've smashed that—St. James's Piccadilly, the Burlington Arcade, Garland's Hotel where we stayed for the pantomime, Maples, and John Lewis. It sounds like a thriller, doesn't it?—but the thrillers are like life—more like life than you are, this lawn, your sandwiches, that pine . . . it's what we've all made of the world since you died. I'm your little Arthur who wouldn't hurt a beetle and I'm a murderer too. The world has been remade by William LeQueux.

Every age has its aesthetic of crime and terror, its attempt to give form to its special psychic or neurotic climate. No age has imposed greater handicaps on the effort than ours. Crime has gone beyond Addison's "chink in the chain armour of civilized communities." It has become the symptom of a radical lesion in the stamina of humanity. The hot violence of the Elizabethans is as different from the cold brutality of Hitlerian or Communist Europe, the heroic sin in Aeschylus or Webster from the squalid and endemic degeneracy in Céline or Henry Miller, the universal proportions of Greek or Shakespearean wrong from the gratuitous calculation and *inconséquences* of Gide's aesthetic criminals, as the worth at which the individual life was held in those times from its worthlessness in ours. A criminal takes his dignity from his defiance of the intelligence or merit that surrounds him, from the test his act imposes on the human community. He becomes trivial when that measure is denied him. So the modern thriller is permitted its prodigies of contrivance and hecatombs of death at the cost of becoming a bore. So film audiences fidget restlessly through the newsreel, waiting to be overwhelmed by the "edifying bilge" of Hollywood. The thrill habit, fed by tabloids, drugstore fiction, headlines, and events, has competed successfully with gin, drugs, and aspirin, and doped the moral nerve of a generation.

The hardship this imposes on the artist is obvious. When felony, by becoming political, becomes impersonal; when the *acte gratuit* elicits not only secret but public approval, its dramatist faces the desperate task of restoring to his readers their lost instinct of values, the sense of human worth. It is not enough that the thriller become psychic: Freudian behavior patterns have become as much an open commodity and stock property as spy rings and torture chambers were fifty years ago. It must become moral as well.

The Victorian *frisson* of crime was all the choicer for the rigor of propriety and sentiment that hedged it in. Dickens' terrors are enhanced less by his rhetoric than by his coziness. The reversion to criminality in Dostoevsky takes place in a ramifying hierarchy of authority—family life, social caste, political and religious bureaucracy, Tzarist militarism and repression. The horror in *The Turn of the Screw* is framed by the severest decorum, taste, and inhibition. James—like Conrad, Gide, and Thomas Mann—felt the seduction of crime but he also knew its artistic conditions. "Everything you may further do will be grist to my imaginative mill," he once wrote William Roughead of Edinburgh in thanks for a book of the latter's criminal histories: "I'm not sure I enter into such matters best when they are *very* archaic or remote from our familiarities, for then the testimony to manners and morals is rather blurred for me by the *whole* barbarism. . . . The thrilling in the comparatively modern much appeals to me—for there the *special* manners and morals become queerly disclosed. . . . then go back to the dear old human and sociable murders and adulteries and forgeries in which we are so agreeably at home." The admonition might have served as the cue for the talent of Graham Greene.[2]

----

[2] The titles and dates of Greene's book-length tales are: *The Man Within* (1929), *The Name of Action* (1930), *Rumour at Nightfall* (1932), *Orient Express* (titled in England *Stamboul Train*, 1932), *It's a Battlefield* (1934), *England Made Me* (1935; republished in America in 1948 as *The Shipwrecked*),

Greene, dealing in a "whole barbarism" equaling or surpassing anything in history, has undertaken to redeem that dilapidation from the stupefying mechanism and inconsequence to which modern terrorism has reduced it. Arthur Calder Marshall has rightly said, in an article in *Horizon*,[3] that "few living English novelists derive more material from the daily newspaper than Graham Greene." His *mise-en-scène* includes the Nazi underground and fifth column (*The Confidential Agent, The Ministry of Fear*), Communist politics riddled by schisms and betrayals (*It's a Battlefield*), Kruger and his international swindles (*England Made Me*), Zaharoff and the alliance between munitions-making and *Machtpolitik* (*This Gun for Hire*), the English racetrack gang warfare (*Brighton Rock*), the Mexican church suppression (*The Power and the Glory*), wartime in the Gold Coast (*The Heart of the Matter*), in London (*The End of the Affair*), and in Indochina (*The Quiet American*); while his *Orient Express* is the same train we've traveled on all the way from *Shanghai Express* to *Night Train* and *The Lady Vanishes*. But where once—in James, Conrad, Dostoevsky, in Dickens, Defoe and the Elizabethans —it was society, state, kingdom, world, or the universe itself that

---

This Gun for Hire (English title *A Gun for Sale*, 1936), *Brighton Rock* (1938), *The Confidential Agent* (1939), *The Power and the Glory* (1940; first titled in America *The Labyrinthine Ways* but reissued under its original English title in 1947), *The Ministry of Fear* (1943), *The Heart of the Matter* (1948), *The End of the Affair* (1951), *The Quiet American* (1956). Some of these were presented as "entertainments" (*Orient Express, The Confidential Agent, The Ministry of Fear*), others being submitted as novels (*It's a Battlefield, The Power and the Glory, The Heart of the Matter, The End of the Affair, The Quiet American*); but since *Brighton Rock* was first called an "entertainment" and later listed as a novel, the force of Greene's distinction is not always clear. There are also several books of shorter tales, two books of travel (*Journey Without Maps*, 1936, and *Another Mexico*, 1939, the latter called *The Lawless Roads* in England), a short study of *British Dramatists* (1942), a *jeu d'esprit* called *Loser Takes All* in 1955, and a number of films, among them *The Fallen Idol* and *The Third Man* in which Greene had a direct hand (not the case in most of the films made from his books). His first play, *The Living Room*, was produced in 1953, and dramatic versions of *Brighton Rock* in 1943 and of *The Power and the Glory* in 1956. A selection of his critical and personal essays appeared in *The Lost Childhood* in 1951.

[3] "The Works of Graham Greene," *Horizon*, May 1940, pp. 367–75.

supplied the presiding order of law and justice, it is now the isolated, betrayed, but finally indestructible integrity of the individual life that must furnish that measure. Humanity, having contrived a world of mindless and psychotic brutality, reverts for survival to the test of the single man. Marked, hunted, or condemned, he may work for evil or for good, but it is his passion for a moral identity of his own that provides the nexus of values in a world that has reverted to anarchy. His lineage is familiar—Raskolnikov, Stavrogin, Kirilov; Conrad's Jim, Razumov, and Heyst; Mann's Felix Krull and Gide's Lafcadio; Hesse's Steppenwolf and Demian, and, more immediately, Kafka's K. He appears in almost every Greene novel—as hero or victim in Drover, Dr. Czinner, the nameless D., and Major Scobie; as pariah or renegade in Raven, Farrant, Rowe, and the whisky priest of *The Power and the Glory;* as the incarnation of pure malevolence in Pinkie, the boy gangster of *Brighton Rock.*

The plot that involves him is fairly consistent. *Brighton Rock* may be taken as showing it in archetype. Its conflict rests on a basic dualism of forces, saved from the prevalent danger of becoming an inflexible mechanism by Greene's skill in suggestion and insight, yet radical in its antithesis of elements. Pinkie is a believing Catholic. He knows Hell as a reality and accepts his damnation. *Corruptio optimi pessima* is the last faith left him to live or die by. Ida Arnold, the full-blown, life-loving tart whose casual lover the gang has killed, sets out to track him down: "unregenerate, a specimen of the 'natural man,' coarsely amiable, bestially kind, the most dangerous enemy to religion." She pursues him with ruthless and convinced intention, corners him, sees him killed. The boy is sped to his damnation and Ida triumphs ("God doesn't mind a bit of human nature. . . . I know the difference between Right and Wrong.") The hostility is crucial. It figures in all of Greene's mature books—Mather the detective against Raven the assassin in *This Gun for Hire;* the Inspector against Drover in *It's a Battlefield;* the Communist police lieutenant, accompanied by the *mestizo* who acts as nemesis, against the hunted, shameless, renegade priest in *The Power and the Glory,* trailing his desecrated sanctity through the hovels and jungles of the Mexican state yet persisting in his office of grace and so embracing the doom that pursues him. It reappears in the hunting down of Major Scobie by the agent Wilson in *The Heart of the Matter,* and it counts in the tragic passion of Bendrix for Sarah Miles in *The End of the Affair.* A critic in *The New Statesman* once put the case concisely: "Mr. Greene is a Catholic, and his novel *Brighton Rock* betrays a misanthropic, almost Jansenist, contempt for the virtues that do not spring from grace." [4]

It is this grace that operates as the principle which makes palpable its necessary enemy, Evil. And it is the evil that materializes out of vice, crime, nightmare, and moral stupefaction in Greene's books that brings him into a notable company. The same evil is made to work behind the dramatic mystery and psychic confusion in *The Turn of the Screw* and beneath the squalid violence in Conrad's *The Secret Agent,* that parent classic in this field of fiction which, appearing in 1907, established the kind of novel that Greene and his generation have carried to such exorbitant lengths. To define and objectify the evil, to extricate it from the relativity of values and abstractions— arbitrary justice, impersonal humanitarianism and pity, right and wrong, good and bad—is the ultimate motive of Greene's work. His pursuit of it has carried him afield among the totems and obscenities of coastal Africa which he conjured in *Journey Without Maps,* his descent to the heart of darkness:

> It isn't a gain to have turned the witch or the masked secret dancer, the sense of supernatural evil, into the small human viciousness of the thin distinguished military gray head in Kensington Gardens with the soft lips and the eye which dwelt with dull lustre on girls and boys of a certain age. . . . They are not, after all, so far from the central darkness. . . . when one sees to what unhappiness, to what peril of extinction, centuries of cerebration have brought us, one sometimes has a curiosity to discover if one can from what we have come, to recall at which point we went astray.

------

[4] *The New Statesman and Nation* (London), March 20, 1943, p. 188. The critic is not named; he was discussing a dramatic production, made at that time in London, of *Brighton Rock.*

An echo clearly sounds here from a passage in T. S. Eliot's essay on Baudelaire (1930) which has become a classic statement of the problem in recent criticism:

> So far as we are human, what we do must be either evil or good; so far as we do evil or good, we are human; and it is better, in a paradoxical way, to do evil than to do nothing: at least, we exist. It is true to say that the glory of man is his capacity for salvation; it is also true to say that his glory is his capacity for damnation. The worst that can be said of most of our malefactors, from statesmen to thieves, is that they are not men enough to be damned.

And Greene has pointed to another definition of his subject in one of the epigraphs he prefixed to his book on Mexico in 1939—a passage, too long to quote here in full, from Newman:

> To consider the world in its length and breadth, its various history, the many races of man, their starts, their fortunes, their mutual alienation, their conflicts . . . the impotent conclusion of long-standing facts, the tokens so faint and broken of a superintending design, the blind evolution of what turn out to be great powers or truth . . . the greatness and littleness of man, his far-reaching aims, his short duration, the curtain hung over his futurity, the disappointments of life, the defeat of good, the success of evil . . . the prevalence and intensity of sin, the pervading idolatries, the corruptions, the dreary hopeless irreligion, that condition of the whole race . . . all this is a vision to dizzy and appal; and inflicts upon the mind the sense of a profound mystery, which is absolutely beyond human solution.
> What shall be said to this heart-piercing, reason-bewildering fact? I can only answer, that either there is no Creator, or this living society of men is in a true sense discarded from His presence . . . *if* there be a God, *since* there is a God, the human race is implicated in some terrible aboriginal calamity.

The drama and present issue of that calamity are what make the continuous theme of Greene's fiction in its development over the past quarter-century.

II

Greene's beginnings in the novel were in a vein of romantic Stevensonian adventure in *The Man Within,* but he emphasized even there,

in a title taken from Thomas Browne, the dualism of the moral personality ("There's another man within me that's angry with me," a
derivation from Paul's "law in my members" in the Epistle to the
Romans). He next applied the motif to the situation of moral anarchy
in modern politics and society and began to adopt for the purpose
the devices of intrigue and mystery as the modern thriller had developed them (*The Name of Action, Rumour at Nightfall, Orient
Express*). These tales, at first crude and exaggerated in contrivance
(Greene has dropped the first two of the last named from his collected
edition), soon advanced into his characteristic kind of expertness, and
all of them implied a dissatisfaction with the current tendencies in
English fiction. This became explicit in his reviews of the modern
novelists. Henry James, possibly Conrad, were the last masters of
the English novel to preserve its powers in anything like their full
tragic and moral potentialities. "After the death of Henry James," he
wrote in an essay on Mauriac, "a disaster overtook the English novel:
indeed long before his death one can picture that quiet, impressive,
rather complacent figure, like the last survivor on a raft, gazing out
over a sea scattered with wreckage."

> For [he continued] with the death of James the religious sense
> was lost to the English novel, and with the religious sense went the
> sense of the importance of the human act. It was as if the world of
> fiction had lost a dimension: the characters of such distinguished
> writers as Mrs. Virginia Woolf and Mr. E. M. Forster wandered like
> cardboard symbols through a world that was paper-thin. Even in one
> of the most materialistic of our great novelists—in Trollope—we
> are aware of another world against which the actions of the char-
> acters are thrown into relief. The ungainly clergyman picking his
> black-booted way through the mud, handling so awkwardly his um-
> brella, speaking of his miserable income and stumbling through a
> proposal of marriage, exists in a way that Mrs. Woolf's Mr. Ramsay
> never does, because we are aware that he exists not only to the
> woman he is addressing but also in a God's eye. His unimportance in
> the world of the senses is only matched by his enormous importance
> in another world.

So the novelist, taking "refuge in the subjective novel," found that
he had "lost yet another dimension": "the visible world for him ceased

to exist as completely as the spiritual." Mauriac accordingly was
rated as belonging to "the company of the great traditional novelists:
he is a writer for whom the visible world has not ceased to exist,
whose characters have the solidity and importance of men with souls
to save or lose, and a writer who claims the traditional and essential
right of a novelist, to comment, to express his views." But if Greene
gave his highest honors among modern novelists to James ("it is in
the final justice of his pity, the completeness of an analysis which enabled him to pity the most shabby, the most corrupt, of his human
actors, that he ranks with the greatest of creative writers. He is as
solitary in the history of the novel as Shakespeare in the history of
poetry"), to Conrad (for his instinct of " 'the mental degradation to
which a man's intelligence is exposed on its way through life': 'the
passions of men shortsighted in good and evil': in scattered phrases
you get the memories of a creed working like poetry through the
agnostic prose"), and to Mauriac ("if Pascal had been a novelist, we
feel, this is the method and the tone he would have used"); if he
granted his secondary respects to writers like Corvo ("he cared for
nothing but his faith . . . if he could not have Heaven, he would
have Hell"), Ford Madox Ford ("he had never really believed in
human happiness"), and De La Mare ("no one can bring the natural
visible world more sharply to the eye"); if he denied the authentic
creative virtue alike to the agnostic Butler ("the perpetual need to
generalize from a peculiar personal experience maimed his imagination") or Havelock Ellis ("invincible ignorance") and to the believing Eric Gill ("as an artist Gill gained nothing from his faith . . .
his rebellion never amounted to much") or the angry mystic Léon
Bloy ("he hadn't the creative instinct . . . the hatred of life . . .
prevented him from being a novelist or a mystic of the first order"),
it appeared that there was another order of talent that had conditioned Greene's own imagination from its earliest workings. He responded to it in the adventure tales of John Buchan ("Now I saw
how thin is the protection of civilization") and Conan Doyle ("think
of the sense of horror which hangs over the laurelled drive of Upper
Norwood and behind the curtains of Lower Camberwell. . . . he

made Plumstead Marshes and the Barking Level as vivid and unfamiliar as a lesser writer would have made the mangrove swamps
of the West Coast"), but its mark had been laid on him long before
he encountered these writers: in childhood when "all books are books
of divination." Its masters then were the literary heroes of his boyhood: "Rider Haggard, Percy Westerman, Captain Brereton, or
Stanley Weyman." But vividly as these ignited his imagination,
much as *King Solomon's Mines* "influenced the future," it "could not
finally satisfy": its characters were too much "like Platonic ideas:
they were not life as one had already begun to know it." The "future
for better or worse really struck" when he discovered *The Viper of
Milan* by Marjorie Bowen. "It was," says Greene, "as if I had been
supplied once and for all with a subject."

"Why?" he asks, and gives his answer. Here for the first time he
learned that while "goodness has only once found a perfect incarnation in a human body and never will again," evil "can always find a
home there"; that there is a "sense of doom" that "lies over success";
that "perfect evil walk[s] the world where perfect good can never
walk again." And he acknowledges that it was Miss Bowen's Italian
melodrama that gave "me my pattern—religion might later explain
it in other terms, but the pattern was already there"; and after "one
had lived for fourteen years in a wild jungle country without a map.
. . . now the paths had been traced and naturally one had to follow
them." [5]

It is apparent from these disclosures that Greene, whatever his
sense of human and moral complexity or his sophisticated insight into
the riddled situation of his time, early decided to address himself to
a primitive order of fiction. But since the social and political conditions of the age had likewise reverted to primitive forms of violence,
brutality, and anarchy he found his purpose matched in the events
of the historic moment. For that moment the thriller was an obvious
and logical imaginative medium, and Greene proceeded to raise it
to a skill and artistry few other writers of the period, and none in

---

[5] All these quotations are from Greene's collection of essays, *The Lost Childhood* (1951).

English, had arrived at. His novels between 1930 and 1945 record the crisis and confusions of those years with an effect of atmosphere and moral desperation perfectly appropriate to the time. If their expert contrivance often seems to descend to sleight of hand; if the surrealism of their action and settings can result in efflorescences of sheer conjuring; if the mechanics of the thriller—chases, coincidences, strokes of accident, and exploding surprises—can at times collapse into a kind of demented catastrophe, these were not too remotely at odds with the possibilities of modern terrorism, police action, international intrigue and violence. His superiority to the convention in which he worked was clear; if at times it ran uncomfortably close to the jigsaw-puzzle manipulation which entertainers like Ambler, Hammett, and Raymond Chandler had made so readable and finally so trivial, there was always working in it a poetry of desperation and an instinct for the rudiments of moral conflict that lifted it to allegoric validity. It was apparently at such validity that Greene was aiming in these books. "What strikes the attention most in this closed Fagin universe," he has said in writing on *Oliver Twist,* "are the different levels of unreality"; and of Mauriac's novels he has said that "One is never tempted to consider in detail M. Mauriac's plots. Who can describe six months afterwards the order of events, say in *Ce Qui Était Perdu?* . . . . We are saved or damned by our thoughts, not by our actions."

In fiction of this kind, action itself becomes less real or representative than symbolic. Disbelief is suspended in acceptance of the typical or the potential; incredulity yields to imaginative recognition; and since the events of modern politics and militarism had already wrenched the contemporary imagination out of most of its accepted habits and disciplines, Greene's plots found the thriller fully conditioned to his purpose. If a writer like David Cecil could say, to the charge that John Webster's plays are "extravagant, irrational, and melodramatic," that "the battle of heaven and hell cannot be convincingly conveyed in a mode of humdrum everyday realism" and that "the wild and bloody conventions of Elizabethan melodrama provided a most appropriate vehicle for conveying his hell-haunted vision of human existence," a similar defense could be argued for Greene's melodrama—the more so because the battle of heaven and hell and the hell-haunted vision had become part of the European and contemporary experience.

Moreover, in tales of this kind (to which the adjective "operatic," used by Lionel Trilling to describe certain features in the novels of Forster, applies) character itself tends to reduce to primary or symbolic terms. The tests of average consistency or psychological realism are not of the first importance. A more radical appeal acts to suspend them. The novel refers to something more than the principles of temperament; the "humors" become not only moral but philosophic. At times, in books like *It's a Battlefield* and *England Made Me,* Greene worked in terms of Freudian or abnormal character types and so brought his characters into an uncomfortable but effective relation with his melodrama. At others—*This Gun for Hire* and *The Confidential Agent*—the psychic pathology submitted openly and conveniently to the claims of political violence and so left the story to rest at the level of the historical or political parable (hence "an entertainment"). In *Brighton Rock* the fable became explicitly religious; in *The Power and the Glory* it perhaps became "metaphysical" as well. The last-named novel is certainly one of Greene's finest achievements, possibly his masterpiece. In it the action and milieu are not only invested with a really convincing quality of legend. The fable itself, and the truth it evokes, are believably enacted by the two central characters—the priest with his inescapable vocation, the police lieutenant with his—in a way that is not pressed to exaggerate or simplify their primitive and symbolic functions in the drama. The book is sustained from first to last by a unity of atmosphere that harmonizes its setting, characters, moral values, and historic reference into a logical consistency of effect, and the result is one of the most haunting legends of our time.

Greene's ambition was not, however, content to rest with this kind of result. His more serious books had already aimed at being more than fables or parables. He had before him the examples of Mauriac and Faulkner, both of whom he has acknowledged as major influences in his work. *It's a Battlefield, Brighton Rock,* and *The Power and the Glory* pointed the way to a fiction of full-bodied and realistic substance, and in *The Heart of the Matter* in 1947 he undertook to write a complete and consistent novel. (His "entertainments" since that time have been frankly written for film production—*The Third Man* and *Loser Takes All.*) This brought him squarely up against the problem of reconciling his religious and didactic premises to the realistic and empirical principles of the novel form; of harmonizing an orthodoxy of belief (however personal or inquisitive) with what George Orwell once called "the most anarchical of all forms of literature." ("How many Roman Catholics have been good novelists? Even the handful one could name have usually been bad Catholics. The novel is practically a Protestant form of art; it is a product of the free mind, the autonomous individual.") [6]

Greene certainly had no intention of conforming to the conventions of religious-literary sentimentalism. In this at least he shared what has been called "one major objective of young English Catholic writers"—"not to resemble Chesterton." On the other hand, he was by conviction committed to a belief in the efficacy and sufficiency of grace as the final test of value in character and conduct. Now that he committed himself equally to the demands of psychological and moral realism which the novel imposes, he met for the first time the tests a novelist faces when he joins the human claims of his art with the theological claims of his faith. And grace is bound to become a question-begging premise on which to rest the arguments of psychic and moral realism. ("The greatest advantage of religious faith for the artist," Gide once noted in his journal, "is that it permits him a *limitless* pride.") [7] The instinctive or lifelong believer—Mauriac, O'Faolain, Eliot, whatever their crises of "conversion" or re-conversion—usually finds a means of harmonizing orthodoxy with experience, dogma with moral inquisition. The voluntary or deliberate convert

---

[6] *Inside the Whale and Other Essays* (London, 1940), p. 173.

[7] "Le plus grand avantage de la foi religieuse, pour l'artiste, c'est qu'elle lui permet un orgueil *incommensurable." Journal 1889–1939,* p. 191 (5 décembre, 1905).

—Claudel, Greene, Waugh, perhaps Bloy and Bernanos—seems never to arrive at such reconciliation, at least not easily or convincingly. Experience and faith refuse to come to natural or practical conjunctions; in fact, it is implied that they were never intended to. Faith becomes for such men the most deadly-serious "vested interest" of their existence. If it does not assert itself in the form of a didactic or inflexible logic, it does so in the form of a perversely ingenious one. There has always been a visible gap between the writer or poet of inherited or habitual faith and the one of converted belief (the same difference shows up in writers of political dogmatism), and it is not lessened by the convert's acquaintance with unbelief. He usually conveys "the perpetual need to generalize from a peculiar personal experience," and his imagination is seldom left unmaimed, however much it may also have been stimulated.

Greene's plots from the first showed a tendency to enforce absolutes of moral judgment—a kind of theological *vis inertiae*—which resulted in the humors to which his characters tended to reduce. The "sanctified sinner" who appears in most of Greene's books is the most prominent of these. The type has become a feature of modern religious literature. Baudelaire, Rimbaud, and Bloy (*Une Femme pauvre*) seem to have combined to give it its characteristic stamp and utility in literary mysticism, and since their day it has become a virtual cliché of religious drama and symbolism. The idea has been put bluntly by its critics: "vice is defined as the manure in which salvation flowers." [8] Orwell made a critical issue of it when he reviewed Greene's *The Heart of the Matter*.[9] It was not only the frivolity of the cult he found suspect: its suggestion "that there is something rather *distingué* in being damned" and its hint of a "weakening of belief" ("when people really believed in Hell, they were not so fond of striking graceful attitudes on its brink"). It was also its results in dramatic artistry: "by trying to clothe theological speculations in flesh and blood, it produces psychological absurdities." The cases

---

[8] Kenneth Tynan, reviewing the dramatic version of *The Power and the Glory* in *The Observer* (London), April 8, 1956, p. 11.
[9] *The New Yorker*, July 17, 1948, pp. 61–63.

of both Pinkie in *Brighton Rock* and Scobie in *The Heart of the Matter* were taken as showing its liabilities for a novelist: that of Pinkie by presupposing "that the most brutally stupid person can, merely by having been brought up a Catholic, be capable of great intellectual subtlety"; that of Scobie "because the two halves of him do not fit together." ("If he were capable of getting into the kind of mess that is described, he would have got into it earlier. If he really felt that adultery is mortal sin, he would stop committing it; if he persisted in it, his sense of sin would weaken. If he believed in Hell, he would not risk going there merely to spare the feelings of a couple of neurotic women.")

In other words, the arguments which such characters enact tend to become increasingly "loaded" as they advance toward explicit theological conclusions. And the fiction that embodies such arguments soon runs into the difficulty which all tendentious or didactic fiction sooner or later encounters. It no longer "argues" the problems and complexities of character in terms of psychological and moral forces; it states, decides, and solves them in terms of pre-established and dictated premises. Grace is always held in reserve as a principle of salvation, a principle which soon becomes too arbitrary and convenient to find justification in conduct or purpose. It descends like a Christianized *deus ex machina* to redeem its vessels when they have driven themselves into the impasse or sacrilege that would, on moral grounds alone, be sufficient to damn them. Greene of course shirks nothing in presenting his men and women as psychically complex and morally confounded. But as he advances out of parable into realism, out of the tale of violence into the drama of credible human personalities, he still keeps an ace up his sleeve, and grace is called upon to do the work that normally would be assigned to moral logic and nemesis. "O God," says Scobie after he has taken communion in a state of mortal sin and is beginning to plan his suicide, "I am the only guilty one because I've known the answers all the time." This admission of his damnation is also his plea for salvation ("I think," says the priest afterward to his widow, "from what I saw of him, that he really loved God"); and what it implies is the kind of presumption or arrogance that has become a feature of recent religious fiction: namely, that neither conduct nor morals are of final importance to the believer. *Corruptio optimi pessima:* it is not only a case of the corruption of the best being the worst. It is by their capacity for corruption or damnation that the best—the believers— qualify for redemption. "The others don't count." [10]

What accompanies this premise in Greene's later novels is likely to take a form which, whatever its theological tenability, can be as repugnant (intentionally repugnant no doubt) to normal religious feeling as it is to aesthetic judgment. "O God, I offer up my damnation to you. Take it. Use it for them," Scobie murmurs at the communion rail; and when, presently, he contemplates future repetitions of his sacrilege, he has "a sudden picture before his eyes of a bleeding face, of eyes closed by the continuous shower of blows: the punch-drunk head of God reeling sideways." On such passages it is difficult not to agree with the critic who acts in revulsion: "a stern theological dogma [is] grossly degraded into melodrama, to an extent which allows even a non-believer to speak of blasphemy. . . . It is intolerable. Whether we accept the dogma or not, it is intolerable that it should be expressed in such luridly anthropomorphic terms as these . . . a hotting-up of religious belief for fictional purposes, a vulgarization of the faith." [11] Greene has made a repeated point of indicting pity as a sin of presumption. Rowe, Scobie, and Bendrix are all made to suffer the consequences of assuming a divine prerogative. It is, however, hard to believe that a similar presumption does not underlie the special pleading that accompanies Scobie's catastrophe. "A priest only knows the unimportant things," says Father Rank to Mrs. Scobie. "Unimportant?" "Oh, I mean the sins," he replies impatiently.

----

[10] Greene took for his motto of *The Heart of the Matter* a passage from Charles Péguy (subsequently shortened to its first three sentences in the published book): "Le pécheur est au coeur même de chrétienté. . . . Nul n'est aussi compétent que le pécheur en matière de chrétienté. Nul, si ce n'est le saint. Et en principe c'est le même homme. . . . C'est une cité. Un mauvais citoyen est de la cité. Un bon étranger n'en est pas." The abbreviation may be significant but the import of the whole passage is conveyed in the novel itself.

[11] Philip Toynbee, *The Observer* (London), December 4, 1955.

"A man doesn't come to us and confess his virtues." To reasoning as conveniently circular as this no practical moral appeal is possible.

The Heart of the Matter is Greene's most ambitious book thus far but in spite of its advance beyond the schematic pattern of its predecessors it is not finally his most convincing one. Its excessive manipulation keeps it from being that. *The End of the Affair* in 1951 showed an important development. It was Greene's first novel to put aside entirely the devices of intrigue, mystery, and criminal motivation. Its scene is modern London, its drama is intimately personal, and though the action takes place in wartime, war does not figure in the events except accidentally. Its plot shows a radical simplicity, and its characters, if tormented to the point of abnormality, remain recognizable as people of credible moral responsibility. It develops a story of secret passion between a modern novelist of brilliant sardonic talent and self-professed agnostic egotism, Maurice Bendrix, and Sarah Miles, the suburban wife who loves him and suffers his selfish claims to the point of immolating herself destructively to save him from death in a bombing. Sarah makes a bargain with God: she will give up her love for Bendrix if his life is saved. Her sacrifice brings on her the sufferings of a religious atonement and finally results in the event of a miracle which reveals to Bendrix the nature and consequences of his selfish corruption. Greene's epigraph here comes from Bloy: "Man has places in his heart which do not yet exist, and into them enters suffering in order that they may have existence."

The tale is closely and powerfully developed, and its three principal characters are perhaps the most subtly drawn and intimately created of any in Greene's gallery. It is true that here again, especially in the final section of the book, they assume a disembodied abstraction of conduct which recalls the cases of Pinkie and Scobie, and the introduction of the miracle, shrewdly handled though it is, risks the dissolution of the entire conflict in an arbitrary conclusion. The symbolic effect that might make such an event convincing is weakened by the realistic basis on which the drama is built; it ends as the later, more schematized novels of Mauriac do, in an unprepared shift from realism to didacticism, an arbitrary change of moral (and consequently of dramatic) premises which has the effect of detaching the characters from their established logic as personalities and forcing them to serve a function outside themselves. The result is an effect of metaphysical contrivance which it would take the powers of a Dostoevsky to justify. But if Greene here resorts to an artificiality of argument that has weakened a share of Mauriac's later work, he also invites in this novel a comparison with Mauriac's psychic and moral insight. By applying himself to an intimate human conflict and laying aside the melodramatic historical framework of his earlier work, he achieves a substance that brings him to a point of renewal and fresh departure in his fiction.[12]

He remains significant, however, because of what he has done to recreate and reassert the moral necessity in his characters, and to project its reality, by symbolic means, into the human and social crisis of his time. He has used guilt and horror for what they have signified in every age, Elizabethan, Gothic, Romantic, or Victorian —as a mode of exploring the fears, evasions, and panic that confuse men or betray the dignity of reason to violence and brutality, but which must always, whatever the historic situation in which they appear, be faced, recognized, and mastered if salvation is to escape the curse of self-deception. The identity Greene's heroes seek is that of a conscience that shirks none of the deception or confusion in their natures. If the "destructive element" of moral anarchy threatens them, it is their passion for a moral identity of their own that redeems them. It is by that passion that they give his work, to quote one of its most

----

[12] I have not included here a discussion of Greene's latest novel, *The Quiet American* of 1956. This is one of his most brilliant feats of dramatic narration, but its drama, which concerns the conflict of American and European foreign policy in the Indo-China war, though announced as representing a "new vein" in which "religion plays little or no part," amounts mainly to a transferring of his argument from a religious to a political basis. It is apparently the cynical English journalist Fowler who is equipped with political and humanitarian "grace," and the innocent, do-gooding, anti-Communist American meddler, Pyle, who is without it. "On every level except the most important one," says Philip Toynbee (an English critic), in the article already quoted, "this is a magnificent novel. But Graham Greene is a novelist who must be judged on the most important level."

acute critics [13]—whatever "its intellectual dishonesty, its ellipses of approximation and selective omissions, as well as its fragmentation of character"—its "sense of history." The drama he presents, "with its evasions and its apologia, is part of our climate of fear and guilt, where it is hard for a man of good-will, lacking good actions, to see straight or to speak plain. The personal tragedy is in the womb of the general one, and pity is their common blood-stream."

It is because he dramatizes the hostile forces of anarchy and conscience, of the moral nonentity with which nature or history threatens man and the absolute tests of moral selfhood, that Greene has brought about one of the most challenging combinations of historical allegory and spiritual argument that have appeared in the present dubious phase of English fiction. His style and imagery can be as melodramatic as his action, but he has made of them an instrument for probing the temper and tragedy of the age, the perversions that have come near to wrecking it, and the stricken weathers of its soul. It still remains for him to get beyond its confusions, negative appeals, and perverse standards—not to mention the tricky arguments by which these are too often condemned in his books and which are too much left to do the work of the honest imagination—to become a fully responsible novelist in his English generation. This is a role to which his acute sense of history and his remarkable gifts in moral drama have assigned him. His skill already puts him in the descent of the modern masters—James, Conrad, Joyce—in whom judgment and

---

[13] Donat O'Donnell, *Maria Cross: Imaginative Patterns in a Group of Modern Catholic Writers* (1952), pp. 63–91, here pp. 88–90. This book, one of the best on its subject, makes an extended analysis of *The Heart of the Matter*. The fullest discussion of Greene's work has appeared in an English study, *The Art of Graham Greene* by Kenneth Allott and Miriam Farris (London, 1951), and in two French books which testify to his popularity in France, where he has been taken as a religious and Catholic answer to Existentialism: Jacques Madaule's *Graham Greene* and Paul Rostenne's *Graham Greene: témoin des temps tragiques* (both Paris, 1949). There are also useful essays by Walter Allen in *Penguin New Writing* (London, 1943) and *Writers of Today* (London, 1946), by Arthur Calder Marshall in *Living Writers* (London, 1947), by Claire Eliane Engel in *Esquisses anglais* (Paris, 1949), and by Henri Lemaître, "Un Romancier chrétien de l'absurde," in *Culture Catholique IV* (Paris, 1949).

imagination achieved their richest combination, as well as in the company of the few living novelists—Mauriac, Malraux, Hemingway, Faulkner—in whom their standard survives. He is one of the few contemporary English talents who insist on being referred to that standard and who give evidence that it means to persist.

1943 [1956]

Readings in Fiction

I. THE POET AS HERO

Lotte in Weimar by Thomas Mann

"As I look back on my work," Thomas Mann once said, "I realize that I have not chosen the subjects of my books. They have chosen me." *Buddenbrooks* "displayed a will of its own. *The Magic Mountain* when its turn came was to be quite as headstrong." "Every piece of work," he added, "is in fact a realization—piecemeal if you like, but each complete in itself—of our own nature; they are stones on that harsh road which we must walk to learn ourselves. No wonder, then, that each one in turn is a surprise to us!"

That Mann, with his lifelong concern for the role of the artist in society, his "profound fascination" by the part the hero of culture plays in the shaping of human action and history—"compelled," moreover, as he has confessed, "to the point of veneration" by the poet "in whom the entire poetical fame of the German people reached its apex"—should one day write a novel on Goethe was clearly on the cards of his life-work from its beginnings. Schopenhauer, Dostoevsky, Nietzsche, Wagner—these sovereign influences in his thought, exponents of daemonic insight and antinomian challenge, might compel him by their "vision through suffering," the "Erfahrung durch Angst, Streit, und Widerstand" which gave the Nineteenth Century its radical strength in self-knowledge and prophecy. But in the dialectic workings of Mann's curiosity there was always an equal attraction toward the genius who, more than any other, resisted the "mystic-sensual" order of revelation, made himself the defendant of the "anti-diabolic principle," and so became the hero of the "pure and disin-terested contemplation" which permits "the only and primary possi-bility of release from the torture of instinct" and grants the artist the supreme felicity of his vocation: "to hold life sacred and to be loyal to it." "Everything in his life was instruction, edification, a means to culture; everything conspired toward a more perfect affirmation of himself and of all creatures": Gide's definition of the Goethean beati-tude expressed the recognition of an even more radically opposed temper and in effect distilled the essence of Mann's. The creator of a gallery of characters who represent above any other in our time the rebellious, guilt-activated, or abnormal compulsions of the aes-thetic or skeptical personality—Hanno Buddenbrooks, Tonio Kröger, Gustav von Aschenbach, Naphtha and Settembrini, Adrian Lever-kühn—was drawn as by a lodestone to the hero who stood in an-tithesis and implicit criticism to these: to the Goethe whose genius it was to convert his own "profound maladjustment and ill humor," his "hampering depression," "mistrust of ideas," and "child-of-nature indifference," his "*médisance*" and "inhuman, elfish irresponsibility" —all of them admitted as elements of his natively "anti-ideal constitu-tion"—into a triumph of "the bourgeois and supra-bourgeois char-acter" whose ultimate patriotism was only to humanity and whose deepest faith committed him to "the victory of the sane." When *Lotte in Weimar* appeared in 1939 (in English in 1940 under the title *The Beloved Returns*) [1] it came as something more than Mann's tribute to the hero of his personal and national culture. It came as the culmi-nation of his lifelong recognition of the principle of genius that had served to correct and stabilize the rebellious sympathies in his own temperament and in the parables that had issued from it.

Yet until its hero appears on page 281, Mann's Goethe novel threat-

---

[1] *Lotte in Weimar* (Stockholm: Bermann-Fischer Verlag, 1939); *The Be-loved Returns,* translated by H. T. Lowe-Porter (New York: Alfred A. Knopf, 1940).

ens to become wholly bogged in the fabulous and confusing legend
of its subject—in the torrents of defensive words and bungling surmises let forth by the garrulous puppets who surround the poet in
his final apotheosis at Weimar. Goethe is here the poet as deity, the
sage and national hero who "has got beyond the pathological and
ripened into greatness" in the *West-Oestlicher Divan.* He appears as
Privy-Councillor, obedient to the fawning whims of Weimar court
and society ("You can resign yourself with dignity now to being a
stiff-legged Excellence and saying grace for your sycophants!"), yet
viewing from the serene couch of Hafiz the toppling thrones and
quaking empires of 1816—a chosen intimate of Nature still, who puts
final touches to his treatises on optics, crystals, and plant morphology
while he pursues in his dreams his "bright vision of the depths." Mann
has subjected him to a species of scientific recovery. Though the form
of the novel obviously derives from his earlier experiments in musical
structure, it more closely suggests the methods of the paleontologist,
and for half its length the fossils of Goethean legend and scholarship
give little sense of the living organism that once inhabited them.

Forty-four years after the Wetzlar idyll that gave the world *Die
Leiden des jungen Werthers* and catapulted its author and heroine
into European fame, the Lotte of that novel, now Frau Councillor
Charlotte Kestner of Hannover, arrives in Weimar. She has not seen
Goethe since her girlhood. She comes ostensibly to visit her sister
Frau Ridel, but secretly she means to win a revenge for having suffered, through half a century of virtuous bourgeois domesticity, the
bondage of being involved in Goethe's "overwhelming life," a symbol
who "from year to year had played an ever greater part in the
thoughts and imaginations of mankind." Through six lengthy chapters of pompously ironical and deflationary dialogue, Frau Kestner
is subjected to the discomforts of a fame she has struggled a lifetime to escape. She suffers the oppressive grovelings of her inn's
major-domo, the clamor of the townspeople, the imbecile gossip of a
roving Irish lion-hunter called Rose Cuzzle, the shamefaced frustrations of Riemer, the great man's secretary, blighted by the proximity
of greatness, the anxious conspiracy of Adele Schopenhauer who is

seeking a confederate to help her circumvent the marriage of Ottilie von Pogwisch to Goethe's mediocre son, and finally the pathetic self-revelation of that son himself, mere "by-blow and after-clap" of his fathers' Jovian love affairs, who comes to deliver Goethe's dinner invitation.

These protracted dialogues, unsustained by the dialectic tension of those in *The Magic Mountain* or by the psychological realism contrived by novelists like James and Conrad for their interminable recitatives, describe the widening periphery of human absurdity and miscomprehension in which genius is compelled to live, but they are recorded with so thick a documentation of Goethean history, so turgid a dressing of period decorum and pontificality, that they almost succeed in laying an irremediable blight on the fact of Goethe's character and existence. They miss entirely the concentrated blend of personal pathos and symbolic precision that marked the art of *Tonio Kröger* and *Death in Venice,* and with it is lost the tragic penetration of those shorter masterpieces, whose concise form Mann decided to be inadequate to the dimensions of his Goethe theme. But for his present purpose the sheerly cumulative persistence of his prose epics proves equally amiss, and for three-fourths of its length his novel threatens to dissipate hopelessly the subject to which it addresses itself.

On page 281, however, the scene and method abruptly change. From Lotte's room at the Elephant we are transported to Goethe's bed-chamber in the Frauenplan and thus into the long interior monologue of the waking poet. The Colossus slowly rears his form. Ponderous with the dignity of fame and power yet still torn by the old conflict of his forces, he is tempted by the remnants of his early antinomian instincts to repudiate the enslaving claims of the nation he has conquered through "the most marvelously compelling matter-of-factness the world has ever heard," so raising to its highest power in the destiny of Europe the "aesthetic autonomy" which his moral passion has brought into harmony with the "Antaean compensation" of the earth, of human fact and necessity. He despises and fears the sinister national ambitions of his "misbegotten race." He defends the pan-European idea of Napoleon, now exiled on St. Helena. He aspires toward "the supra-personal, supra-partisan, supra-racial standards and values" of art and humanitarianism. He becomes Mann's supreme token of the artist's mission among men—of the poet compelled out of visionary illusion and impotence by his saving manhood, "a Titanism that has been pressed back by temporal contingency."

He also becomes, in effect, the antagonist and critic of the genius of dissent which has always held for Mann a rival attraction. When, a few years later, Mann for the first time in his life undertook to "render his intimate homage" to Dostoevsky,[2] he defined the power that balances Goethe's in the culture of Europe. "It was easy for me to render intimate and rapturous homage, tempered with tender irony, to the images of the divine and the fortunate, the children of nature in their exalted simplicity and their exuberant healthfulness: to the autobiographic aristocratism of the molder of a majestic personal culture, Goethe"; but he found himself "filled with awe, with a profound, mystic, silence-enjoining awe, in the presence of the religious greatness of the damned." "It seems impossible to speak of Dostoevsky's genius," he said, "without being forced to think of the word 'criminal.'" "Undoubtedly the subconsciousness and even the consciousness of this titanic creator was permanently burdened with a heavy sense of guilt, a sense of the criminal, and this feeling was by no means of purely hypochondriac nature. It was connected with his infirmity, the 'sacred' disease, the pre-eminently mystic disease, epilepsy," and this is what "accounts for the terrific moral force, the religious frightfulness, of Dostoevsky's knowledge of the soul." Thus it became a conviction with Mann that "life has never been able to do without the morbid," that "disease bears fruits that are more important and beneficial to life and its development than any medically approved normality," and that "the great invalids are crucified victims, sacrificed to humanity and its advancement, to the broadening of its knowledge,—in short, to its more sublime health." It is by dissent, otherness, and estrangement that the radical insights

----

[2] In his introduction to *The Short Novels of Dostoevsky* (New York: Dial Press, 1945).

of art are won; and in an age where society and culture willingly surrender their authority by permitting depravity and disaster to overwhelm them, it is to the resisting and unreconciled individual, guard-
ing his secret knowledge of guilt and truth, that men must turn for
their clues to sincerity and value.

But if Dostoevsky became for Mann the primary and heroic example of the man marked by the genius of dissent and disputation,
Goethe remained primary in a complementary and equally irrefuta-
ble sense: in the sense of his affirmative recognition of a moral unity
in nature and mankind and of the moral health that makes that unity
operative. Goethe provides a balance and counterweight in the dialectic of Mann's aesthetic; he redresses the Manichean tendency of
his sympathy with evil, disease, and abnormality as sources of power.
In the ninety-five pages of Goethe's reverie in *Lotte in Weimar,* and
in the ten closing pages of farewells between the old poet and Lotte,
a static novel springs to life and gives searching expression to Mann's
lifelong concern with the meaning of art, the role of the artist as mediator between idealism and resolution, the androgynous temper of
the creative vision, the fatal consequences of "an ambition for universal truth," the unremitting struggle against disillusionment that
must engage the aging man and the expanding consciousness of his
conceiving mind. Here Goethe becomes the pre-eminent marked man
of modern times, for he is marked by the widest contemporary fame
and suspicion ever gained by a poet. But if we leave him in a final
aura of ambiguity ("I am the flame . . . I am the candle too . . .
And finally I am the drunken butterfly that falls to the flame—figure
of the eternal sacrifice, body transmuted into soul and life into
spirit"), it is because Mann has not found here the clarifying allegory
that distinguishes his greatest work. He has written his novel out of
a major preoccupation of his career, but he has written it more with
ideas than with words—more with historical documentation and
philosophic speculation than with the dramatic and poetic reality
that would crystallize its meaning and permit its characters to become effective solvents of the mystery of the artist's vision and authority.

The reasons for this defect are not elusive. Mann's own strongest work suggests them, and *Lotte in Weimar* represents the same kind of lapse from his radical powers in the later phase of his fiction as *Royal Highness,* another exercise in affirmation, does in his earlier. The novel of moral affirmation is so at odds with the critical and tragic necessity in modern thought—so particularly at odds with Mann's own prolonged conditioning in the problem of decadence—that it usually ends where this one does: in an ambiguity of sentiment, an evasive abstraction of moral commitment, which has the effect of begging the question of moral positivism and of hovering finally in the void of the ideal. Secondly, the discursive method in fiction, raised by Mann to its greatest powers when he was able to employ his skill in dialectic analysis (*The Magic Mountain, Dr. Faustus*), is likely to collapse when the agents of such analysis, characters capable of embodying the terms of a moral argument, remain uncreated as minds or sensibilities in action. Goethe in this book, though beset by the distractions that threaten to annul his vision, lacks the antagonist that would have made a genuine drama of his victory and so misses the greater reality that defeat gave to Aschenbach in *Death in Venice.* But what finally and decisively daunts Mann in this book is the problem of the sage or magus as hero—the mind so transcendant in vision, so aloof to the tests of human absurdity and conflict, that it refuses to lend itself to the requirements of moral and dramatic realism. The actuality in error, dissent, diabolism, or evil that makes classic figures of Aschenbach, Leverkühn, and Felix Krull becomes unavailable to the re-creation of Goethe's triumphant moral amenity. "Body" is all too thoroughly "transmitted into soul and life into spirit," and it is with the abstractions of soul and spirit that we are finally obliged to remain content and dissatisfied in *Lotte in Weimar.* Yet short as the novel is in imaginative force and critical lucidity, it will always have its importance, its appointed place, in the program of Mann's work and thought. In the final phase of his achievement it defines a necessary term in his study of the artist's role in society and so joins with *Dr. Faustus,* eight years later, in rounding out the half-century he gave to debating the question of genius and its laws—the anti-diabolic principle challenging the diabolic in the claims they impose on mankind and its capacity for survival and sanity.

1940 [1956]

II. THE WHISPER OF THE DEVIL

The Pilgrim Hawk by Glenway Wescott

The Pilgrim Hawk, with which Glenway Wescott returned to fiction in 1940 [1] and so resumed what had been in the 1920s one of the most gifted talents of that decade, is less the "love story" its subtitle suggests than a fable, and it shows again, but more explicitly and with greater critical weight, his natural inclination toward symbolic and legendary values in narrative. Where once—in *The Apple of the Eye,* *The Grandmothers,* and *Goodbye, Wisconsin*—he elaborated the mythic clues of the pastoral and folk tale, the tribal ritual of the family photograph album, or the local daemon that haunts the hearsay, superstitions, and country legends of his midwestern homeland, he here reverts to a time and place grown more fabulous than Wisconsin ever could—to the France of the expatriates after the First World War, a lost paradise removed to lunar distance by war and change, whose delusions of emancipation linger in the memory with the unreality of life on another planet. He tells of the rich Irish Cullens, whose love, fixed by psychic necessity, is sped to its crisis by Mrs. Cullen's pet falcon, which figures both her husband's enslavement and tormented jealousy and the wife's mastery of her lover. The relations of the pair and their bird dramatize the tyranny of love, its restless antagonisms, and the long debt it imposes on life; and the drama of marital conflict is given depth by two contrasting images—

---

[1] *The Pilgrim Hawk. A Love Story* (New York: Harper and Brothers, 1940).

the animal passion of two French servants and the enervating Platonic friendship of Alexandra Henry, a wealthy American in whose house near Paris the story takes place one summer afternoon in the 1930s, and the narrator, who watches the crisis and struggles to grasp and interpret its meaning.

The art of fable, with its cognates in primitive myth and in the moral or critical allegory of more modern times, has become a prepossession of contemporary novelists. It comes to them as a means of resisting the pedantry of facts, a corrective of the servility of realism, a plea for poetic values in fiction, a mode of the imagination at a time when psychic and moral claims resist the determinism of science and seek fresh contact with the "realm of essence" where spirit, however elusive or enigmatic, exists in the strength of its primary impulses. It has always been an art of great appeal to Americans: the enthusiasm for it of Poe, Hawthorne, Melville, Crane, and James has reappeared—now enriched by the devices and insights of Mann, Gide, Lawrence, and Kafka—in writers as different as Katherine Anne Porter, Faulkner, and Hemingway. The radical problem of the art exists in its necessary quality of ambiguity and symbolic tension—in the degree to which symbolic or allegorical purpose must remain implicit in the experience or rooted in the matter of the genre as against the degree to which that purpose may derive from the conscious intention or moral intelligence of the author. The balance of these factors is basic to the authority of any successful fable. Without such balance the form either lapses into the static or conventional condition of a parable or becomes artificial through the effort toward originality or critical didacticism and so results in the pedantry which too often cripples the natural impulse that is necessary to animate the tale. To strike the necessary delicacy of analogy or allegory of the valid fable calls for a supreme instinct for evocation and subtlety in a writer. It also calls for the firmest possible integration of his moral idea with his dramatic substance, and for the unobtrusive control of a natural poetic insight. When it shows these, the art of fable escapes the excessive didactic calculation of stories like *St. Mawr*,

"The Gentleman from San Francisco," and the characteristic parables of Gide and takes on the surer authority we get in *Mario and the
Magician*, in Kafka's "The Burrow," or, in more substantial dramatic
terms, in tales as different as "The Turn of the Screw" and "Flowering
Judas."

Mr. Wescott's story is one of the remarkable works of its kind in
recent American fiction. Its deft shaping, sensitive and disciplined
insight, and hypnotic suggestive force show it to be the work of a
scrupulous craftsman and fully conscious critical intelligence. It
shows the studied effect and stylistic scruple that point to a serious
effort in a classic tradition. Yet in spite of its distinction it must be
said of it that the balance essential to its genre is never clearly defined
or resolved. The dramatic substance of his scenes and characters
does not succeed in sustaining the elaborate commentary and moral
deliberation he has imposed upon it. The annotation of the situation
becomes too elaborate, ingenious, and uncomfortably self-conscious.
A tendency toward a worrying preciosity of inference and analysis
is never genuinely subdued to the natural impulse of the events, the
given qualities of the characters, and the result becomes something
too urgently contrived and at times almost desperately *voulu*.

These effects certainly do not minimize the beauty of conception
that declares itself in its pages, the great superiority of its style and
feeling to the general ruck of fiction, or its always subtly considered,
often brilliant observations. The hieratic mystery of the bird, with
its suggestions of the fatality of love, of ruthless energy in nature,
and of the secret ordeal of art, does manage to surmount the elaborate rites of falconry that have been imposed on the action of the
animal; and repeatedly Mr. Wescott condenses his insight into judgments that express his story's motive with admirable point and precision:

> Unrequited passion; romance put asunder by circumstances or
> mistakes; sexuality pretending to be love—all that is a matter of little
> consequence, a mere voluntary temporary uneasiness, compared with
> the long course of true love, especially marriage. In marriage, insult
> arises again and again and again; and pain has to be not only en-

dured, but consented to; and the amount of forgiveness that it necessitates is incredible and exhausting. When love has given satisfaction, then you discover how large a part of the rest of life is only payment for it. . . . To see the cost of love before one has felt what it is worth, is a pity; one may never have the courage to begin.

He can be reminded how "all pets, all domesticated animals, no matter how ancient or beautiful or strange, show a comic aspect sooner or later; a part of the shame of our humanity that we gradually convey to them," and again of "the absurd position of the artist in the midst of the disorders of those who honor and support him, but who can scarcely be expected to keep quiet around him for art's sake." He can define his personal difficulty and yet overshoot the mark of creative humility: "Again and again I give way to a kind of inexact and vengeful lyricism; I cannot tell what right I have to be avenged, and I am ashamed of it. Sometimes I entirely doubt my judgment in moral matters; and so long as I propose to be a story-teller, that is the whisper of the devil for me."

Such lucidity of scruple produces a valuable alertness in the conscience of a writer, but its insistence over and above the volition of his drama soon involves him in a radical difficulty: it leads not only to a serious enervation of the tone, force, and unity of his story and to the exaggerated preciosity which is the major weakness of this particular book, but to something more dangerous still—an enervation of his imaginative substance itself and of the impulse that must be counted on to project it as drama and reality. *The Pilgrim Hawk* is by way of being a serious assessment of talent and purpose, one of the most incisive examinations of the imaginative conscience recent American writing has produced. In what it does to sublimate the aesthetic inflation and self-regard of Wescott's earlier work it indicates a renewal of discipline that may recover the exquisite pastoral lyricism of *The Apple of the Eye* and direct it toward finer and more substantial uses. The tale leaves the question hanging in suspense. It marks a revival of courage and critical insight in its author, and it serves as a word of warning, an act of cautionary artistry and admirable dedication to the most serious purposes a writer of fiction can address himself to, for a new generation of American talents. But in itself the book tests and exercises, rather than masters, the faculties that have given us the finest examples of the modern fable.

1940

III. THE COOL HAND

Up at the Villa by Somerset Maugham

Though *Up at the Villa,* his novel of 1941,[1] may not represent Somerset Maugham at what his admirers call—and what his detractors, in all fairness, should call—his best, it may be taken as a fair example of the work he has produced at punctual intervals during the greater part of his sixty years of fiction-writing, and one's temptation to dismiss it as a triumph of servant-girl's entertainment is given pause by the phenomenal value that still attaches to Maugham's name among modern authors. The standard argument on his case has become a byword. He is the complete cool hand and past master in the arts of popular fictional entertainment. He has never been taken in by literary gangdom, aesthetic pretensions, or anything else in the life around him or in the profession he practices. He is a walking model of his own no-nonsense, fact-facing, smooth-tooled gentleman heroes. He is always perfectly aware of what he is doing and is as fully in control of his faculties when turning out a piece of commercial rubbish as when producing a "masterpiece." This reputation has been as carefully fostered by Maugham himself as by his protégés. *The Summing Up,* his book of personal reminiscence and stock-taking, was a shrewdly calculated exercise in his favorite virtue— professional sincerity; so expertly calculated, in fact, that even its author seemed unaware that his elaborately cold-blooded realism

----

[1] *Up at the Villa* (New York: Doubleday, Doran and Company, 1941).

gave his show away more readily than the bewildered ardors and protestations we usually get in literary memoirs.

Popular critics are always captivated by the complacent brand of aesthetic amorality Maugham has made the hallmark of his career. "His cynicism has advanced so far as to become candor," Mr. Clifton Fadiman has said; "it's a positive pleasure to be sold so smooth and shiny a gold brick." And since longevity and commercial success are taken by a large part of the reading public as endorsements of quality, it has become fairly common during the last ten or fifteen years— in England perhaps more frequently than in America—to hear Maugham called "the foremost living English novelist," the suggestion always being conveyed that had he been so disposed, he could have produced another *Cakes and Ale* or *Of Human Bondage* —granting, that is, that he felt sufficient respect for his public to make the effort.

One is moved to ask: Why then hasn't he done so? Following the exceptional skill of *Cakes and Ale* in 1930 he has preferred to turn out a succession of luxurious pot-boilers, *Cosmopolitan* thrillers, and Hollywood slick-jobs equaled only by the similar procession of banalities that followed *Of Human Bondage* in 1915. His plays, shrewdly carpentered problem-pieces and drawing-room comedies in the fagged line of Pinero and Wilde, are hard to discuss seriously even among the arid wastes of the contemporary commercial drama. One has only to see them in revival a few years after their glamorous first nights and shorn of their original stars to realize the prodigies of mechanical contrivance, mawkish dialogue, and trumped-up moral pretension they encompass. Modern fiction, especially in England, has largely represented a triumph of the higher journalism, but the more serious members of Maugham's generation—Bennett, Wells, Galsworthy—at least respected the more urgent social sympathies, class conflicts, and psychological interests of their time. Maugham has never allowed these worries to get the better of him. He has brought unusual gifts—in storytelling, in humane observation, in suspense and humor, even in more serious matters of passion or decadence—to the most trivial of uses. His two notable novels have issued from the only two experiences in which he has allowed himself to become deeply or personally involved: his youthful sufferings in love, moral distress, and physical disability, and his ordeal of personal exoneration as a professional writer. The first struggle he sublimated by a patient, disillusioned, carefully documented, unoriginal, but convincing realism; the second by a brilliant feat of satire. Yet one has only to look at the conclusions at which those books arrived—their commitment to cautious compromise and unabashed cynicism—to understand why their author has lapsed almost without exception in his other work into a perfect model of the literary journeyman, aloof to artistic risk or innovation, actively hostile to original talent, invulnerable to the serious claims of his profession, and apparently without conscience when it comes to lending his remarkable equipment to the highest sales values that tawdry smartness and banality command.

If any doubt remains on this score, *Up at the Villa* should dismiss it (though almost any of his later books, from *The Painted Veil* and *The Narrow Corner* to *The Razor's Edge* and *Then and Now* will serve equally well). The incredible falseness of its dialogue (on pages 39–43 or 87–99, for instance) should alone be enough to convince even moderately sensitive readers; it would put to shame the humblest employee of the Hollywood or television script-mills. One may exaggerate the importance of all this. But Maugham continues to be influential. His claim to importance is highly respected in college classes, rental libraries, and newspaper columns. He figures as a guide for ambitious talents. He has come in his later years to stand as a kind of distinguished example and father-figure not only for purveyors of journalistic entertainment and mass-fiction but for more ambitious apprentices in novel and story writing. His career in the fashionable social circles and international cocktail sets of America and Europe, in Riviera villas, in theatrical circles, on P. and O. liners, or among the glamorous places of the Orient has become a model of envy to innumerable aspirants who take this kind of success as a sign of valid literary distinction. And it is quite in line with his elaborately groomed, no-nonsense attitude toward art that he should use the pulpits to which he has access—the *Saturday Evening Post,* the films, the television, the numerous anthologies he has compiled—to disseminate a large skepticism about modern literature, to expound his man-to-man common sense on the aesthetics of the mystery thriller and the detective story, to indulge himself in sneers or commiseration at the expense of Proust and Joyce, and to reduce the labors of Henry James to an ultimate refinement of futility.

The motive behind these Literary Lessons for Rotarians is not difficult to glimpse. No man likes to be shown up by his betters quite as ruthlessly as the slightest comparison between James and Maugham shows up Maugham. At the age of sixty-seven James had not only written an almost unbroken succession of original novels and tales (in which, contrary to the opinion of Maugham and, it might be added, of Van Wyck Brooks, he was taken in by *nothing* in the world of pretences and ambition in which he mixed), but was writing, in the fullness of his age and powers, one of the most searchingly pathetic and beautifully wrought stories ever set to paper, "The Bench of Desolation." At the age of sixty-seven Maugham could do no better than turn out *Up at the Villa* for the delectation of drugstore readers, movie audiences, and the boudoirs. One of its features that provided Mr. Fadiman with special pleasure is that it does not contain "a wasted word." The truth has seldom been more perfectly reversed. All the words are wasted.

It is usually rated as Maugham's greatest feat in satire and outstanding service to authorship in our time that he should have exposed to the death-ray of his merciless sarcasm the self-promoting, double-dealing, and unconscionable careerism of one of his most popular literary contemporaries in the character of Alroy Kear in *Cakes and Ale.* The demolition was complete and probably beneficial, but as in many cases of its kind, it may have been as much inspired by a guilty conscience as out of respect for the ethics of the satirist's profession. Nothing Maugham has written since *Cakes and Ale* has done much to exempt him from his own indictment. But since he has consistently prided himself on having made a virtue of cynicism, he has doubtless armed himself with one of the professional cynic's oldest consolations: "We but teach bloody instructions, which, being taught, return to plague the inventor."

1941   [1956]

IV. THE STRAIGHT WAY LOST

The Middle of the Journey by Lionel Trilling

When we meet John Laskell he is thirty-three, crossing the perilous Dantean decade in which the risks, doubts, and challenges of a man's life declare themselves and his personality first begins to contract into the limitations and decisions to which it is fated. He is a "fortunate young man of the middle class" who has disciplined his privileges by an earnest if skeptical liberal faith. After giving up his youthful creative ambitions he has become an authority on housing, so justifying in his own mind the social bearings of his political sympathies. He has loved once, a healthy intelligent girl called Elizabeth Fuess, and they loved in the intelligent way of an emancipated modern passion. She however died suddenly, and he has not yet subjected himself again to the risk of so inexplicably violated a confidence in life.

His friends are mostly liberals like himself. One is Arthur Croom, assistant professor and Socialist, a man "in whom the drive for power did not destroy intelligence and character," a "man of the near future." Another is Croom's wife Nancy, charming, domestic, college-bred, and soon to reveal "a passion of the mind and will so pure that, as it swept through her, she could not believe that anything that opposed it required consideration." A third is Kermit Simpson, rich publisher of the leftist-liberal *New Era*, "very handsome, a big rangy man who was good at field sports, court games, and boating," but also "all too bland." "There was no roughness in him. He never followed passion where it led, nor did necessity ever constrain him to resistance. The blandness was fatal to his character." There is finally Gifford Maxim, member and secret agent of "the Party," a "man of the far future, the bloody, moral, apocalyptic future that was sure to come," who has become the standard of dogmatic conviction around which the lesser faiths and good intentions of his friends have come to take their bearings.

Laskell, when the crucial summer of the novel begins, has just recovered from an almost fatal attack of scarlet fever. It has laid open the lesions and doubts of his character. He has learned for the first time the difference between the sick and the well, between the meaning of death and the healthy world that dreads to hear death mentioned, between the will to live and the wish to die, between security and fear and what these mean in the problem of existence. Just as he is about to emerge into the world again to go to Connecticut for the curative summer the Crooms have arranged for him, Maxim drops a bomb among his friends. He reveals that he has renounced the Party.

Laskell goes to the country, lives down the road from the Crooms' house with the Folger family, and presently meets the semi-derelict family of the Caldwells—Duck Caldwell, selfish, honest, alcoholic, imperative, with a mind "not wicked" but asserting "the pure will of nothingness," his wife Emily who once ran a tearoom and still echoes a feebly Bohemian past, and their child Susan, to whom Laskell becomes unwittingly attached. Laskell, his wounds still open, thus becomes involved in a drama of faiths that soon includes not only the latent conflict between himself, the Crooms, and Simpson, but also the deeper conflict between these middle terms of the modern moral and political argument and the antagonisms that hedge them—the derelict Caldwells on one side, the passionately dogmatic Maxim, driving from Communist absolutism to religious, on the other. The drama grows in tension. Its debate proliferates until it arrives at a climax of passion—Laskell and Emily Caldwell—and another of death—Susan's at the hand of her father. It tests the group of friends to their foundations. And the summer ends with their relations profoundly and permanently disturbed. One autumn morning Laskell,

now tested in more than health yet stronger in more than body, takes
the train back to the city.

These are the characters and outward events of Lionel Trilling's
first novel—*The Middle of the Journey* [1]—and readers who know
not only his critical writings but his earlier stories will know what
to expect in the way of a narrative keenly sustained and subtly ar-
ticulated. It is a novel of remarkable, of almost unflinching, austerity.
Little or nothing has been conceded to the conventional inducements
of current fiction. Effects of action and background are reduced to
a minimum. Humor, byplay, color, incident, are pared to the quick.
The treatment is stark in its economy of detail and atmosphere. But
it defines a milieu that has become a new area in fiction, possibly
the setting of a new type of novel that has emerged from the critical
thought and intellectual conflict of the past ten years—it finds differing versions in Edmund Wilson's *Memoirs of Hecate County,* in
Eleanor Clark's *The Bitter Box,* and in John Kelly's *All Souls' Night.*

It is the milieu of the contemporary literary and political intelli-
gentsia. One must admit that nothing the realists or naturalists of
the Nineteenth Century tackled in the way of unromantic discourage-
ments when they undertook to bring the drab lives of servant girls,
nuns, shopkeepers, miners, and wage slaves into the novel is missing
for the present-day novelist who attempts to dramatize a world as
generally bleak, unpromising, and denatured as the world of contemporary thinkers, writers, and professors. Those flats in the Village,
cottages on the Cape, houses in Connecticut, and campus colonies!
Is it possible that the slightest spur to imagination may be found in
them? One may, moreover, be inclined at first to complain that Mr.
Trilling has abstracted his characters from their real roots and conditions in modern society; that he has endowed their acts and words
with an obtrusive self-consciousness and absence of human spontaneity that reduces their dramatic appeal and pathos to a disobliging
minimum. We are told little of where or how they originated in
American life. All of them—the Crooms, Laskell, Simpson, even the
more localized Caldwells, Folgers, and Walkers—are suspended in

-----

[1] *The Middle of the Journey* (New York: The Viking Press, 1947).

a kind of social and moral void. Their talk is strung to a painful pitch of abstraction. Exceptions do occur: two admirable nurses and a country clergyman who put in brief appearances; but too often their performances—especially the high-strung, bright-minded speeches of Nancy Croom, the pathetic soul-hungers of Emily Caldwell, or the efforts of the child Susan to recite a Blake poem "with expression" —are calculated to set the teeth on edge.

What Mr. Trilling has written is, quite overtly, a dialectic novel. The term appears in his pages. His language is analytical, his structure polemic, his sequence of scenes and confrontations virtually syllogistic. Yet it is a remarkable evidence of his skill and sincerity, and of the tenacious probity of his thinking, that he has been able to keep his plotting sharply dramatic; that as we read we lose our sense of lacking familiar fictional properties; and that we become seriously absorbed by his story, not only as an argument keenly sustained but as the record of an essential experience in our time, one fully equal in validity to the actualities of proletarian fiction and far more salient than the attenuations and enfeebled appeals that have lately overtaken the novel of sensibility.

By that time also, convinced by the passion with which ideas and dogmas can possess the modern mind, we feel the authenticity of his scenes and people. Nancy Croom, with her socialist logic and scarifying affection, becomes a definitive portrait of a recognizable type of modern woman. The little girl with her Blake poem is a pathetic image of cultured childhood (anticipated by the progressive-school girl in Mr. Trilling's story "The Other Margaret"). Kermit Simpson is a muzzy-minded prototype of a dozen wealthy patrons of the Left. The scenes of the drama precisely define the orbit of middle-class gentility, academic inhibition, and well-to-do patronage that has nurtured the cautious self-deceptions and guilty fears which have lamed the liberal position in modern thought and made the triumph of absolutes so sinister in our time.

For the theme of the novel is the fate of the liberal critical intelligence—its confusions and its necessity. John Laskell's is the mind in which that fate is tried, the focus, made vulnerable by illness and a fresh access of clarity, of the conflict between the political and moral passions that surround him. Mr. Trilling is probably the finest analyst and historian of the liberal predicament we have. His account of that problem in his critical books and essays is a permanent one. We are kept fully aware, in this novel, of his rigorous insight and schooling in the liberal dilemma. It is inevitable that we should be reminded of his admirable study of E. M. Forster in this connection —particularly if one emphasizes the fact that *The Middle of the Journey* is quite independent of Forster's work in its style, method, and content—and likewise of his searching book on Matthew Arnold. It is also unavoidable that we should recall how fully aware he is of the existence of modern classics of dialectic art like *The Princess Casamassima, The Ivory Tower, The Magic Mountain, Howards End,* and *The Counterfeiters.* Such books have schooled his imagination; he has not denied himself the most formidable models; but they have not deprived him of his own language and insights. What he said in his book on Forster about that novelist's dissection of the "undeveloped heart" is as relevant here as what he said about the role which Forster assigns to the "relaxed will" and to "the Primal Curse . . . the knowledge of Good-and-Evil" in modern morality. What men like Forster and Gide share in their conception of the novel is shared also by Mr. Trilling: for him also the novel is what Gide once called it, "a crossroads—a meeting place of problems." He knows the importance to the critical imagination of believing that "whatever your station or country, you should believe only what is true, and what you would be disposed to believe if you were of another country, another station, another religion."

When John Laskell, at the end of his momentous summer, faces the rival angers of his friends—the Crooms with their inflamed conviction of the guilt of society which permits no responsibility in the individual; Maxim with his dogmatic belief in individual responsibility which admits the mitigation of mercy—he knows at last why they are angry with him. It is "the anger of the masked will at the appearance of an idea in modulation. The open will does not show that anger; only the will masked in virtue shows it." But against their accusations Laskell holds to his position. It *is* the will in modulation that must survive if absolutes are to be denied their tyranny and the intelligence is to survive for the uses of justice and truth. The charge of defending "individual morality" against "social morality" is one that Mr. Trilling has not escaped in his experience of political controversy. This novel, with its subtle, athletic, and unsimplified articulation of "the double truth" of social and individual values shows how honestly he sees the complex actuality of values which the simplistic moralism of dogmatic or abstracting minds, hot for action and accusation, ignores. On that score alone *The Middle of the Journey* becomes a significant document. But it is more than a document: it is a searching example of a new mode in fiction, one whose function in the moral dilemmas of our age his acute critical instinct has sensed and whose claim on the imaginative resources and personal responsibility of his generation the human faith evident in his pages demonstrates. It is a book that brings the best critical intelligence now discernible in America into play with an absolutely honest creative purpose, and it shares with only a few recent works of fiction the honor of establishing that cooperation of talents on a sound footing.

1947

V. HEMINGWAY 1950 AND 1952

Across the River and into the Trees and The Old Man and the Sea
by Ernest Hemingway

I

The story opens two hours before daylight on the lagoons north of Venice. "The Colonel"—Richard Cantwell, ex-Brigadier General, aged fifty, and already under sentence of death—is going out to the duck-shooting. It is another of Hemingway's mornings—we've known them before and unforgettably, in Michigan, in Paris, in Wyoming, Africa, Spain, and Cuba—and for a moment an old spell is revived: the cold half-light breaking above the islands, the ice-sheeted waters, the angry boatman flinging decoys from the boat, the first birds in the sky. Presently we cast back a day or two. The Colonel drives from his postwar station at Trieste to Venice. The Adriatic country he has known and loved since he fought in it as a boy in the other war unfolds its panorama of history and memories. He arrives at the Gritti Palace Hotel where he is greeted as an old patron and then goes to Harry's Bar to meet the nineteen-year-old girl, Renata, whom he loves. From then on the tale recounts their last meetings, pledges of devotion, and defiance of despair until the Colonel, driving back to Trieste with his orderly, is killed in the car by his heart and dies. His farewell to arms comes thirty years after Frederick Henry's and a dozen after Robert Jordan's, but he is the same man, this time "half a hundred years old."

This is the novel—*Across the River and into the Trees,* Hemingway's fifth in thirty years of writing [1]—that has been awaited for ten years, certainly with every hope that it would show the renewal of a talent that has given us several of the most memorable and original books of the century. But there is little use in hedging on an unpleasant but emphatic fact: it doesn't. What might, in, say, thirty pages, have been an effective *conte* on the order of "The Short Happy Life of Francis Macomber" or "The Snows of Kilimanjaro" has been stretched, beaten out, and enervated to the length of three hundred. The drama is almost completely static. The talk, retaining only occasional hints of its old living accents, develops unbelievable prodigies of flatness, mawkishness, repetition, and dead wastes of words. The Colonel, advertised as "perhaps the most complex character that Hemingway has ever presented," who does, in fact, offer possibilities as a man of stoic habit and action in the face of death, proves very soon to be a stereotype of earlier Hemingway heroes: another existen-

----

[1] *Across the River and into the Trees* (New York: Charles Scribner's Sons, 1950).

tial man at his rope's end, faithful only to the ritual of soldiering and love; and the girl Renata repeats the submissive child lover of *For Whom the Bell Tolls*, serving also as counterfoil to another familiar type in earlier stories, the bitch ex-wife—an ambitious woman journalist in this case—who has sealed Cantwell's skepticism of all but the most rudimentary forms of human or sexual sympathy.

The reader inevitably comes to this book with a complex conditioning. It is, first of all, offered as an interim work or by-product of the larger novel Hemingway has been writing since 1940. Its style and manner, however debased from their earlier authority, continuously echo those of the novels and tales that have stamped the modern imagination with some of its most memorable fables and images and with a language whose firmness of accent and truth of sensibility will certainly remain a permanent quality in the American style. But we are also perforce reminded on every page of how many other assaults the force and stubborn integrity of these have met in the last twenty years—confused performances like *Death in the Afternoon* and *To Have and Have Not,* the severe miscalculation of *Green Hills of Africa,* a fiasco of ineptitude like *The Fifth Column,* the muddled power of *For Whom the Bell Tolls,* not to mention the dismal exhibitionism of the *Esquire* articles in the thirties or the self-exploiting public character of the interviews and photographs. The misgiving inevitably and cumulatively induced by all this has hardly been improved at hearing Hemingway deliver himself of statements like the following: "I started out very quiet and I beat Mr. Turgenev. Then I trained hard and I beat Mr. de Maupassant. I've fought two draws with Mr. Stendhal. . . . But nobody's going to get me in any ring with Mr. Tolstoy unless I'm crazy or I keep getting better." The modesty vis-à-vis Tolstoy is appreciated, but one wonders if a little less certainty about having worsted the Messrs. Turgenev, Maupassant, and Stendhal might not, to put it mildly, have been tactful or done Mr. Hemingway a little good. The celebrated *New Yorker* profile in which this pronouncement appeared (May 13, 1950), while it obliged the reader to make every possible allowance for calculated malice, left one wondering what, in so exaggerated a display of professional infantilism, Indian talk, self-typed histrionics, and willing exposure, could possibly survive for the serious business of art and writing. The only answer permitted by *Across the River* is unavoidable: very little.

The obvious truth is that this novel is the poorest thing its author has ever done—poor with a feebleness of invention, a mawkishness of language, and a self-parodying crudity of style and theme even beyond *The Fifth Column* and *To Have and Have Not*. There is hardly a trace in it of the latent rigor that enabled Hemingway, in tales like "The Undefeated," "Old Man at the Bridge," "The Capital of the World," "Francis Macomber," and "The Snows of Kilimanjaro," to pull himself together after several earlier lapses and to declare his old powers. A few favors are granted: the book at least lacks the supremely inept "(obscenity)" device that disfigured the ̶ ̶ ̶ ̶ *For Whom the Bell Tolls*, even if its four-letter words are ̶ ̶ ̶ in with a clumsiness that does little to redeem the situatio ̶ ̶ ̶ one is left with—the analogous case of Kipling, once suggested by Edmund Wilson, is again pertinent—is the impasse of mechanism and contrivance a talent arrives at when a narrowly formulated conception of experience or humanity is pushed to the limits of its logic, progressively excluding any genuine exploration of moral complexity or any but the most inflexibly prejudiced responses to character and conduct. Colonel Cantwell and his girl, the mystique of duty and death, the ritualized conception of war, hunting, and danger, the secret brotherhood of the "Order" at the Gritti—these, with their unmistakable echoes of Kipling and reminders of what Kipling meant to the young readers of Hemingway's generation in the early years of the century, here give the effect of exhausting a formula once sufficiently austere and disciplined to create a number of the genuine masterpieces of our time but now betrayed in its potential sterility and solipsism.

Hemingway was perhaps right on one score when he measured himself against Turgenev, Stendhal, and Maupassant. They too centered their vision of life in a specific and critical judgment on human experience; insisted on their verdict even at the risk of formulation;

adhered to it stubbornly from first to last. But none of them rejected the values of possibility or made of their temperamental bias a principle of exclusion; and not even the least of them—Maupassant—permitted himself the self-defeating rigidity of attitude and simplification of expression to which Hemingway has become increasingly addicted in the last twenty years. We are left to conclude that this talent, while nothing can cancel what it achieved in at least two novels and a score or more of brilliant tales, will be subjected to some severely revised judgments in the coming years, and that when it is measured against the richer resources of some of its closest rivals—Fitzgerald, for one, or Faulkner—it will meet rougher tests than the unlikely cases of Stendhal and Turgenev provide. *Across the River and into the Trees* can be an occasion for little but honest and ungrateful exasperation. But we are promised another novel soon. We must wait for it. And see.

1950

II

Two years after *Across the River* Hemingway has followed it with another novel, not the long one he has been rumored to be writing during the past decade but a short tale or *conte* called *The Old Man and the Sea*.[2] It will bring to his readers one of those shocks of confidence and reassurance that can be among the most heartening experiences in modern writing. If the preceding book discouraged his most loyal admirers, this one should dispel the doubts of his most convinced skeptics, and it will reaffirm the expectation which even in the most dubious passages of his career he has never wholly failed to excite.

One of the puzzling features of American talent, especially talent of an original and positively creative strength, is the frequency of its lapses and its capacity for generating suspense. The more average or middling endowment is unlikely to test its public in this fashion. Men like Howells, David Graham Phillips, Frank Norris, or Sinclair

---

[2] *The Old Man and the Sea* (New York: Charles Scribner's Sons, 1952).

Lewis write out of a given stock or *donnée* of method and material, work it out to its logical capacities or conclusion, show comparatively little deviation from an established line of purpose, and disappoint few hopes even when the method becomes routine or the material runs thin. The men of keener gifts and invention have seldom shown this stability. American fiction, particularly during the past fifty or sixty years, has been a record of flights and drops, of brilliant energy and recurring exhaustion, of superb feats of invention or discovery and of desperate reversals. A factor of the spasmodic and the fractious seems to have operated in the native novelist and story writer—remarkable powers of concentrated vision or revelation and an equivalent tendency to fall into fatigue, perversity, disgust, or a contempt of confidence. These are, of course, always likely to be liabilities of unusual energy, symptoms of the dissatisfaction or restlessness the more equable temper is unlikely to suffer or a lower vitality to subject itself to. Poe and Melville provide the classic examples of the type; to name later cases would be to list most of the talents that are to be counted as the authentic originals of modern American fiction, from Stephen Crane and Dreiser to Sherwood Anderson, Scott Fitzgerald, Faulkner, Ring Lardner, Dos Passos, Hemingway himself.

The problem probably has complex origins. How far it must be referred to the strain and tension of American experience, how much to an overtaxing of that "heightened sensitivity to the promises of life" that Fitzgerald called the spring of action and energy in our character, how much to the exaggerated pressures of literary reputation, how much to a lack of the established métier of the European literary profession, how much to the climate of insecurity that has become prevalent in a distracted century—such influences it would take a good deal of careful investigation to determine. The one thing that appears to be certain is that it has become impossible as well as unwise to be final in one's estimate of the authentic American talent. It is as likely to confound the most confirmed pessimism as to startle or embarrass the most convinced complacency. Its capacity for recovery seems to be equal to its capacity for mortification. The American novelist often produces one of his most exciting dramas in the fluctuations and uncertainties of his own career.

When Hemingway published *Across the River and into the Trees* he gave his strongest followers reason to believe that his resources had been depleted. This was not a new experience for them, but it had never been quite so emphatic. The novel gave every possible sign of marking an impasse not only in his subject matter and moral assumptions but in its style and method. The book was, as we now know, written at a point of crisis in his life. He found himself seriously, perhaps fatally, ill. The tale was apparently conceived as a personal valedictory, an act of conscious stock-taking and intimate moral self-projection. And as so often in books of such motivation— *Pierre, The Sacred Fount, The "Genius," L'Immoraliste, The Arrow of Gold,* to some extent in a finer novel than any of these, *Tender is the Night*—it showed, but in an extreme degree, the liability of that order of inspiration. The writer's persona proved almost abjectly inadequate to the use exacted of it; the personal usurped the functions of the intimate; imaginative projection yielded to defensive apology. The result was a failure not only of imagination but of language, of insight and expression as much as of drama, with results not only embarrassing but fundamentally disastrous in fiction or any other kind of writing: the book gave away its secret and so offended the first law of its art. *Across the River* has already been treated to some misspent ingenuity of analysis and symbolic interpretation by unflinching admirers of its author. This has possibly yielded some interesting psychological evidence; on the score of its critical or aesthetic relevance it has amounted to little but a documentation of the obvious. For let us make no mistake about it. It was a bad book, an almost desperately miscalculated performance; it had the effect of certifying the latent weaknesses in Hemingway's equipment; and to rate it as anything else is to do his finer powers a disservice.

Those powers, which for thirty years have been among the major assets and one of the surest reasons for pride in the American creative achievement, reappear in strength in *The Old Man and the*

Sea. The tale is so admirably written, so beautifully conceived and stated, so firmly controlled and so accurately condensed to its essence, that it invites rating as one of the finest things Hemingway has ever done. Perhaps it should be said at the outset that this may not be the case. It does not show the strongest implicitness of conception and feeling he has been capable of in the past, in "Big Two-Hearted River," or "The Killers," or "The Undefeated," or "Fathers and Sons." It does not show the specific dramatic force of "Francis Macomber" or "Fifty Grand," or the intensity of tragic pathos of "An Alpine Idyll," "A Canary for One," "Cat in the Rain," and "Hills Like White Elephants." Its emblematic theme of heroism and endurance in old age recalls the similar themes of "The Undefeated" and "Old Man at the Bridge" without quite achieving the emotional reality of the first or the steel-cut precision, so perfectly laconic yet so bitterly and classically accurate, of the second. And of course it deliberately avoids the fuller dramatic and psychological body of the longer novels. Hemingway has always shown the integrity which only the true masters of a style or a subject can claim: he has from the first supplied his own standard of value, and it asserts itself as urgently in relation to his best work as to his weakest. *The Old Man* recapitulates his powers as unmistakably as *Across the River* summed up his failings, and both of them do so by measures he himself has supplied. Just as there has been something remorseless about the lengths to which he has indulged his shortcomings, so there is something ruthless about the test to which he can rise when he recovers his strength and about the way he in turn imposes that test on his readers.

Another matter in which he has always kept company with the masters of his art is the combination in his work of an intense personal necessity for expression and self-realization and of the objective intelligence, severe and unsparing, by which his art judges and controls that intimate personal need. Everything he has written—including this story—has issued from his own personality, ordeal, conflict, self-doubt and self-concern. His themes, all the way from the stories of boyhood in Michigan and soldiering in war, to the tales of France, Africa, Spain, and Cuba, suggest their autobiographical origins. He is always himself present in his lines, whether they describe action or dream, objective events and characters or the moral commentary drawn from these. (*In Our Time,* with its alternation of anecdote and personal asides or epiphanic comments, gave a perfect and permanent definition of the elements at work in his mind and imagination, and its method has been projected for better or worse into everything he has written since.)

But against this insistent personal claim in his work there has always operated the critical force of his style and symbolic insights—the severe language, the spare accuracy of statement, the lean form, the precision in allegoric suggestion, the austere authority of his imagery and symbols. The intimate personality that speaks in his pages has never spared itself the checks and severity of this implicit discipline. The moment the personality indulges itself extravagantly, defensively, apologetically, or histrionically, it is made to feel the lash of the critical whip in his words, images, and rhythms. The overwrought reveries in "The Snows of Kilimanjaro," the selfjustifying diatribes in *Death in the Afternoon* or *To Have and Have Not,* the excesses of melodrama in *For Whom the Bell Tolls,* never escape the reproof of that latent honesty, even when the surface appearances of those books give every sign that it has been violated. Hemingway has been from the beginning his own first, last, and consistent critic. His essential art and drama derive from a persistent critical instinct in his style and method. It has made possible the authority of his genius, given him his originality and success, provided the surest standard by which to judge his lapses, made a continuous moral drama of his career in art, and made of himself a classic example of the aesthetic conscience in his age and generation.

His own moral drama has given him the subject of *The Old Man and the Sea.* Its story of the old Cuban fisherman Santiago, famous for his skill and cunning, now deserted by his sacred luck, abandoned by everything but his hope and courage, desperate to catch the fish that still eludes him after eighty-four days of failure, successful at last in catching a fabulous giant marlin only to have it attacked by sharks and reduced to a skeleton, returning finally to port with his mutilated trophy, defeated in everything but faith and his determination to try once more, and blessed in nothing but his knowledge that life is tragic and survival alone a reason for gratitude—this is obviously susceptible to a large amount of personal interpretation. The degree to which it overtly invites such a reading may keep it from achieving the purer integrity of "The Undefeated" and "Old Man at the Bridge," but its superb sincerity of language and moral dignity removes it by miles from the messy apologetic and crude rancors of *Across the River*. As by a kind of systolic rhythm, the moral force of Hemingway's art has reasserted itself. Once more he has recovered the essential powers that have enabled him to mark a stage in the maturity of American writing and to declare his authority in the literature of his time. The authority has redefined itself; it returns unmistakably; but what makes it a particular lesson for his fellow-artists is the struggle that has gone into its making, the self-respect that has survived its abuses, and the hard tenacity by which it has endured.

1952

Note on Sources

NOTE ON SOURCES

As noted in the Foreword, a considerable share of the material of this book has appeared in a different form in books and periodicals. While all the essays have been extensively revised or rewritten and some are new essays, the following acknowledgments indicate the sources of material that has now been incorporated in the present versions.

PART I

"Dickens: The Reputation Revised"—from *The Nation*, Vol. CLXIX, pp. 279–81 (September 17, 1949), including material also from "Dickens as Historian and Reformer," *The Nation*, Vol. CLIV, pp. 434–37 (April 11, 1942), and further additions.

"Dickens: The Undivided Imagination"—written as the "Introduction" to *Bleak House*, Riverside Editions (Boston: Houghton Mifflin Company, 1956). Reprinted by permission of Houghton Mifflin Company.

"Dickens: The Revolutionary Fate"—written as the "Introduction" to *A Tale of Two Cities*, New Harper's Modern Classics Series (New York: Harper and Brothers), to be published. Included here by permission of Harper and Brothers.

"Hardy in Defense of His Art: The Aesthetic of Incongruity"—from *The Southern Review*, Vol. VI, pp. 125–49 (Summer 1940: The Thomas Hardy Centenary Number), with revisions.

"Samuel Butler: The Victorian Insolvency"—written as the "Introduction" to *The Way of All Flesh* (New York: The Modern Library, 1950), here revised. Copyright 1950 by and included by permission of Random House, Inc., New York.

"Henry James: The Act of Life"—based in part on the author's "Introduction" to *The Portable Henry James* (New York: The Viking Press, 1951, new edition, 1956), and here including material from "The Poetics of Henry James," *Poetry: A Magazine of Verse*, Vol. XLV, pp. 270–79 (February 1935), which was reprinted in *The Question of Henry James*, edited by F. W. Dupee (New York: Henry Holt and Company, 1945), pp. 212–17; and from "The Act of Life," *The New Republic*, Vol. CXXXIV, pp. 25–26 (April 30, 1956).

PART II

"Conrad: Chance and Recognition"—from *The Sewanee Review*, Vol. LIII, pp. 1–22 (January–March 1945), here revised. Earlier versions of this essay were printed as "Joseph Conrad" in *Orígenes* (La Habaña, Cuba), Año II, No. 11, pp. 27–41 (Otoño 1946), and in *Critiques and Essays on Modern Fiction 1920–1951*, edited by John W. Aldridge (New York: Ronald Press Company, 1952), pp. 270–85. Material from this essay and from those listed under "Conrad in His Age," below, was incorporated in the author's "Introduction" to *The Portable Conrad* (New York: The Viking Press, 1947).

"Conrad: The East and the Sea"—from the "Introduction" to *The Nigger of the "Narcissus,"* New Harper's Modern Classics Series (New York: Harper and Brothers, 1951), here revised. Copyright 1951 by and reprinted by permission of Harper and Brothers.

"Conrad: The Threat to the West"—from the "Introduction" to *Under Western Eyes*, New Classics Series (New York: New Directions, 1951), here revised. Reprinted by permission of New Directions and Mr. James Laughlin.

"Conrad in His Age"—here a new essay, based on material in "Conrad: Nel Mezzo del Cammin," *The New Republic*, Vol. CIII, pp. 873–74 (December 23, 1940); "Conrad: The Secret Sharer," *The New Republic*, Vol. CIV, pp. 567–74 (April 21, 1941); and "Conrad in His Age," *The New Republic*, Vol. CVII, pp. 644–45 (November 16, 1942).

"E. M. Forster: The Trophies of the Mind"—an essay based on "Introducción al Arte de E. M. Forster" in *Sur: Revista Bimestral* (Buenos Aires, Argentina), Numero 236, pp. 35–52 (Septiembre–Octubre 1955); incorporating material from "E. M. Forster," *The Nation*, Vol. CXLVII, pp. 412–16 (October 22, 1938); "A Forster Revival," *The Nation*, Vol. CLVII, pp. 158–59 (August 7, 1943); and "The Trophies of the Mind," *The Nation*, Vol. CLXXIII, pp. 480–82 (December 1, 1951).

"Ford Madox Ford: Yesterday and After"—the first part from "The Career of Ford Madox Ford," *The Nation*, Vol. CXXXIV, pp. 403–04 (April 6, 1932); the second part from "Ford Madox Ford," *The Nation*, Vol. CLXIX, pp. 110–11 (July 30, 1949); with additions.

"Willa Cather: The Tone of Time"—from "Willa Cather," *The Nation*, Vol. CLXIV, pp. 713–16 (June 14, 1947), with material from "The Tone of Time," *The Nation*, Vol. CLI, pp. 574–76 (December 7, 1940).

"Graham Greene: The Best and the Worst"—from "Graham Greene," *The Nation*, Vol. CLVII, pp. 18–20 (July 3, 1943), here revised and expanded. Earlier versions of this essay were included in *Forms of Modern Fiction*, edited by William Van O'Connor (Minneapolis: University of Minnesota Press, 1948), pp. 287–93; in *Critiques and Essays on Modern Fiction 1920–1951*, edited by John W. Aldridge (New York: Ronald Press Company, 1952), pp. 518–25; and in *Der Monat* (Berlin), in 1953.

"The Poet as Hero"—from "Lotte in Weimar," *The Nation*, Vol. CLI, pp. 175–76 (August 31, 1940), and in part from "Literature and Anarchy," *The American Scholar*, Vol. XV, pp. 370–80 (Summer 1946).

"The Whisper of the Devil": from *The Nation*, Vol. CLI, pp. 636–37 (December 21, 1940), revised.

"The Cool Hand": from *The Nation*, Vol. CLII, pp. 534–36 (May 3, 1941), revised.

"The Straight Way Lost": from *The Nation*, Vol. CLXV, pp. 413–16 (October 18, 1947).

"Hemingway 1950 and 1952": the first part from "A Good Day for Mr. Tolstoy," *The Nation*, Vol. CLXXI, p. 230 (September 9, 1950); the second part based on material in an article in the *Times Literary Supplement* (London), No. 2746 (September 17, 1954).

Certain passages in the essays on Henry James, Willa Cather, Glenway Wescott, Lionel Trilling, and Ernest Hemingway have been used in chapters of the author's books *A Literatura dos Estados Unidos: Suas Tradições, Mestres e Problemas* (Rio de Janeiro, Brazil: Editora Agir, 1947) and *Historia de la Literatura Norteamericana: Desde Los Orígenes hasta el Dia* (Buenos Aires, Argentina: Editorial Losada, 1950), as well as in articles published in *A Manhã* and *Correio da Manhã* (Rio de Janeiro) and *Sur* (Buenos Aires), and in *Les Nouvelles littéraires* (Paris).